DICTIONARY OF RIDDLES

DICTIONARY OF

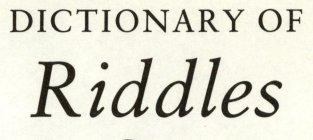

Riddles

MARK BRYANT

London and New York

First published 1990
by Routledge
11 New Fetter Lane, London EC4P 4EE
29 West 35th Street, New York, NY 10001

© 1990 Mark Bryant

Typeset by Mayhew Typesetting, Bristol
Printed in Great Britain
by Richard Clay, Bungay, Suffolk

British Library Cataloguing in Publication Data

Bryant, Mark
    Dictionary of riddles.
    1. Folk riddles
    I. Title
    398.6

    ISBN 0–415–02676–8

Library of Congress Cataloging in Publication Data

Bryant, Mark, 1953–
    Dictionary of riddles / Mark Bryant.
        p. cm.
    Based on: Riddles, ancient and modern. 1983.
    Includes bibliographical references.
    ISBN 0–415–02676–8
    1. Riddles – History and criticism. 2. Riddles
    I. Bryant, Mark, 1953–   Riddles, ancient
    and modern. II. Title.
PN6367.B78   1990
398.6–dc20   89-39374 CIP

FOR MY PARENTS

Some people have an unconquerable love of riddles.
They may have the chance of listening to plain sense,
or to such wisdom as explains life; but no, they must
go and work their brains over a riddle, just because
they do not understand what it means.

Isak Dinesen, 'The Deluge at Nornderney', *Seven
Gothic Tales* (1934)

Et quid amabo nisi quod aenigma est?

Giorgio de Chirico from *Self-Portrait* (1908)

Would'st thou divert thyself from melancholy?
Would'st thou be pleasant, yet be far from folly?
Would'st thou read *riddles* and their explanation?
Or else be drowned in contemplation?
, , , O then come hither
And lay this book, thy head and heart together.

John Bunyan, 'The Author's Apology for His Book'
from *The Pilgrim's Progress* (1678)

CONTENTS

Preface

Part One: A Brief History of Riddles   1

Introduction   3
Ancient riddles: sacred and profane   12
Modern beginnings   20
The Renaissance and beyond   30
Revival and decline   43
The last laugh?   51

Part Two: Dictionary of Riddles   65

Solutions to the riddles   333
Appendix   352
Further reading   357
Acknowledgements   358
Index   359

PREFACE

The history of riddling is a rich and varied one and stretches back far into the antiquity of our culture. Indeed, man's observations of analogies in nature led him to invent oral riddles long before he could shape letters and communicate them to others, many of the earliest literary enigmas being reworkings of far older spoken forms. However, the attraction of the riddle in all its many guises – literary, oral, and pictorial – has apparently flagged in recent years, most of the surviving relics being allotted a lowly position amongst the comic books and video machines of playroom and amusement arcade. Occasional flames of interest still flicker from time to time, but somehow the spark that was able to set the Middle Ages and the Renaissance ablaze in a riot of enigmatic jollification has come to rest on damp kindling in recent years.

In this book, in what must of necessity be a highly selective and personal choice from the chronicles of the art, I have skimmed fairly rapidly through the history of the riddle, giving a brief overview of the development of the form from its ancient beginnings to the present day, and have added what is, hopefully, a representative sample of what the field has to offer. Obviously there will be many sources I have been unable to consult and though I have tried to be as accurate as possible no pretensions to scholarship are made; I merely commend what follows to the reader as a cursory glimpse of a currently rather neglected form of entertainment in the hope that some fun, and perhaps even a little further interest, may result.

This book is generally based on an earlier work, *Riddles Ancient and Modern* (Hutchinson, 1983), but the anthology section has been considerably expanded – doubled, in fact. On the whole, apart from small alterations and corrections of fact, the historical survey and my conclusions remain the same as in the original, despite the fact that, happily, there has indeed been a mushrooming of interest in riddles, both literary and pictorial, in the last few years – largely as the result of publishers offering valuable prizes for their solution to promote the sale of books etc. But these verbal puzzles bear little resemblance to the poetic enigmas of the great literary figures of the past, and many indeed are just reworkings of ancient folk riddles, so the thesis still stands – when contemporary Nobel, Pulitzer, and Booker prize-winners start penning riddles a new era will have dawned. Until then, I am inclined to the view that the art of enigmatography has, if not entirely died out, been appropriated by the composers of cryptic crossword-puzzle clues, for better or worse. As Will Shortz of the National Puzzlers' League of the USA remarked in recent correspondence: 'Everything in modern life is speeded up . . . riddles are just part of the trend – they've been pared down to the bare essentials.' But the history of the subject is fascinating, and it is with this, and in particular the literary riddle, that this book is concerned.

I am greatly indebted to the following individuals and institutions for the invaluable help that they have given in preparing this book: University of London Library, Senate House; The British Library; The Folklore Society; Tessa Chester of The Renier Collection, Bethnal Green Museum of Childhood; and Will Shortz and Philip Cohen of the National Puzzlers' League of the USA. Thanks too, must go to Danny Nissim, Belinda Thompson, Dione Johnson and Laurence Guernet for much-needed renderings of hitherto untranslated material; to Daphne Wright, Elizabeth Handford and Mina Patria for helping to piece it all together; to Ib Bellew whose crazy idea got the whole thing started and Peter Bedrick who launched it in the USA; and finally to my family and friends who always wondered where I was. It only remains for me to wish the reader, as the renowned English emblematist Francis Quarles does in the Preface to his own book *Emblemes*, 'as much pleasure in the reading, as I had in the writing'. And I hope you laugh once, at least.

Mark Bryant
London

PART ONE

A Brief History of Riddles

Introduction

It may come as some surprise to those who have only
encountered riddles in the guise of jokes wrapped round party
hats in Christmas crackers, or who have been on the receiving
end of witticisms from precocious infants, such as 'Why did the
chicken cross the road?', that this skittish footnote to the austere
chronicles of our folk-culture heritage has itself an ancient and
learned history. All those saloon-bar teases over a glass of beer,
or stammered opening gambits at not-so-informal cocktail parties
are examples of verbal sleights-of-hand whose ancestry can be
traced back to classical Greece and beyond.

Did you know that Swift, Schiller, Edgar Allan Poe, and Jane
Austen all wrote riddles? Or that enigmas were known and
discussed by Aristotle and Homer centuries before Freud
analysed their relation to jokes and the unconscious? Riddles
appear in the Bible, the Koran, and ancient Sanskrit and Norse
manuscripts. Writers from St Aldhelm and Cervantes to Goethe,
Galileo, and Shakespeare either composed riddles themselves or
drew on sources from elsewhere to embroider their works. And
closer to our own time Puccini, Tolkien, and Lewis Carroll have
all made use of enigmas in their world-renowned compositions.

One of the earliest known riddles is inscribed on an ancient
tablet believed to date from Babylonian times, and reads as
follows:

> Who becomes pregnant without conceiving?
> Who becomes fat without eating?

to which the answer is 'clouds'; whilst the oldest Greek riddle is
that propounded in the search for Glaukos, son of Minos, King
of Crete and custodian of the infamous Minotaur. As a child, it
is said, the unfortunate Glaukos was chasing a mouse through

3

the palatial store-rooms when he tripped and fell into an enormous vat of honey and expired. Minos, failing to find the boy anywhere, consulted his soothsayers, who in true oracular form came up with the following:

> In the fields grazeth a calf whose body changeth hue thrice in the space of each day. It is first white, then red, and at the last black. He who can unravel the meaning of this riddle will restore thy child to thee alive.

The answer, 'a mulberry', was supplied by one Polyidos, who subsequently discovered Glaukos in the vat and miraculously restored him to life. Minos forced Polyidos to tell Glaukos the secret of his resurrection. The seer eventually did so, but was so incensed at his treatment that as he sailed off he spat into the boy's mouth, stopping his memory of the secret for ever.

But the history of the riddle goes back even beyond these records to the very infancy of the human race, arising spontaneously along with folk-songs and proverbs in the dawn of man's primitive existence on this planet.

ANATOMY OF THE RIDDLE

So just what exactly is a riddle? On closer inspection this proves to be a thornier subject than it first appears, as many authorities hold differing opinions as to what should and what should not be included under this rubric. Indeed, one of the most influential thinkers of modern times, Ludwig Wittgenstein (1889–1951), had very definite views of riddling, as he shows in *Tractatus Logico-Philosophicus* (1921):

> The *riddle* does not exist.
> If a question can be framed at all, it is also possible to answer it.

This view was shared by Edgar Allan Poe (1809–49) who wrote, in a short story called 'The Gold Bug':

> It may well be doubted whether human ingenuity can construct an enigma of the kind which human ingenuity may not, by proper application, resolve.

It is curious that the great philosopher should assume that riddles are unanswerable by definition and hence do not exist.

However, academic wrangles apart, I shall outline here a general working description of what I think most people would agree to be the essential bones of the topic, which, though of necessity somewhat skeletal, should be adequate for the purposes of this brief introduction.

To clear the ground it is of course first necessary to distinguish our word from that meaning 'a coarse-meshed sieve' or 'a board or metal plate set with pins used in straightening wire' which derives from the Old English *hriddel*, 'to sift'. According to the *Oxford English Dictionary* the word 'riddle' in the sense of this book has its origins in the Old English *raedels* meaning 'advice' or 'opinion', and the definition given there is the following rather general description:

> A question or statement intentionally worded in a dark or puzzling manner, and propounded in order that it may be guessed or answered, especially as a form of pastime; an enigma, a dark saying.

If, from this kind of 'dark saying', we follow the cross-reference to 'enigma', we find that this comes from the Greek verb meaning 'to speak allusively (or obscurely)' and the noun 'a fable'. But what distinguishes a riddle from other kinds of 'dark sayings', such as parables, proverbs, fables, or simple grammatical and arithmetical puzzles, is its use of metaphor. Broadly speaking, a 'true' riddle is one that compares two otherwise unrelated things in a metaphorical manner and is usually verbal, either written or spoken. Obviously the descriptions must be as accurate as possible or the point will be lost, but they are deliberately phrased in such a way as to baffle and puzzle the reader or listener. A riddle may take the form of a statement or a question, sometimes prefixed by an interrogative formula such as 'Riddle me, riddle me ree' (itself a corruption of 'Riddle me a riddle, riddle my riddle').

The oral riddle is a simple unembellished puzzle which has been passed down by word of mouth and whose solution is usually a familiar object, natural phenomenon, etc. These riddles can be found in all societies at all times in history, but are particularly prevalent in those areas which are technologically underdeveloped. A very simple example of such a riddle is the children's rhyme of Humpty Dumpty, who appears to be a man but is in fact nothing more than an egg.

Almost by definition, most *recorded* oral riddles have become slightly more literary in the very act of writing them down, but the true literary riddle is one which has been deliberately crafted around the written form. Thus they may have complicated metres and/or rhyming schemes and may be embroidered with delicate metaphors. Their solutions are also generally far more wide-ranging, and often include some of a more abstract nature. Here is an example, on a rainbow, by one of the acknowledged masters of the art, Friedrich von Schiller (1759–1805):

5

A bridge of pearls its form uprears
   High o'er a grey and misty sea;
E'en in a moment it appears,
   And rises upwards giddily.

Beneath its arch can find a road
   The loftiest vessel's mast most high,
Itself hath never borne a load,
   And seems, when thou draw'st near, to fly.

It comes first with the stream, and goes
   Soon as the wat'ry flood is dried.
Where may be found this bridge, disclose,
   And who its beauteous form supplied!

Apart from the 'true' riddles, or *enigmas*, there are also a number of related forms of puzzle which would normally be called 'riddles' and which, for that reason, I have included in this book.

The *conundrum* is a riddle whose solution is based on the punning use of words in the question. Thus the conundrum 'What is black and white and red all over?', which seems to signify a strange multi-coloured beast, is answered by the solution 'a newspaper' – the puns working on 'red' and 'all over'. Conundrums are apparently quite a recent addition to the riddler's armoury and today appeal particularly to children.

A *charade* is a variety which appears to have had its origins in the Languedoc region of France (the word itself being French). Again a relatively recent development in riddling history, it is essentially a literary exercise playing on letters or syllables, and as such has been called the *Silbenrätsel* (syllable riddle) in German. A well-known charade by the eighteenth-century Whig statesman Charles James Fox runs as follows:

My *first* is expressive of no disrespect,
   But I never call you by it when you are by;
If my *second* you still are resolved to reject,
   As dead as my *whole*, I shall presently lie.

The answer is 'herring' (her-ring). Charades can also be acted out and in this form are still a very popular kind of parlour game. (A good example, on 'nightingale', is described in Thackeray's *Vanity Fair*, Chapter 51.)

Logogriphs, also known as *Worträtsel* or *calembours*, are riddles based on single words in which letters are removed to make new words. They are thus concerned with the form of the word and its components rather than its meaning. A French version drawn from the eighteenth-century literary magazine *Mercure de France* will serve to illustrate this: '*Je brille avec six pieds, avec cinq je te couvre.*' This signifies the word '*étoile*' (star) which, by losing a leter, becomes '*toile*' (tablecloth). The logical development of this form, involving the transposition of the letters themselves, is the anagram.

Even more concerned with the position of words and letters is the *literary rebus*. A very simple rebus using the letters on their own would be 'IOU' (for 'I owe you'), or the caption of Duchamp and Picabia's notorious bearded version of the Mona Lisa (1919), 'LHOOQ' (*Elle a chaud au cul*). A simple but even cleverer French rebus consists of just two letters, G and a, to be read '*J'ai grand appetit*' (*G grand, a petit*). Many rebuses also involve the positioning of words and letters, such as the following representation of 'I understand he undertook to overthrow the undertaking':

stand	took	to	taking
I	he	throw	this

or the French:

pir	vent	venir
un	vient	d'un

which is to be read '*Un soupir vient souvent d'un souvenir.*'

'*Catch*' riddles are, strictly speaking, hardly riddles at all in any sense of the word but are more like jokes, whose humour derives from the fact that they seem to imply by their riddle-like form that a witty solution is in order, when in fact the answer really is the obvious one. 'Why did the chicken cross the road? To get to the other side' is a widely used example of this kind. Another, from Mark Twain's *The Adventures of Huckleberry Finn*, is: 'Where was Moses when the candle went out? In the dark'. Related to these are other kinds of trick riddle either in the form of arithmetical puzzles such as:

> A priest, and a friar, and a silly auld man,
> Gaed [went] to a pear tree, where three pears hang.
> Lika [each] ane took a pear – how many hang there?

– the answer being 'two', as the three men are the same person – or those of the 'hidden name' variety:

> There was a king met a king
>   In a straight lane;
> Says the king to the king
>   Where have you been?
> I've been in the wood,
>   Hunting the doe:
> Pray lend me your dog,
>   That I may do so.

> Call him, call him!
>   What must I call him?
> Call him as you and I,
>   We've done both.

The dog's name is 'Been'.

There are also *pictorial riddles*, where allegorical statements are made by images, leading to a moral that is revealed by the 'solution' of the picture. In other varieties a name or saying may be discovered by punning use of the words used to describe the objects. Pictorial puzzles of this kind obviously owe much to the hieroglyphics of the ancient Egyptians and other picture-based languages and find their modern counterpart in emblems, visual rebuses and, ultimately, via the cryptic paintings of de Chirico and *Pittura metafisica*, in certain aspects of the work of the Surrealist Movement.

Riddles of a kind occur too in the world of music. Tchaikovsky is on record as having described his Sixth Symphony ('Pathétique') as being something of a riddle, based on a programme which 'is of a kind which remains an enigma to all – let them guess it who can'. Solutions such as Life, Love, Disillusionment, and Death have been suggested but the programme remains a mystery. In a similar vein are the *Enigma Variations* of Edward Elgar. Composed in 1899, they are a deliberate attempt to capture in music the personalities of certain of Elgar's friends. Although he gave clues to the solutions of the musical riddles in the form of their subjects' initials, and later identified the personalities themselves, a further puzzle remains, as the overall theme running through the whole piece is supposed to conceal a popular melody. Various suggestions have been made, from 'God Save the King' to 'Auld Lang Syne' (the current favourite of musicologists being 'Rule Britannia'). But the secret of the *Enigma* theme died with its composer.

Moving on to vocal music, one of the characters in Gilbert and Sullivan's *The Yeoman of the Guard* (1888), the prankster Jack Point, is renowned for his riddling and jokes and is most put out when the conversation takes a change of direction after he has put his 'best conundrum' – 'Why is a cook's brain like an overwound clock?' – thereby depriving us of the answer for ever. However, perhaps more accessible to final solution are the riddles contained in Puccini's romantic opera *Turandot*, in which the eponymous heroine, the daughter of a Chinese emperor, consents to marry the first royal suitor who can solve her three riddles – on penalty of death for failure. Prince Calaf, travelling incognito, solves them but is nearly executed when Turandot reneges on her promise. However, all turns out happily in the end and they are eventually married. The riddles, which differ somewhat from those in Gozzi's original (1762) version and those in Schiller's translation, occur in the second act. Here is one on 'hope':

> In the dark night flies a many-hued phantom.
> It soars and spreads its wings
> above the gloomy human crowd.
> The whole world calls to it,
> the whole world implores it.
> At dawn the phantom vanishes
> to be reborn in every heart.
> And every night 't is born anew
> and every day it dies!

THE USES OF RIDDLES AND RIDDLING

Riddles have many uses, but the most widespread throughout their history has been in deciding contests of wit. Such contests have varied from light-hearted entertainments to dramatic battles with a man's fortune or life itself at stake.

In some parts of the world it was once traditionally the custom to grant a condemned man the opportunity of putting a 'neck' riddle to his captors which, if they failed to solve it, would literally save his neck. Naturally the riddles tended to be as esoteric as possible, involving enough specialist and personal knowledge to make them virtually insoluble to any but the propounder. A very famous example is the Ilo riddle: 'On Ilo I walk, on Ilo I stand, Ilo I hold fast in my hand', where Ilo was in fact the riddler's dog, out of whose skin he had made a pair of shoes and a pair of gloves. A still more macabre version of this kind of riddle is the following:

> I sat wi' my love, and I drank wi' my love,
> > And my love she gave me light;
> I'll give any man a pint o' wine,
> > That'll read my riddle right.

(I sat in a chair made from my wife's bones and drank from her skull under a candle made from the fat of her body.)

A natural variant of the 'neck' riddle is that used in a contest for someone's hand in marriage. It was just such a contest that led to the final tragedy of Oedipus. The goddess Hera was angered by the news that the club-footed prince had killed King Laius of Thebes (his father) at the crossroads to the city, and took it upon herself to destroy the good citizens of Boeotia. To this end she sent from Ethiopia the horrendous monster known as the Sphinx, which was the terrible issue of the hundred-headed Typhon and Echidna. Transmogrified from three separate

9

animals, the Sphinx had the head and breasts of a woman, the body, feet, and tail of a lion, and the wings of a bird, and, as though that was not monster enough to sort out the Boeotians, the canny creature also posed the following riddle to every passer-by:

> What is it that goes on four legs in the morning, two legs at noon and three legs in the evening?

All who failed to solve it were summarily killed. Oedipus, however, guessed the answer to be 'man', who crawls on all fours as a child, walks on two legs as an adult, and hobbles on three (the third being a stick) in old age. The Sphinx was so enraged at its defeat that it hurled itself into the nearest abyss. But the winner of the contest was no luckier: the prize for defeating the monster was the hand of Laius's wife and all his worldly goods. Oedipus accepted, still unaware of his true identity, thus fulfilling the prophecy that he would murder his father and marry his mother.

An equally grim contest was that between Thor and the astute underground dwarf Alvis ('all-wise'), who wished to marry Thor's daughter Thrud. Described in the 'Alvissmal' in the *Elder Edda*, this is the earliest known account of a riddle contest for the hand of a lady. Thor puts to the dwarf thirteen questions about the nature of the universe. The god is impressed by Alvis's knowledgeable answers but in the end confesses that the whole test was a ruse to prevent the dwarf's marriage to Thrud, saying:

> Never have I met such a master of lore
> > With such a wealth of wisdom.
> I talked to trick you, and tricked you I have:
> > Dawn has broken, Dwarf,
> > Stiffen now to stone.

(which is apparently what they do if caught in daylight).

However, somewhat more light-hearted competitions are narrated in the riddle ballads of the eighteenth century such as 'Captain Wedderburn's Courtship' and 'A Noble Riddle Wisely Expounded'. And light-hearted is indeed what the riddle-session became in the hands of some exponents, as the delightful frivolity of Straparola's *Facetious Nights (Tredeci Piacevoli Notti)* bears witness. In the introduction to this source-book of drollery the author (whose pseudonym means 'the babbler') explains how Sforza, Duke of Milan, having been ousted from his own court by intrigue, has removed himself to the island of Murano near Venice, and that the book is supposed to be a documentary of the happenings at his palace there during the thirteen nights of Carnival when members of his daughter's circle of friends draw lots to relate stories, sing songs, and propound riddles. First published (in a complete edition) in 1557, the book immediately scandalized the local authorities with its earthy enigmas and ribald tales, but surprisingly it was not banned until fifty years later. And even then it was only the allusions to impropriety on the part of various clerical characters in the stories and not the overall licentiousness of the book itself that provoked the Vatican censor's displeasure.

To be fair, though, Straparola was not the only riddler to be tempted into scurrility. Owing to the natural propensity of the riddle form to be used to depict harmless objects in an apparently obscene way, riddles have also been used by many other authors (a surprising number of them from clerical backgrounds) to titillate, shock, and scandalize those who hear them. Amongst these must be classified a fair number of the output of the fourteenth-century Bohemian monk Dr Claretus, a good many from the anonymous author of the *Demaundes Joyous* (the first riddle book ever printed in England) and the vast majority of the works of many Italian enigmatographers of the sixteenth, seventeenth, and eighteenth centuries, notably the exceedingly licentious Tommaso Stigliani whose books, along with those of Straparola, were on the Vatican's index of prohibited titles (1605) to protect public morals.

Political as well as personal use was made of 'dark sayings' both by soothsayers and their audiences at the oracles of Ancient Greece and Rome. During the eighteenth century groups of young French lawyers in Picardy used pictorial riddles to lampoon local dignitaries without risk of libel, and it is even said that Lorenzo de' Medici went so far as to employ professional riddlers to distract the populace from his political intrigues.

Another major use of the enigma has been in the performance of religious ceremonies. The telling of riddles on the Jewish Passover Eve is a well-known and long-established tradition, and the long, questioning, 'Who knoweth one?' verse is close to the hearts of all members of the faith from rabbi to bar mitzvah boy. Again we hear of riddles being used almost like a charm in wedding, fertility, harvest, and rain-making ceremonies in Africa and elsewhere, Sir James Frazer in *The Golden Bough* (1890–1915) recording examples from an Indonesian ritual to make the rice grow involving the incantation of riddles of every variety. Riddles were also enjoyed at the Roman festival of Saturnalia; the Greeks indulged in the pastime during Agrionia; and it still survives in a lesser form in some modern Christmas celebrations.

Riddles have also been used in teaching everything from religion to grammar. Catechetic and other kinds of 'clever question' involving intimate knowledge of certain scriptures are cases in point. The first section of Pseudo Bede's *Flores*, parts of the

11

somewhat bawdy *Demaundes Joyous* (1511), certain Hindu texts, and many of the medieval 'dialogues' all contain examples. Here is an illustration from the fourteenth-century *Dialogue of Salomon and Saturnus*:

> Tell me, who was he that was never born, was then buried in his mother's womb, and after death was baptized?

to which the solution is 'Adam'. And, on the grammatical side, the eleventh-century Arab scholar, story-teller and intelligence chief Al-Hariri includes the following riddle in his twenty-fourth 'assembly':

> And in what place do males put on the veils of women, and the ladies of the alcove go forth with the turbans of men?

which refers to the grammatical ambiguity in Arabic in which the feminine numerals from three to ten are used with masculine nouns and the masculine numerals with feminine nouns. And earlier still, the eighth-century Archbishop of Canterbury, Tatwine, had even composed an enigma on prepositions and the cases they govern in Latin.

Few modern teachers would go to such lengths to thrust learning down the unwilling throats of their pupils, but riddling remains as popular as ever with children. Indeed, the timelessness of the riddle form, and the fact that there are certain kinds of enigma whose humour maintains its freshness all down the ages, seems to suggest that the art of enigmatography is ingrained in our collective unconscious. For as the philosopher Franz Brentano says in the foreword to his book *Neue Räthsel* (1878), '"Astonishment [*Erstaunung*]," said Aristotle, "is and was from the beginning what led men to philosophize; they felt a yearning to the solution of riddles."'

Ancient riddles: sacred and profane

Most of the myths of classical antiquity, whether sacred or profane, Greek, Roman, Hebrew, Scandinavian, or Asian, are steeped in accounts of riddle contests between men, gods, and sundry wise monsters, many of which will already be familiar to the modern reader. Some contests, such as those between Oedipus and the Sphinx, Solomon and Sheba, or Samson and the Philistines, are immediately recognizable, though others, such as the Norse saga of Heidrek and Gestumblindi or the riddle hymn of the Rig-Veda, may be less well known. But all are examples of a riddlemania that had become firmly established as a major art form alongside the traditions of poetry-, epitaph- and song-writing long before the new civilizations of mainland Europe had even begun to stir from inarticulate barbarity.

THE CLASSICAL RIDDLE

The Greeks in particular were great riddlers. Whether it was a friendly bout of wit after a meal, as described in Athenaeus's *Deipnosophistae* where the loser was condemned to quaff a great mug of wine mixed with brine, or whether in deadly earnest – with rather more sobering penalties – the enigmatic form was a recognized part of classical Greek culture. As in later genera-tions, to be able to give a good account of oneself in this tortuous art was a sign of intellectual prowess and the mark of a wise man.

Though Aesop's *Fables* and some of the pithy pronouncements of Pythagoras of Samos were described as enigmas in their day, the first use of the word with its modern connotation was by the poet Pindar (*c*.522–442 BC), though there is good reason to believe that the form had existed before. The great pre-Socratic philosopher Heraclitus – now sadly perhaps only generally known as the subject of William Johnson Cory's jingle 'They told me Heraclitus, they told me you were dead,/ They brought me bitter news to hear, and bitter tears to shed' – was so well known for his cryptic remarks about the nature of the universe that even Cicero and Diogenes Laertius referred to him as 'the Riddler' and 'the Obscure'. Plato refers to the pastime of riddling in *The Republic* and mentions (Book V.479) 'the children's riddle about the eunuch hitting the bat and what he threw at it and what it was sitting on' (this is a variant of Panarces's riddle, viz: a man who was not a man [a eunuch] threw a stone that was not a stone [a pumice stone] at a bird that was not a bird [a bat] sitting on a twig that was not a twig [a reed]). Indeed, the very nature of the riddle itself became a topic for philo-sophical debate, with Aristotle's Cypriot pupil, Clearchus of Soli, even going so far as to write an entire treatise specifically devoted to the subject (not unnaturally entitled *On Riddles*) in which he distinguished seven different kinds. And Diogenes Laer-tius, in his *Lives of Eminent Philosophers*, profiles the venerable enigmatographer Cleobulus (*c*.600 BC) who is said to have writ-ten over 3,000 lines of songs and riddles. Cleobulus also appears as one of the seven in Plutarch's *Dinner of the Seven Wise Men* as does his equally famous daughter Cleobulina who composed enigmas in hexameters. Another guest at the dinner, Cleodorus, is rounded upon by Aesop for saying of her:

13

Perhaps it is not unbecoming for her to amuse herself and to weave these as other girls weave girdles and hair-nets, and to propound them to women, but the idea that men of sense should take them at all seriously is ridiculous.

On the less esoteric side, though perhaps more ridiculous, we hear of Pindar's riddling ode against the letter S; and numerous examples occur in the writings of Antiphanes (including some put in the mouth of the heroine in *Sappho*) and other notable playwrights of the period. There are enigmas in Theognis's *Elegies*, Sophocles's *Ichneutae*, the *Idylls* of Theocritus, Alexis's *Sleep*, Diphilus's *Theseus*, and Aristophanes's *Wasps*, as well as umpteen examples in Book 10 of Athenaeus's gallimaufry of classical lore, the *Deipnosophistae*, when the grammarian Aemilianus Maurus decides it is time to turn their discussion away from the pleasures of drink and drinking.

In the surviving fragment of Hesiod's *Melampodie* a riddle contest to the death between the two seers Colchos and Mopsos is described, and in real life the great bard Homer – himself a distinguished enigmatographer – is reputed to have died from chagrin at being unable to solve the following riddle on lice, posed by the fishermen of Ios:

> What we caught we threw away; what we didn't catch we kept.

Tales also abound of how Alexander the Great (no doubt well prepared by his tutor Aristotle) picked the wits of the Hindus with riddles, and how Aesop was forever coming to the rescue of King Lyerus of Babylon in his intellectual battles with the riddling Nectanebo of Egypt.

The well-known riddles of Glaukos and Oedipus can be found throughout Greek literature and many other traditional enigmas of every variety may also be discovered in Book 14 of *The Greek Anthology*. The following anonymous contribution may serve as a good illustration here:

> I am the black child of a white father; a wingless bird, flying even to the clouds of heaven. I give birth to tears of mourning in pupils that meet me, and at once on my birth I am dissolved into air.

The answer is 'smoke' (the pupils are those of the eyes).

Even the Romans, whose comparatively modern culture was based on a regimentation so severe that the reader might be forgiven for doubting their inclination to riddling, are known to have indulged in the art, and riddling continued to flourish during the great age of Latin civilization. The story survives that when Marcus Aurelius asked the Jewish sage Judah the Patriarch how he should go about filling his empty treasury, the patriarch is reported to have gone into his garden and uprooted all the old flowers and planted new ones in their stead. This enacted riddle was taken to mean that the emperor should oust his old councillors and recruit new ones in their place (who would presumably pay for the privilege). A similar story is told of how Tarquin the Great lopped off the heads of the biggest poppies in his garden to signify to Sextus that the chief citizens of the recently conquered Gabii should be executed.

The Roman grammarian Pompeius described the employment of the ice riddle ('My mother brought me forth, then shortly I her daughter brought her forth again') by small boys playing in the streets of classical Rome, and on a more literary note Virgil's third eclogue ('Are these Meliboeus' Sheep?') from the *Pastoral Poems* involves a light-hearted riddling contest between the two shepherds, Menalcas and Damoetas, for the love of a certain Phyllis.

The Egyptian Greek Athenaeus, though describing events in the Golden Age of Greek literature, was of course himself writing in the time of the Roman Empire (second–third centuries AD) and riddles can also be found in the *Noctes Atticae* of Aulus Gellius, like the following from Book XII, vi:

> I know not if he's minus once or twice,
> Or both of these, who would not give his place
> As I once heard it said, to Jove himself.

The answer to this is 'Terminus' (once *minus* plus twice *minus* is thrice [*ter*] *minus*) and the allusion is to a statue of this god which could not be moved from the temple of Jupiter on the Capitol. The great orator Cicero is also alleged to have penned a few enigmas; Apuleius's lost work *Liber ludicorum et gryphorum* is supposed to have contained a fair number; and riddles also occur in Plutarch's *Dinner of the Seven Wise Men*. The following triple enigma occurs in Petronius's *Satyricon*:

> 'What part of us am I? I come far, I come wide. Now find me.'
> I can tell you what part of us runs and does not move from its place; what grows out of us and grows smaller.

The answers 'foot', 'eye', and 'hair' have been suggested.

SANSKRIT AND NORSE ENIGMAS

The oldest Sanskrit riddles (*c*.1000 BC) occur in the riddle hymn of Dirghatamas (Hymn 164) in Book I of the Rig-Veda. Of the fifty-two verses all but one are riddles and tend to be on cosmological themes. A good example is the following to which the solutions 'wind' and 'lightning' have been suggested:

The one who made him does not know him. He escapes from the one who has seen him. Enveloped in his mother's womb, he is subject to annihilation, while he has many descendants.

Again in the 'Vana Parva' of that enormous epic the *Mahabharata* (seven times longer than the *Odyssey* and *Iliad* put together) we find that the riddles form an integral part of the story. Here Yudhisthira and his four royal brothers are dying of thirst in a forest when they come to an enchanted pool. As Yudhisthira arrives he discovers to his horror all the princes lying dead and the pool presided over by a *yaksha* (a servant of the gods normally friendly to man) in the shape of a crane. As he's about to drink the water the *yaksha* threatens to kill him (like all the rest) unless he can first answer its riddles. The questions posed mostly require answers of a moral or religious kind, thus:

> *Yaksha*:
> Still, tell me what foeman is worst to subdue?
> And what is the sickness lasts lifetime all through?
> Of men that are upright, say which is the best?
> And of those that are wicked, who passeth the rest?
> *Yudhisthira*:
> Anger is man's unconquered foe;
> The ache of greed doth never go;
> Who loveth most of saints is first;
> Of bad men cruel men are worst.

There are nine groups of questions in all, mostly of four lines, and Yudhisthira's reward for answering all correctly is to drink the water and choose one brother's life. He chooses Nakula, a step-brother by another marriage in preference over his own direct kin so that both mothers might rejoice. The *yaksha* is so impressed by this decision that it revives all four of the dead princes.

Apart from the story of Alvis and Thor mentioned earlier, one of the most famous instances of riddling in Norse literature occurs in the tale of King Heidrek in the *Hervarar Saga*. In this we are told how the wise King Heidrek had made a vow to the god Frey that however deeply a man had wronged him he would either be given a fair trial by his seven judges or would be let off scot-free if he could propound a riddle that the king could not answer. Now in his realm dwelt one Gestumblindi who was not on good terms with Heidrek and was in the course of time summoned to be judged according to the custom. Knowing that he would be no match for the king's wit and fearing for his life, Gestumblindi prayed fervently to Odin to help him. His prayers were answered and Odin, dressed as the old man, appeared at

Heidrek's hall and posed a number of short riddles like the following:

> I saw maidens like dust. Rocks were their beds. They were black and swarthy in the sunshine, but the darker it grew, the fairer they appeared.

– to which the solution is 'embers on the hearth'. Heidrek solved all these without much difficulty, but when Odin asked, 'What did Odin whisper in Balder's ear, before he was placed on the pyre?', the king realized that his opponent could only be Odin himself to know the answer and threw his sword Tyrfing at the god. Odin, however, made good his escape in the form of a falcon but was so piqued by Heidrek's unsporting behaviour that he caused his slaves to murder him that very evening. An attractive variant of this story, set in verse, occurs in the *Gátu Ríma*, or 'Faroese Riddle Ballad'.

THE JUDAEO–CHRISTIAN TRADITION

Riddles abound in the Old Testament, and we are constantly reminded in Judaeo–Christian literature that skill in the art of riddling was the mark of a true sage. This astuteness is mentioned in the first chapter of Proverbs which suggests that by following its dictates the reader can acquire wisdom:

> If the wise man listens, he will increase his learning, and the man of understanding will acquire skill to understand proverbs and parables, the sayings of wise men and their riddles.

The One True God himself spoke in riddles and 'dark sayings', though to his chosen few (such as Daniel or Moses) all great knowledge was made plain:

> But my servant Moses is not such a prophet; he alone is faithful of all my household. With him I speak face to face, openly and not in riddles. He shall see the very form of the Lord.
>
> (Numbers 12:7–8)

Many of the Proverbs are also believed to have been originally current as riddles before being written down. For example, Proverbs 17:12 could be redrafted as: 'What is worse than meeting a bear? Meeting a fool in his folly.' Proverbs 30 also riddles about the four mysterious things, the four little wise things, and the four stately things, the second group of which I quote here:

17

Four things there are which are smallest on earth yet wise beyond the wisest: ants, a people with no strength yet they prepare their store of food in the summer; rock-badgers, a feeble folk, yet they make their home among the rocks; locusts, which have no king, yet they sally forth in detachments; the lizard, which can be grasped in the hand, yet is found in the palaces of kings.

The prophet Daniel, dragged off to Babylon in captivity with the rest of the Israelites when they were conquered by the Chaldeans, could not only hold his own with the odd lion but also had an enviable reputation as a solver of puzzles, and was much sought out by the noble insomniacs and perplexed dignitaries of the day:

This same Daniel . . . is known to have a notable spirit, with knowledge and understanding, and the gift of interpreting dreams, explaining riddles and unbinding spells.
(Daniel 5:12)

To this end, it was Daniel who was summoned to untangle the meaning of the celestial graffiti that became manifest at the feast of King Belshazzar: '*Mene, mene, tekel, upharsin.*' Literally, 'mina, mina, shekel, half-mina' (units of currency), Daniel took this to mean that Belshazzar had been 'numbered, numbered, weighed and found wanting', which in concrete terms signified that his time was up and that his kingdom would be split up and given to the Medes and Persians, which is indeed what happened.

The riddle proposed by the Hebrew judge Samson to a group of Philistines gathered at his wedding reception is justly acclaimed, and apart from its appearance in Holy Writ has been widely disseminated throughout the Western world in recent years on the green-and-gold tins of Tate & Lyle's Golden Syrup:

Out of the eater came something to eat;
Out of the strong came something sweet.
(Judges 14:14)

Samson in his wisdom gave the fellows seven days to solve the riddle and stipulated a forfeit of 'thirty fine linen wrappers and thirty gala dresses' for the loser. Admittedly it was a somewhat unfair contest as the solution relied on special knowledge – the fact that Samson had seen in the desert a lion's carcass in which bees had made a hive – but with the help of his new bride the Philistines returned to the court with the answer, itself phrased in the form of a riddle: 'What is sweeter than honey? What is stronger than a lion?' (to which some commentators have appended the solution 'love'). Samson, somewhat peeved at this subterfuge, riddled out his anger in the following words: 'If you had not ploughed with my heifer, you would not have found out my riddle,' and paid his debt by murdering thirty Philistines and giving *their* clothes to the winners.

But perhaps the greatest of all the biblical enigmatographers, and certainly one of the wisest men in the Hebrew tradition, was King Solomon of Jerusalem, architect of the great temple, author of the Song of Songs and Ecclesiastes, and constantly quoted worthy in all matters of judgement and law. In the first Book of Kings the scribe tells us how Bilqis, Queen of Sheba, travelled many miles to Solomon's court with the express purpose of testing out his prodigious wisdom, posing many 'hard questions' to the great man in cryptic form. Though these are not reported in the Bible itself, some held to be the genuine article can be found in the 2nd Targum to the Book of Esther and elsewhere in rabbinical literature – the best of them being:

> There is something which when living moves not, yet when its head is cut off it moves.

and

> What is that which is produced from the ground, yet man produces it, while its food is the fruit of the ground?

The solution to the former is 'tree', which when its head (branches) is cut off can be made into a ship, and to the latter is 'wick'. Solomon's riddling talent appears again in the chronicles of the great Jewish historian Josephus (*Antiquities of the Jews*, Chapter 8: 3) where we learn of Solomon and Hiram of Tyre sparring at riddles by post:

> . . . the king of Tyre sent sophisms and enigmatical sayings to Solomon and desired he would solve them, and free them from the ambiguity that was in them.

In this case the forfeit was cash and Hiram soon began to lose heavily until he found a riddle-solver called Abdemon who quickly won back the money from Solomon, and more besides.

Apart from those of the Old Testament, a number of riddles can also be found in the Talmud, many of which play on letters of the Hebrew alphabet, while some, like 'What animal has one voice living and seven voices dead?' (answer: 'ibis', from whose carcass many instruments can be made), are genuine riddles.

There is even a poetical riddle, the solution to which has never clearly been established:

> High from heav'n her eye looks down,
> Constant strife excites her frown;
> Winged beings shun her sight,

She puts the youth to instant flight.
The aged, too, her looks do scout;
Oh! oh! the fugitive cries out.
And by her snares whoe'er is lured
Can never of his sin be cured.

Another as yet unsolved riddle occurs in the Revelation of St John (the only riddle in the Christian New Testament):

He that hath understanding let him count the number of the beast; for it is the number of a man, and his number is six hundred and sixty and six.

A number of interpretations have been put forward over the centuries but none seems to be wholly satisfactory, a fact that might lead one to conclude, as did G. K. Chesterton generally, that 'The riddles of God are more satisfying than the solutions of man.'

Modern beginnings

The roots of modern literary riddling in the western world can be traced back to the incursions of the Saxons and Norsemen into England in the centuries following the departure of the Romans in AD 406. With them the Teutonic hordes brought to these windy isles a tradition of wandering minstrel poets who related sagas of heroes from former times, and a craze for enigmatic and metaphorical descriptions of all kinds. The Anglo-Saxons quickly developed their own cryptic sayings from these earlier Germanic 'kennings' and developed an enigmatic art form that was soon to hold its own amongst the other varieties of literature of the period. But more than anything it was the growth of classical erudition, particularly as encouraged by King Alfred – who imported scholars like Hadrian from the ancient cultures of the Mediterranean with their already-established heritage of enigmatography – that gave rise to the important Anglo-Latin school of riddle-masters who in their turn paved the way for all riddling, whether in Latin or the vernacular, to follow. Starting with the 'century' (100) of enigmas finely crafted by an anonymous learned scribe some time around the fifth century AD, renewed interest in the art of riddling, both pagan and religious, spread across the mainland of Europe and into the Far East where it mingled with indigenous traditions of cryptic utterance formed from time immemorial.

SYMPHOSIUS AND THE ANGLO-LATIN SCHOOL

The father of modern literary riddling and inspiration for all subsequent riddle-masters up to the Renaissance is himself surrounded in clouds of enigma. He is acknowledged as 'Symphosius' by his great successor Aldhelm, but whether this was his real name, a pseudonym for one of the minor Latin poets, Firmianius Symphosius Caelius or Lactantius (under whose names his work was widely disseminated), or whether the name merely describes what the riddles were used for – i.e. postprandial intellectual discourse (cf. Plato's *Symposium*) – is a matter for academic dispute. What is certain is that one hundred hexameter triplets in good, if prosaic, Latin on subjects varying from everyday items to celestial phenomena were carefully copied out and grouped under the title *Symphosii Aenigmata*. Generally believed to have been composed somewhere around the fifth century AD, and decidedly pagan in character, they were enormously popular in Anglo-Saxon England and have remained so ever since. Indeed, such has been Symphosius's influence that he has come to be regarded as doing for the riddle what Martial did for the epigram, being held up as a model and ideal to be strived towards by all the great riddlers that followed. The riddles were originally devised for recitation at the ancient feasts of Saturnalia, a traditional forum for enigmas and jests, and the carnival atmosphere is reflected in the verse.

The collection, which contains many literary inventions as well as versifications of folk themes, also includes a rendering of Homer's lice riddle. Here is an example of a riddle on an anchor:

> My twin points are joined together by crooked iron; with the wind I wrestle, with the depths of the sea I fight; I search out the midmost water, and I bite the very ground itself.

The next addition to the history of Anglo-Latin riddling is a collection of sixty-two riddles discovered in a monastery in the northern Italian city of Bobbio near Genoa, subsequently described as the 'Berne Riddles'. Believed to have been written by an Irish monk by the name of Tullius in the seventh century, they represent the work of the first-ever Italian riddle-master of the Middle Ages. The subject matter of these enigmas is still very much concerned with folk themes, but though the collection was popular and was still being reprinted in the nineteenth century, the first major figure after Symphosius is unquestionably Aldhelm, the riddling saint.

St Aldhelm was an extraordinarily talented man. As well as being a brilliant scholar and theologian, the Abbot of Malmesbury and Bishop of Sherborne (one of the top dioceses in

Wessex) was also an inveterate enigmatographer. Noted in the Venerable Bede's *Ecclesiastical History* as one of the fathers of the modern Church, he was an excellent musician, and his poems were greatly loved by Alfred. Indeed, the king himself related that in order to induce more people into church, Aldhelm would sing to them as they passed and drop sacred lyrics into his refrains. His riddles are one hundred in number and occur in the *Epistola ad Acircium*, a treatise on prosody written between AD 685 and 705 addressed to his friend Aldfrith ('Acircius'), King of Northumberland.

The subject matter of the riddles, which are again in hexameters, is much the same as that of Symphosius, with the exception that for the first time a Christian element is introduced together with a substantial amount of classical mythology and fable. The following is a simple folk-oriented riddle on wind:

> None can espy me, none lay hands on me;
> My rushing voice shrills swift through all the earth.
> I shatter oaks with harsh and hideous might,
> Yea, beat upon the skies, and sweep the fields.

In the wake of the literary saint came a succession of theological dignitaries, all of whom managed to find time between building churches, converting the heathen, and studying the Scriptures to jot down some riddles to amuse, test, and sometimes shock their sacred brethren. The Archbishop of Canterbury, Tatwine, published forty hexameter riddles before his death in 734, about a third of which were on religious topics. All are between four and sixteen lines long, and he employed an ingenious acrostic to preface his work in which the first letters of the answers to all forty riddles were contained:

> *Sub deno quater haec diverse enigmata torquens*
> *Stamine metrorum exstructor conserta retexit.*

> (Twisting these riddles diversely in ten four times he who built them up revealed them by the thread of their metres.)

The first line contains the initial letters of the first words of all the riddles and the second line contains, in reverse order, the initial letters of the last word in their first lines!

Though by all literary yardsticks a competent poet, Tatwine's riddles are rather dull, but perhaps not so turgid as those of his successor in this brief history – Abbot Eusebius of Wearmouth (d.747) – who wrote sixty hexameter riddles which were published together with the Archbishop's to complete the 'century' after the fashion of Symphosius.

The great Devonian missionary bishop Winfrid, later known

as Boniface, composed twenty pithy enigmas, ten each on the moral virtues and vices, though again these are rather stilted. A great peripatetic, Boniface swept all before him in his religious fervour and showed the true light to large sections of pagan Germany and France in the time of Charles Martel (no doubt riddling as he went). A story is told of how he instantly won over a tribe of Hessian tree-worshippers by felling their sacred Oak of Jupiter, somehow making it fall in such a way that the trunk split into four neat sections as it hit the ground. A lifelong friend and correspondent of an expatriate Anglo-Saxon princess named Bugga (who had become a nun in Italy), Boniface was murdered by a gang of recalcitrant pagans on 5 June 755 – a fountain is said to have sprung immediately from the spot.

The Venerable Bede himself is credited with having written out some riddles, though these are now generally held to be apocryphal, the manuscript indicating a hand much later than the great scholar's. The most notable of these works is generally known by its abbreviated title *Flores* and contains twelve original riddles together with direct quotations from other enigmatographers and a short colloquy. A rather clever riddle on a horse drawn by a pen will serve to illustrate the style:

> I am sitting above a horse which was not born, whose mother I hold in my hand.

Next came the ninth-century Lorsch manuscript of somewhat derivative riddles, and the works (mostly logographs) of the Byzantine school (*fl.* 950–1300), including Psellus and Christophorus of Mytilene. The last major enigmatist in the Latin tradition of this period was Dr Claretus of Bohemia, who composed 150 mostly single-line folk-oriented enigmas in the fourteenth century, some of which were distinctly spicy whilst others, though more decent, tended to give the game away. Here is a rather longer one:

> A layman comes with an iron spoon, shoves it in and opens up his mother; he salts her, and sews up her skin; then he takes his mother's children, grinds all their bones, and feeds his own children.

(The solution is 'a crop in a field'.)

RIDDLERS OF THE HEBREW GOLDEN AGE

The period from the middle of the tenth century to the end of the fifteenth century saw the flowering in Spain of the Golden Age of modern Hebrew literature. For it was at this time, under Moorish rule, that the Jewish community in the region of Andalusia, with its cultural centre at Cordova, suddenly burst forth with a host of talent in verse, song, prose – and riddles. To Jews of the Middle Ages, whether threadbare children or venerated rabbis, the elaborate construction and telling of riddles was, as with the Ancient Greeks, a regular and accepted mode of table entertainment, and all the major Hebrew poets of this era composed enigmas and acrostics of great merit. Philosophical riddles appeared in monumental ethical works such as Solomon ibn Gabirol (a.k.a. Avicebron)'s eleventh-century *Choice of Pearls*, and some (e.g. the famous 'Who knoweth one?' number riddle for Passover Eve) even managed to find their way into the Jewish prayer-book.

Dunash ben Labrat (*c.*920–90) is generally regarded as being the founder of Spanish Hebrew poetry and the motivating power behind this literary industry, for it was he who first introduced the Arabic metre into Hebrew verse, thus setting a trend that was to be much imitated throughout the Jewish world. He is particularly important in the history of enigmatography in that he stands midway between the Anglo-Latin school and the advent of riddling in the vernacular as represented in such works as the Anglo-Saxon *Exeter Book*. Very few of his riddles survive today, but to give an example of his style here is his enigma on a candle:

> What weeps tears without an eye, and makes everything visible and does not see its own garment? At the time when it approaches death that which cuts off its head revives it.

Murdered by a jealous Muslim poet, his body was hidden under a fig tree and was only discovered some time later when suspicions were aroused by the amazing fruit the tree produced.

One of the most popular of the Hebrew riddles of this period was a long and highly technical grammatical treatise written by Abraham ibn Ezra (1089–1164), who is also believed to have used riddle-like phrases to conceal his unorthodox views on Judaism. Always a wanderer, his travels eventually led him to London and he is held to have been the inspiration for Robert Browning's poem 'Rabbi ben Ezra'. That the Victorian poet knew of ibn Ezra's writings is evidenced by the fact that he incorporated one of the riddler's verses into his own 'Holy Cross Days' in 1854.

Influential though the work of ibn Ezra may have been, it was his great contemporary Jehudah (or Judah) Halevi (*c.*1086–1141) who is credited with being, not only the foremost Hebrew poet since the Bible and a religious philosopher of the first order, but also the Jewish enigmatographer *par excellence*. The German poet Heinrich Heine included a poem singing his praises in *Romancero* (1851):

And Jehuda ben Halevy
Was not merely skill'd in reading,
But in poetry a master,
And himself a first-rate poet.

Yes, he was a first-rate poet,
Star and torch of his own age,
Light and beacon of his people,
Yes, a very wondrous mighty

Fiery pillar of all song,
That preceded Israel's mournful
Caravan as it was marching
Through the desert of sad exile.

Halevi's patron, the venerated poet and contemporary of Omar Khayyam, Moses ibn Ezra (who also wrote riddles), once described him as 'the star from Castile which will illuminate the world'. Born into a wealthy and learned family in Toledo, c.1086, Halevi studied medicine for some years at Lucena and later set up practice in Cordova, where he quickly became the town's foremost physician. Halevi's riddles are contained in his *magnum opus* known as the *Cuzari* (or *Al-Khazari*), described by some as the Song of Songs of modern Judaism. Over three hundred of his poems are included in the Jewish liturgy but to give an example of his enigmatic skill, here is his riddle on a needle:

What is it that's blind with an eye in its head,
    But the race of mankind its use cannot spare;
Spends all its life in clothing the dead,
    But always itself is naked and bare?

The last major Hebrew riddler of this period was an Italian, a friend and imitator of Dante Alighieri. Immanuel ben Solomon ben Jekuthiel, known as Immanuel of Rome (1260–c.1328), was by all accounts a cheerful young man (another friend of Dante's once described him as 'the happily laughing soul'). He led a profligate youth and there are innumerable tales of his womanizing, reading of 'improper books', and taste for Greek philosophy – a habit then considered totally unorthodox. One day, however, to his own bad fortune and posterity's good luck, Immanuel suddenly lost his entire wealth. In his subsequent wanderings he met a patron who encouraged him to collect his writings into a single book. But such was the Jewish community's opinion of their wayward bard that this anthology, in which are also included his riddles, was instantly banned as being too erotic and irreligious. Indeed, although a version appeared in 1535, another complete edition of the work, entitled *Mahberot Immanuel*

(Compositions of Immanuel), did not appear until well into the eighteenth century.

RIDDLES FOR EVERYMAN: THE VERNACULAR

Riddles in the vernacular abound in the Middle Ages. We hear of riddles in the bazaars of twelfth-century China, of the teasers of 'Ali the Enigmatic', Fani and others in Turkey, and of countless examples both literary and oral in western Europe. However, it is only possible to scratch the surface of this huge treasury in a book of this size and mention just a few of the larger and more famous collections.

One of the most celebrated source-books of vernacular riddles and one of the most important general anthologies of early modern English literature is the Anglo-Saxon *Exeter Book*. Apart from ninety-six (presumably originally one hundred) magnificent riddles, it also includes some of the major extant writings of the early Anglo-Saxon period: poems like 'The Wanderer', 'The Seafarer', and 'The Whale'.

Originally believed to have been the product of the eighth-century Anglo-Saxon poet Cynewulf's pen, the *Exeter Book* was probably written in the last quarter of the tenth century and was presented to Exeter Cathedral in 1072 by Leofric, the city's bishop. The riddles are of varying length (the average is 15 lines; the longest 108) and are on common natural topics (many being on weapons or pastoral/agricultural themes) in both folk and literary form. Most of the answers have now been largely agreed upon amongst the academics, with the help of clues in the form of runes attached to some of the riddles in the manuscript.

Some of the riddles are mildly obscene but the majority are perfectly respectable, a good example being the following one on a plough:

> My beak is below, I burrow and nose
> Under the ground, I go as I'm guided
> By my master the farmer, old foe of the forest;
> Bent and bowed, at my back he walks,
> Forward pushing me over the field;
> Sows on my path where I've passed along.
> I came from the wood, a wagon carried me;
> I was fitted with skill, I am full of wonders.
> As grubbing I go, there's green on one side,
> But black on the other my path is seen.
> A curious prong pierces my back;
> Beneath me in front, another grows down
> And forward pointing is fixed to my head.
> I tear and gash the ground with my teeth,
> If my master steer me with skill from behind.

Whoever the author of the *Exeter Book* may have been, we can be sure that the composer of the Arabic literary masterpiece known as the *Maqamat* (or *Makamat*) was none other than the distinguished raconteur, poet, philologist, and enigmatographer Al-Hariri. Born in the ancient city of Basra in Iraq, then renowned for its learning and its famous school of Arabic grammar, Abu Muhammad Al-Qasim Al-Hariri (1054–1122) seemed destined to write riddles, for his lifelong occupation was *sahib al Khabar* – chief of local intelligence. Noted for his ugliness and described as being 'of mean aspect', Al-Hariri is reputed to have informed an offended student: 'I am a man to be heard of, not seen.'

The *maqamat* (or collection of 'assemblies') was a literary form pioneered some years before, in which a narrator relates stories told by a wandering rhetorician as he journeys from town to town, living off the donations given by appreciative audiences who *assemble* to hear him. The idea of writing such a collection was suggested to Al-Hariri by his patron Anushirwan of Baghdad, who, having read his first tale (the forty-eighth in the final version), encouraged him to write more. On completing forty, Al-Hariri presented them at the court of his benefactor, but when he failed to produce others on the spot he was accused of plagiarism. He returned home and wrote a further ten to complete the fifty that survive today. This stymied the critics and Al-Hariri achieved tremendous popularity, becoming greatly celebrated in his own lifetime and receiving acclaim from princes and poets alike. One contemporary of his, named Zamakhshari, even went as far as to say:

> I swear by God and His marvels,
> By the pilgrims' rite and their shrine:
> Hariri's *Assemblies* are worthy
> To be written in gold each line.

Written to please rather than instruct, the *Assemblies* contain a wealth of classical Arabic lore, including commentaries on the Koran, grammatical exercises, poetry, and jokes, as well as riddles. And the enigmas themselves are of various kinds, involving plays on Arabic words, grammatical quizzes, etc. Here is an example of a more conventional type of riddle, taken from Chapter 42:

> What groom is it who weds, both in secret and openly, two sisters, and no offence at his wedlock is ever found? When waiting on one, he waits as well on the other eke: if husbands are partial, no such bias is seen in him. His attentions increase as the sweethearts are growing grey, and so does his largess: what a rare thing in married men!

to which the solution is 'kohl pencil'.

The continued success of the book – which has become a classic of the Arabic tongue second only to the Koran itself – is partly due to the fact that almost without exception the stories are, unusually for this period, entirely decent. Many translations and imitations have appeared both in the Orient and in European countries, though a complete authoritative English version was not available until 1898.

Riddles also occur in the tale of Abu al-Husn and his slave-girl Tawaddud in *The Arabian Nights Entertainment*, whose earliest stories date from the eighth century, but perhaps the best oriental enigmas of this period occur in the *Shanamah*, or 'Book of Kings', of Persia. This beautifully illustrated book has been much admired over the years and stands as the major literary monument of Persian writing. It consists of 60,000 rhyming couplets tracing the history of the Persians until their conquest by the Arabs in the seventh century. It was written by Firdusi (b.*c*.950), who took thirty years to complete the work. When he presented it to Sultan Mahud the Great (998–1030), however, he was shabbily treated. Instead of a piece of gold for every line as promised, he received silver, and was so incensed that he divided the money between a beer vendor and an attendant at a local baths before leaving the city in disgust. Heinrich Heine immortalized the story in his 'The Poet Ferdusi' and tells how:

> Then his pilgrim staff he straightway
> Grasp'd, and left at once the city,
> And before the gate the dust he
> From his very shoes rejected.

The riddles, mostly on cosmological themes, appear in the section where the hero Zal (son of Sam) is tested by Menucheich, Emperor of Iran. (Zal, of course, is well-versed in the art and passes the test with flying colours.) Here is an example on day and night:

> There are two splendid horses, one black as pitch, the other of shining crystal; each runs ahead of the other but never catches it.

The *Shanamah* also inspired Matthew Arnold's poem 'Sohrab and Rustum' (1853).

APOLLONIUS OF TYRE AND THE INCEST RIDDLE

No account of riddling of this period, whether in Latin or the vernacular, would be complete without some reference to the story of Apollonius of Tyre and the evil king Antiochus. One of the best-known romances of the Middle Ages and the Renaissance, the tale appeared in over a hundred different Latin manuscript editions, the oldest of which dates from the ninth century, although allusions to previous accounts seem to indicate an ancestry more venerable still, perhaps dating back to a Hellenistic novel in the manner of Xenophon.

Simply put, the plot is as follows: King Antiochus has committed incest with his daughter and wants to prevent her marrying anyone else. To this end he decides to test each royal suitor with the following riddle:

> The branch's leaf is like the root.
> The father eats the mother's fruit.

Success wins the lady's hand, failure the suitor's death. After many challenges, King Apollonius of Tyre sails into town to try his hand and solves the riddle easily but is justifiably upset:

> ' . . . This riddle is unfair.
> It brings all guessers shame and care.
> If its dark words are plainly said,
> They mean you take your child to bed.

> 'You are the root, your child the tree.
> In mortal sin through her you be.
> Your child inherits the fleshly act
> Her mother did in marriage pact.'

Needless to say King Antiochus is enraged at being exposed and seeks to murder Apollonius, who sets sail with Antiochus's hitman Talliarchus hot on his heels. Shipwreck brings the luckless Apollonius to Pentapolis where he marries the king's daughter, Luciana. Hearing some time later that Antiochus and his daughter have died, Apollonius and his queen set sail homewards, but Luciana dies in childbirth at sea and in his grief Apollonius leaves the baby, Tarsiana, to be brought up at Tarsus and goes into self-imposed exile in Egypt until his daughter's wedding day. Returning ten years later and being shown Tarsiana's supposed grave, the poor fellow in his misery sails to his home town of Tyre to die. However, a storm drives him to Mytilene where his daughter had in fact been taken into slavery by pirates and has become well known for her singing. Sent to entertain the noble visitor, the girl refuses to accept his money until he either cheers up or answers a number of riddles such as the following:

> Downy inside, and smooth to the air,
> Inside my breast I wear my hair.
> From hand to hand I go in play.
> When men go eat, outside I stay.

to which Apollonius gives the solution 'ball'. The king guesses all the riddles and Tarsiana is so moved by his sadness that she hugs him. Apollonius throws her off and, upset, she recounts her whole unhappy life, on hearing which Apollonius discovers that she is his daughter. Sailing home they happen upon Luciana who had been washed ashore, still alive, at Ephesus, and the whole family live happily ever after.

The Renaissance and beyond

After the passionate outpourings of the Golden Age of Hebrew literature, the finely honed enigmas of the Anglo-Latin poets and their successors, and the superb forays into riddling in the vernacular by the likes of Al-Hariri and the author of the *Exeter Book*, the opening to the great renaissance of fine art and architecture of the sixteenth and seventeenth centuries was at first unpromising for the history of enigmatography. Strangely, the first stirrings of renewed interest came not from the formerly intensive breeding grounds of enigmatic composition but rather from the pens of a small number of German scribes writing in Latin. Once begun, however, the great machinery of enigmatography soon got into gear and cruised massively and with even greater finesse through the reigns of Henry VIII to Cromwell, past Caxton and Columbus to the Reformation, Lepanto and Shakespeare. A new generation of master riddlers would soon emerge and the subtle wit of Cervantes, Malatesti, Straparola and the anonymous English collections would once again tease the public imagination to the limits of its collective endurance with this maddening yet delightful literary exercise.

THE GERMAN ENIGMA

In the wake of such early riddling classics as the contest between Wolfram and Klingsor in the medieval *Wartburgkrieg* and the closely guarded enigmas of the famous 'Meistersingers', the first major collection of riddles to emerge in this period was the anonymous German anthology culled from many sources and known as the *Strassburger Räthselbuch* (1505).

After this came a number of German Protestant academics composing literary enigmas in Latin. The first of these, Ludovicus Helmbold (1532–98), was a teacher and minister of the church in Muhlhausen, Thuringia; he published a hundred rather pedestrian riddles under the title *Aenigmatum centuria*.

30

Next, William of Orange's lawyer, Johannes Lorichius Secundus (also known as Hadamerius from his birthplace near Koblenz), published a three-volume collection entitled *Aenigmatum libri tres* in 1545, which was followed twenty years later by the *Emblematum et aenigmatum libellus* of the emblematist Hadrian Junius.

Though Junius was regarded by many as the most distinguished writer of Latin riddles in northern Europe in this period, it is perhaps his successor, Nicolaus Reusner, Rector of Jena University (where years later another enigmatist, Schiller, was to further the art), who is best known today. Not only did Reusner compose riddles on his own account, he also compiled an enormous collection, *Aenigmatographia*, in which he preserved for posterity many examples that might otherwise have been lost. Here is the riddle for smoke taken from his volume *Aenigmata*, published in the last year of his life (1602):

> *Lacryma multa mihi, sed nulla est causa doloris,*
> *Coeli affecto vitam, sed gravis aer obest.*

> (Many are the tears I give but there is no cause for grief. I strive for life in the sky, but the weighty air engulfs me.)

A year earlier, 120 enigmas from the hand of Johannes Lauterbach (1531–93), a teacher in Heilbronn, were published, and later another teacher, Johannes Buchler of Gladbach in north Germany, put together an equally popular collection. This book, whose abbreviated title is *Gnomologia*, was first issued in 1602 and contained a variety of folklore pieces including proverbs and songs as well as riddles. Joachim Camerarius of Papenberg also wrote some riddles at this time and 420 enigmas were published by Huldrich Therander in 1605, though most of these are merely German versions of older Latin originals.

RIDDLING IN ENGLAND

The passion for riddling, ever strong in medieval Britain, grew apace during the Renaissance and many collections circulated during this period, noteworthy both as works of literature in their own right and for the influence they had on the great poets, playwrights, and thinkers of the day – the most notable of whom was, of course, William Shakespeare.

Shakespeare would have known the works of the great riddle-masters of the past and those of his own time, and there are innumerable allusions to riddles and riddling in his plays. Lysander 'riddles very prettily' in *A Midsummer Night's Dream*; 'riddling confession finds but riddling shrift' for Romeo in *Romeo and Juliet*; and a rather grim enigma also appears in the

31

gravediggers' scene of *Hamlet* (Act V, Scene 1) thus:

First Clown:
What is he that builds stronger than either the mason, the shipwright or the carpenter?
Second Clown:
The gallows-maker; for that frame outlives a thousand tenants.

That Shakespeare had read the *History of Apollonius of Tyre* in some shape or form is evidenced by his dramatization of the basic plot in his play *Pericles*. In fact, the choice of name for his continuity character, Gower, seems to suggest that it was the version of the tale in John Gower's *Confessio Amantis* (1390) that had fired his imagination. Be that as it may, the substance of the plot is much the same, though Shakespeare's version – unlike, say, the Spanish *El Libro di Apolonio* – lacks the sequence of riddles when Apollonius (Pericles in Shakespeare) confronts his long-lost daughter Tarsiana (Shakespeare's Marina). However, his treatment of the key Antiochus riddle is masterful:

I am no viper, yet I feed
On mother's flesh which did me breed.
I sought a husband, in which labour
I found that kindness in a father.
He's father, son, and husband mild;
I mother, wife and yet his child:
How they may be, and yet in two,
As you will live, resolve it you.
(*Pericles*, Act I, Scene 1, 65–72)

Riddling was practised in all walks of life under the Tudors, from the fireside jokes and pleasantries of the peasant to the razor-sharp wit of the court *littérateurs*.

The metaphysical poet John Donne alludes to the power of the enigmatic art when he describes the complexities of the soul in his *Sermons*: 'Poor intricated soul! Riddling, perplexed, labyrinthine soul!'; and Thomas Campion in 'Winter Nights' talks of filling the long evenings:

This time doth well dispense
    With lovers' long discourse;
Much speech hath some defence,
    Though beauty no remorse.
All things do not all things well;
    Some measures comely tread,
Some knotted riddles tell,
    Some poems smoothly read.

And 'labyrinthine' the riddle had certainly become at the hands of some of the finer exponents of the art with the massive upsurge in learning brought by the Renaissance. However, a certain earthiness can still be found in many of the enigmas of this period. This was, after all, the time of the riddles of Stigliani and Straparola, and even official court riddlers could still get away with the occasional uncensored ribaldry, as the following exchange between the far-from-prudish Henry VIII and his jester Will Sommers testifies:

> 'Now tell me,' says Will, 'if you can, what it is, that being born without life, head, lip or eye, yet doth run roaring through the world till it die?'
> 'This is a wonder,' quod the king, 'and no question. I know it not.'
> 'Why,' quod Will, 'it is a fart.'
> At this the king laughed heartily and was exceeding merry . . .

> (from R. Armin, *Foole upon Foole*, 1600)

The first riddle book printed in the English language was *The Demaundes Joyous*, produced by Wynkyn de Worde in 1511. Essentially a selective translation of a French book (by an anonymous author) known as *Demandes joyeuses en manière de quodlibets* and published at the end of the previous century, it contains a series of fifty-four questions prefaced by the word 'Demaunde' and followed by the solutions; it is quite short, only six pages in all. Some of the riddles are mildly obscene (though the worst have been edited out by the English printer), and some are rather dull, being just questions testing one's knowledge of the Bible. None the less this little book, originally published in the reign of Henry VIII, has remained immensely popular over the years. Here is a short example of the kind of riddle it contains:

> What thing is it, the less it is the more it is dread?

to which the answer is 'a bridge'.

Another popular collection of the sixteenth century, again anonymous, was *The Riddles of Heraclitus and Democritus* (1598), printed by Arnold Hatfield. Heraclitus was long regarded as the arch-riddler of pre-Socratic philosophy and this collection, though certainly in no way connected with the work of the ancient Greek seer, gained a certain kudos from using his name in the title. There are sixty riddles in all, of varying lengths and metres, on subjects ranging from animals to household objects – like the following riddle on a pound of candles:

On an evening as colde as colde might bee,
  With frost and haile, and pinching weather,
Companions about three times three
  Lay close in a pound together:
Yet one after one they took a heate
  And died that night, all in a sweate.

The little-known poet Humphrey Gifford (*fl.*1580) produced a commendable collection of eighteen enigmas at this time, which were published at the end of a volume of his verse entitled *Posie of Gillowflowers* (1580). The somewhat more famous poet and emblematist George Wither is credited with having composed a number of enigmas. Other collections creating interest at this time were *Wit's Extraction* (1664) by William Bagwell and *Wit's Academy, or Six Peny'worth for a Penny* (1656), reputed to have been the work of Ben Jonson, though published nineteen years after his death. John Florio (*c.*1553–1625), Jonson's friend and the translator of Montaigne, included a number of enigmatical questions in his Anglo-Italian book, *First Fruites* (1578), and Sir Thomas Wyatt also seems to have turned his hand to fashioning a few riddles, like the following verse on a gun:

Vulcan begat me; Minerva me taught:
Nature, my mother; Craft nourisht me year by year:
Three bodies are my foode: my strength is naught.
Anger, wrath, waste, and noise are my children dear.
Guess, my friend, what I am: and how I am wraught:
Monster of sea, or of land, or of elsewhere.
Know me and use me: and may thee defend:
And if I be thine enemy, I may thy life end.
                    (from *Tottel's Miscellany*, 1557)

The soldier-poet, George Gascoigne (*c.*1534–77) and even Isaac Newton himself have had riddling stanzas ascribed to them.

During this period a number of volumes of enigmas appeared with titles that varied on the theme of 'A Book of Merry Riddles' (in various spellings). These are all believed to draw on a rather salacious collection called *A Hundred Merry Riddles*, produced by William Rastell in about 1530. A cleaned-up edition of this book, containing only seventy-six riddles, was extremely popular in Shakespeare's time and may well have been the 'Book of Riddles' that Slender loses in *The Merry Wives of Windsor*:

Slender:
. . . How now, Simple, where have you been? I must wait on myself, must I? You have not the book of Riddles about you, have you?

34

Simple:
Book of Riddles? Why, did you not lend it to Alice Short-cake upon All-hallowmas last, a fortnight afore Michaelmas?

(Act I, Scene 1, 181–6)

Another important collection from this time is the one now commonly referred to as *The Holme Riddles*, an anthology of over 140 enigmas collected by the Randle Holme family of Chester. There were four Randle Holmes (b. 1571, 1601, 1627 and 1659) and the manuscript is written in three different hands. Many of the riddles, which are on the usual folk themes and are sometimes obscene, can be traced back to other sources, but one particularly striking and original example is the following on a rose-bud:

> there is a thing wch hath five chins 2 hath beards 2 hath none, & one it hath but half an one.

(The rose's outward green leaves are both jagged and plain.)

THE ITALIAN SCHOOL

In Italy enigmatography reached a degree of sophistication hitherto undreamt of. Immanuel of Rome, Dante's riddling Jewish friend, had set the pace with his *Mahberot*, and following in his wake all the major scribes of the day sharpened up their quill pens and set to, it being quite the thing to be known to be engaged in this high-society fad in one's spare time. It is said that Dante wrote riddles, as did Petrarch; Boccaccio included a number of acrostics in his unfinished work *Amorosa Visione*; Leonardo da Vinci is credited with some enigmatic pronouncements; and seven salacious enigmas flowed from the hand of the renowned man of letters and namesake of Francesco Griffo's excellent seriffed typeface, Cardinal Pietro Bembo (1470–1547). The great astronomer Galileo Galilei also wrote a number of riddles such as the following on the riddle itself:

> *Monstro son io più strano, è più difforme*
>   *Che l'Arpia, la Sirena, o la Chimera;*
>   *Nè in terra, in aria, in acqua è alcuna fiera,*
>   *Ch'abbia di membra così varie forme.*
> *Parte a parte non ho che sia conforme,*
>   *Più che s'una sia bianca, o l'altra nera;*
>   *Spesso di cacciator dietro ho una schiera,*
>   *Che de' miei piè van rintracciando l'orme.*
> *Nelle tenebre oscure è il mio soggiorno;*
>   *Che se dall'ombre al chiaro lume passo,*
>   *Tosto l'alma da me sen fugge, come*

Sen fugge il sogno all'apparir del giorno,
  E le mie membra disunite lasso,
  E l'esser perdo con la vita, e'l nome.

> (I am a monster, stranger and more alien than the Harpy,
> the Siren, or the Chimera. Neither on land, in the air, nor
> in the sea is there a beast whose limbs can have so many
> shapes; no one piece of me conforms with another, anymore
> than if one is white, the other is black. A band of hunters
> often follows behind me looking for the tracks made by my
> feet. I inhabit the darkest places, and if I pass from the
> shadows into bright light my soul quickly slips away with
> the coming of the day and my tired limbs fall away, and I
> lose my being with my life and with my name.)

The composition of riddles in Latin continued to flourish
during this period. Lilio Gregorio Giraldi's *Aenigmatum ex anti-*
quis . . . (1551) collected together in one book all the enigmas
from classical antiquity known at that time, and Julius Caesar
Scaliger (*Poetices*, 1561; *Poemata*, 1591), whose complete works
run to over 1,000 pages, is credited with having written more
Latin enigmas than any other Italian – in his own words '*plurima*
fecimus nos'. A good example is this specimen on a plough from
Poemata:

Ore gero gladium, matrisque in pectore condo
  Ut mox, qua nunc sunt mortua, viva colas.
Dux meus a tergo caudamque trahens retrahensque
  Hasta non me ut eam verberat ast alios.

> (I carry a sword in my mouth, and I bury it in my mother's
> breast so that soon you may cultivate, alive, what is now
> dead. My leader from behind me sticks a tail on me and
> drags it back and forth, and lashes not me but others, in
> order to beat her.)

However, it was with riddles in the vernacular that the Italians
really excelled. One of the best and certainly the most prolific
Italian enigmatographer of the sixteenth century was the
blacksmith-riddler Giulio Cesare Croce (1550–1609). Born at
San Giovanni in Persiceto in northern Italy, Croce settled in
Bologna, siring no less than fourteen children and giving birth to
an incredible 478 literary works of various kinds. He is
especially noteworthy in that not only are the riddles in his two
major collections (*Notte sollazzevole di cento enigmi* . . . (1599)
and *Seconde notte* . . . (1601)) perhaps the most original of his
time, but they are also exceptional in being almost entirely
'decent'. Nearly all the other riddlers of Renaissance Italy
included among their works subjects of a highly obscene nature.

Indeed, thirty-six of Stigliani's forty-three octaves and sonnets are still deemed too foul to reprint even today. Here is Croce's riddle on the earth:

> Sospesa in aria stò, nè tocco nulla,
>   E circondata son di lumi intorno,
> Hor di novo mi vesto, hora son brulla,
>   E al caldo, al freddo stò la notte, e'l giorno,
> Ogn'un di calpestarmi si trastulla,
>   Fino alle bestie mi fan danno, e scorno,
> E tai tesori ascondo nel mio seno,
>   Che chi gli trova fò felice a pieno.

(I am suspended in the air, I touch nothing, and I am surrounded by lights. Now I dress myself afresh, and now I am naked, and I am in the heat and the cold, by night and by day. Everyone amuses himself by trampling upon me, even the animals abuse and scorn me, and yet I have such treasures hidden in my bosom that he who finds them I can make full of happiness.)

Gifted writers such as Cenni (another blacksmith) and the pseudonymous author of seventy-one riddling sonnets known as 'Madonna Daphne' must, for reasons of space, be passed over quickly here. However, no account of riddling in Renaissance Italy would be complete without giving due consideration to the superb irreverent creations of Giovanni Francesco Straparola. Despite the banning of his *Facetious Nights* and the 'castrated' versions that appeared following it, this book was tremendously successful and went into twenty editions in as many years (Boccaccio had to wait fifty years before the eighteenth edition of *The Decameron* appeared), influencing many subsequent riddle-masters and supplying fables to be retold later by such major figures as Perrault and Molière. Though many of the seventy-four uproarious tales derive from Boccaccio, the *Gesta Romanorum*, *Arabian Nights*, Morlini's *Novellae*, and ancient Sanskrit yarns, some – notably the story of Belphegor – are the product of Straparola's own pen. Perhaps most memorable of all his creations is the fairy-tale of *Puss in Boots*, reworked for posterity by Perrault, the Brothers Grimm, and the German poet Tieck. Stories taken from the *Facetious Nights* also appear in Painter's *Palace of Pleasure* (1566) and it was also drawn on by the versatile riddler Alexandre Sylvain. Not all Straparola's riddles were rude, as the following example on a football attests:

> Dead to men I seem to be,
> Yet surely breath there is in me;
> Cruel is my fate, I trow,
> Buffeted now high, now low.

But assaults of fist and heel
Vex me not, for naught I feel.
Blameless I midst all my woes,
Yet find all men my bitter foes,
Backwards, forwards, urged and driven,
Soaring high from earth to heaven.

Moving on to the seventeenth century, the first enigmatist of note – or perhaps it would be more accurate to say notoriety – was another riddling scandal-monger, Tommaso Stigliani. Born in 1573, Stigliani was employed in the court of Charles Emmanuel I and seems to have spent a large part of his spare time composing outrageous enigmas which were published (including the thirty-six unrepeatable ones) in the still prohibited *Rime* (1605). A slightly cleaner version appeared as *Canzoniero* in 1623.

Another wayward riddler of this period was the Franciscan friar Francesco Moneti. Perhaps best known as one of the greatest humorous satirical poets of his age, Moneti is reputed to have lacked the humility and brotherly love required of one of his calling. Born in 1635, Antonio Moneti changed his Christian name as a mark of respect when he entered the order at the age of sixteen. Such was his reputation for writing scurrilous verse that when a lampoon appeared on the death of Pope Clement X (1669) Moneti was immediately seized and imprisoned for nearly twelve months as being the most likely author (he was in fact innocent on this occasion).

His riddles are contained in three books published around 1699 which overlap somewhat; perhaps the most complete edition is *Apollo énnimatico*, which contains 150 riddles in the form of octaves, sestinas, and quatrains on everyday topics such as candles and salt, with a sprinkling of more abstract subjects like vice, truth, and death.

Michelangelo Buonarroti the Younger (1568–1646), grand-nephew of the artist and a poet in his own right, wrote seventy-one very 'decent' riddles, and a very large anonymous collection known as the *Genoa University Manuscript* also dates from this period.

The unquestioned master of Italian seventeenth-century riddling was Antonio Malatesti. Born in Florence in 1610 Malatesti was a friend of the poet Lorenzo Lippi and features in the latter's classic poem *Malmatile Racquistato* as 'Amostante Latoni' (which is an anagram of the riddler's name). His play *La Tina* was dedicated to Milton (who is supposed to have met Malatesti while travelling in Italy) but it is for his riddle collection *La Sfinge* – in three parts (1640, 1643, and 1683) – that he is best remembered. This book inspired many subsequent riddlers and though some of the subject-matter can hardly be classified as altogether proper, it certainly cannot be termed vulgar. In total the three parts contain 269 sonnets, 57 octaves, and 66 quatrains. The riddle on a mirror warrants inclusion here to give an impression of the master's touch:

> Chi vuol vedere quel che fuggir non può,
>   venga venga una volta innanzi a me,
>   che s'avrà gli occhi e la ragion con sè,
>   conoscerà quel ch'io gli mostrerò.
> In virtù dell'argento il tutto fo
>   non avend'io religïon, nè fè;
>   ignudo mostro il corpo com'egli è,
>   se dal fiato dell'uom panni non ò.
> Nè m'importa, se un brutto in odio m'à,
>   mentre un bello si val di mia virtù,
>   perchè chiara i'vo'dir la verità.
> Piccola o grande vaglio meno e più;
>   ma se non fusse la fragilità,
>   varrei più, che non val tutto il Perù.

(He who wants to see what is escaping, and cannot, let him come once first to me, for if he has got his eyes and his reason with him, he will know what I will show him. I do everything in the virtue of silver, having no religion or faith; I show the body, naked as it is, if I am not clothed by the breath of man. Nor does it matter to me, if I am held in hatred by someone ugly whilst a beautiful person values my worth, because I will speak the truth clearly. The small or the large I consider less and more; but if it were not for my fragility, I would be worth more than the whole of Peru.)

THE FRENCH TRADITION

The celebrated essayist Michel de Montaigne (1533–92) is credited with having declared:

> I have a backward and torpid mind; the least cloud stops its progress. I have never, for example, found a riddle easy enough for me to solve.

However, this is not to say that French enigmatography of this period was of a particularly complicated kind. In fact, the folk-riddles of the highly successful *Les Adevineaux amoureux*, produced by an anonymous author in 1478, owe much of their popularity to the simplicity of their presentation, as this enigma on lice, fingers, and eyes testifies:

Two who run and ten who chase them, two who look on, and one who puts them to death.

Another bestselling riddle book from this period was the original of Wynkyn de Worde's *Demaundes Joyous*, an anonymous collection of enigmas entitled *Demandes joyeuses en manière de quodlibets*, printed some time before 1500. The original contained eighty-seven *demandes* whilst de Worde's has only fifty-four.

Two spoof riddles occur in Rabelais's *Gargantua* (1534), whilst Chapter 19 of *Pantagruel* (1532) depicts a dumb-show exchange of rebuses between the witty buffoon Panurge and the English philosopher Thaumast. And in Chapter 11 of the so-called 'Fifth Book' of the series Panurge and company are arrested by the monster Grippeminault, Archduke of the Furrycats, a race of terrible creatures that eat little children and feed on marble stones. From his seat of justice, the monster demands an answer to the following riddle:

A pretty creature, young and fair and slender,
Conceived, without a sire, a swarthy son
And bore him painlessly, the little tender
Suckling, although his birth was a strange one.
For, like a viper, through her side he bored
Impatiently, a truly hideous thing,
And then o'er hill and valley boldly soared,
Riding the air, and o'er land journeying;
Which drove the Friend of Wisdom out of his mind,
For he had thought him of the human kind.

After some humming and hawing Panurge eventually comes up with the solution, which is a black weevil born from a white bean. (Pythagoras – 'Friend of Wisdom' equals 'philosopher' – believed it to have received a human soul from somewhere by metempsychosis.)

Tabourot des Accords's study of rebuses and other kinds of puzzles, entitled *Les Bigarrures du Seigneur des Accords*, also appeared at about this time (1582) and was well received. As well as examples of the pictorial form the book included chapters on literary and even musical rebuses. A good example is the following lover's riddle:

which reads '*Deux coeurs en un coeur*' and '*S'entre-aymer, iusques à la fin comme au commencement*' ('Two hearts in one heart' and 'To love one another the same at the end as at the beginning').

Charles Fontaine is credited with a collection of *Odes, énigmes et épigrammes* dating from 1557, but it seems that the only French riddler of any renown in the sixteenth century was Alexandre Sylvain (in reality the Belgian poet and enigmatist Alexander van den Bussche), whose *Cinquante aenigmes françoises* appeared in 1582. These riddles draw mainly on Italian sources, such as Straparola, and are generally of sonnet form. Here is an example on an oyster:

> *Ie n'ay ny pieds, ny mains, ny teste, mais un corps,*
> *Qui est tousiours armé d'une armure bien forte*
> *Qui me sert de rampart, de fenestre, & de porte,*
> *Et par fois est ouverte à ceux qui par dehors*
> *Guettent: pour me manger, car plus que moy sont forts.*
> *Mais pour mieux leur monstrer combien celà m'importe*
> *Ie les retiens captifs, & prins de telle sorte*
> *Que malgré leur effort souvent demeurent morts.*
> *Ie ne les mange point, car ce qu'est ma viande*
> *Est si tres delicat qu'à peine se peut voir,*
> *En fin ie suis mangé tant ma misere est grande,*
> *Qui me sçaura nommer fera bien son devoir.*

(I have neither feet, nor hands, nor head, but only a body, which is always protected by very strong armour that serves as rampart, window and door, and is sometimes opened to those who are outside lying in wait: to eat me, for they are stronger than me. But in order to show them how much I resent this, I keep them captive and prisoner so that in spite of all their efforts they often die. But I do not eat them, because the kind of food I eat is so dainty that you can hardly see it. In the end, though, I am eaten and my misery is great. He who can name me will have performed his task well.)

The following century saw the publication in 1694 of a remarkable treatise on enigmatography entitled *La philosophie des images énigmatiques*. Composed by the Jesuit historian and heraldic scholar Claude-François Menestrier, this thorough study discusses the background and significance of most varieties of riddle from oracles to hieroglyphics and includes a section of sample enigmas of each sort.

This period also saw the composition of the poet Boileau's famous riddle on the flea:

> *Du repos des Humains implacable Ennemie,*
> *J'ay rendu mille Amans envieux de mon sort;*
> *Je me repais de sang, et je trouve ma vie*
> *Dans les bras de celui qui recherche ma mort.*

(Implacable enemy of human rest, I have made a thousand lovers jealous of my lot; I feast on blood, and find my life in the arms of those who seek my death.)

This fine enigma was communicated to Boileau's friend, the advocate Brossette, in a letter of 29 September 1703. Boileau claimed it was his first-ever literary work, as he had composed it around 1652, when he was only seventeen.

Riddling questions can be found in *Les Aventures de Télémaque* (1699), the best-known work of Fénélon, Archbishop of Cambrai (1651–1715), and another popular collection dating from this time in Abbé Cotin's *Recueil des énigmes de ce temps*, containing over a hundred riddles, including a number of the riddle itself.

CERVANTES AND RIDDLING IN SPAIN

On the Iberian peninsula, the tradition of *preguntas* (a kind of riddling question in rhyme) was already well established by 1545 when Spain's first important collection of riddles, Luis Escobar's *Respuetas a las cuatrocientas preguntas* was published. This was followed by Sebastian de Horozco's *Cancionero*, containing many excellent enigmas both respectable and obscene. In 1581 Sylvain appeared again, this time in the guise of Alexandro Sylvano, with a collection of forty riddles entitled *Quarenta aenigmas en lengua espannola*.

However, dominating the seventeenth century – master of the riddle as well as every other aspect of Spanish literature of this period – is Miguel de Cervantes Saavedra, author of the masterpiece *Don Quixote*. Some particularly notable examples of his riddling skill occur in Book 6 of the pastoral epic *La Galatea*, written before *Don Quixote* in 1585, in which the heroine (after whom the book is named) is engaged in an outdoor exchange of wits with her friends. The riddling session, however, is cut short by the sound of a struggle between some shepherds and a person attempting suicide on the banks of a nearby river. This riddle on a riddle is perhaps best representative of Cervantes's style.

> Dark 'tis, yet very clear,
> Containing infinite variety,
> Encumbering us with truths,
> Which are at length declared.
> 'Tis sometimes of a jest produced,
> At others of high fancy.
> And it is wont defiance to create,
> Of airy matters treating.

Any man its name may know,
Even to little children,
Many there are, and masters have
In different ways.
There is no old woman it embraces not,
With of these ladies, one
At times in good odour,
This tires, that satisfies.

Wise ones there be who overwatch
Sensations to extract.
Some run wild
The more they watch o'er it.
Such is foolish, and such curious,
Such easy, such complex,
Yet, be it something, be it nought,
Reveal to me what the said thing may be?

It is sad to think that Cervantes, whose works were enormously popular in his own lifetime, should none the less die a pauper – another riddle perhaps.

Revival and decline

As every schoolboy knows (and every schoolgirl too), the eighteenth century was the great *Wendepunkt* of modern European history. Hard on the heels of the glittering grand monarchies of Louix XIV and Frederick the Great of Prussia came the 'Age of Revolutions', when justice was meted out to the spendthrift aristocracy, the starving masses received their due and the yoke of a medieval form of government was cast off for ever. This was the period of the American War of Independence (1775–83) and the French Revolution (1789–99), of Paine and Rousseau and the Romantic Movement that drew its ideals from them, and of the great satirists Pope and Swift. And, quite apart from 'Madame Guillotine', it was also a time of great advances in technology, particularly in the media, with broadsheets and magazines reaching the general public to an extent undreamt of only a short while before. In company with the polemics, lampoons, news items, and poems, one of the literary forms that took advantage of the widespread dissemination of the printed word was the riddle. There was a renewed upsurge of interest in riddle ballads collected later by Sir Walter Scott and others in Great Britain.

* *
5/2
—
91

43

see p. 49

Through the influence of the beautifully worked creations of Schiller in Germany, Swift in England, and many of the Italian enigmatographers (notably Catone l'Uticense Lucchese), riddling once again became a major public entertainment and private pastime, and fashionable folk fairly buzzed with the latest enigmas from the new breed of virtuosi. Riddlemania seemed to have permeated all levels of society, but particular impact during this age of turmoil came from the higher intellectual strata – even the great French *philosophe* François Voltaire being credited with some erudite riddling verses. And his equally great contemporary, Jean Jacques Rousseau also wrote a few *énigmes* such as the following on a portrait, published in 1776:

> *Enfant de l'Art, Enfant de la Nature,*
> *Sans prolonger les jours j'empêche de mourir:*
> *Plus je suis vrai, plus je fais d'imposture,*
> *Et je deviens trop jeune à force de vieillir.*

(Child of Art, Child of Nature, without prolonging life, I prevent death: the truer I am, the more false I appear, and I become too young as age creeps on.)

With the riddle-masters of the eighteenth century the sun of western enigmatography had reached its zenith and, though commendable work continued to be published in the following decades and beyond, the light of this particular form of literary wit had begun to fade in the popular imagination and never again would public enthusiasm for them wax so great.

"STURM UND DRANG" ... AND RIDDLES

Johann Wolfgang von Goethe took an active interest in the riddle form and a number of witty enigmas by him were circulated to friends between 1802 and 1827. But it was with Goethe's friend and co-director (along with Herder) of the German *Sturm und Drang* Movement in European Romanticism – Friedrich von Schiller – that the literary riddle arguably received its highest expression of all time.

Schiller (b. 1759) stands in the front rank of German playwright-poets of this period and was also highly esteemed as an historian, succeeding to the chair of History at Jena University in the year that the Paris mob laid waste the Bastille prison. His riddles still carry much of their delightful mystery in translation. Here is an example taken from a miscellaneous collection entitled *Parabeln und Rätsel* (1803).

> A bird it is, whose rapid motion
>   With eagle's flight divides the air;
> A fish it is, and parts the ocean,

That bore a greater monster ne'er;
An elephant it is, whose rider
　　On his broad back a tower has put:
'Tis like the reptile base, the spider,
　　Whenever it extends its foot;
And when, with iron tooth projecting,
　　It seeks its own life-blood to drain,
On footing firm, itself erecting,
　　It braves the raging hurricane.

The solution is 'a ship'.

Many of these enigmas had already had a public airing in another of Schiller's plays, *Turandot* (1802), translated from Carlo Gozzi's Italian original. In order to keep the audiences guessing, Schiller would depart from Gozzi's three basic riddles and introduce different ones at every performance. Gozzi's original riddles were:

Who is the creature which belongs to every country, is a friend of the entire world, and does not tolerate its equal?

Who is the mother that gives birth to her children, and devours them when they grow up?

What is the tree whose leaves are white on one side and black on the other?

to which the solutions are, respectively, 'the sun', 'the sea', and 'the year'.

SWIFT AND THE ENIGMA IN ENGLAND

Meanwhile in England interest in riddling had recommenced with increased vigour. Notable public figures such as William Pitt (1708–78) and the Whig statesman Charles James Fox (1749–1806) composed enigmas. And many more have been ascribed to Lord Chesterfield, Garrick, Canning, Thomas Moore, and Horace Walpole. The pastoral poet William Cowper wrote the following riddle in July 1780 between his many fits of despondency:

I am just two and two, I am warm, I am cold,
And the parent of numbers that cannot be told.
I am lawful, unlawful – a duty, a fault,
I am often sold dear, good for nothing when bought;
An extraordinary boon, and a matter of course,
And yielded with pleasure when taken by force.
Alike the delight of the poor and the rich,
Tho' the vulgar is apt to present me his breech.

which when printed in *The Gentleman's Magazine* some years later (December 1806) received this riddling reply:

> A riddle by Cowper
> Made me swear like a trooper;
> But my anger, alas! was in vain;
>   For, remembering the bliss
>   Of beauty's soft Kiss,
> I now long for such riddles again.

Another notable contribution at this time was by the poet Catherine Maria Fanshawe (1765–1834) who wrote the famous 'A Riddle on the Letter H', once mistakenly credited to Lord Byron. Here is the 'amended' version with the now generally accepted alteration to the opening line:

> 'Twas whispered in heaven, 'twas muttered in hell,
> And echo caught faintly the sound as it fell;
> On the confines of earth 'twas permitted to rest,
> And the depth of the ocean its presence confessed . . .
> Yet in shade let it rest, like a delicate flower,
> Ah, breathe on it softly, – it dies in an hour.

A number of fine riddles were also composed by members of the famous 'Blue Stocking Circle' and their followers, in particular by Mrs Delany, Hannah More, Mrs Barbauld, and Esther Vanhomrigh (Swift's 'Vanessa').

Various anonymous collections appeared with titles such as *A Choice Collection of Riddles, Charades, Rebusses* (1792), *Thesaurus Ænigmaticus* (1725), *The Masquerade* (1797), *The Polite Jester* (1796), and *John Falkirk's Cariches*.

Perhaps the most significant enigmatographer in England during this period was the satirist, poet, and author of *Gulliver's Travels*, Dean Swift (1667–1745). These stylish, high-brow, literary enigmas were published in serial form in journals like *The Muses Mercury* and the *Miscellanies* (of Pope, Swift, Arbuthnot, and Gay) printed by Faulkner in 1727. The subjects vary considerably, as does their length and metre, but perhaps this riddle on gold serves as well as any to illustrate his right to immortality in the pantheon of the world's greatest riddle-masters:

> All-ruling Tyrant of the Earth,
> To vilest Slaves I owe my birth.
> How is the greatest Monarch blest,
> When in my gaudy Liv'ry drest!
> No haughty Nymph has Pow'r to run
> From me; or my Embraces shun.
> Stabbed to the Heart, condemned to Flame,
> My Constancy is still the same.

The fav'rite Messenger of *Jove*,
And *Lemnian* God consulting strove,
To make me glorious to the Sight
Of Mortals, and the Gods Delight.
Soon would their Altars Flame expire
If I refus'd to lend them Fire.

RIDDLING MAGAZINES

Swift was not the only riddler to take advantage of the new
technology as manifested in the publication of popular and
literary magazines in the eighteenth century. In France the Paris-
based *Mercure de France* (first published in 1672) soon
established itself as the frontrunner of a flourishing industry in
society riddling journals, and published occasional writings from
many of the leading literary figures of the day. *Énigmes*,
logogriphs, and charades would appear regularly in this fortnightly pot-pourri of poetry, news, and views, with their solutions being given in the following issue. A frequent contributor
in the years up to 1810 (after which time the magazine seems to
have deemed such bagatelles too frivolous to grace their pages)
was the enigmatist Lamotte (or Lamothe), an example of whose
work from the revolutionary month of 'Brumaire' (October) in
Year 9 (1800) I give here:

> *Avec un guide impitoyable,*
> *Je parcours les monts chevelus,*
> *Où je poursuis un monstre, aux humains redoubtable;*
> *C'est aux jeunes taillis que je chasse le plus,*
> *Et souvent j'y vais faire un carnage effroyable*
> *De ces monstres cruels, sous mes dents, abattus.*

(With a ruthless guide, I wander over hairy mountains where
I pursue a monster, dreaded by humans. It is in the young
brushwood that I hunt the most and often I inflict a frightful
carnage on those cruel monsters, slaughtered under my teeth.)

The solution is 'a comb'. Journals devoted to riddling mush-
roomed all over France in this period, which also saw the
publication of the riddle treasury (437 *énigmes*) *Magasin
énigmatique*, edited by Duchesne.

Meanwhile in England, apart from the pages of *The Muses
Mercury: Or the Monthly Miscellany* edited by John Oldmixon
and *The London Magazine and Monthly Chronicler* (1732–85),
perhaps the most significant forum for the enigmatic art was the
Universal Magazine of Knowledge and Pleasure. First published
in 1747, this monthly periodical gives perhaps the most representative image of English riddling in the eighteenth century.

Contributors would pose riddles to be solved (hopefully, but not always) by the next issue and a veritable stampede would follow in which budding literati would attempt to be the first to guess the answers. Here is an example, together with its solution in verse (as was common), by one 'E.R.' from the October issue of 1747:

> Nor wings, nor feet, unto my share have fell,
> Yet I in swiftness do the best excel.
> Arms I have none, nor weapons do I wear,
> And yet I daily wound the brave and fair.
> My name is odious, both to friends and foes,
> Yet I'm admired by all the Belles and Beaus.
> And when my name's concealed, I've many friends,
> The best man fears me, and his fault amends.
> All wise men hate me, as their common foe,
> Take C from me, I keep you from the snow.
> Old maids caress me, for this world I hate,
> As it hates them, so we receive our fate.
> From these short hints, to tell my name's your task,
> That well performed, I've nothing more to ask.

The answer coming in the form:

> She needs no wings: she makes but too much haste.
> She needs no weapons; for she wounds too fast.
> Old maids, and belles, and beaus caress the quean.
> And why? She kills their time, and vents their spleen.
> The brave, the wise, the good, she will defame.
> A cursed fiend! and SCANDAL is her name.

Though the magazine, like the *Mercure de France*, was published well into the nineteenth century, the practice of including riddles amongst its items did not, and by the time of the new series in 1814 they had disappeared from its pages for ever.

THE CHAPBOOK ENIGMA

Though multifarious magazines and journals circulated in urban literary society at this time, such periodicals would rarely find their way across the length and breadth of the country. And in the days before national newspapers (*The Times*, then known as *The Daily Universal Register*, did not appear until 1785), penny post, TV and radio, the chapman – a pedlar of household goods, sundry broadsides and cheap pamphlets – was a commonplace and welcome figure in the small communities that dotted the English countryside. Carrying his wares from village to village, the itinerant chapman was often the only contact that many citizens of the realm had with the doings of their own government, let alone the outside world. Among his political tracts, news-stories (usually somewhat distorted), and varied amusements to while away the long dark evenings were small collections of riddles. Two very popular examples which survive from the eighteenth century are *A Whetstone for Dull Wits* and *The True Trial of Understanding or Wit Newly Reviv'd*. Each only a few pages long, they contain fifteen and nine riddles respectively, beautifully illustrated with explanatory woodcuts. The riddles are of varying lengths and on subjects of a folk-oriented kind such as the following (from *A Whetstone for Dull Wits*):

> By the help of a guide
> I often divide
> What once in a green forest stood;
> Behold me, tho' I
> Have got but one eye,
> When that is stopt I do the most good.

The answer is given as 'A Hatchet, with which they cleave Wood; till the Eye is stopped with the Haft, it cannot perform business.'

RIDDLE BALLADS

Another strand in the history of enigmatography in the eighteenth century was the tradition of anonymous riddle-ballad composition in Britain. These tales took three basic forms:

(i)   a riddling contest in which the loser forfeits his life or a wager;
(ii) one where the prize is someone's hand in marriage; and
(iii) a competition in which the 'clever lass' outwits the menfolk.

An example of the first variety is the well-known ballad of 'King John and the Abbot of Canterbury', which appears in many versions in the literature of the period. The Abbot of Canterbury has accumulated such wealth and power that King John believes he is plotting treason and puts to him three questions which he must answer or lose his head. The Abbot begs three weeks to solve the riddles, but after consulting the best university brains of the time is none the wiser until he meets up with a shepherd who offers to change places with him. The answer the latter gives to the first riddle 'Tell me to one penny what I am worth' is as follows:

> For thirty pence our Saviour was sold
> Among the false Jews, as I have bin told;
> And twenty-nine is the worthe of thee,
> For I thinke thou art one penny worser than hee.

49

The shepherd solves the other two riddles in similarly humorous vein, which so amuses the king that he offers to make the shepherd Abbot of Canterbury. However, the king relents when the shepherd refuses on the grounds of illiteracy, accepting instead a reward and the release of the Abbot.

Examples of the second kind of riddle can be found in ballads such as 'Proud Lady Margaret' – which appears in Sir Walter Scott's *Minstrelsy* (1803), communicated 'by Mr Hamilton, music-seller, Edinburgh with whose mother it had been a favourite' – and 'Captain Wedderburn's Courtship'. And the 'clever lass' comes into her own in 'A Noble Riddle wisely Expounded or The Maid's Answer to the Knight's Three Questions', though there are more than three questions in most versions. Here are a few from Motherwell's MS:

> O what is whiter than the milk?
> Or what is softer than the silk?
>
> O what is sharper than the thorn?
> O what is louder than the horn?

To which the maid responds:

> . . . snow is whiter than the milk,
> And love is softer than the silk.
>
> O hunger's sharper than the thorn,
> And thunder's louder than the horn.

FURTHER SOUTH: ITALY IN THE EIGHTEENTH CENTURY

Anonymity and pseudonymity were also prevalent in Italian riddling of this period and sometimes the writer would go to great lengths to prevent his true identity being discovered.

One of the finest composers of enigmas of this time was Catone l'Uticense Lucchese (Leone Santucci) whose 142 riddling sonnets entitled *Enimmi* first appeared in 1689, were reprinted many times, and were translated into Latin in 1760. Believed to have been a priest, Santucci had a fine sense of humour and is highly esteemed in the history of Italian riddling – some consider his verses even better than Straparola's. The subjects dealt with are all totally 'decent' and vary from the learned to the popular, from books to fungus, but are primarily intended as literary exercises, not for general public consumption.

Giovanna Statira Bottini (an anagram for Giovanni Battista Taroni) was a secular priest who died in 1727 having composed numerous oratorios and a highly popular collection of a hundred enigmatic octaves entitled *Cento nodi*. Bottini's riddles, first published in 1718, were much plagiarized in his day and are largely on folk themes. Passing quickly over the work of Chiariti (1784) and Silvano's hundred sonnets (*Ennimi di Lucio Vittore Silvano*, 1793), we come to the enormous enigmatic outpourings of the Venetian 'Fosildo Mirtunzio'. Each of the five *veglie* that make up his *Veglie autunnali* (1796) consists of a hundred octaves and covers an incredible range of subjects, rarely overlapping.

But perhaps the best collection in eighteenth-century Italy, along with the works of Malatesti and Catone, is the *Enimmi di Moderno Autore*. First published in Florence in 1797 it contains 152 carefully written sonnets on subjects such as household objects; there are very few riddles on living things apart from insects. The authors also expanded the scope of riddling metres by adding the ancreontic form to the already-established octave and sonnet.

The last laugh?

With the coming of the nineteenth century there began a gradual decline in the esteem in which the riddle was held. From being at times the quintessential vehicle of high-society humour and literary drollery, it deteriorated at last into a childish amusement. In the same way that the once-subtle art of emblem-writing had lost its prestige almost completely with the advent of Bunyan's *A Book for Boys and Girls* (1686), so too with the publication of such bagatelles as *Pretty Riddle Book* (1805) and *Guess Again or Easy Enigmas & Puzzles for Little Folks* (*c*.1824) the skills of the enigmatist became debased into punning parlour games, simple verses in nursery-rhyme books, and jokes in Christmas crackers.

It is perhaps symptomatic that this was the period of the great folklore collectors – Wossidlo, Rolland, Friedreich, and, more recently, Archer Taylor – who had begun the painstaking task of clearing up after the cryptic carnival, codifying and pigeon-holing with a dexterity that typified an age when genius was regarded, in Jane Ellice Hopkins's immortal phrase, as being 'an infinite capacity for detail'.

This is not to say that top-class riddling had entirely died out: many society figures produced occasional pleasantries to while away the winter evenings, particular interest being aroused by word-puzzles, especially logogriphs and charades. The celebrated

German scientist G. T. Fechner wrote a number of enigmas under the pseudonym 'Dr Mises', and *Neue Räthsel* (1879), by his equally famous compatriot Franz Brentano, was held by Freud to be one of the best modern collections of riddles. Edgar Allan Poe was an accomplished enigmatist (see Part 2, pages 252–3) and fine charades were composed by William Bellamy and the humorous poets C. S. Calverley (1831–84) and Winthrop Mackworth Praed (1802–39). Peacock, William Whewell, and even Pope Leo XIII also have riddles ascribed to them and the great historian Thomas Babington Macaulay is credited with penning the following charade:

> Cut off my head, how singular I act!
> Cut off my tail, and plural I appear!
> Cut off my head and tail – most curious fact!
> Although my middle's left, there's nothing there!
> What is my head, cut off? A sounding sea!
> What is my tail, cut off? A flowing river!
> Amid their mingling depth, I fearless play,
> Parent of softest sounds, though mute forever.

The solution is 'cod'. But somehow the excitement had gone from the art and even the ribald riddle had begun to lose its charm, though bawdy collections such as the *Royal Riddle Book* still appeared (1820). A clear indication of the decline of enigmatography can be seen in the description of Emma Woodhouse's efforts to educate her silly pupil, Harriet Smith, in Jane Austen's *Emma*:

> ... the only literary pursuit which engaged Harriet at present, the only mental provision she was making for the evening of life, was the collection and transcribing of all the riddles of every sort that she could meet with, into a thin quarto of hot-pressed paper, made up by her friend, and ornamented with cyphers and trophies.

Her efforts were mostly confined to charades like the following (on courtship):

> My first displays the wealth and pomp of kings,
>   Lords of the earth! their luxury and ease.
> Another view of man, my second brings,
>   Behold him there, the monarch of the seas!
>
> But ah! united what reverse we have!
>   Man's boasted power and freedom, all are flown:
> Lord of the earth and sea, he bends a slave,
>   And woman, lovely woman, reigns alone.
>
> Thy ready wit the word will soon supply,
> May its approval beam in that soft eye!

Although riddling as a serious entertainment gradually declined in nineteenth-century Europe, it nevertheless continued to flourish in a form more adapted to the whims of the childish prankster and survives in this guise even today. From the 'Mother Goose' treasury to the fiendish Gollum of Tolkien's *The Hobbit* there can be no doubt that the telling and invention of riddles plays a very important part in the psychological development of the modern child.

Although strictly speaking a work of the eighteenth century, Robert Samber's translation of Charles Perrault's *Contes de ma mère l'Oye* (1697), which first appeared in John Newbery's edition as *Mother Goose's Tales* (c.1729), was a favourite amongst Victorian children. As well as such well-known fairy stories as 'Cinderella' and 'The Sleeping Beauty', it also contained a number of riddles. Typical of the rhyming sing-song style of this collection is the following:

Black I am and much admired,
Men seek me until they're tired;
When they find me, break my head,
And take me from my resting bed.

to which the solution is 'coal'. The themes centre on everyday objects, animals, heavenly bodies, etc., and they are of varying lengths. Most of them can be found in similar form in general collections of folk riddles from across the globe, as is common with these kinds of enigma.

In a similar vein a good collection of Scottish nursery-rhymes and riddles was made by the publisher Robert Chambers in 1870. Entitled *Popular Rhymes of Scotland*, some of the examples are rather fine, such as this one on a cock:

There was a prophet on this earth,
His age no man could tell;
He was at his greatest height
Before e'er Adam fell.
His wives are very numerous,
Yet he maintaineth none;
And at the day of reckoning
He bids them all begone.
He wears his boots when he should sleep;
His spurs are ever new;
There's no a shoemaker on a' the earth
Can fit him for a shoe.

Riddles also appeared in diverse books published specifically with the modern child in mind, such as *The Boy's Own Book*

(1829) and its companion volume *The Girl's Own Book* (1832), and later on in the various 'annuals' edited and published by S. O. Beeton (1831–77), husband of the author of *Household Management*. (And, I might add, the publications of George Routledge (1812–88), whose company has produced the book you are currently holding.) Such was the popularity of the enigma amongst children of school age that books entirely devoted to the subject began to grace booksellers' shelves, with titles such as *Pretty Riddle Book* by Christopher Conundrum (1805), *Mince Pies for Christmas* (1805), *The Frolics of the Sphinx* (1812), *Guess Again or Easy Enigmas & Puzzles for Little Folk* (*c*.1824) and a number of penny and halfpenny chap-books such as *Peter Primrose's Books for Boys and Girls: Riddles* and *The Guess Book* (*c*.1820), from which the following is taken:

> The beginning of *e*ternity,
> The end of tim*e* and spac*e*,
> The beginning of *e*very *e*nd,
> And the end of *e*very plac*e*.

The answer is 'the letter E'.

A number of Victorian writers better known for their adult literary works also composed enigmas for the playroom, notably D. G. Rossetti's sister Christina. Here is an example of hers on pins and needles:

> There is one that has a head without an eye,
> And there's one that has an eye without a head,
> You may find the answer if you try;
> And when all is said,
> Half the answer hangs upon a thread.

And Tom Hood (1835–74), the son of the celebrated poet, was both editor of *Fun* magazine and author/illustrator of such delightful volumes as *Excursions into Puzzledom*, which contains both literary and pictorial riddles.

The Reverend C. L. Dodgson ('Lewis Carroll') also wrote a number of books for children, the most famous of which are the Alice books. In Chapter IX of *Through the Looking Glass* (1872) the White Queen tells the following riddle whose answer is not given in the story, but we know from *Fun* (30 October 1878), where a similarly rhyming answer was published by an anonymous author, that it is 'oyster':

> 'First the fish must be caught.'
> That is easy: a baby, I think, could have caught it.
> 'Next, the fish must be bought.'
> That is easy: a penny, I think, would have bought it.

'Now cook me the fish!'
That is easy, and will not take more than a minute.
'Let it lie in a dish!'
That is easy, because it is already in it.

'Bring it here! Let me sup!'
It is easy to set such a dish on the table.
'Take the dish-cover up!'
Ah, *that* is so hard that I fear I'm unable!

For it holds it like glue –
Holds the lid to the dish, while it lies in the middle:
Which is easiest to do,
Un-dish-cover the fish, or dishcover the riddle?

A famous conundrum also occurs in Chapter VII, 'A Mad Tea-party', of *Alice's Adventures in Wonderland* where the Mad Hatter asks, 'Why is a raven like a writing desk?' This caused an enormous amount of speculation at the time and though apparently not meant to be taken seriously, Carroll did eventually publish an answer years later: 'Because it can produce a few notes, tho' they are *very* flat; and it is never put with the wrong end in front.' Other good solutions, proposed by the American puzzle genius Sam Loyd are: 'Because Poe wrote on both' and 'Bills and tales are among their characteristics.' Carroll also wrote a number of charades and logogriphs such as the following on a tablet – the first riddle he ever composed.

A monument – men all agree –
Am I in all sincerity,
    Half cat, half hindrance made.
If head and tail removed should be,
Then most of all you strengthen me;
Replace my head, the stand you see
    On which my tail is laid.

And he would often tease his little girl friends with pictorial rebuses like the one depicted overleaf taken from a letter written to Georgina Watson from his family's house 'The Chestnuts' in Guildford.

The art of writing books for children which also attract a more adult readership is admirably exemplified in our own time by the works of the late Professor J. R. R. Tolkien. In *The Hobbit* (1937) young Bilbo Baggins is confronted in Chapter 5 by the odious slimy creature Gollum who has lost his magic ring in the labyrinths within the Misty Mountains. A riddle contest ensues, with the object of continuing until one or the other is unable to solve a riddle in three guesses. If Bilbo wins he is to be allowed to go free; if not Gollum will eat him. Not surprisingly, after nine genuine riddles such as Gollum's

The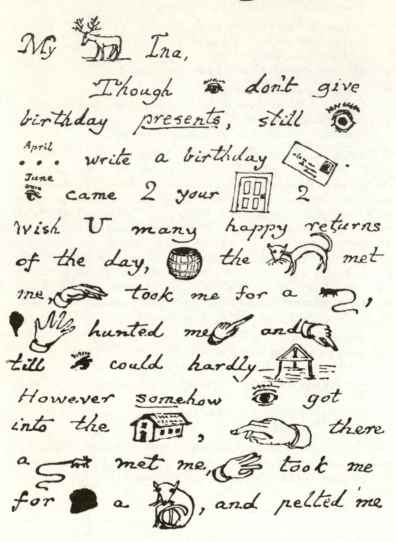

My [deer] Ina,

Though [eye] don't give birthday presents, still [I] ... write a birthday [letter]. April [came] 2 your [door] 2 wish U many happy returns of the day, [barrel] the [cat] met me, [hand] took me for a [mouse], [hand] hunted me and [hand] till [hedgehog] could hardly [house]. However somehow [eye] got into the [house], [hand] there a [eel] met me, [hand] took me for a [blot] a [owl], and pelted me

June

with , , . Of course ran.
into the street again, a
met me took me
for a , dragged me
all the way 2 the
the worst of all was when
a met me took
me for a . I was
harnessed 2 it, had
2 draw it miles and miles,
all the way 2 Merrow. So
U C I couldn't get 2 the
room where U were.
However I was glad to

hear U were hard at work learning the [multiplication table grid] for a birthday treat.

I had just time 2 look into the kitchen, and your birthday feast getting ready, a nice [bowl] of crusts, bones, pills, cotton-bobbins, and rhabarb and magnesia— "Now," I thought, "she will be happy!" and with a [face] I went on my way—

Your affᵗᵉ friend

CLD

> This thing all things devours:
> Birds, beasts, trees, flowers;
> Gnaws iron, bites steel;
> Grinds hard stones to meal;
> Slays king, ruins town,
> And beats high mountain down.

to which the answer is 'time', Bilbo decides to cheat a bit and asks, 'What do I have in my pocket?' Gollum suggests 'Handses', a knife, and 'String or nothing'. The object is in fact Gollum's ring which Bilbo has found and now slips on to make himself invisible, because though he knew that 'the riddle-game was sacred and of immense antiquity, and even wicked creatures were afraid to cheat when they played at it . . . he felt he could not trust this slimy thing to keep any promise at a pinch'. He guesses correctly and eventually makes good his escape. (The ring, incidentally, is later the salvation of Baggins and his little troop of dwarves and is the mainspring of the plot of the enormously popular sequel *The Lord of the Rings*.)

The modern tradition in children's riddling books continues to the present day with the publication of such excellent collections as Ennis Rees's *Riddles, Riddles Everywhere* (1964) and John Cunliffe's *Riddles, Rhymes and Rigmaroles* (1971), both of which are delightfully illustrated. A recent addition is Kit Williams's intriguing picture-book *Masquerade* (1979). Only thirty-two pages long, this charming tale contains in all eight riddles of varying lengths, the solution to each being given in a full-page cryptic illustration facing the text. One such example is a traditional folk riddle to which the answer is 'a hare':

> A hopper o' ditches,
> A cropper o' corn,
> A wee brown cow,
> And a pair of leather horns!

The phenomenal commercial success of this slim volume may be at least partly due to the fact that the solution to all of the riddles provides clues as to the whereabouts of a finely worked piece of jewellery in the form of a golden hare, valued at £5,000, which the author had buried in an undisclosed location before publication. (The hare has now been discovered.)

THE NEW MAGAZINES

The same tale of decadence that can be traced in the publication of books of riddles also unfolds in the history of the riddle as it is found in magazines and journals of the modern period. To be fair, a number of enigmas did appear at intervals in *Notes and Queries* for the year 1865, variously entitled 'Yorkshire Household Riddles' and 'Lincolnshire Household Riddles', but these were merely folk riddles that had been collected by readers. More important, perhaps, were the contributions to *Bentley's Miscellany* (1837–69), *The New Monthly Magazine* (1814–84), Henry E. Dudeney's teasers in *The Strand Magazine*, and the newspaper columns of the American puzzle-king, Sam Loyd (1841–1911). *Punch* has also published a number of conundrums in its pages from time to time, either under the rubric 'Whys and whens, by an eminent professor' (usually eight at a time), or at the bottoms of columns as fillers, a particularly good illustrated example from an issue of 1843 being:

Why is a solar eclipse like a mother thrashing her own child? –
Because it's a hiding of the sun.

(The picture shows a recalcitrant child being set about with a stick by a hard-faced old matron wearing a mob cap.)

However, apart from *The Riddle Magazine* (1873), *Ennimistica moderno* (1924), and periodicals such as *Enigma*, the journal of the National Puzzlers' League of the USA (founded 1883), riddles now increasingly only occurred in the schoolboy's 'Penny Dreadfuls' or more respectable juvenile publications like *Little Folks* (1871–1932) and *The Prize* (1863–1931). And today's riddler-in-the-street is hard put to find any regular serious publication to cater for his whims, as most modern quiz magazines deal largely with acrostics and crossword puzzles. Indeed, perhaps the most widely read examples of magazine enigmas available in modern times are those that appear in children's comics – the antics of such arch-fiends as the enigmatic villain known as 'the Riddler', who terrorizes the Gotham City of the American D.C. Comics' Batman series, being a case in point. Today's youngsters are well acquainted with his cryptic clues to the 'Dynamic Duo' concerning the whereabouts of his next crime – an example being the scrap of paper which Batman finds in the episode entitled 'Riddles in the Dark' (August 1980 issue), on which is written 'When is a horse most like a stamp collection?' The answer is 'When it's a hobby horse', which indicates that the Riddler is at Hobby Airport, Houston.

CONTEMPORARY RIDDLING IN THE THIRD WORLD AND ELSEWHERE

In spite of its apparent decline in the west, riddling is still practised by adults in many countries of the Third World, from the Indians of the Americas to African tribesmen, and from the villagers of Asia to the peasantry of rural Russia. Serious contests and riddle rituals can still be seen taking place amongst Yoruba, Afrikaners, and Parsees, and adult games involving the telling of enigmas continue to be popular throughout the Third World.

In South Africa the oral tradition survives amongst the Hottentots; Bushmen puzzle over enigmas involving all kinds of animals and hunting; and the Bantu have a very wide-ranging collection with examples like the following: 'What shows no mark when it is hit?', to which the answer is 'water'. According to Sir James Frazer in *The Golden Bough* (written at the turn of the century), the rain-making ceremonies of one African tribe involve naked women dancing and shouting, and if any men are found in the neighbourhood while this is going on they are beaten and quizzed with obscene riddles alluding to their circumcision rituals.

Riddles of the English-speaking inhabitants of the country tend to reflect those disseminated in Europe and so do not concern us here, but among the Afrikaners a great many original riddles have been found and over 2,000 were published in G. A. van Rooyen and S. H. Pellisier's book *Raai, raai, riepa, of Die Afrikaanse raaiselbok* (1954). Many of them rhyme, like the following:

It is coloured and round.
It has a pot belly,
It lies on the ground,
It blows at a fellow.
A dog it kisses
And kills while it hisses.

to which the answer is 'a puff-adder'.

The Yoruba of Nigeria also have a large store of enigmas, though many are based on knowledge of their particular institutions and are hence difficult for an outsider to appreciate. One example of a more general nature is this riddle on a drum:

They cut off his head; they cut off his waist; his stump says he will call the town together.

The Kxatla enjoy riddle contests with subjects such as fingers: 'Ten boys with their hats on the back of their heads'; or bread: 'The white horse goes into the stable and comes out brown'. The Nyanja have 'The hide in the middle, the meat outside' as a riddle for the gizzard, and the Tlokwa signify snowing in the description 'The white goats are descending from the mountain'.

The Parsees of India also have a long-established tradition of riddling that continues today. For example: 'Coat after coat do I put on and hot-tempered am I' is an onion, and a lighted lamp is described as a 'golden parrot drinking water with its tail'. A Latin-American riddle on a bell runs:

61

A lazy old woman
has a tooth in her crown,
and with that tooth
she gathers the people.

whilst a collection of Macedonian folklore provides us with the
following on a chestnut:

Without as smooth as glass,
Within a woolly mass.
But hid amid the wool
There lurks a nice mouthful.

THE END OF THE ENIGMA?

Exactly *why* riddling in modern, highly industrialized societies
seems to have deteriorated from being an adult literary entertainment into a pastime for children, yet continues undaunted in
rural communities of the Third World and elsewhere, is an
enigma in itself. Has it something to do with the different
cultural backgrounds of the civilizations involved, the
dependence or alienation created by the presence/absence of
increased technology, or just varying temperaments? Is riddling
something only relevant to cultures at the so-called 'mythological'
stage of thought or has all the fun gone out of the western
world?

Sir James Frazer racked his brains over this issue nearly a
hundred years ago to no avail and it is certainly beyond the
scope of this book to investigate the matter further. However,
recent research by a number of eminent psychologists, socio-
logists, and anthropologists, together with the novel light shed
on our thinking processes by the work of writers such as Edward
de Bono, and new insights into play behaviour by Johann Huiz-
inga (*Homo Ludens*) and Opie and Opie (*The Lore and
Language of Schoolchildren*) have begun to make some inroads
into this shady area of our knowledge.

One interesting insight that *has* emerged from these early
exploratory attempts is that, in the west at least, interest in riddles
seems to coincide with seasons of intellectual awakening – something that has been borne out by the researches for the present
anthology. Whether during the classic period of Greek culture,
early Anglo-Saxon Britain, the flowering of the Middle Ages and
Renaissance in Europe, or the stately grandeur of court life in the
seventeenth and eighteenth centuries, the riddle has always
appeared hand in hand with a resurgence in artistic activity,
almost as a touchstone of cultural finesse. And who knows? With
the advent of executive toys, 'Space Invaders' in pubs, high-brow
lectures on Tolkien and Lewis Carroll, international crossword

62

(and even tiddlywink) competitions, not to mention *Masquerade*, 'Dingbats', the maddeningly successful 'Cube', and the increased audiences for cryptic quiz programmes and 'whodunnits' (many of which are currently being filmed), could it be that the play instinct, and specifically a delight in mystery games and puzzling, really is returning to our microchip-manacled society? Or will that great riddle-master, Time, have the very last laugh?

PART TWO

Dictionary of Riddles

Author's note

This section of the book is intended primarily as a dictionary of nearly 1,500 riddles selected from the enormous literature on the subject, with the aim of trying to give a representative cross-section of the material currently available. Some riddles, especially those in Latin, French and Italian, appear here in translation for the first time, though no attempt has been made to imitate the (usually exquisite) verse forms of the originals. The riddles are generally arranged alphabetically by author, except in cases where the authorship is not known, when the entries can be found under the title of the work in question. Solutions for all the riddles can be found on pages 333–51.

ADEVINEAUX AMOUREUX, Les (1478)
Anonymous French riddle collection printed in Bruges.

1   *Entre deux jambes le vis amble;*
    Entre deux fesses le vif trepple,
    Et quant il vient a la porte,
    Son maistre hurte a l'anel.

    (Between two legs the living flesh ambles,
    Between two buttocks the living flesh trembles,
    And when it comes to the door,
    Its master knocks.)

2   *Adevinez que c'est:*
    Quand il nait il brait,
    Et quand il est nait
    Il se tait.

    (Guess what this is: as it is born it cries out, and when it is born it becomes silent.)

3   *Plus petit que ung boeuf,*
    Plus menu que ung oeuf,
    Plus amer que sieue,
    Et trop plus doulz que lettue.

    (Smaller than an ox, tinier even than an egg. Sharper than sap yet sweeter than lettuce.)

4   *J'en ay et vous en avez.*
Aussi ont les bois et les prez,
Les eaues et ainsi les mers,
Les poissons, les bestes et les blez,
Et toutes aultres choses du monde,
Ainsi que il tourne a la reonde.

(I have one and you have one. So do the woods, fields, streams and seas, fish, beasts and crops, and everything else in this revolving world.)

5   *En quel temps de l'an est il le moins de fruits?*

(At which time of year is there the least fruit?)

6   *Je fus nez avant mon pere*
Et engendré avant ma mere,
Et ay occis le quart du monde,
Ainsi qu'il gist a la reonde,
Et si despucelay ma taye.
Or pensez se c'est chose vraie.

(I was born before my father, begotten before my mother and have slain a quarter of the world's population. How can this be?)

7   *Blanc est le champ et*
Noire est la semence.
Ly homs qui la semme est
De moult grant science.

(White is the field and black the seed. The man who sows it has great learning.)

8   *Deux qui courent, dix qui les chacent, deux qui les regardent, et ung qui leur fait la moe.*

(Two who run and ten who chase them, two who look on, and one who puts them to death.)

AELIA LAELIA CRISPIS (N.P.)

Enigmatic inscription from a Roman tombstone found near Bologna in the eighteenth century, also known as the 'Bononian Enigma'. Many solutions have been attempted. This translation, by Peacock (q.v.) omits three further lines from an MS version in Milan as these are believed to be a separate epigram on Niobe.

9
D. M.
AELIA . LAELIA . CRISPIS .
NEC . VIR . NEC . MULIER . NEC . ANDROGYNA .
NEC . PUELLA . NEC . JUVENIS . NEC . ANUS .
NEC . CASTA . NEC . MERETRIX . NEC . PUDICA .
SED . OMNIA .
SUBLATA .
NEQUE . FAME . NEQUE . FERRO . NEQUE . VENENO .
SED . OMNIBUS .
NEC . COELO . NEC . AQUIS . NEC . TERRIS .

68

SED . UBIQUE . JACET .
LUCIUS . AGATHO . PRISCUS .
NEC . MARITUS . NEC . AMATOR . NEC NECESSARIUS .
NEQUE . MOERENS . NEQUE . GAUDENS . NEQUE . FLENS .
HANC . NEC . MOLEM . NEC . PYRAMIDEM .
NEC . SEPULCHRUM .
SED . OMNIA .
SCIT . ET . NESCIT .
CUI . POSUERIT .

TO THE GODS OF THE DEAD.

Aelia Laelia Crispis,
Not man, nor woman, nor hermaphrodite:
Not girl, nor youth, nor old woman:
Not chaste, nor unchaste, nor modest:
But all:
Carried off,
Not by hunger, nor by sword, nor by poison:
But by all:
Lies,
Not in air, not in earth, not in the waters:
But everywhere.
Lucius Agatho Priscus,
Not her husband, nor her lover, nor her friend:
Not sorrowing, nor rejoicing, nor weeping:
Erecting
This, not a stone-pile, nor a pyramid,
Nor a sepulchre:
But all:
Knows, and knows not,
To whom he erects it.

AFRICAN FOLK RIDDLES
Yoruba, Bantu, Afrikaans, and Nandi riddles from a variety of sources,
largely *The Nandi* (1909) by A. C. Hollis.

10   *Anyiny ingua tere'-'p-oiin.*

(What is the sweet vegetable that comes out of the cooking-pot
of the spirits of the deceased?)

11   *A-tinye cheptán-nyō ne-'ngo-wendi kâp-tich ko-'sīk-ot ta-nyo-ne
ka ko-sis-anu.*

(What are the things which as they go to the cattle-kraal sing,
whilst as they return home are silent?)

12   *A-tinye cheptán-nyō ne-piiy-onyi mutai ko-rukut lakat.*

(I have a daughter who gets a good meal every morning, but she
goes to bed hungry at night.)

13   *A-tinye lakōk pokol añg tukul ko-chuchun-o.*

(I have a hundred children and I support them all.)

14   *Iut-yin-dos a-ma-par-i-ke.*

(What are the things which make a noise at one another, like bulls bellowing before a fight, but which do not hurt one another?)

15   *Ki-a-mwok-te kôtén-nyō ko-ma-tar-at, tun te-'p-a-ip-u ko-tar-at.*

(I shot off my arrow and it was not feathered, but when I went to fetch it, it was feathered.)

16   *Ki-ki-ñgot kaita, kut ki-ñgot-e tilatit.*

(A hut has been made and the thorn enclosure is in course of construction.)

17   *Ñgurur-in a-ma-am-in.*

(What is the thing which looks down at you but which does not eat you?)

18   *Nīr ma-ñget.*

(What is it that does not break though you may draw it out as far as you like?)

19   *Oon-w-a piich che-koiin kelien.*

(Who are the long-legged people who have made me fly back home?)

20   They cut off his head; cut off his waist; his stump says he will call the town together.

21   They tell him to sit beside the fire, he sits beside the fire; they tell him to sit in the sun, he sits in the sun; they tell him to wash, he says, 'Death comes'.

22   Elephant dies, Mangudu eats him; buffalo dies, Mangudu eats him; Mangudu dies, there is no one who wants to eat him.

23   What shows no mark when it is hit?

24   What is it that a mother loves very dearly, but which can never welcome her when she comes home?

25   It is coloured and round,
It has a pot-belly,
It lies on the ground,
It blows at a fellow.
A dog it kisses
And kills while it hisses.

26   It has no liver and no lung.
It has no heart and no tongue,
And yet calls thousands together
At their duties to gather.

27   Crooked his head, saw at his paunch, tortoise-bull scream.

ALDHELM of Malmesbury, St (d.709)
Bishop of Sherborne and Abbot of Malmesbury. Riddles contained in
Epistola ad Acircium.

28   *Dudum lympha fui squamoso pisce redundans;*
       Sed natura novo fati discrimine cessit.
       Torrida dum calidos patior tormenta per ignes.
       Nam cineri facies nivibusque simillima fulget.

       (Once I was water, full of scaly fish;
       But, by a new decision, Fate has changed
       My nature: having suffered fiery pangs,
       I now gleam white, like ashes or bright snow.)

29   *Sum mihi difficilis vultu membrisque biformis,*
       Cornibus armatus; horrendum cætera fingunt
       Membra virum, fama clarus per Gnossia rura.
       Spurius incerto in Creta genitore creatus,
       Ex hominis pecudisque simul cognomine dicor.

       (Incongruous is my visage to my frame:
       Though horns are on my head, the rest of me
       Appears a hideous man; by fame well known
       Through all the Gnossian land, a bastard, born
       In Crete of unknown sire, by double name
       Of man and beast together I am called.)

30   *Candida forma nitens, necnon et furva nigrescens*
       Est mihi, dum varia componor imagine pennæ;
       Voce carens tremulo faxo crepitacula rostro.
       Quamvis squamigeros discerpam dira colubros,
       Non mea lethiferis turgescunt membra venenis.
       Sic teneros pullos prolemque nutrire suesco
       Carne venenata, tetroque cruore draconum.

       (Both shining white am I and dusky black
       Together, decked with parti-coloured plumes.
       No trilling voice is mine, for with my beak
       I utter ugly sounds. Though scaly snakes
       I catch and rend – to them a fearsome foe –
       Death-dealing venom never swells my veins;
       Nay more, I even feed my fluffy chicks
       With poisoned flesh and loathful serpents' blood.)

31   *Roscida me genuit gelido de viscere tellus,*
       Non sum setigero lanarum vellere facta,
       Licia nulla trahunt, nec garrula fila resultant,
       Nec crocea seres texunt lanugine vermes,
       Nec radiis carpor, duro nec pectine pulsor;
       Et tamen en vestis vulgi sermone vocabor.
       Spicula non vereor longis exempta pharetris.

       (The dewy earth's cold vitals gave me birth;
       I am not made of rough wool, and no loom
       Has ever stretched me, nor its humming thread
       Leapt back and forth, nor have the Chinese worms

Woven me of their saffron floss. By wheels
I was not tortured, nor by carding combs.
Yet, lo, the people christen me 'a coat'.
No arrow in the quiver frightens me.)

32   *Grandia membra mihi plumescunt corpore denso,*
Par color accipitri, sed dispar causa volandi.
Nam summa exiguis non trano per æthera pennis,
Sed potius pedibus spatior per squalida rura,
Ovorum teretes præbens ad pocula testas.
Africa Pœnorum me fertur gignere tellus.

(My heavy body and great limbs sprout plumes;
I have the falcon's hue, but not his flight,
For through the upper air my scanty wings
Could never bear me; rather, I must pace
On foot through dirty fields. Smooth eggs I lay,
To make men cups. Phoenician Africa,
So runs the rumour, is my native land.)

33   *Lurida per latices cœnosas lustro paludes,*
Nam mihi composuit nomen Fortuna cruenta.
Rubro dum bibulis vescor de sanguine buccis.
Ossibus et pedibus careo geminisque lacertis,
Corpora vulneribus sed mordeo dira trisulcis,
Atque salutiferis sic curam præsto labellis.

(I haunt, all pale, the waters of foul fens;
Fortune has fashioned me a bloody name,
For greedy gulps of red blood are my fare.
No bones, or feet, or arms at all have I,
Yet bite with three-forked wounds unlucky men,
And by health-bringing lips thus conquer care.)

34   *Me pater et mater gelido genuere rigore,*
Fomitibus siccis dum mox rudimenta vigebant,
Quorum vi propria fortunam vincere possum;
Cum nihil in latices mea possunt vincere fata;
Sed saltus, scopulos, stagni ferrique metalla
Comminuens penitus naturæ jura resolvam.
Cum me vita fovet, clari sum sideris instar;
Post hæc et fato victus pice nigrior exsto.

(Of cold and hardness did my sire and dam
Beget me, but I speedily grew strong
Upon dry tinder; nourished by such food,
I now can conquer fortune, for no thing
But water ever can subdue my power.
The wooded uplands, rocks – yea, iron and tin –
I menace, when I loose my natural force.
While life is warm in me, no star of heaven
Outshines me; when at last my race is run,
The blackest pitch is not so black as I.)

35

Sponte mea nascor fœcundo cespite vernans,
Fulgida de croceo flavescunt culmina flore;
Occiduo claudor, sic orto sole patesco.
Unde prudentes posuerunt nomina Græci.

(Born of my own free will, on fertile sod
I flourish. Yellow flowers adorn my head.
At morn I open, close at setting sun,
And hence the clever Greeks devised my name.)

36

Materia duplici palmis plasmabar apertis,
Interiora mihi candescunt viscera lino,
Seu certe gracili junco spoliata nitescunt;
Sed nunc exterius flavescunt corpora flore
Quæ flammasque focosque larem fumantia fundunt.
Et crebro lacrimæ stillant de frontibus udæ.

(Of two materials have open palms
Moulded me, gleaming white am I within –
My vitals are the shining spoil of flax,
Or slender rush; but all my outer parts
Are yellow with a colour born of flowers;
They vomit forth hot, fiery flames, and melt,
Dripping a rain of tear-drops from my brows;
Thus I dispel the fearful shades of night.
My vitals burn, and naught but ashes leave.)

37

Me pridem genuit candens onocrotalus albam,
Gutture qui patulo sorbet de gurgite lymphas.
Pergo per albentes directo tramite campos,
Candentique viæ vestigia cærula linquo,
Lucida nigratis fuscans amfractibus arva.
Nec satis est unum per campos pandere callem;
Semita quin potius milleno tramite tendit,
Quæ non errantes ad cœli culmina vexit.

(The shining pelican, whose yawning throat
Gulps down the waters of the sea, long since
Produced me, white as he. Through snowy fields
I keep a straight road, leaving deep-blue tracks
Upon the gleaming way, and darkening
The fair champaign with black and tortuous paths;
Yet one way through the plain suffices not,
For with a thousand bypaths runs the road,
And them who stray not from it, leads to heaven.)

38

Cum Deus infandas jam plecteret æquore noxas,
Abblueretque simul scelerum contagia lymphis,
Prima ego præcepti complevi jura parentis,
Portendens fructu terris venire salutem.
Mitia quapropter semper præcordia gesto,
Et felix præpes nigro sine felle manebo.

(When God by flood was punishing vile sin,
And by those waters cleansing evil's stain,
I first fulfilled the patriarch's command,
As by a fruitful bough I signified
Salvation to the earth was come. Thenceforth
My heart is ever gentle, and in me,
A happy bird, no black bile ever flows.)

39   *Me pedibus manibusque simul fraudaverat almus*
      Arbiter, immensum primum dum pangeret orbem.
      Fulcior haud volitans veloci præpetis ala,
      Spiritus alterno vegetat nec corpora flatu,
      Quamvis in cœlis convexa cacumina cernam,
      Non tamen undosi contemno marmora ponti.

(The Lord Creator both of feet and hands
Defrauded me, when first he set in place
The world immeasurable. I do not fly,
Borne on the pinions of a bird; no breath
Livens my body with recurrent gusts.
I may behold the vaulted arch of heaven,
Yet scorn not rolling ocean's broad expanse.)

40   *De rimis lapidum profluxi flumine lento,*
      Dum frangunt flammæ saxorum viscera dura,
      Et laxis ardor fornacis ardet habenis.
      Nunc mihi forma capax, glacieque simillima lucet.
      Nempe volunt plures collum confringere dextra,
      Et pulchræ digitis lubricum comprendere corpus.
      Sed mentes muto dum labris oscula trado.
      Dulcia compressis impendens bacchia buccis,
      Atque pedum gressus titubantes sterno ruina.

(In sluggish stream I flowed from rifted rocks,
As flames broke up the stones, and fire applied
The unleashed ardour of the furnace-heat;
My form capacious now is clear as ice.
Yea, many long to hold me in their hand,
Fingering my slippery shape in dainty grasp;
But I befool their minds, the while I lay
Sweet kisses on their lips that press me close,
And urge their tottering footsteps to a fall.)

41   *Nunc mihi sunt oculi bis seni in corpore solo,*
      Bis ternumque caput, sed cætera membra gubernat.
      Name gradior pedibus suffultus bis duodenis,
      Sed novies deni sunt et sex corporis ungues.
      Synzygias numero pariter simulabo pedestres,
      Populus et taxus, viridi quoque fronde salicta
      Sunt invisa mihi, sed fagos glandibus uncas,
      Fructiferas itidem florenti vertice quercus
      Diligo, sic numerosa simul non spernitur ilex.

(Now in one body I have twice six eyes
And twice three heads, but all my other parts
Rule these. Upborne on twice two feet I walk,
And yet my body's nails are ninety-six.
In number like a metric syzygy
I thus appear. The poplar and the yew
And green-leaved willow-tree I hate, but love
The crooked beech-tree with its nuts, and oaks
With thick-crowned head that juicy acorns bear,
Nor do I scorn the holm-oak with its shade.)

42   *Jam referam verbis tibi, quod vix credere possis,*
      Cum constet verum, fallant nec frivola mentem.
      Nam dudum dederam soboli munuscula grata
      Tradere quæ nunquam poterat mihi quislibet alter,
      Dum Deus ex alto fraudaret lumine claro,
      In quo cunctorum gaudent præcordia dono.

(Now I shall tell what you can scarce believe,
Though true it is, not foolish trickery:
For once I gave my son a pleasing gift,
A gift which none could ever give to me,
Since God on high withheld this glorious boon,
In which all other men rejoice their hearts.)

43   *Callidior cunctis aura vescentibus æthræ,*
      Late per mundum dispersi semina mortis,
      Unde horrenda seges diris succrevit aristis.
      Quam metit ad scelera scortator falce maligna.
      Cornigeri multum vereor certamina cervi,
      Namque senescenti spoliabor pelle vetustus,
      Atque nova rursus fretus remanebo juventa.

(Of all that breathe refreshing air of heaven,
I am most cunning, who through all the world
Flung wide the seeds of death, whence sprang a crop
Of grim and hideous grain; there with his scythe,
Measuring the yield to serve his evil plans,
Roams the Defiler. Never dare I fight
The stag with branching antlers. When old age
Falls on me, I cast off my worn-out skin,
And find my body staunch, my youth renewed.)

44   *Sunt mihi sex oculi, totidem simul auribus exsto;*
      Sed digitos decies senos in corpore gesto;
      Ex quibus ecce quater denis de carne revulsis;
      Quinquies at tantum video remanere quaternos.

(Six eyes are mine; as many ears have I;
Fingers and toes twice thirty do I bear.
Of these, when forty from my flesh are torn,
Lo, then but twenty will remain to me.)

45 *Quæ res in terris armatur robore tanto*
Aut paribus fungi nitatur viribus audax?
Parva mihi primo constant exordia vitæ,
Sed gracilis grandes soleo prosternere letho;
Quod lethum proprii gestant penetralia ventris.
Nam saltus nemorum densos pariterque frutecta,
Piniferosque simul montes cum molibus altos,
Truxque, rapaxque, feroxque, sub æthere spargo.
Et minor existens gracili quam corpore sciniphs;
Frigida dum genitrix dura generaret ab alvo
Primitus ex utero producens pignora gentis.

(What earthly thing is armed with might like mine,
Or boldly strives to use such force and strength?
Small was my life's beginning, but great things,
Though I am slender, low I lay in death,
A death my belly's inmost hollow hides.
For woodlands dense, groves, shrubs, and mountains tall,
Pine forests on their flanks, I murderously –
Savage and greedy, with capacious maw –
Lay waste, and scatter wide beneath the sky;
And yet my form was slighter than a gnat's
When first my icy mother brought me forth,
Producing offspring from her stony womb.)

46 *Nos denæ et septem genitæ sine voce sorores,*
Sex alias nothas non dicimus adnumerandas,
Nascimur ex ferro rursus ferro moribundæ,
Necnon et volucris penna volitantis ad æthram;
Terni nos fratres incerta matre crearunt;
Qui cupit instanter sitiens audire, docemus,
Tum cito prompta damus rogitanti verba silenter.

(We are seventeen sisters voiceless born; six others, half-sisters,
we exclude from our set; children of iron, by iron we die, but
children too of the bird's wing that flies so high; three brethren
our sires, be our mother as may; if anyone is very eager to hear,
we tell him, and quickly give answer without any sound.)

ALEXIS (c.375–c.275 BC)
Ancient Greek poet and dramatist. Riddle cited in Athenaeus's *Deipnosophistae*.

47 It is not mortal nor yet immortal; rather, it has a nature so
mixed that its life is neither in man's estate nor in a god's, but
its substance ever grows fresh and then dies again; it may not
be seen by the eye, yet it is known of all.

AL-HARIRI, Abu Muhammad Al-Qasim (1054–1122)
Arab grammarian and intelligence officer from Basra, Iraq. Riddles
contained in *Maqamat* ('Assemblies').

48 Rise, my dear son, may thy luck not set, nor thy adversary
keep on foot, take with thee the one of full-moon face and

of pearly hue, of pure root and tormented body, who was pinched and stretched, imprisoned and released, made to drink and weaned, and pushed into the fire, after he had been slapped. Then career to the market the career of the longing swain, and bring back instead of it the pregnant that impregnates, the spoiler who enriches, the saddener who gladdens, the possessor of a puff that sets on fire, and of a germ that breaks forth in light, of an emission [utterance] that satisfies, and of a gift that profits, who, when he is struck, thunders and lightens, and reveals himself in flames, and who sputters on tinder-rags.

49   A maiden I know, brisk, full of speed in her ministry, returning the same track that she went by when starting off:
A driver she has, kinsman of hers, who is urging her, but while he thus is speeding her on, is her helpmate too.
In summer she is seen dew-besprinkled and moist and fresh, when summer is gone, her body shows flabby and loose and dry.

50   A son there is of a mother fair, whose root has sprung from her lofty plant:
He hugs her neck, though for some time, she had erewhile discarded him:
He who reaps her beauty ascends by means of him and none forbids and blames.

51   One split in his head it is through whom 'the writ' is known, as honoured recording angels take their pride in him;
When given to drink he craves for more, as though athirst, and settles to rest when thirstiness takes hold of him;
And scatters tears about him when ye bid him run, but tears that sparkle with the brightness of a smile.

52   One restless, although firmly fixed, bestowing gifts, not working mischief,
Now plunging, now uprising again, a marvel how he sinks and soars:
He pours down tears as one oppressed, yet is his fierceness to be feared:
For then he brings destruction on, although his inmost heart is pure.

53   One of whose sharpness I fight shy, he grows without either food, or drink . . .

54   What is the thing, that when it corrupts, its error turns to righteousness,
And when its qualities are choice it stirs up mischief where it appears:
Its parent is of pure descent, but wicked that which he begets.

55   And people who in their flight in eagle's wake sped along, although they were heavily arrayed in helmet and steel.

56   And oftentimes passed me by a dog in whose mouth there was a bull, but know ye, it was a bull without any tail.

57   What groom is it who weds, both in secret and openly, two
      sisters, and no offence at his wedlock is ever found? When
      waiting on one, he waits as well on the other eke: if husbands
      are partial, no such bias is seen in him. His attentions increase
      as the sweethearts are growing grey, and so does his largess:
      what a rare thing in married men!

ALL THE YEAR ROUND (1859–95)

Weekly periodical edited by Charles Dickens which later incorporated
his *Household Words*. Riddles cited (including one from Henry VIII's
time) in an unsigned article in the issue for 16 December 1876.

58   It came, though I fetched it; when come it was gone;
      It stayed but a moment, it could not stay long;
      I ask not who saw it, it could not be seen,
      And yet might be felt by a king or a queen.

59   Of us five brothers at the same time born,
      Two from our birthday our beards have worn,
      On other two none ever have appeared,
      While the fifth brother wears but half a beard.

60   'Tis seen each day, and heard of every hour,
      Yet no one sees or ever hears its power;
      It is familiar with the prince and sage,
      As well as with the peasant. In each age,
      Since time began, it has been known full well;
      And yet no earth, nor heaven, nor even hell
      Has e'er contained it, or e'er known its worth.
      It does exist, and yet it ne'er had birth;
      It nowhere is, and yet it finds a home
      In almost every page of every tome;
      The greatest bliss to human nature here
      Is having it to doubt, and dread, and fear.
      It gives us pain when measuring the esteem
      Of those we fondly worship in love's dream.
      It gives us pleasure instantly to hear
      From those we love; sweet friendship it can sear.
      Thought cannot compass it, yet ne'ertheless
      The lip can easily its sense express.
      'Tis not in sleep, for sleep hath worlds of dreams;
      Yet plain and easy to each mind it seems;
      For men of all degrees and every clime
      Can speak of it. Eternity nor time
      Hath it beheld. It singularly sounds
      To foreign ears. Title, wealth, and fame,
      However great, must end in it the same.
      It is, is not. It can be heard, although
      Nor man, nor angel e'er its sound can know.

61   'Twas not on Alpine snow or ice,
          But honest English ground,
        'Excelsior' was their device;
          But sad the fate they found.
        They did not climb for love or fame,
          But follow'd duty's call;
        They were together in their aim,
          But parted in their fall.

62   The beuety of the nyght ys shee,
        And mother of all hwmors that be,
        And lykwyse lady of the seys,
        That tyme doth mesure as she fleys;
        The sonn shee follows everywhere
        And shee ys changen of the ayer.
        Thys ladys name fayne woold I know,
        That dwells so high and rules so low.

63   My first two letters are a man, my first three a woman, my first
        four a brave man, my whole a brave woman.

64   I went to a wood, and caught it;
        Then I sat me down and sought it;
          The longer I sought
          For what I had caught,
        The less worth catching I thought it;
        I would rather have sold than bought it.
          And when I had sought
          Without finding aught,
        Home in my hand I brought it.

65   Misery, myself, and my wife.

66   The reverse of fourteen,
        The extremes of eleven,
          United you'll certainly have
        The name of a woman
        Six husbands in seven
          Would gladly see laid in the grave.

AMUSING RIDDLE BOOK, The (1830)

67   My habitation's in a wood,
        And I'm at any one's command.
        I often do more harm than good:
        If once I get the upper hand,
        I never fear a champion's frown;
        Stout things I often times have done;
        Brave soldiers I can fell them down,
        I never fear their sword nor gun.

ANONYMOUS

A selection of riddles, mostly of folk origin, drawn from a wide variety of sources including Chambers's *Popular Rhymes of Scotland* (1870) and Taylor's *English Riddles from Oral Tradition* (1951).

68   Riddle me, riddle me, riddle me ree,
     I saw a nut cracker up in a tree.

69   I never was, am always to be,
     None ever saw me, nor ever will,
     And yet I am the confidence of all
     Who live and breathe on this terrestrial ball.

70   I am taken from a mine, and shut up in a wooden case, from which I am never released, and yet I am used by almost everybody.

71   What runs all day and all night and never stops?

72   What is it that goes uphill and downhill yet never moves?

73   What goes out but never comes back?

74   What goes up and never comes down?

75   What goes through the woods and never touches a thing?

76   What goes round the house and in the house and never touches the house?

77   Over the water and under the water and never touches the water.

78   What goes away above the ground and returns under it?

79   What goes over the water and under the water and never touches the water?

80   What can pass before the sun without making a shadow?

81   What walks all day on its head?

82   What goes to the wood facing home?

83   What is it goes from house to house and never goes in?

84   Runs smoother than any rhyme,
     Loves to fall but cannot climb.

85   What makes a lot of noise
     In a house with one door,
     And if it sits in a draft,
     You can't hear it no more?

86   Never sings a melody, never has a song,
     But it goes on humming all day long.

87   If you feed it it will live,
     If you give it water it will die.

88   I'm in everyone's way,
     Yet no one I stop;
     My four arms in every way play,
     And my head is nailed on at the top.

89   What has a head but cannot think?

90   What kind of ear cannot hear?

91   What has a mouth but cannot talk?

92   What has teeth but cannot eat?

93   What has four legs and one back but can't walk?

94   Two-legs sat upon three-legs,
      One-leg knocked two-legs off three-legs,
      Two-legs hit four-legs with three-legs.

95   At night they come without being fetched, and by day they are
      lost without being stolen.

96   The calf, the goose and the bee,
      The world is ruled by these three.

97   It was neither fish, flesh, nor bone,
      And they said it had horns and wasn't a beast.

98   Little Jessie Ruddle, sitting in a puddle, green garters and yellow
      toes. Tell me this riddle or I'll smash your nose!

99   What is it that, after we have fastened, bolted, locked, barred
      the house, placed a watchman on guard, and taken the keys
      with us, yet before morning, goes out in spite of us?

100   I tremble at each breath of air,
      And yet can heaviest burdens bear.

101   No principal or teacher, I can make everyone in the world talk
      without saying a single word.

102   What gets wet when drying?

103   What force or strength cannot get through.
      I, with gentle touch, can do;
      And many in the street would stand,
      Were I not, as a friend, at hand.

104   Three men going to heaven: one goes halfway and turns back,
      one goes right up, and one doesn't go at all.

105   Behind the king's kitchen there is a great vat,
      And a great many workmen working at that,
      Yellow is their toes, yellow is their clothes.
      Tell me this riddle and you can pull my nose.

106   Out in the garden
      I have a green spot,
      And twenty-four ladies dancing on that;
      Some in green gowns,
      And some in blue caps.
      You are a good scholar,
      If you riddle me that.

107   Four boys were walking along the street.
      Two were big and two were small,
      And the two in front were walking quick,
      And the two behind were walking quick.
      Although the two in front stop,
      The two behind could not catch them.

108 There were five men walking along and it started to rain. The four that ran got wet and the one that stood still stayed dry.

109 There is a thing that when it has a root, it has no leaves; and when it pulls up its root, the leaves appear.

110 What is round as a dishpan, deep as a tub, and still the oceans couldn't fill it up?

111 Patch upon patch without any stitches, Riddle me that and I'll buy you a pair of breeches.

112 What is black and white and red all over?

113 My first is in south but not in north, My second is in picture but not in film, My third is in fourth and also in worth, My fourth is in book and also in cook, My fifth is in toe but not in sew, My sixth is in life but not in death.

114 What comes once in a minute, twice in a moment, but not once in a thousand years?

115 The more you take, the more you leave behind. What are they?

116 My first is in apple and also in pear, My second is in desperate and also in dare, My third is in sparrow and also in lark, My fourth is in cashier and also in clerk. My fifth is in seven and also in ten, My whole is a blessing indeed unto men.

117 There is a flying thing, which stays anywhere – even in the forests; its face is the face of a cow, its neck the neck of a horse, its breast the breast of a man, its wing is like a leaf in blossom, its tail resembles a snake and its feet look like the feet of a bird.

118 When one does not know what it is, then it is something; but when one knows what it is, then it is nothing.

119 A water lock and a wooden key, the hunter is captured and the game escapes.

120 To ease men of their care I do both rend and tear Their mother's bowels still; Yet though I do, There are but few That seem to take it ill.

121 I saw a wonderful thing. It has four legs but no soul, it gets many thousand thrusts but does not feel them, it has tulips and violets in full bloom, but you cannot hear the sigh of a nightingale.

122 There is a city, people go about in it, but one sees no streets.

123 Who flays himself, does not die from it, and walks without feet?

124   What has four wings and can't fly, no legs but can go?

125   What is as black as a priest, leaps like a horse, and a hundred men can't bridle it?

126   A rooster without trousers with a red moustache runs all over woods and mountains, and when he finds water, he perishes.

127   A hollow ship with freight of slops,
      Inside a cave her anchor drops.

128   What is it that a man buys for three pence, boils in a quart of salt, and then salts some more when it has boiled?

129   Not bigger than a grain of barley, and it covers the table of a king.

130   Who is it who has neither bones nor a skeleton, who carries fire on his head?

131   A little rod in Alexander's wood, neither pine is it, nor oak is it, it is no wood on earth, and you will not guess it till nightfall.

132   A hundred-year-old man and his head one night old.

133   A tree which you cut down today and the next it begins to sprout.

134   Every girl has one. Boys have none.
      Miss Granville had a capital one until she married Mr Roberts, when she lost it.
      Her daughter Gertie has a large one in front, her daughter Margaret has a small one near the centre, her sister Mrs Miggs had one twice in the same place.

135   It has neither mouth, nor teeth, nor bowels;
      Yet it eats its food steadily.
      It has neither village, nor home, nor hands, nor feet;
      Yet it wanders everywhere.
      It has neither country, nor means, nor office, nor pen;
      Yet it is ready for fight always.
      By day and by night there is wailing about it.
      It has no breath; yet to all it appears.

136   White are the walls, green are the men, brown are the priests, who sleep in the monastery.

137   What holds water yet is full of holes?

138   What goes into the water red and comes out black?

139   What goes into the water black and comes out red?

140   What goes up and down stairs without moving?

141   Round the rocks
      And round the rocks
      The ragged rascal ran,
      And every bush he came to
      He left his rags and ran.

142   What grows in the woods,
Winters in the town,
And earns its master many a crown?

143   As round as an apple,
As deep as a pail;
It never cries out
Till it's caught by the tail.

144   Crooked as a rainbow,
Slick as a plate,
Ten thousand horses
Can't pull it straight.

145   Humpty Dumpty sat on a wall,
Humpty Dumpty had a great fall,
All the king's horses and all the king's men
Couldn't put Humpty Dumpty together again.

146   The man who made it did not want it;
The man who bought it did not use it;
The man who used it did not know it.

147   Brothers and sisters have I none but that man's father is my
father's son.

148   What is big at the bottom, little at the top, and has ears?

149   What is green on the mountain, black in the market-place, and
red in the house?

150   What has a head like a cat, feet like a cat, tail like a cat, but
is not a cat?

151   What small chest is full of mouse bones?

152   He who has it doesn't tell it;
He who takes it doesn't know it;
He who knows it doesn't want it.

153   It has cities, but no houses;
It has forests, but no trees;
It has rivers, but no fish.
What is it?

154   What is this: there's a sweet shop inside a lumber shop inside a
leather shop inside a thorn shop?

155   Who spends the day at the window, goes to the table for meals
and hides at night?

156   Why is a good meerschaum like a water-colour artist?

157   Lives without a body, hears without ears, speaks without
mouth, to which the air alone gives birth.

158   Why is O the noisiest of the vowels?

159 Without as smooth as glass,
Within a woolly mass.
But hid amid the wool
There lurks a nice mouthful.

160 A pitcher with a thousand chinks,
Yet ne'er lets out the water it drinks.

161 My back as frying-pan does appear;
  Beneath a snowy breast;
A pair of scissors jut in the rear;
  What am I? Have you guessed?

162 I keep a tiny something in a tiny box,
Secured under many keys and many locks:
If the tiny something breaketh loose,
Of the tiny box what is the use?

163 He feeds on beef the livelong day,
At night he scans the Milky Way.

164 Though it is not an ox, it has horns; though it is not an ass,
it has a pack-saddle; and wherever it goes it leaves silver behind.
What is it?

165 I bind it, and it walks; I loose it, and it stops.

166 A messenger that could not speak, bearing a letter that was not
written, came to a city that had no foundations.

167 In daytime I have nothing to do
And am left quietly in a corner.
But at night I'm brought out
And swallow fire and flame.

168 First I was burnt, then I was beaten,
Then I was drowned and pierced with nails.
What am I?

169 A red maiden is sitting in a green summerhouse,
If you squeeze her she will cry
And her tears they are as red as blood,
But yet her heart is made of stone.

170 What goes round and round the wood and never gets into the
wood?

171 As I went out one moonlight night,
I saw a thing that made me fright.
I hit it hard and heavy blows
Till it bled gallons at the nose.

172 I sat on my hunkers,
I looked through my peepers,
I saw the dead burying the living.

173 A hopper o'ditches,
A cropper o'corn,
A wee brown cow,
And a pair of leather horns!

174   He comes to you amidst the brine,
       The butterfly of the sun,
       The man of coat so blue and fine,
       With red thread his shirt is done.

175   My first denotes company;
       My second shuns company;
       My third summons company;
       My whole amuses company.

176   What is that which sweetens the cup of life, but which, if it loses
       one letter, embitters it?

ANTIPHANES (4th century BC)
Ancient Greek dramatist. Riddle cited in Athenaeus's *Deipnosophistae*.

177   There is a feminine being which keeps its babes safe beneath its
       bosom; they, though voiceless, raise a cry sonorous over the
       waves of the sea and across all the dry land, reaching what
       mortals they desire, and they may hear even when they are not
       there; but their sense of hearing is dull.

APOLLONIUS OF TYRE, The History of (9th century)
Popular medieval romance; versions in *Gesta Romanorum* and Gower's
Confessio Amantis (1390). Riddles taken from Spanish edition, *El Libro
di Apolonio* (13th century).

178   . . . Tell me now this thing.
       What house is always murmuring,
       Though the indwellers are all dumb?
       Now please me with the answer. Come!

179   The river's kin and friend am I.
       My lovely hair I raise on high.
       My trade is to make black of white.
       That one is hard to solve aright.

180   I am the forest's child most swift.
       Furrows I cut and leave no rift.
       I fight the winds. I'm dangerous.

181   I have no limbs, no parts inside,
       But two teeth like an elephant goad.
       The one who bears me I hold still.

182   I'm soft as wool, soft as a bog.
       When I swell up, I'm like a frog.
       I grow in water, where I plunge.

183   I am not black, nor white nor red;
       No tongue by which wise saws are said
       Have I. I win when I am opposite.
       I can be bought for a small bit.

184   Downy inside, and smooth to the air,
       Inside by breast I wear my hair.
       From hand to hand I go in play.
       When men go eat, outside I stay.

ARABIAN NIGHTS ENTERTAINMENT, The (8th–16th centuries)
Also known as *The Thousand and One Nights*, this collection of Indian, Persian, and Arabic tales was first translated into English in 1705. The best-known version is that by Sir Richard Burton (1885–8) from which the examples below are taken. Riddles occur in 'Abu al-Husn and His Slave-girl Tawaddud' (Story 113, Nights 437–62), though religious questions also occur in the story of the Linguist-Dame in the 'Supplemental Nights' volume.

185   A dweller in the tomb whose food is at his head,
        When he eateth of that meat, of words he waxeth fain:
        He riseth and he walketh and he talketh without tongue;
        And returneth to the tomb where his kith and kin are lain.
        No living wight is he, yet in honour he abides;
        Nor dead yet he deserveth that Allah him assain.

186   An eater lacking mouth and even maw;
        Yet trees and beasts to it are daily bread:
        Well fed it thrives and shows a lively life,
        But give it water and you do it dead.

187   Two lovers barred from every joy and bliss,
        Who through the live-long night embracing lie:
        They guard the folk from all calamities,
        But with the rising sun apart they fly.

188   She wears a pair of ringlets long let down
        Behind her, as she comes and goes at speed.
        An eye that never tastes of sleep nor sheds
        A tear, for ne'er a drop it hath at need;
        That never all its life wore stitch of clothes;
        Yet robes mankind in every mode of weed.

ARISTOPHANES (c.450–c.385 BC)
Ancient Greek comic dramatist. Riddle found in *Wasps*.

189   What is that brute which throws away its shield
        Alike in air, in ocean, in the field?

ASHMORE, A. C. Stevenson (fl. 1920s)
Compiler of popular puzzle books. Examples taken from *Word Games and Word Puzzles* (1929).

190   When frost and snow o'erspread the ground,
          And chilly blows the air,
        My first is felt upon the cheek
          Of every maiden fair.
        In earth's cold bosom lies my next,
          An object most forlorn;
        For often cruelly 'tis used,
          And trampled on with scorn.
        Amid the darkest shades of night
          My whole looks bright and gay,
        Though dull and gloomy it appears
          Exposed to light of day.

191   What has four legs and only one foot?

192   My first is in sorrow, but not in sad,
My second's in girl, but not in lad,
My third is in near, but not in far,
My fourth is in tram, but not in car,
My fifth is in sure, but not in slow,
My sixth is in reap, but not in sow,
My whole is the season of frost and snow.

193   My first is a fowl of good eating,
Though not at all times of the year;
My second, without any treating,
Is found in the hedge that is near.

My whole is a fruit that is seen
To flourish in gardens near bowers;
'Tis red, it is yellow, or green,
And you much prefer it to flowers.

194   What is it that you can keep after giving it to someone else?

195   My first is in add, but not in take,
My second's in joint, but not in steak,
My third is in stack, but not in heap,
My fourth is in thick, but not in deep,
My fifth is in veal, but not in lamb,
My sixth is in ounce, but not in dram,
My seventh's in smile, but not in frown,
My whole is a writer of highest renown.

196   My first is called bad or good,
    May please you or offend you;
My second in a thrifty mood
    May very much befriend you.

My whole, though called a 'cruel word',
    May yet appear a kind one,
It often may with joy be heard,
    With tears may often blind one.

197   My first is in sharp, but not in keen,
My second's in jealous, but not in mean,
My third is in love, but not in hate,
My fourth is in friend, but not in mate,
My fifth is in dear, but not in cheap,
My sixth is in wake, but not in sleep,
My seventh's in slay, but not in slain,
My whole is a time when we hope it won't rain.

198   My first often rests on the floor,
And mostly not far from the door;
And sometimes the word we employ
As the shortened name of a boy.

My second grows thick on the head –
It may be auburn, yellow, or red,
But be it dark, or be it fair,
I do assure you, 'tis not *hair*.

My whole I like when soft; when hard
My beauty slumber is quite marred.

199 My first is in iron, but not in gold,
My second's in sell, but not in sold,
My third is in swim, but not in sink,
My fourth is in pens, but not in ink,
My fifth is in cup, but not in mug,
My sixth is in mat, but not in rug,
My seventh's in happy, but not in glad,
My eighth is in wicked, but not in bad,
My ninth is in brick, but not in clay,
My whole brings the news to you day by day.

200 What animal is equal to nothing added to ten?

201 What paper is like a sneeze?

AUSTEN, Jane (1775–1817)
English novelist. Riddles appear in *Emma* (1816). (See also *Garrick*.)

202 My first displays the wealth and pomp of kings,
  Lords of the earth! their luxury and ease.
Another view of man, my second brings,
  Behold him there, the monarch of the seas!

But ah! united what reverse we have!
  Man's boasted power and freedom, all are flown:
Lord of the earth and sea, he bends a slave,
  And woman, lovely woman, reigns alone.

Thy ready wit the word will soon supply,
May its approval beam in that soft eye!

BAGWELL, William (*fl.* 1655)
London merchant and writer on astronomy born *c.* 1593. Fifty riddles
appear in *Wit's Extraction* (1664). The enigmas are accompanied by an
Observation, an Explanation, and a Moral.

203 Black am I as a coal, yet well belov'd
Of those that have much of my goodness prov'd.
Teeth I have none, and yet I shall him bite
That hath good Teeth, though he in me delight.
Beaten and bruis'd am I, when o'er-power'd
As well by him that's Valiant, as the Coward.
He that's with me o'er bold, tho' ne'er so strong,
I'll smite his Nose, be't ne'er so great or long.
And when I have thus done, I'll make him yield,
As he that's over thrown i' th'open field.

204 I am of general use, much in request,
In all parts of the North, South, East and West.
With me some do much good, and'ts well accepted;
And some much ill, as they are so affected.
Many are griev'd that have not me obtain'd;
And others careless when they have me gain'd.

A Master and a Servant both I have;
The one commands me, th'other is my slave.
But when the Messenger for them does come,
They leave me quite, and others take their room.

205   He's quick and nimble, yet cannot abide
To go from's food till he be satisfi'd.
He nips him whom he loves, then gets away;
Turns to's food, then scores, but doth not pay.
The greatest mischief he does, is i'th'night;
Then like a cunning Shark, plays least in sight;
Yet this Vexatious course he'll not forbear,
Till he be taken in the Hunters snare.
Who when this busie-body there doth find,
He's prest to death, yet's marks are left behind.

206   He that deals gently with me, though he's sad
And melancholy, yet I'll make him glad.
He that abuses me, and means to swagger,
I'll knock his pate, and make him forthwith stagger.
If he persist, nothing shall intervene;
For though he's plump & fat, I'll make him lean.
Nay more then this, let him be ne'er so tall,
I'll trip up's his heels, and give him a sound fall.
When I him have thus us'd, he'll then me hate,
And turn me out of doors when 'tis too late.

207   I Ride without a Saddle on a thing
That hath no legs nor bones, yet thus stradling,
Am thereon stately mounted, to the end
I may two friends (that are decay'd) befriend.
Wherefore, when I before them do appear,
That which to them seems doubtful, I make clear.
Now when this business I have thus begun,
I'll not dismounted be till I have done:
Then shall I to my Lodging be convey'd,
Till I in this kinde am again employ'd.

208   Her back is round, her belly's flat withal;
Her metamorphis'd guts are great & small.
Her Navel's comely, and her Neck is long,
Bedeck'd with Ornaments, though small, yet strong.
B'ing thus compleat, her Masters chief ambition
Is to make known to all her sweet condition:
Her neck therefore, and other parts below,
He gently handles: he'll not from her go,
Till he receives from her his full content;
Which all the standers by do much resent.

BARBAULD Mrs A. L. (1743–1824)

Poet, editor, and author (with her brother John Aikin) of children's books including *Evenings at Home* (1792–6). Friend of Hannah More (q.v.).

209   We are spirits all in white,
On a field as black as night;
There we dance, and sport, and play,
Changing every changing day:
Yet with us is wisdom found,
As we move in mystic round.

Mortal! wouldst though know the grains
That Ceres heaps on Libya's plains,
Or leaves that yellow autumn strews,
Or the stars that Herschel views,
Or find how many drops would drain
The wide-scoop'd bosom of the main,
Or measure central depths below?
Ask of us, and thou shalt know!
With fairy step we compass round
The pyramid's capacious bound,
Or, step by step, ambitious climb
The cloud-capped mountain's height sublime.
Riches, though we do not use,
'Tis ours to gain and ours to lose.
From Araby the Bless'd we came;
In every land our tongue's the same;
And if our number you require,
Go count the bright Aonian quire.
Wouldst thou cast a spell to find
The track of light, the speed of wind?
Or when the snail, with creeping pace,
Shall the swelling globe embrace?
Mortal! ours the powerful spell:
Ask of us, for we can – tell.

210   I often murmur, yet I never weep;
I always lie in bed, but never sleep;
My mouth is wide, and larger than my head,
And much disgorges, though it ne'er is fed:
I have no legs or feet, yet swiftly run –
And the more falls I get, move faster on.

211   There's not a bird that cleaves the sky,
With crest or plume more gay than I,
   Yet guess me by this token –
That I am never seen to fly
   Unless my wings are broken.

212   I never talk but in my sleep,
I never cry, but sometimes weep;
My doors are open day and night;
Old age I help to better sight.
Chameleon-like, I feed on air,
And dust to me is dainty fare.

BARHAM, Rev. R. H. (1788–1845)
Popular writer for *Bentley's Miscellany* (q.v.) and *The New Monthly Magazine*. Charade occurs in 'My Letters' in his most well known work, *The Ingoldsby Legends* (first collected edition 1840).

213   My first is follow'd by my second;
        Yet should my first my second see,
        A dire mishap it would be reckon'd,
        And sadly shock'd my first would be.

        Were I but what my whole implies,
        And pass'd by chance across your portal,
        You'd cry, 'Can I believe my eyes?
        I never saw so queer a mortal!'

        For then my head would not be on,
        My arms their shoulders must abandon;
        My very body would be gone,
        I should not have a leg to stand on.

BEDE, The Venerable (AD 673–735)
English historian and scholar. Riddles attributed to him occur in *Excerptiones patrum, collectanea, flores ex diversis, quaestiones et parabolae* ('Flores') and *Jocoseria*.

214   *Dic mihi, quæso, quæ est illa mulier, quæ innumeris filiis ubera porrigit, quæ, quantum sucta fuerit, tantum inundat?*

        (Tell me, I beg you, who is the woman who offers her breasts to countless sons, and who, however much she is sucked, pours out as much?)

215   *Dic mihi quæ est illa res quæ caelum totamque terram replevit, silvas et surculos confringit, omniaque fundamenta concutit: sed nec oculis videri aut manibus tangi potest.*

        (Tell me, what is it that fills the sky and the whole earth and tears up new shoots, and shakes all foundations, but cannot be seen by eyes or touched by hands?)

216   *Quid est quod mater me genuit et mox eadem gignetur a me?*

        (What is it that bore me as a mother and soon will be born from me?)

217   *Sedeo super equum non natum, cujus matrem in manu teneo.*

        (I am sitting above a horse which was not born, whose mother I hold in my hand.)

BEETON'S BOY'S ANNUAL (1870)
One of many publications by S. O. Beeton (1831–77), founder of *Boy's Own Magazine* and *Boy's Own Volume* (q.v.), and husband of the household management writer, Mrs Beeton. As well as 'fact, fiction and adventure' could be found a number of puzzles, riddles, etc.

218   I had existence ere the world begun,
And now I'm told I'm new beneath the sun;
Thought cannot grasp me; I am hardly sought,
The pauper buys me, yet I go for naught;
Speech, too, can frame me, though I can't be *said*;
Some will pursue me, while by some I'm fled.
Cut off my head, I then become a thing
From which a part of everything must spring;
My head the centre of a knot will be;
The poor who eat me whole, live frugally.
I'm scarcely seen, save when you shut the eyes,
And he who gains me sure will lose a prize.
However much one may have had before,
The more he gets he always wants me more.
Yet people occupy themselves full well
Enjoying me, as all the papers tell,
The *whole*, in dullest seasons oft you hear me
Spoken of, while all good people fear me!

219   Upon my head, and eke my eldest boy,
I take it in, but not without alloy,
My *first* is this. My *second* makes a gown;
My *whole* oft to my *first* is handed down.

220   My *first* in a quiver
          You'll see as a river,
And oftentimes painted as grasped by grim Death.
          My *second* will be
          Always down by the sea,
In the *best* wat'ring places inhaling a breath,
While under the shelter of Devon's sweet coast
My *whole* of Britannia's best guard can well boast.

221   My *first* is rapid, yet a sluggish stream
It used to be, as antiquaries deem.
My *second* rather *sticks* as you will see,
And is the usual offshoot of a tree.
My *whole* a town in Lancashire is found,
Yet once it might be said on Scottish ground
A certain forest for my name had served
Ere Macbeth met the death he well deserved.

222   My *first* is a fellow; my *whole* is oft so,
Yet through my *second* both surely can go.
My *first* with my *whole* you can anywhere meet,
While my *second's* obliged to run out of a street.
Contain'd in the Army and Navy, the fate
Of my *whole*'s to be linked to a bishop in state.
Now, reader, come guess, leave me not in 'the lurch',
You're my *first* and my *whole* if you are in the Church.
Put this aside, and then my *second* down
The volume will be, and you naught but a clown.

BELLAMY, William (1846–?)

American writer best known as the author of a number of fine charades. Examples taken from *A Century of Charades* (1894) to which the answers are given in a highly complicated numerical key.

223   My first the anxious mother often hears;
       My second is the vaunted cup that cheers;
       When coming through my third, two bodies met;
       Before you ride, my fourth you have to get.

       You'll guess my whole if you will think a bit;
       It is a sort of touchstone for your wit.

224   My first was once a king uncouth,
         The lord of subterranean fires;
       And, if its people told the truth,
         My second was the land of liars.

       Undoing by night the labour of each day,
       Ulysses' queen her suitors kept at bay.
       A pattern wife, as husbands all agree,
       She was my whole, if wife my whole can be.

225   My first has led a blameless life,
       He never quarrels with his wife,
       His inmost thoughts are free from sin,
       He's happy when the tide is in,
       He never seeks my whole to raise,
       His taste is worthy of all praise.
       Yet such existence who would wish to live
       Long as my last presents alternative?

226   My hair is falling down my first,
         I'm sure I must a perfect fright be,
       I think my corset lace has burst,
         Oh, how I wish my third I might be!
       For if my whole could work the spell,
         Or some kind-hearted wizard hear me,
       I'd take my second in a shell,
         I'd play baseball and none would jeer me.
       Without my skirts, how queer 't would seem;
         No mouse would fright, no tramp appall me;
       'T would be just lovely as a dream,
         And all the girls my fourth would call me.

227   From tennis courts my first ascends;
       My second in commotion ends.
       No martyr's crown my whole secured,
       Who worse than martyrdom endured;
       They found who tore his limbs apart
       A lady's image at his heart.

BENTLEY'S MISCELLANY (1837–69)

Popular literary journal published by Richard Bentley. Originally edited by Dickens, contributors included Thackeray, Longfellow, Cruikshank, and Leech. Also contained occasional riddles. Examples taken from issues for 1838 and 1840.

228   As a skaiter was sporting his elegant make
In the Regent's Park, he was ask'd this con.:
'Why is this sheet of ice like a Canada lake?
Give it up?' – 'Because it's the lake *you're on* (Huron).'

229   'Up, lady, up to the turret's height,
   Gaze far as eye can strain;
There are glittering spears and armour bright,
And pennon and plume – 'tis a glorious sight
   On the peaceful hill and plain;
For the iron rule of my *First* hath pass'd,
And the loved and the brave are return'd at last.

'With my *Second* still close to his faithful heart,
   Doubt not thy knight is there;
That golden shield has repell'd each dart,
And the cruel sword has not dared to part
   Those links so soft and fair.
The pledge at the moment of parting given
Has found mercy on earth and mercy in heaven.' –

'Peace, boaster vain!' a stern voice said,
   And my *Whole* before us stood, –
'Peace! for thou speak'st of the long since dead,
And long has that vaunted pledge been red
   In the gallant wearer's blood!' –
He said, – and ere night-fall the lady knew
That the words of the prophet of ill were true.

230   There was once a knight both young and tall,
   And blessed with a handsome face,
When he rode at the ring, or danced at the ball,
   'T was done with a wonderful grace;
By the leaguered wall, in the battle's burst,
   'Mid the foremost his name was reckoned;
But, alas! he always was my *First*,
   Because he had not my *Second*.

Fair ladies turned with a scornful look
   When he ventured to draw near;
And fathers and mothers shuddered and shook
   If he gazed on their daughters dear;
Often apart from the crowd he stole,
   And cried as his fate he cursed,
'If my *Second* I had, I might e'en be my *Whole*,
   But I never should be my *First*.'

231   Gentle and fair the maiden is,
   And many a lover tries

With flatt'ring looks and honey'd words
　　To win so sweet a prize.
But still unmoved and calm she hears
　　Their vows of deep affection,
And courteous though her answer be,
　　'Tis firm in its rejection.
Each suitor sees the hopes destroy'd
　　His pride so fondly nurst,
And, mortified, they all agree
　　The maiden is 'My First.'

But there's a blush on that fair cheek
　　The charge seems to deny;
The tear that's check'd before the world
　　But falls when none are by.
Sadness that will not be dispell'd,
　　Indifference to please,
When mark'd by an observing eye,
　　Strong symptoms, maidens, these!
There's love within that heart; but though
　　A hidden love it be,
'My Second' mid the Alpine rocks
　　Is not more pure than she.

Oh! Fortune, well they judge of thee
　　Who drew thine image blind,
For still thy shadows darkest fall
　　Where fate had else been kind.
No stain is on the maiden's choice,
　　Save one her guardians see,
Unpardonable in their eyes, –
　　'Tis that of Poverty.
And they forbid the sacrifice
　　Which she would gladly make,
Of wealth, and worldly splendour, all
　　For the beloved one's sake.

And so they part, with bitter tears,
　　But still unchanged, they'll keep
The mem'ry of that treasured love
　　Which soothes them while they weep.
And yet, young lovers, I will hope
　　The time may come at last,
When, rich in present happiness,
　　You'll smile at sorrows past;
For never fairer maidens graced
　　The dance in courtly hall,
And nobler heart than *his* ne'er beat
　　'Mid the brave ranks of 'my all.'

BERNE RIDDLES, The (7th century)

Collection of sixty-two riddles from Bobbio, Italy, believed to have been written by Tullius, an Irish monk.

232   *Mortem ego pater libens adsumo pro natis*
Et tormenta simul, cara ne pignora tristem.
Mortuum me cuncti gaudent habere parentes
Et sepultum nullus paruo uel funere plangit.

(I, as father, freely take up sad death for my son's sake, and torments too, lest my children suffer. All parents rejoice to have me dead and none laments at my burial with its tiny funeral.)

233   *Mortua maiorem quam uiuens porto laborem.*
Dum iaceo, multos seruo; si stetero, paucos.
Viscera si mihi foris detracta patescant,
Vitam fero cunctis uictumque confero multis.
Bestia defuncta quae nulla . . . memordit,
Et onusta currens uiam nec planta depingo.

(I carry a greater load dead than alive. While I lie, I serve many men: if I were to stand, I should serve a few. If my entrails are torn out to lie open out of doors, I bring life to all, and I give sustenance to many. A lifeless creature which . . . bites nothing, when loaded down I run on my way yet never show my feet.)

234   *Nullam ante tempus lustri genero prolem*
Annisque peractis superbos genero natos,
Quos domare quisquis ualet industria paruus,
Cum eos marinus iunctus percusserit imber,
Asperi nam lenes sic creant filii nepotes,
Tenebris ut lucem reddant, dolori salutem.

(I shall bear no offspring before the lustral period of five years, and when the time has passed I shall bear superb sons; anyone who can make some small exertion will be strong enough to tame them, as soon as some sea storm has come and shaken them thoroughly. And thus rough sons will bring forth gentle grandsons, to give light for those in darkness and health for the afflicted.)

235   *Dissimilem sibi me mater concipit infra,*
Et nullo uirili creata de semine fundor.
Dum nascor sponte, gladio diuellor a uentre.
Caesa uiuit mater: ego nam flammis aduror.
Nullum clara manens possum concedere quaestum
Plurimum fero lucrum, nigro si corpore mutor.

(My mother conceived me below, a different thing from herself, and I poured forth created by no male seed. While I was born spontaneously, I was torn from her belly by a sword. But my mother lives on, though cleft open, for I cauterize all wounds. I bring most profit if I am changed to having a black body.)

BIBLE, The

Judaeo-Christian religious text. Riddles occur in Proverbs, Judges, *et passim*. Those cited are from Proverbs 30.

236   Three things there are which will never be satisfied,
        four which never say, 'Enough!':
        The grave and a barren womb,
        a land thirsty for water
        and fire that never says, 'Enough!'

    Three things there are which are too wonderful for me,
        four of which I do not understand:
        the way of a vulture in the sky,
        the way of a serpent on the rock,
        the way of a ship out at sea,
        and the way of a man with a girl.

    At three things the earth shakes,
        four things it cannot bear:
        a slave turned king,
        a churl gorging himself,
        a woman unloved when she is married,
        and a slave-girl displacing her mistress.

    Four things there are which are smallest on earth
        yet wise beyond the wisest:
        ants, a people with no strength
        yet they prepare their store of food in the summer;
        rock-badgers, a feeble folk,
        yet they make their home among the rocks;
        locusts, which have no king,
        yet they sally forth in detachments;
        the lizard, which can be grasped in the hand,
        yet is found in the palaces of kings.

    Three things there are which are stately in their stride,
        four which are stately as they move:
        the lion, a hero among beasts,
        which will not turn tail for anyone;
        the strutting cock and the he-goat;
        and a king going forth to lead his army.

BISHOP'S RIDDLE, The (19th century)

Perhaps the most debated enigma of recent times, this riddle has appeared in many forms and has been attributed to Hallam the historian, Byron, Fox, and Sheridan, amongst others, with a number of possible solutions. General consensus, however, now seems to point to the author as being Dr Denison, Bishop of Salisbury (from 1837–54). A number of versified answers appear in the Appendix.

237   I sit on a rock whilst I'm raising the wind,
        But, the storm once abated, I'm gentle and kind:
        I've kings at my feet who await but my nod
        To kneel in the dust on the ground I have trod.
        Tho' seen to the world, I'm known to but few;
        The Gentile detests me, I'm pork to the Jew;

I never have passed but one night in the dark,
And that was with Noah alone in the Ark;
My weight is three pounds, my length is a mile:
And when I'm discovered you'll say with a smile,
That my last and my first are the best of our Isle.

BOILEAU (DESPRÉAUX), Nicolas (1636–1711)

French literary critic and poet. Riddle contained in a letter to Brossette
(1703) but composed in 1652.

238   *Du repos des Humains implacable Ennemie,*
       J'ay rendu mille Amans envieux de mon sort;
       Je me repais de sang, et je trouve ma vie
       Dans les bras de celui qui recherche ma mort.

       (Implacable enemy of human rest, I have made a thousand lovers
       jealous of my lot; I feast on blood, and find my life in the arms
       of those who seek my death.)

BOOK OF MERRY RIDDLES, The (1629)

Anonymous riddle collection printed in London

239   He went to the wood and caught it;
       He sate him downe and sought it;
       Because he could not finde it,
       Home with him he brought it.

240   What work is that: the faster ye worke, [the] longer it is ere ye have
       done; and the slower ye worke, the sooner ye make an end?

241   What is that that is rough within, and red without,
       and bristled like a bares snowt:
       there is never a Lady in this Land
       but will be content to take it in her hand.

242   What Kings, Queens, and their servants be they that be burnt once
       a yeere, and be cut and torne as small as flesh to pot?

243   Three prisoners, such as it was,
       were shut up in a prison of glasse.
       The prison doore was made of bread,
       and yet they were for hunger dead.

244   Who bare the best burthen that ever was borne at any time since,
       or at any time before?

245   What is the most profitable beast, and that men eat least on?

246   What is that one seeketh for, and would not finde?

247   What is that:
       as high as a hall,
       as bitter as gall,
       as soft as silke,
       as white as milke?

248   What is he that getteth his living backward?

249   What is it that goeth to the water, and leaveth his guts at home?

250   What is that which 20 will go into a tankard, and one will fill
a barn?

251   What is it that goes to the water, and the first that touches the
water is the arse?

252   Ten men's strength, and ten men's length, and ten men cannot
set it on end; yet one man may beare it.

253   Thorow a rocke, thorow a reele,
thorow an old spinning wheele,
thorow a hard shining bone:
such a riddle you have none.

254   Downe in a meddow I have 2 swine; the more meat I give them the
lowder they cry, the lesse meat I give them the stiller they lye.

255   Beyond the sea there is an oake,
and in that oake there is a nest,
and in the nest there is an egge,
and in that egge there is a yolke,
which cals together Christian folke.

256   I consume my mother that bare me,
I eat my nurse that fed me,
then I dye leaving all blinde that saw me.

BOOKE OF MERRIE RIDDLES, A (1631)
Anonymous riddle collection printed in London for Robert Bird. Also
known as *Prettie Riddles*.

257   A maid there was that married a man, by whom was many children
gotten; yet all they died, and went away, before the mother was
begotten.

258   In what place crew the cock so lowd,
that all men heard it out of doubt?

259   When I am old, I cast my skinne,
whereby I doe come young againe.

260   White I am, and blacke withall,
I have eyes, and yet am blind.
Gaine and losse not without braule
I doe procure, as you shall find.

261   I am within as white as snow,
without as greene as hearbs that grow;
I am higher then a house,
and yet am lesser then a mouse.

262   There dwels foure sisters near this town,
in favour like, and like in gowne.
When they run for a prise to win,
all at once they doe begin.
One runnes as fast as doth the other,
yet cannot overtake each other.

100

263   Sixe haires did come within a plain,
whom hounds had started out the nest.
Hill up, hill downe they runne amaine,
till they were weary and then did rest.
They caught him once, and scapt again,
more eager went they then before,
and tooke more paine then (as I win)
to beare away the game and more.
The hounds and hunters all were one,
each liked his game and took his prey.
But when their sport was past and done,
they left their haires and came away.

264   In open field I cannot lye,
and yet may rest quietly
within a boxe of ivory.

265   A ship there drives upon the tide,
that sailes doth beare, she hath no mast.
But one oare she hath on each side;
her sailes the snow in whitenesse passe.
In her front weares two lanthorns bright;
but when she is upon point to fall,
then lend an eare, for great delight
of musicke she affords to all.

266   What man is he of wit so base,
that wears both his eyes in a case;
for feare of hurting them it is,
and I doe find it not amisse.

267   My prey I seek the fields and weeds about,
and have more teeth then beasts within the land,
and whensoever my game I have found out,
then safe I bring it to my master's hand.
Upon my back the deere he layes
and there doth kill one, sometimes more:
he shuts me up and goes his wayes,
better contented then before.

268   A tree there is that boughes doth beare
in number five, as I doe know:
no equall length they never were,
and on their tops doe hornes grow.
Yet they are tied about with gold,
except the longest, without doubt,
which for use sake might be controld,
if it with gold were hoopt about.

269   In what place of the earth doth the skie seeme
to be no larger then a yard, or twaine?
Which? I pray thee,
tell mee.

270 What doth with his roote upwards grow,
and downward with his head doth show?

271 What is lesser then a mouse,
and hath more windows then a house?

272 When we by the way do goe,
upon our shoulders we beare our way;
if we were not, then many should be
wet to the skin in a rayny day.

273 In the last minute of my age
I doe waxe young againe.
And have so still continued,
since world did first begin.

274 Trip trap in a gap,
as many feete as a hundred sheepe.

275 I know a child borne by my mother,
naturall borne as other children be,
that is neither my sister nor my brother.
Answer me shortly: what is he?

276 I have a smith without a hand,
he workes the worke that no man can.
He serves our God, and doth man ease
without any fire in his furnace.

277 As round as a hoope I am,
most part when it is day;
but being night, then am I long
as any snake, I say.

278 What is it [that] more eyes doth weare
then forty men within the land,
which glister as the christall cleare
against the sunne, when they doe stand?

279 My coate is greene, and I can prate
of divers things about my grate.
In such a prison I am set
that hath more loope holes then a net.

BOOK OF RIDDLES, The (1851)
229 enigmas, charades, etc., by 'the Editress of "The Lady's Library"'.

280 My *first* is Latin for a book,
   Which boys, at least, must know quite well;
My *second*'s two thirds of, to knot,
   And this you'll also quickly tell.
My *whole*'s the proudest boast of those
   Who dwell within this favoured land;
'Tis England's boon to every slave
   Whose foot has pressed our sea-girt strand.

281   Where'er my *first* may meet your eyes,
        A lovely colour it will be, –
    My *second*'s formed of earth, stones, sand, –
        Almost all things except the sea.
    My *whole*'s a country dark and wild,
        The people honest, poor, and free,
    Who from *reflection* gain much light,
        Yet seldom trees or flowers see.
    The strangest thing about this land,
        Where snows are deep, and stars are bright,
    Is – in a year as long as ours,
        They only have one day – one night!

282   My *first* is a member used most in a fight;
        My *second*'s a part of a General, known
    In the first wars with Erin, e'er England's brave knight
        Won that gem of the West, to embellish her throne;
    Whilst my *whole* is the name of as gallant a band
    As e'er caused raid or riot in Scotia's land.

BOTTINI, Giovanna Statira (d.1727)
Pseudonym (anagram) of Giovanni Battista Taroni. Riddles published in
Cento nodi (1718).

283   *Quel, che m'ha in odio, ognor mi va cercando,*
        E da quel, che mi cerca io sempre fuggo,
        Senza timor di qua, di là volando
        E gigli e rose ogn'or lambisco e suggo:
        Per le vie più segrete io vado errando,
        E chi mi nutre ingratamente io struggo,
        Ma a forza di rotture al fine esangue
        In man di chi mel diede io rendo il sangue.

(He who hates me is always searching for me, and from he who
searches for me, I am always fleeing, without fear, flying here and
there. Lilies and roses I always glide over and suck: I wander
through the most secret ways, and, ungratefully, I destroy that
which nourishes me. But finally bloodless because of being broken
I render the blood into the hand of he who gave it me.)

284   *Ardito, senza brando, e quasi ignudo*
        Quante volte fugai le armate schiere;
        Fui del Duce primier sostegno, e scudo,
        Portai spoglie nemiche, armi, e bandiere;
        Pugnai ne' boschi ancor contro il più crudo
        Furor de' mostri, e di voraci fiere,
        E per unico vanto il Ciel mi diede
        Tutte le glorie, e le fortune al piede.

(Bold, without a sword, and almost naked, how many times
have I escaped from armed bands. I was the prime support and
shield of the chief, I carried enemy spoils, arms and flags. I still
fought in the woods against the most vicious fury of monsters,
and of voracious wild beasts, and, as a unique honour, Heaven
gave me all glory and fortune at my feet.)

BOURNE, Vincent (1695–1747)

Latin poet and teacher at Westminster School. Riddles occur in *Poemata, Latine partim reddita, partim scripta* (1734). Translation by his pupil William Cowper (q.v.), published 1803.

285   *Parvula res, et acu minor est, et ineptior usu:*
      Quotque dies annus, tot tibi drachma dabit.
    Sed licet exigui pretii minimique valoris,
      Ecce, quot artificum postulat illa manus!
    Unius in primis cura est conflare metallum;
      In longa alterius ducere fila labor.
    Tertius in partes resecat, quartusque resectum
      Perpolit ad modulos attenuatque datos.
    Est quinti tornare caput, quod sextus adaptet;
      Septimus in punctum cudit et exacuit.
    His tandem auxiliis ita res procedit, ut omnes
      Ad numeros ingens perficiatur opus.
    Quæ tanti ingenii, quæ tanti est summa laboris?
      Si mihi respondes, Œdipe, tota tua est.

(A needle small, as small can be,
In bulk and use, surpasses me,
    Nor is my purchase dear;
For little, and almost for nought,
As many of my kind are bought
    As days are in the year.

Yet though but little use we boast,
And are procur'd at little cost,
    The labour is not light,
Nor few artificers it asks,
All skilful in their sev'ral tasks,
    To fashion us aright.

One fuses metal o'er the fire,
A second draws it into wire,
    The shears another plies.
Who clips in lengths the brazen thread
For him, who, chafing every shred,
    Gives all an equal size.

A fifth prepares, exact and round,
The knob, with which it must be crown'd;
    His follower makes it fast,
And with his mallet and his file
To shape the point, employs awhile
    The seventh and the last.

Now therefore, Œdipus! declare
What creature, wonderful and rare,
    A process, that obtains
Its purpose with so much ado,
At last produces! – Tell me true,
    And take me for your pains!

BOY'S NEWSPAPER, The (1880–82)

First published on 15 September 1880, this paper, which contained a number of riddles contributed by readers, was incorporated with *Youth* from 26 July 1882. The first example was composed by 'A. W. Harris, aged 13'.

286   I'm used to compose every play,
        No monarch without me can reign,
    In palace acknowledged my sway,
        Yet to live in a cottage I deign.

    No scholar, whatever his rank,
        Can dispense with my valuable aid,
    Without me there's never a bank
        Its interest duly hath paid.

    Although I'm no lover of sport,
        In racing I'm well to the fore,
    You will find me the leader in aught,
        That's connected with lawyers and law.

    And now to conclude, I must say
        A painting is only a blot;
    A poor worthless thing of to-day,
        If the painter's companion I'm not.

287   Oh what a blessing to the human race!
        Shorn of its pow'r what would mankind be?
    Art and aesthetics would be out of place,
        An o'er the dado none would disagree.

    Pupils have I to serve me true and well,
        A lash to scourge them if they disobey;
    And 'cheek' below my surface when I swell,
        As a memento of a glorious fray.

    How useful to the housewife who would mend,
        By strict economy her ways and means,
    'Tis where bucolic farmers oft attend,
        To sell East Anglian horses, peas, and beans.

288   I am a very simple word, and composed of letters four;
    But when carefully refined they always make me more;
    My appearance oft is smooth, and sometimes very soft;
    Schoolboys often feel me when fighting they are caught;
    I am often with you when you take a walk,
    And sometimes by the seaside where thither you resort.
    You'll see me in the cottage for seats I'm often used;
    I am a juicy sort of wood and very often bruised;
    And once for all I am not an Englishman,
    But come from the mighty shores of Hindostan.

289   In the clouds it is found
        May be seen in the ground;
        'Tis the first sound we hear
        From our baby-boy dear,
        'Tis the last word that's spoken
        Ere the thread of life's broken.

        'Twill be seen if we go
        To the regions below.
        'Twill be found in the throne,
        In the Court and the crown
        Of her whose renown
        Is o'er the world known.

        It's seen in all books,
        In all thoughts, words, and looks.
        We have it in poverty,
        And in prosperity;
        'Tis in every relation,
        And found in temptation.

        Now search this through well,
        All your fears 'twill dispel;
        But if you regard *it*,
        It goes from your view.

290   Upon my *first* in sports engage
            Full many a youth and maid,
        Whilst oft in sheltered woodland glade
            Its depths the beasts invade.

        Go get a glass, and look therein,
            Now, what do you espy?
        My *second*, when *you* speak of it,
            Can you this fact deny?

        Red, rosy lips,
            A heart of stone,
        To taste most sweet
            My *third* you'll own.

        Central station of the French
            My *whole* was at a time,
        When they had a hold upon
            India's fruitful clime.

BOY'S OWN BOOK, The (1861)
Children's compendium published by Lockwood & Co., including
puzzle section called 'The Riddler'.

291   Round is my shape, as broad I am as long,
        Firm is my frame-work and my nerves are strong;
        With double breast, and buttons round my waist,
        With hoops, and loops, and stays and braces graced;
        The colours, titles, and the arms I bear,
        Blazon my fame, and speak my character.

Ten thousand vassals at my levee stand,
Come when I call, and move at my command.
By me inspired, men keep or break the peace;
I fire their rage, or make their fury cease.
Myself obnoxious to a tyrant's will,
Who wreaks unpitying vengeance on me still;
Racking my limbs, he turns me o'er and o'er,
He lugs my ears, and thumps me till I roar.

292　In every hedge my second is,
　　　As well as every tree;
　　And when poor school-boys act amiss,
　　　It often is their fee.
　　My first, likewise, is always *wicked*,
　　　Yet ne'er committed sin:
　　My total for my first is fitted,
　　　Compos'd of brass or tin.

293　My first is part of a day,
　　　My second at feasts overflows,
　　In cottage my whole is oft seen,
　　　To measure old time as he goes.

294　A cat does my first, and men drink at my second,
　　My whole is the drift of an argument reckon'd.

295　My first gave us early support,
　　　My next is a virtuous lass;
　　To the fields if at eve you resort,
　　　My whole you will probably pass.

296　Though I'm nothing that breathes yet I'm dreaded by all
　　And strange to declare owe my rise to a fall.
　　'Mid the poor and the rich, e'en 'mid princes intrude;
　　At their banquettings, too, I have often been rude,
　　But say of intrusion who justly complains?
　　The feasting enjoyed I but seize the remains;
　　The course being finished, my glass gone about,
　　By orders I hand all the company out:
　　This duty completed here ends my employ;
　　And I leave rich and poor their deserts to enjoy.

297　My first is to ramble; my next to retreat
　　My whole oft enrages in summer's fierce heat.

298　A riddle of riddles, it dances and skips,
　　It is read in the eyes, though it cheats on the lips;
　　If it meet with its match it is easily caught;
　　But when money will buy it, it's not worth a groat.

299　Form'd half beneath and half above the earth,
　　We, sisters, owe to art a second birth;
　　The smith's and carpenter's adopted daughters,
　　Made on the earth to travel o'er the waters.
　　Swifter we move, as tighter we are bound,
　　Yet neither touch the water, air, nor ground.

We serve the poor for use, the rich for whim,
Sink when it rains, and when it freezes, swim.

300   Sharp is my form, my nature sharper found,
When I am forced to give the fatal wound,
Steeped in black venom, then, I strike the heart,
And keenest pains with slightest touch impart.
Yet I am used to give the wretched rest,
And of its burden ease the woe-fraught breast.
My birth is various, but in every land
I still can bear the ensign of command.
Silent – I speak; my voice in every clime
Is heard, and shall be to remotest time;
Honour and praise of right to me belong;
'Tis I immortalise the poet's song.
'Tis I that can transmit the patriot's name,
Sacred to ages, on the lists of fame;
Yet short my date of life, however high,
Soon I'm worn out, and then neglected die.

BOY'S OWN VOLUME, The (1865)

One of many publications by S. O. Beeton (1831–77), founder of *Boy's Own Magazine* and *Beeton's Boys Annual* (q.v.), and husband of the household management writer, Mrs Beeton. As well as 'fact, fiction and adventure' could be found a number of puzzles, riddles, etc.

301   'Tis an April dawn, and the air is balm,
The sea like a mirror is bright and calm,
And reflects the clouds as they come and go
Over the Gulf of Mexico.
And down 'neath the water clear as glass,
The bright-hued fishes dart and pass,
And the fairy forests of seaweed grow,
And wave in the far-off depths below,
Where the turtles feed, and the strange things dwell,
Old Ocean hides in his crystal cell.
And now a canoe shoots from the shore,
Till it reaches two hundred yards or more.
A party of fishers, intent on spoil,
Make themselves ready to ply their toil.
Nor turtle, nor fish, nor weed seek they,
But to wrest from old Ocean a richer prey.
For each is my *whole*, and they seek my *first* –
A dangerous trade; of their foes the worst
Is that pest of the seas, whose fin will mark
His terrible presence – 'A shark! a shark!'
Now my *second* rises, and bending low,
Gazes intent on the depths below;
A quiet plunge – a ripple – no more,
And the sea is unruffled as before.
With his iron spud, and his net for spoil,
My *second* pursues his dangerous toil,
And gathers the oysters in whose shells

My beautiful *first* enshrouded dwells.
Then up to the surface of the sea
Rises my *second* joyfully,
Happy indeed if his net contain
A plentiful harvest from the main,
Of rough old shells, in whose wrinkled case
The best of my *first* oft find a place.
Happy, if safe in life and limb,
The shark has made no meal of him.
Oh, lady fair! when you gaily deck
With my shining *first* your arms and neck,
Like frozen dewdrops pure and fair,
Meet for a princess's raven hair,
Do you cast a thought how my *second* doth go
Down in the Gulf of Mexico,
Daring the perils of shark and deep,
To steal your gems from their ocean sleep?

302   When Spring comes dancing o'er the land,
      And clothing hill and lea,
My *second*'s seen in every hedge,
      My *first* on many a tree.
My *second*, with its varied hues,
      Its buds and blossoms bright,
Doth gladden every nook of eart[h],
      The peasant child's delight.

My *first*, how welcome is his note
      The harbinger of spring!
The little dark brown bird herself
      Can scarce more sweetly sing;
And through the early budding days
      He blithely tells his tale,
And only when the summer comes
      His merry note doth fail.

My *second*, added to my *first*,
      Was aptly styled my *whole*,
Whereby two pleasant memories
      In one name we enrol,
By linking Spring's sweet buds and blooms,
      Her traces fresh and new,
With her blithe herald's name as well
      Her merriest songster, too!

303   There's a sweet little dell
      Clad in tenderest green,
Where a soft rippling brook
      Flows green rushes between.
'Tis the haunt of my *first*,
      And the home of my *whole*,
While the sound of my *second*
      Above it doth roll.

The tall ferns bend over
　My *first*'s timid head,
As he nestles secure in
　His soft mossy bed.
My *second* at intervals
　Falls on the ear,
And blends with the sound
　Of the brook singing clear;

While my *whole* dwells there ever,
　And lifts her slight form
Secure from the ravage
　Of wind or of storm.
She's the nymph of the spot,
　And the brook thinks so too,
As it mirrors her form,
　With its cup of pale blue!

304　My *first* is a masculine name,
　　My *second*'s the colour of war,
My *third* is ambitious of fame,
　　And hope shineth therein as a star.

(To guide us o'er life's troubled sea,
　To cheer an existence like this;
May it ne'er set for thee or for me,
　But guide us to regions of bliss!)

Thus formed, a gentle, winged creature, I ween,
May, warbling, midst gardens and orchards be seen;
And oft, when chill frost binds the bosom of earth,
He claims our protection, and flies to our hearth.

BRITISH FOLK RIDDLES
Folk riddles taken from a variety of sources including Robert Chambers *Popular Rhymes of Scotland* (1870), J. O. Halliwell-Phillips *Popular Rhymes and Nursery Tales* (1849), and *Nursery Rhymes of England* (1886).

305　There was a man o' Adam's race,
　　He had a certain dwalling-place;
　　It was neither in heeven, earth, nor hell –
　　Tell me where this man did dwell!

306　Hair without, and hair within,
　　A' hair, and nae skin.

307　A beautiful lady in a garden was laid,
　　Her beauty was fair as the sun,
　　In one hour of her life she became a man's wife,
　　And she died before she was born.

308　The first letter of our fore-fadyr,
　　A worker of wax,
　　An I and an N;
　　The colour of an ass:
　　And what have you then?

110

309 In the middle of the garden was a river,
     In the middle of the river was a boat,
     In the middle of the boat was a lady,

     Who wore a red petticoat.
     Eve ye dinna ken her name
     It's yer ain self to blame,
     'Cause I telt ye in the middle of the riddle.

310 I am become of flesh and blood,
         As other creatures be;
     Yet there's neither flesh nor blood
         Doth remain in me.
     I make kings that they fall out,
         I make them agree;
     And yet there's neither flesh nor blood
         Doth remain in me.

311 Arthur Bower has broken his band;
     He comes roaring up the land;
     The King of Scots, with all his power,
     Cannot turn Arthur of the Bower.

312 Formed long ago, yet made today,
     Employed while others sleep;
     What few would like to give away,
     Nor any wish to keep.

313 As black as ink and isn't ink
     As white as milk and isn't milk
     As soft as silk and isn't silk
     And hops about like a filly-foal.

314 Long legs, crooked thighs
     Little head and no eyes.

315 Hitty Pitty within the wall
     Hitty Pitty without the wall
     If you touch Hitty Pitty
     Hitty Pitty will bite you.

316 As I went over Lincoln Bridge,
     I met Mister Rusticap;
     Pins and needles on his back,
     A-going to Thorny Fair.

317 It's as round's the moon,
     An' as clear's crystal;
     An ye dinna tell ma riddle,
     I'll shoot ye wi' ma pistol!

318 As I was going over London Bridge, I saw something in the
     hedge. It had four fingers and one thumb, and was neither fish,
     flesh, fowl nor bone.

319   I have a cock on yonder hill,
I keep him for a wonder,
And every time the cock do crow,
It lightens, hails and thunders.

320   Goes to the door and doesn't knock,
Goes to the window and doesn't rap,
Goes to the fire and doesn't warm,
Goes upstairs and does no harm.

321   A cow calved it; it grew in the woods; and a smith made it.

322   We have a horse
Without any head;
He is never alive,
And never will be dead.

323   My back and belly is wood,
And my ribs is lined with leather.
I've a hole in my nose and one in my breast,
And I'm oftenest used in cold weather.

324   There was a prophet on this earth,
His age no man could tell;
He was at his greatest height
Before e'er Adam fell.
His wives are very numerous,
Yet he maintaineth none;
And at the day of reckoning
He bids them all begone.
He wears his boots when he should sleep;
His spurs are ever new;
There's no a shoemaker on a' the earth
Can fit him for a shoe.

325   Fatherless and motherless,
Born without a skin,
Spoke when it came into the world
And never spoke again.

326   Brass cap and wooden head,
Spits fire and spews lead.

327   What shoemaker makes shoes without leather,
With all four elements put together?
Fire and water, earth and air;
Every customer has two pair.

328   As I went over Padstow Bridge
Upon a cloudy day,
I met a fellow, clothed in yellow,
I took him up and sucked his blood,
And threw his skin away.

329   The robbers came to our house,
When we were all in.
The house lap out at the windows,
And we were all taken.

112

330   Behind the bush, behind the thorn,
I heard a stout man blow his horn,
He was booted and spurred, and stood with pride,
With golden feathers at his side;
His beard was flesh, and his mouth was horn,
I am sure such a man never could have been born.

331   As I went over London Bridge,
I saw a little house: I looked in
Through the window, and there was
A red man making a black man sing.

332   Yonder stands a tree of honour,
Twelve limbs grow upon her;
Every limb a different name,
It would take a wise man to tell you the same.

333   Lives in winter,
Dies in summer,
And grows with its root upwards.

334   The land was white,
The seed was black.
It'll take a good scholar
To riddle me that.

335   In marble walls as white as milk,
Lined with a skin as soft as silk;
Within a fountain crystal clear,
A golden apple doth appear.
No doors there are to this stronghold
Yet thieves break in and steal the gold.

336   As I was going to Worcester, I met a man from Gloucester. I
asked him where he was going, and he told me to Gloucester to
buy something that had neither top nor bottom but which could
hold flesh, blood, and bones.

337   Hoddy-doddy,
With a round black body!
Three feet and a wooden hat;
What's that?

338   Riddle me, riddle me, what is that
Over the head and under the hat?

339   What God never sees,
What the king seldom sees;
What we see every day;
Read my riddle – I pray.

340   I've seen you where you never was,
    And where you ne'er will be;
And yet you in that very same place
    May still be seen by me.

341   Over the water,
And under the water,
And always with its head down!

342   I saw a fight the other day;
A damsel did begin the fray.
She with her daily friend did meet;
Then standing in the open street,
She gave such hard and sturdy blows,
He bled ten gallons at the nose;
Yet neither seem[ed] to faint nor fall,
Nor gave her any abuse at all.

343   There is a bird of great renown,
Useful in city and in town;
None work like unto him can do;
He's yellow, black, red, and green.
A very pretty bird I mean;
Yet he's both fierce and fell:
I count him wise that can this tell.

BROUGH, Robert B. (1828–60)

British dramatist and journalist. Wrote considerable amount of verse and humorous essays for weekly magazines as well as popular burlesques with his brother William.

344   Cut off my head, and you'll quickly see
Something disliked by you and by me;
Cut off my tail, and then it is clear
The past of a verb will quickly appear;
Cut off my head and my tail also,
You'll have a conjunction then, I trow.
Whole, I'm an insect, not over clean,
Dreaded at picnics in meadows green.
To critics, to publishers, intimate friends,
My name a most delicate piquancy lends,
When they smile in their guile, and hiss as they sing,
And hide under flatteries a venomous sting.

BUONARROTI, Michelangelo the Younger (1568–1646)

Grand-nephew of his more famous namesake. Ten riddles occur in *Fiera* and 71 in *Indovinelli*.

345   *Io porto sempre una scala addosso,*
     Ma senza adoperarla, in alto ascendo;
     E senza piedi ogni erto cammin prendo
     (Gran cosa!), e ho le polpe dentro all'osso.

(I always carry a spiral staircase with me, but I never use it myself to climb up to the heights; yet without feet I travel the steepest roads (amazing fact!), and have flesh inside my bones.)

BYRON, George Gordon, 6th Baron (1788–1824)
English poet. Complete text of riddle ascribed to him.

346   I am not in youth, nor in manhood, nor age,
        But in infancy ever am known;
        I'm a stranger alike to the fool and the sage,
        And though I'm distinguished in history's page,
        I always am greatest alone.

        I am not in the earth, nor the sun, nor the moon –
        You may search all the sky – I'm not there;
        In the morning and evening – though not in the noon –
        You may plainly perceive me, for like a balloon,
        I am midway suspended in air.

        I am always in riches, and yet I am told
        Wealth ne'er did my presence desire;
        I dwell with the miser, but not with his gold,
        And sometimes I stand in his chimney so cold,
        Though I serve as a part of the fire.

        I often am met in political life –
        In my absence no kingdom can be –
        And they say there can neither be friendship nor strife,
        No one can live single, no one take a wife,
        Without interfering with me.

        My brethren are many, and of my whole race
        Not one is more slender and tall;
        And though not the eldest, I hold the first place
        And even in dishonour, despair and disgrace,
        I boldly appear 'mong them all.

        Though disease may possess me, and sickness and pain,
        I am never in sorrow nor gloom;
        Though in wit and in wisdom I equally reign,
        I'm the heart of all sin, and have long lived in vain,
        And I ne'er shall be found in the tomb!

CALVERLEY, Charles Stuart (1831–84)
Barrister and poet who wrote light verse under the initials 'C.S.C.'
Riddles taken from *Verses and Translations* (1862)

347   Evening threw soberer hue
            Over the blue sky, and the few
            Poplars that grew just in the view
        Of the hall of Sir Hugo de Wynkle:
            'Answer me true,' pleaded Sir Hugh,
            (Striving to woo no matter who,)
            'What shall I do, Lady, for you?
        'Twill be done, ere your eye may twinkle.
        Shall I borrow the wand of a Moorish enchanter,
        And bid a decanter contain the Levant, or
        The brass from the face of a Mormonite ranter?
        Shall I go for the mule of the Spanish Infantar –

(That *r*, for the sake of the line, we must grant her) –
And race with the foul fiend, and beat in a canter,
Like that first of equestrians Tam O'Shanter?
I talk not mere banter – say not that I can't, or
By this my *first* – (a Virginian Planter
Sold it me to kill rats) – I will die instanter.'
The lady bended her ivory neck, and
Whispered mournfully, 'Go for – my *second*.'
She said, and the red from Sir Hugh's cheek fled,
And 'Nay,' did he say as he stalked away,
      The fiercest of injured men:
'Twice have I humbled my haughty soul,
And on bended knee I have pressed my *whole* –
      But I never will press it again.'

CANNING, George (1770–1827)

Tory statesman (Prime Minister 1827) and author; also penned a number of riddles.

348   Though weak to a proverb my *first* has been reckoned,
The game is so constantly made of my *second*;
Yet, to hosts without number, my *whole* bade defiance,
And the world stood amazed at the beauteous alliance.

349   A noun there is of plural number,
Foe to peace and tranquil slumber;
Now any other noun you take,
By adding *s* you plural make,
But if you add an *s* to this
Strange is the metamorphosis:
Plural is plural now no more,
And sweet what bitter was before.

CARROLL, Lewis (1832–98)

Pseudonym of Charles Lutwidge Dodgson, English writer and mathematician. Riddles contained in *Through the Looking Glass* (1872) and miscellaneous journals, etc.

350   'First the fish must be caught.'
That is easy: a baby, I think, could have caught it.
   'Next, the fish must be bought.'
That is easy: a penny, I think, would have bought it.

   'Now cook me the fish!'
That is easy, and will not take more than a minute.
   'Let it lie in a dish!'
That is easy, because it is already in it.

   'Bring it here! Let me sup!'
It is easy to set such a dish on the table.
   'Take the dish-cover up!'
Ah, *that* is so hard that I fear I'm unable!

For it holds it like glue –
Holds the lid to the dish, while it lies in the middle:
    Which is easiest to do,
Un-dish-cover the fish, or dishcover the riddle?

351

I. My First

The air is bright with hues of light,
    And rich with laughter and with singing:
Young hearts beat high in ecstasy,
    And banners wave, and bells are ringing:
But silence falls with falling day,
And there's an end to mirth and play.
        Ah, well-a-day!

II. My Second

Rest your old bones, ye ancient crones!
    The kettle sings, the firelight dances:
Deep be it quaffed, the magic draught
    That fills the soul with golden fancies:
For youth and pleasance will not stay,
And ye are withered, worn, and gray.
        Ah, well-a-day!

III. My Whole

O fair cold face! O form of grace,
    For human passion madly yearning!
O weary air of dumb despair,
    From marble won, to marble turning!
'Leave us not thus!' we fondly pray.
'We cannot let thee pass away!'
        Ah, well-a-day!

352
They both make a roaring, a roaring all night:
They both are a fisherman-father's delight:
They are both, when in fury, a terrible sight!

The first nurses tenderly three little hulls,
To the lullaby-music of shrill-screaming gulls,
And laughs when they dimple his face with their skulls.

The second's a tidyish sort of a lad,
Who behaves pretty well to a man he calls 'Dad',
And earns the remark, 'Well, he isn't so bad!'

Of the two put together, oh, what shall I say?
Tis a time when 'to live' means the same as 'to play':
When the busiest person does nothing all day.

When the grave College Don, full of love inexpressi–
Ble, puts it all by, and is forced to confess he
Can think but of Agnes and Evie and Jessie.

353
A monument – men all agree –
Am I in all sincerity,
    Half cat, half hindrance made.
If head and tail removed should be,

117

Then most of all you strengthen me;
Replace my head, the stand you see
On which my tail is laid.

354 My First is singular at best
More plural is my Second:
My Third is far the pluralest –
So plural-plural, I protest,
It scarcely can be reckoned!

My First is followed by a bird,
My Second by believers
In magic art: my simple Third
Follows, too often, hopes absurd,
And plausible deceivers.

My First to get at wisdom tries –
A failure melancholy!
My Second men revere as wise:
My Third from heights of wisdom flies
To depths of frantic folly!

My First is ageing day by day;
My Second's age is ended:
My Third enjoys an age, they say,
That never seems to fade away,
Through centuries extended!

My Whole? I need a poet's pen
To paint her myriad phases.
The monarch, and the slave, of men –
A mountain-summit, and a den
Of dark and deadly mazes!

A flashing light – a fleeting shade –
Beginning, end, and middle:
Of all that human art hath made,
Or wit devised! Go, seek *her* aid,
If you would guess my riddle.

CASSELLS COMPLETE BOOK OF SPORTS AND PASTIMES (1888)

Contains many examples of riddles as well as arithmetical and alphabetical puzzles.

355 In other days, when hope was bright,
You spoke to me of love and light,
But now you tell another tale,
That life is brief and beauty frail;
Away, ye grieve, and ye rejoice,
In one unfelt, unfeeling voice.

356 Enough for one, too much for two, and nothing at all for three.

357 To half-a-dozen add six, and to the result add five hundred. The whole will represent a word signifying clear, lucid, bright, or glowing.

358   First in the path of Duty,
       And ranking first in Art,
       Foremost in Virtue and in Vice,
       Leading all in Immortality,
       And foremost in Devotion.
       Pore over these with studious care,
       A kingly name is hidden there.

359   Ride on, ride on, thou traveller bold,
           And cast thy looks on *first*;
       See how the tempest clouds do lower,
           That soon in storm shall burst.
       Ride on, ride on, thy *second* leads
           Across the lonely heath,
       Where gibbets tell of darksome deeds,
           And culprits swing beneath.
       Ride on, ride on, my *third* thou art
           An honest one and true;
       Beware! a *third* is lurking near,
           Who would his hands imbrue.
       Ride on, ride on, ride for thy life,
           Spur on thy faithful steed,
       For now my *whole* thy second bars,
           Nerved for his lawless deed.

360   Safe on my fair one's arm my *first* may rest,
       And raise no tumult in a lover's breast.
       My *second* does the want of legs supply,
       To those that neither creep, nor walk, nor fly.
       My *whole*'s a rival to the fairest toast,
       And when it's most admired, it suffers most.

361   Write one thousand down, quite plain,
       Then half of two, then add again
       Fifty and one's final letter;
       You can then do nothing better
       Than, after every evening meal,
       Walk the distance I reveal.

362   My *first* is near the dear bright sea,
           The green waves oft it lave;
       It glitters in the sunshine,
           Lies in the deep dark cave.
       My *second* is quite endless,
           Like the love of which it tells,
       A bright idealisation
           Of Love's eternal spells.
       My *third* alas! to say the truth,
           Suggests a vacant sty.
       My *whole*, a royal residence;
           Now, prithee, tell me why.

363   A thousand and fifty and one transpose,
       'Twill produce a fruit in Spain that grows.

CERVANTES SAAVEDRA, Miguel de (1547–1616)

Spanish novelist and dramatist. Riddles contained in *La Galatea* (1585).

364   *¿Cuál es aquel poderoso*
que desde oriente a occidente
es conocido y famoso?
A veces, fuerte y valiente;
otras, flaco y temeroso;
quita y pone la salud,
muestra y cubre la virtud
en muchos más de una vez,
en más fuerte en la vejez
que en la alegre joventud.

Múdase en quien no se muda
por estraña preeminencia,
hace temblar al que suda,
y a la más rara elocuencia
suele tornar torpe y muda;
con diferentes medidas,
anchas, cortas y estendidas,
mide su ser y su nombre,
y suele tomar renombre
de mil tierras conocidas.

Sin armas vence al armado,
y es forzoso que le venza,
y aquel que más le ha tratado,
mostrando tener vergüenza,
es el más desvergonzado.
Y es cosa de maravilla
que en el campo y en la villa,
a capitán de tal prueba
cualquier hombre se le atreva,
aunque pierda en la rencilla.

(What is that powerful thing
Which, from the orient to the drooping west
Is known and is renowned?
Now strong and valiant,
Now timorous and weak,
Taking and giving health,
Virtue both shows and conceals
In more than a single time.
Stronger is in age,
And in the cheerful growth,
Changeth it doth in that which changeth not.
By some unusual pre-eminence
It makes him tremble who perspires,
And for the rarest eloquence
Can it to baseness and to silence turn.
With divers means,
It measures its being and its appellation,
Is wont to seize renown,
Such as is known in lands innumerable.

Armless itself, it yet subdues the armed,
And to be victorious is compelled,
Seeming directly vengeance to pursue
The most disgraced is,
A thing of wonder is it,
Which in field and city,
At the head of proof,
That any man may boldness feel,
Yet doth in the scuffle lose.)

365   ¿Quién es la que es toda ojos
de la cabeza a los pies,
y a veces, sin su interés,
causa amorosos enojos?

    También suele aplacar riñas,
y no le va ni le viene,
y aunque tantos ojos tiene,
se descubren pocas niñas.

    Tiene nombre de un dolor
que se tiene por mortal,
hace bien y hace mal,
enciende y tiempla el amor.

(Who is that which all eyes is,
From the crown to the feet.
Occasionally his own interest without,
Is cause of amorous annoyances?
Accustomed is he quarrels to appease,
Yet neither goes nor comes,
And though possessing eyes so many,
Few children doth discover,
Of grief bearing the name,
Which is accounted mortal,
Both good and harm he doth,
Love moderates and inflames.)

366   Es muy escura y es clara;
tiene mil contrariedades;
encúbrenos las verdades,
y al cabo nos las declara.

    Nace a veces de donaire,
otras, de altas fantasías,
y suele engendrar porfías
aunque trate cosas de aire.

    Sabe su nombre cualquiera,
hasta los niños pequeños;
son muchas, y tiene dueños
de diferente manera.

    No hay vieja que no se abrace
con una destas señoras;
son de gusto algunas horas:
cuál cansa, cuál satisface.

    Sabios hay que se desvelan
por sacarles los sentidos,

y algunos quedan corridos
cuanto más sobre ello velan.
    Cuál es necia, cuál curiosa,
cuál fácil, cuál intricada,
pero sea o no sea nada,
decidme qué es cosa y cosa.

(Dark 'tis, yet very clear,
Containing infinite variety,
Encumbering us with truths,
Which are at length declared.
'Tis sometimes of a jest produced,
At others of high fancy,
And it is wont defiance to create,
Of airy matters treating.

Any man its name may know,
Even to little children,
Many there are, and masters have
In different ways.
There is no old woman it embraces not,
With of these ladies, one
At times in good odour,
This tires, that satisfies.

Wise ones there be who overwatch
Sensations to extract.
Some run wild
The more they watch o'er it.
Such is foolish, and such curious,
Such easy, such complex,
Yet, be it something, be it nought,
Reveal to me what the said thing may be?)

367   *¿Quién es el que, a su pesar,*
mete sus pies por los ojos,
y sin causarles enojos,
les hace luego cantar?
    El sacarlos es de gusto,
aunque, a veces, quien los saca,
no sólo su mal no aplaca,
mas cobra mayor disgusto.

(What is that which to its displeasure
Measures its feet by its eyes,
Without discomfort causing,
Making them quickly sing?
It is pleasant to extract them,
Though ofttimes he who them fairly extracts,
Not only does not his sure ill assuage,
But more disgust conceals.)

Muerde el fuego, y el bocado
es daño y bien del mordido;
no pierde sangre el herido,
aunque se ve acuchillado;
  mas si es profunda la herida,
y de mano que no acierte,
causa al herido la muerte,
y en tal muerte está su vida.

(Fire bites, and the mouthful
Is the damage, and the profit of the masticator,
The wounded wight loses no blood,
Though he should be well slashed.
But if the wound is deep,
Its point the hand not hitting,
Death to the stricken party doth ensue,
And in that death stands life.)

CHARADES, ENIGMAS, AND RIDDLES (1859)

Various riddles collected by 'A. Cantab.' and published by J. Hall &
Son, Cambridge.

369   Ye riddling Bards, explore my name
And to the Ladies shew it;
For they by me increase their fame
And therefore ought to know it.
My usual make is nearly square,
Quite different are my prices;
And I am always near the Fair
Soon as the charmer rises.
The foppish beau with empty head
Must needs have my advice
To tie his cravat, brush his hair
And make his toilet nice,
In park and playhouse I attend,
Much wanted, to be sure;
But when I Celia thus befriend
I'm drest in miniature.
Me the old maid who wants a spouse
Oft wears with great regard;
I'm found in every peasant's house,
And broken oft, though hard.

370   From the third Harry's reign, I my pedigree trace,
Though some will contend that more ancient's my race;
But in those early days my importance was small,
I ne'er came by choice, but obeyed other's call:
Now, so willing am I, no entreaties I need,
But tremble with fear lest I should not succeed:
I'm a mere human creature like you or another,
But to make me requires no aid from a mother:
I was born amid tumult, and riot, and noise,
With a numerous family, all of us boys;
We are none of us dumb, some of language profuse,

123

But two words are as much as most of us use:
One little hint further to give I think fit, –
We all of us stand before we can sit.

371
Our high rank and station by all must be known,
By birth we are twins, as can clearly be shown;
But though we're so nearly allied to each other
Yet sometimes the one will forsake his dear brother;
One part of our story you'll say is absurd,
We oftentimes speak yet ne'er utter a word;
We're full of expression, though silence we keep,
We laugh with the gay, with the wretched we weep;
We're tell-tales by nature, and sometimes reveal
A secret that prudence would bid us conceal;
But to give us our due, the delight we supply
No station can purchase, no money can buy.

372
Though I am dumb, I oft impart
The secret wishes of the heart;
I oft deceive – oft make amends,
Foes I create, and yet make friends:
For me the Lawyer quits his fee
For me the statesman bends his knee;
For me ye all have made a rout –
Me ye shall have who find me out.

373
A monosyllable am I, fatal to mortals here below,
First minister of grisly Death, I fell down thousands at a blow:
Take off two letters and you'll find, another syllable I gain;
Though not so fatal to mankind, I rack the wretch with varying
        pain:
The Hero like a coward shakes whene'er he feels my influence dire,
And as I change my fitful shape, I burn him with consuming
        fire.

374
Two patient creatures and a preposition,
Produce a monster worthy of perdition.

375
O'er all the world my Empire does extend
And while that lasts my reign shall never end,
By all I'm loved, and almost all deceive;
Yet when I promise next they all believe;
To Heaven I lead, but must not enter there,
Elsewhere I cannot be – Earth is my sphere:
If yet in vain you study for my name,
Search your own heart, for there I surely am.

376
If you my letters place aright
They'll note the present hour;
Reversed, they shew the fate of Troy
When Greece arose in power.
Reader, transpose them once again,
They'll quickly bring to view
What, when you're ill or when you're wrong
It would be right to do.

377   Within a secret cavern I'm confined,
       Yet range about as freely as the wind;
       Round the vast globe with winged step I roam,
       And yet I never leave my native home;
       O'er all the glowing sky sublime I stray,
       Explore the azure plains, the Milky Way,
       Survey each radiant orb, range the pale moon
       And rove from star to star, from sun to sun;
       With daring step the heavenly road I climb,
       And still on Earth ne'er pass the bounds of Time;
       The fetters of the world with scorn disown
       And make its treasures and its powers my own.
       Unhurt on Etna's burning top I stand,
       Yet cool as when by gentle zephyrs fanned;
       Warm, when on mountains of eternal snow,
       Unfrozen, through the Polar ice I go;
       Such is my power that I am always free,
       No chains can rob me of my liberty.

378   What object do the vulgar often see,
       Converse and deal with most familiarly;
       While Emperors and Princes seldom meet it,
       And when they do, with state and pomp they treat it.
       Some, of a haughty self conceited throng
       Though oft they meet it, do the fact disown;
       But falsely these; – yet Solomon 'tis true
       With all his sapience, this thing never knew;
       And what the paradox does more advance,
       It was his wisdom caused his ignorance.
       If then, this wondrous secret you would know,
       Ask Death, the leveller of all below.

379   With Monks and with hermits I chiefly reside,
       From courts and from camps keep at distance;
       The ladies who ne'er could my presence abide
       To banish me lend their assistance:
       I seldom can flatter but oft shew respect
       To the Patriot, the Preacher, the Peer;
       But sometimes, alas, a sad mark of neglect
       Or proof of contempt I appear.
       I once, as the chief of our Poets records
       Was pleased with the nightingale's song,
       But such is my taste, I leave ladies and lords
       To wander with thieves the night long.
       By the couch of the sick I am frequently found,
       And ever attend on the dead:
       With recent affliction I sit on the ground,
       But when call'd for am instantly fled.

380   My first may pass for horse or ass,
          If they are not too old,
       And if you can a measure scan
          My next you will unfold.

These parts when found will soon expound
　　My whole, you'll frankly own;
For on the plain scarce lives a swain
　　To whom it is unknown.

381　Kings, Queens, and Peers my first adorn,
　　Without their presence 'tis no more;
And Commerce by my next is borne
　　From north to south, from shore to shore:
My whole in hope is ever gay
　　When Love and Honour join their flame,
Yet mutual vows invoke the day
　　That sees me lose my once loved name.

382　My first in Summer all are made
　　By Sol's meridian heat;
My next the indolent most need,
　　'Tis worn upon the feet.

My whole, a rash misguided man
　　Who feared nor good nor bad;
A Knight in Hal's usurped reign
　　Who mighty valour had.

383　More numerous subjects has my first
　　Than any mortal king can boast,
And yet for more he's still athirst
　　Till all the world compose his host.

My second, made with wondrous skill
　　To men and boys importance gives,
And when the night is dark and still
　　The fearful Town from dread relieves.

When fear with Superstition's joined
　　My fancied whole my first foretels,
And thus th' enfeebled sick man's mind
　　To dread it constantly impels.

384　My first some do with smiling hope,
　　And some with fierce despair;
My second lies in vols of Pope,
　　The Baron's prize and care;
My whole must ever blissful prove
To those who wisely fix their love.

385　My first in Winter loads the burthen'd plain,
　　My next, of fluid is a portion small;
My whole, when Spring resumes her gentle reign
　　Smiles on the mead, and Hope restores to all.

386　My first to Chloe's voice attention lends;
To find my next, the boy his leisure spends;
　　My whole a merchant most intent on gain
　　Still gives, in hopes his bargain to maintain.

126

387   My first for ages out of mind
All men have always worn behind,
And yet 'tis found in every land
They carry it upon the hand:
My next within a cell matured
Though never ill, is often cured.
My whole within its mystic lines,
Black men and white, alike confines.

388   My first matures the lovely Spring
And tempts the feathered choir to sing
    In many a varying note;
My next to carriages belong,
Or in neat order ranged along
    Support the ripening fruit.

Soon as my blooming first appears,
Both old and young forget their cares
    To dance around my whole;
While rustic mirth and honest glee
With the loud laugh of jollity
    Delight the peasant's soul.

389   Deprived of my first, e'en fifty were nought,
In my second the proof of affection is sought;
My third you will find in every sea,
And say what a soul without it would be?
My last, though 'tis first in woman's heart,
In hatred and horror takes principal part:
My whole I consider a rich repast
Though Papists will say that on him they fast.

390   My third in my first is most awful at sea,
Yet many outlive it, so therefore may we:
My first in my third is the charm of the wood
And type of whatever is noble and good;
Do you ask for my second? – I've mentioned it twice,
Nay, in these very lines you will meet with it thrice.

391   size
                    Antoinette
                   age

CHARADES OF EVERY VARIETY (1872)

By 'A. B. L. Riddel, R.S.' One of a series of puzzle pamphlets entitled 'Home Amusements for the Family Circle' published by Dean & Son, priced sixpence each. Other authors had equally improbable names, e.g. 'S. P. Hincks, the Younger', 'O. E. Dipus, Junior' and 'A. C. Rostick'. See also *Enigmas of Every Variety*.

392   My *first* in the kitchen solemnly stands,
    And warns me to my *second*,
And the neighbours oft declare I am
    As regular as my *whole*.

393   Sir Roland he was as brave a knight
       As ever the Red Cross wore;
    With his trusty sword he held his right,
       In the brave old days of yore.

His heart was bold, and his hand was strong,
    And he loved a lady fair;
He wooed her true and he wooed her long,
    And he hoped her hand to share.

For Lady Ella was fair to see,
    And blue and bright was her eye,
As the star that beams on the dark, dark sea,
    From the gemmed and quiet sky.

'Fair Ella, my own, my lady-love,'
    Sir Roland said with a tear;
'Let my sorrow thy soft compassion move,
    To my *first*, oh, lend an ear;

'For I pledge my troth, my *next* you are,
    That I am as loyal a knight,
As e'er lifted a lance in the Paynim war,
    Or bled in the gory fight.'

'Thy prayer is heard, and my heart is thine,'
    Fair Ella she said with a smile;
'And now in peace or war thou art mine,
    For well hast thou stood the trial.'

Sir Roland his eye was bright with my *whole*,
    And his heart leapt up for joy;
A warm impassioned kiss he stole,
    And his rapture knew no alloy.

And when she was his at her own sweet will,
    He loved her more and more;
And when he was old he loved her still,
    As he loved in days of yore.

394   My *first* garotters fear, and soldiers can't abide,
Though sleek it is, and fair to see, when by the fireside;
My *second* is an animal, though very much abused,
That, ever patient, struggles on, however ill he's used;
My *third* upon the battle-field from struggling foes is torn,
To deck our halls and rooms of state, it proudly home is borne;
My *whole* is what, I fondly hope, whate'er our fate may be,
May ne'er, throughout this stormy life, befall both you and me.

395   O'er a snow-white, trackless waste,
    Guided by a cunning hand,
    Swiftly glides my *first* to glad,
    Loved ones far from fatherland.

In my *second* may be traced,
    The reflector of the heart;
'Tis a pronoun though it forms
    Of a word the smallest part.

'Neath Arabia's cloudless sky,
You will often see my *third*;
Emblem of our bodies frail,
Teaching us our loins to gird.

When at mercy's door we knock,
Pleading that our sins may roll
Burden-like from off our back,
Then are we in truth my *whole*.

396   Like my *first*, at most hours of the day you may meet
In London's fine squares, or far-famed Regent Street;
But in either of these should my *second* appear,
Your cheek might be blanched, and expressive of fear;
Yet my *whole* is as harmless, as harmless can be,
You may eat it as salad, or drink it as tea.

397   Jem Jenkinson waited on Brown,
    To ask for the hand of his daughter;
He held a snug berth in the town,
    And felt pretty sure he had caught her.
But queer are the fortunes of love,
    And Jem's was one of the worst;

For Brown, in my *second*, most unlike a dove,
    Right speedily showed him my *first*.
Our hero, abashed and confounded,
    Lost over his feelings control,
And hurrying home deeply wounded,
    Spoke of it when there as my *whole*.

398   Feathered songsters blithely singing,
Hills and rocks with echoes ringing,
Zephyrs sighing in the trees,
Truly are my *first* all these.
Softly o'er my *second* stealing,
Comes a blissful, happy feeling,
As the thoughts are fixed above
All else, upon my *whole*, and love!

399   My *first* is a sportive but timorous thing,
Which bounds through the coverts with joy in its spring,
Darting off at the fall of a leaf,
My *second*'s oft heard in the day's busy round,
Striking full on the ear with its echoing sound,
And proclaiming now joy and now grief.
My *whole* may be seen in the meadows and glades,
Where it brightens the earth with its hue ere it fades.

400   A traveller, weary and sinking from thirst,
With joy threw him down at the brink of my *first*,
And a copious draught drank he.
My *second* is seen in the autumn's late day,
And foretells that its beauties will soon pass away.
My *whole* dashes on with a rush and a bound,
Appalling the ear with the might of its sound,
Like the roar of a troubled sea.

CHESTERFIELD, Philip Dormer Stanhope, 4th Earl of (1694–1773)
Lord Lieutenant of Ireland and friend of Pope, Gay, etc. Best known for his letters to his son and godson, in which the following occur.

401   *Quoique je forme un corps, je ne suis qu'une idée;*
        Plus ma beauté vieillit, plus elle est décidée;
        Il faut, pour me trouver, ignorer d'où je viens;
        Je tiens tout de lui, qui réduit tout à rien.

        (Although I form a body, I am only an idea. With age my beauty increases. To find me you must not know where I come from. I take after him who reduces everything to nothing.)

402   Scorn'd by the meek and humble mind,
            And often by the vain possess'd,
        Heard by the deaf, seen by the blind,
            I give the troubled spirit rest.

403   The noblest object in the works of art;
        The brightest scene that nature doth impart;
        The well-known signal in the time of peace;
        The point essential in a tenant's lease;
        The ploughman's comfort when he holds the plough;
        The soldier's duty and the lover's vow;
        A planet seen between the earth and sun;
        A prize which merit never yet has won;
        A wife's ambition, and a parson's dues;
        A miser's idol, and the badge of Jews:
        If now your happy genius can divine
        The correspondent word to every line,
        By the first letters will be plainly found
        An ancient city that is much renowned.

CHOICE COLLECTION OF RIDDLES, CHARADES, REBUSSES, A (1792)

404   In a garden was laid
        A most beautiful maid
        As ever was seen in the morn;
            She was made a wife
            The first day of her life,
        And died before she was born.

CHRISTOPHORUS of Mytilene (*fl.* 1050)
Byzantine poet and enigmatographer.

405   You seized me and yet I fled; you see me flee and cannot hold me tight; you press me in your hand but I escape and your fist is left empty.

CLARETUS, Dr (14th century)
Bohemian monk. Riddles appear in untitled MS.

406   *Ut gramen viride, non est gramen tamen inde;*
        Ceu sanguis rubeum, non est sanguis tamen ipsum;
        Est teres et tritum velut ovum.

130

(Like grass it is green, but it is not grass;
Like blood it is red, but it is not blood;
It is round and smooth like an egg.)

407 *Dulcifluum modicum, ossis quae tenet ollam.*

(It's small and sweet and comes in a bony pot.)

408 *Visceribus careat volitans.*

(What flies without flesh?)

409 *Intrans bos stabula sibi cornua destitit extra.*

(The ox is entering the stable, and has left his horns outside.)

410 *Dum moritur, generat semper.*

(What dies and always gives birth?)

411 *Possideo phialam, mihi more pirique rotundam
Et viscelosam medio, circumque pilosam;
Saepius acciderat, ex hac quod et unda fluebat.*

(A vessel have I,
That is round as a pear,
Moist in the middle,
Surrounded with hair;
And often it happens
That water flows there.)

412 *Das hoc, quod nec habes?*

(Who gives what he does not have?)

413 *Sunt sexaginta volucres cum quinque trecentae,
Atque duodeni griffones, tres quoque nidi;
Hi simulac unum generant ovumque per annum.*

(Three hundred and sixty-five birds, twelve griffins, and three
nests, together produce but a single egg.)

414 *Mundus agens audit.*

(What did the whole world hear?)

415 *Ab strepitu venit inque stubam sine porta.*

(What enters a room without any noise, without using the
door?)

416 *Abs radice manens in campo quoque crescens.*

(What grows in the field without roots?)

417 *Dat paries assum cum glande nucem.*

(Inside the wall, when it is cooked, you will find two kinds of
nut.)

418 *Ens mas rugosus dominis exstat amandus.*

(The thing I have is male and wrinkled, and the ladies love it.)

419   *Expellens et oves stabulum mulgebo per omnes.*

(If I drive out all the sheep, I can milk the fold.)

420   *Circum crinosum, medio pulchrum, sed ad anum*
Fert arulam tenuem.

(It is hairy round about, it is pretty in the middle, but at the bottom it wears a little thorn.)

421   *Unum tento specum, quo nat carnis mihi frustrum. Vivi precari mihi.*

(In cavern moist my flesh doth lie,
And with this wriggling piece pray I.)

422   *Est veniens laicus, coclear ferri tenet intus;*
Perforat hic matrem, sale condit, consuit utrem;
Postea fert pueros ex hac, teret ossa per omnes.
Et nutrit proprios pueros.

(A layman comes with an iron spoon, shoves it in and opens up his mother; he salts her, and sews up her skin; then he takes his mother's children, grinds all their bones, and feeds his own children.)

423   *Hic pendet rasum; si nunc subtus foret hirtum,*
Hirsutum cuperet rasum.

(Here hangs a shaven one; if you were to put a hairy one beneath, the hairy one would want the shaven one.)

CLEOBULUS (*fl. c.*600 BC)
Ancient Greek poet. Riddles cited in *Greek Anthology* and Diogenes Laertius's *Lives of Eminent Philosophers*. The second riddle is ascribed to his daughter, Cleobulina, by Aristotle.

424   There is one father and twelve children. Each of these has twice thirty children of different aspect, some of them we see to be white and the others black, and though immortal, they all perish.

425   I saw a man glue brass on another with fire.

COLLECTION OF BIRDS AND RIDDLES, A (n.d.)
By 'Miss Polly and Master Tommy'. Chapbook published by J. Kendrew of York containing poems on various birds interspersed with riddles and illustrated with woodcuts.

426   My back is bare,
My belly thin,
          My guts are all
Without my skin,
          I'm often scrap'd,
But never fill'd,
          As many have
Oft times beheld.

Four teeth I have,
But got no tongue,
    Yet when I speak,
Please old and young;
    My voice it is
A pleasing sound,
    Which makes them oft
To trip it round.

427   Tho' I both foul
And dirty am,
And black as pitch can be,
    There's many a lady
That will come
And by the hand take me.

428   How many hundreds for my sake have died!
    What frauds and villanies have not been tri'd?
And all the grandeur which my race adorns
Is like the Rose beset around with thorns.

429   When mortals are involv'd in ills,
    I sing with mournful voice;
If mirth their hearts with gladness fills,
    I celebrate their joys.
And as the lark with warbling throat,
    Ascends upon the wing;
So I lift up my cheerful note,
    And as I mount I sing.

COWPER, WILLIAM (1731–1800)

English poet. This riddle, written in July 1780, appeared in *The Gentleman's Magazine* for December 1806.

430   I am just two and two, I am warm, I am cold,
And the parent of numbers that cannot be told.
I am lawful, unlawful – a duty, a fault,

I am often sold dear, good for nothing when bought;
An extraordinary boon, and a matter of course,
And yielded with pleasure when taken by force.

Alike the delight of the poor and the rich.
Tho' the vulgar is apt to present me his breech.

CREATION RIDDLE, The (17th century?)

This riddle has appeared in many forms but the earliest record seems to be that of a correspondent in *Notes and Queries* who found it handwritten in notes to a copy of Patrick Symon's *History of the Church* (1634). This version, dated 30 September 1744 and described as an old riddle, is reproduced below.

431   Before creating Nature will'd
    That attoms into form should jar,
    The boundless space by me was fill'd,

On me was built ye first made star.
For me a Saint will break his word,
  By ye proud Atheist I am rever'd
At me the Coward draws his sword,
  And by the Hero I am fear'd.
Than Wisdom's sacred self I'm wiser,
  And yet by every blockhead known,
I'm freely given by ye Miser,
  Kept by ye Prodigal alone.
Scorn'd by ye meek and humble mind,
  But often by ye vain possest,
Heard by ye deaf, seen by ye blind,
  And to the troubled Conscience rest.
The King, God bless him, as 'tis said,
  Is seldom with me in a passion,
Tho' him I often can persuade
  To act against his inclination.
Deform'd as vice, as virtue fair,
  The Courtier's loss, the Patriot's gains,
The Poet's purse, the Coxcomb's care,
  Read, you'll have me for your pains.

CROCE, Giulio Cesare (1550–1609)

Italian blacksmith-poet. Riddles published in *Notte sollazzevole di cento enigmi* (1599) and *Seconde notte sollazzevole di cento enigmi* (1601).

432   *In verde selva nacqui, e a l'aria, al vento,*
       Come volle mia sorte, un tempo stetti;
       E del mio stato mi vivea contento,
       Nè mai mi lamentai in fatti, o in detti;
       Ma poi tagliato con pena, e tormento,
       A corpo vuoto fo diversi effetti,
       Che mentre per lo naso m'è soffiato
       Grido, e per gl'occhi fuor rimando il fiato.

(I was born in a green wood, and in the open air and in the
wind, it was my fate for me to stay for a time; and I was happy
to live in my state. Nor did I ever complain in word or in deed;
but then cut down with hurt and torment, with an empty body
I produce various effects, such that when my nose is blown into
I shout, and I send out my breath through my eyes.)

433   *Io sono al mondo tanto sventurato,*
       che quasi non vorrei esser nasciuto;
       poi che, misero me, son bastonato
       in vita, e in morte ogn'hor pesto e battuto;
       pur tanta contentezza hò in simil stato,
       ch'io fo tacer la cetra, & il liuto:
       e mentre ch'un mi batte, e mi martella,
       col ferro altri si foran le budella.

(I am so unfortunate in the world that I almost wish that I had
never been born; since, unhappy me, I am beaten in my life, and
in death kicked and hit every hour. Yet I am so content in such

a state, that I silence the zither and the lute. And whilst one is hitting and hammering me, others have their entrails punched with iron.)

434   *Sospesa in aria stò, nè tocco nulla,*
        E circondata son di lumi intorno,
        Hor di novo mi vesto, hora son brulla,
        E al caldo, al freddo stò la notte, e'l giorno,
        Ogn'un di calpestarmi si trastulla,
        Fino alle bestie mi fan danno, e scorno,
        E tai tesori ascondo nel mio seno,
        Che chi gli trova fò felice a pieno.

(I am suspended in the air, I touch nothing, and I am surrounded by lights. Now I dress myself afresh, and now I am naked, and I am in the heat and the cold, by night and by day. Everyone amuses himself by trampling upon me, even the animals abuse and scorn me, and yet I have such treasures hidden in my bosom that he who finds them I can make full of happiness.)

CURTIS, Sir William (1752–1829)

Banker, MP and Lord Mayor of London much ridiculed in his day by satirical poets such as Peter Pindar. A number of cockney conundrums playing on puns requiring dropped Hs ascribed to him.

435   My first's a little bird as 'ops,
        My second's needful in 'ay crops,
        My 'ole is good with mutton chops.

436   Why is a crane like a well-known shell-fish?

DAVIES, Sir John (1569–1626)

Solicitor-General for Ireland, poet and author of a number of acrostics. Also wrote riddles.

437   There was a man bespake a thing,
        Which when the owner home did bring,
        He that made it did refuse it:
        And he that brought it would not use it,
        And he that hath it doth not know
        Whether he hath it yea or no.

DELANY, Mrs Mary (1700–88)

Eminent member of 'Blue Stocking Circle' that also included Hannah More (q.v.). The wife of Swift's friend Patrick Delany.

438   What a good boy will do, when he chooses, at school,
        To remember his lessons and not play the fool;
        My *second* great travellers often have seen,
        Now pitch'd on the sands, and now spread on the green;
        Some transient view of the *whole* you secure,
        While honour, and riches, and health you procure;
        And 'tis Virtue alone that will make it endure.

439   My *first* is the terror of timid and young;
My *second* disguises the head and the tongue;

But when *join'd together*, the grave and the wise
Are gain'd by my charms and award me a prize.

DEMAUNDES JOYOUS, The (1511)

Anonymous translation and selection from the French *Demandes joyeuses en manière de quodlibets* (*c*.1500). Printed by Wynkyn de Worde.

440   Which is the broadest water and least jeopardy to pass over?

441   Why come dogs so often to the church?

442   Why doth a dog turn him thrice about ere he lieth him down?

443   What thing is it that hath horns at the arse?

444   What is it that freezeth never?

445   What thing is it, the less it is the more it is dread?

446   Wherefore is it that young children weep as soon as ever they be born?

447   What time in the year beareth the goose most feathers?

448   What was he that slew the fourth part of the world?

449   What thing is that which hath no end?

DES ACCORDS, Éstienne Tabourot (1549–90)

French lawyer and poet. A number of *rébus de Picardie* and literary rebuses appear in *Les Bigarrures du Seigneur des Accords* (1582).

450   *G a c o b i a l*

451   *ooooo eeee sont aaaaa pons*

452   *trop   vent   bien*
           tils   sont   pris

453   *hait   en   tient*
           le   pens   le coeur

454   *G a p pour mes aa*
              d tenter

455   *comme* 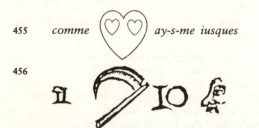 *ay-s-me iusques*

456

p
comme

457

458 *Pri-bonne-se pren-fait bon-dre*

DIALOGUE OF SALOMON AND SATURNUS, The (14th century)

459 Tell me, who was he that was never born, was then buried in his mother's womb, and after death was baptized?

460 Tell me, what is the heaviest thing on earth to bear?

461 Tell me, what is that which pleaseth one man and displeaseth another?

462 Tell me, what are the four things that never were and never will be full?

DRAWING ROOM SCRAP SHEET, The (1831–2)
Series of twenty-six coloured sheets with ornamental borders containing two pages of poetry, puzzles, etc., sold in selected bookshops from 5 November 1831.

463   If you cure me of my first
I will give you my second,
And my *tout* you shall have in the evening.

464   My first is chiefly made of stone,
     My second grows on trees,
My *tout* is sweet when fully grown –
     Now guess it if you please.

465   My first is always good in France,
     My second clean when there;
My whole is now in general use
     And decks the British fair.

466   Look well upon me, and you'll trace
The despot mark'd upon my face,
The stamp of pow'r, of sov'reign sway,
To which the English homage pay;
To shorten life, and rule the hour,
To aggrandize, I have the pow'r;
Both wealth and lands I can bestow,
With joy and grief, despair and woe;
And fire I give to beauty's eyes,
Or call up beauty's tears and sighs;
There's not a passion in the soul,
That is not sway'd by my control;
The wretched seek me for relief,
And cling to me with firm belief
That I have pow'r to soothe their pain,
And bring them happiness again;
It is most strange that, when entire,
I'm harmless as the glowworm's fire;

Yet power's law's revers'd in me –
My strength's divisibility;
And that which men may deem disgrace,
In me bestows the pow'r of place;
To listlessness I owe my birth,
Yet none excite like me on earth;
But study well, and you may draw
My strong affinity to law;
Indeed in me you also see
The symbols of divinity;
And yet (th' anomaly most sad!)
Religionists all say I'm bad,
But still allow, e'en while they hate,
The perfect order of my state.
In short, in ev'ry polish'd land,
I find a ready open hand,
   And welcome from my slaves;
And although contumely I meet,
Alike the frowns and smiles I treat,
   Of heroes and of knaves.

And now my story's told, farewell!
In almost ev'ry clime I dwell,
   Unlimited in sway;
Except in England – here, I own
A power, before whose might alone
   I freely homage pay.

DUDENEY, Henry E. (1857–1930)

British puzzle-master whose brain-teasers first appeared in *Tit-Bits* and the *Strand Magazine* under the pseudonym 'Sphinx', and who was universally acknowledged as puzzle-king on the death of the American Sam Loyd (q.v.) in 1911. Examples taken from *The World's Best Word Puzzles* (1925) and *Strand Magazine* issues of 1914.

467   A sentry, with an eager eye,
     And steady step and slow,
   Walked o'er my *first*, whilst thickly fell
     The downy flakes of snow.

His face was thin, his aspect sad,
   For fierce the war had raged,
And long it was since my *second* had
   His hungering lips engaged.

At length there was a rustling;
   He challenged the parole,
Yet there came to him no answer,
   But the fluttering of my *whole*.

468   Untouched I tell of budding growth and life;
     Beheaded I lead upward, more or less;
   Again – with varied fragrance I am rife;
     Again – but little value I express.

469   It is a welcome gift to man – but stay!
        'Tis yet a stumbling block in some men's way.
        Behead, and many a person to it flies
        To gain a glow of health from exercise.
        Behead, again; the secret's out, I vow,
        For every reader's looking at it now.

470   My *first* you'll admit is a kind of a squeeze,
        Not always intended exactly to please.
        My *second*, no doubt, is just simply a sign.
        My *whole* is a metal not found in a mine.

471   By nature's law to me is given
        The greatest power under heaven.
        The proudest monarch I confine,
        Who silently themselves resign,
        And own obedience by a nod
        To me, their more than demi-god.
        So universal is my sway
        That high and low my laws obey.
        If more of me you wish to know,
        Inquire not of the sons of woe,
        But of the weary and the gay,
        Who to me their homage pay;
        Though while they in my power remain
        Should you inquire 'twill be in vain.

472   Ladies, a riddle I submit.
          To fifty just add one,
        And having thereby shown your wit,
          You may my whole put on.

473   In Noah's time, when from the Ark
          Came animals in pairs,
        Who was it then would suffer most
          From trampling on the stairs.

474   My name declares my date to be
          The morning of a Christian year.
        I'm motherless, as all agree,
          And yet a mother am, 'tis clear;
        A father, too, which none dispute,
        And, when my son comes, I'm a fruit.
        And, not to puzzle you too much,
        'Twas I took Holland for the Dutch.

475   A Bible character without a name,
        Whose body never to corruption came,
        Who died a death that none have died before,
        Whose shroud is found in every household store.

476   Take away my first letter and I remain unchanged; take away
        my second letter and I remain unchanged; take away my third
        letter and I remain unchanged; take away all my letters and still
        I remain exactly the same.

477   I needed *three* and *four*,
      And started for the door,
To get a *three*, *four*, *five* resolved to strive.
    I had not gone a square,
      When by chance I *total* there,
By which I mean my *one, two, three, four, five.*

478   Five hundred begins, five hundred ends it,
      Five in the middle is seen;
The first of all figures, the first of all letters,
      Take up their stations between.
Join all together, and then you will bring
Before you the name of an eminent king.

479   **G·4·E TXTX_N B**

480   One evening through my study window crept
An enemy to harm me; but I leapt
Upon my feet, and, whipping out my knife,
Struck off its head, hoping to take its life.
But lo! 'twas now seen creeping on the floor –
A horrid thing more dreadful than before.
I faced the foe, cut off its tail, and then
Fixed down the wretched creature with a pen.
It seemed to change, and, as I stood aghast,
Into the vegetable kingdom passed.

481

482

483   My head and tail both equal are,
My middle slender as a bee.
Whether I stand on head or heel
Is quite the same to you or me.

But if my head should be cut off,
The matter's true, though passing strange
Directly I to nothing change.

ENIGMAS OF EVERY VARIETY (1872)

By 'I. S. Olveall'. One of a series of puzzle pamphlets entitled 'Home Amusements for the Family Circle' and published by Dean & Son. See also *Charades of Every Variety*.

484   What every man prefers to life,
Fears more than death or deadly strife;
What the contented man deserves,
The poor man has, the rich requires –
The miser spends, the spendthrift saves,
And all men carry to their graves.

485   I love to roam when the Curlew's wing
    Is dipp'd in the deep blue wave
Of the rock-bound bay, when moonbeams play
    O'er many a lov'd one's grave.
Down, too, in the dell, to the trysting tree
    I stray with happy pair,
And bright hopes bring, of the bridal ring,
    To the maiden young and fair.
To crimson poles on the battle fields
    Of a stricken land I flee,
And I sorrow start in the widow'd heart,
    From the depths of every sea.
And though to the peasant bard I kneel,
    And the fairest of treasures bring,
I wield the power, in an evil hour,
    To humble the proudest king.

486   O'er lawns I rove, and often climb the hill,
And change my colour often as you will;
The courtier vain, philosopher, and beau,
I often please, yet by strict rule I go;
Midst ladies fair, at routs and balls I'm seen,
Yet with the cottage maid trip o'er the green;
With British tar, on topsail-yard, I shine,
Or with the collier sink into the mine;
Where armies march I constantly attend,
Ay, and each soldier owns me as his friend.
Of me the pious Baptist mention makes,
Shakspere, too, when of Niobe he speaks;
The greatest kings and princes bend to me,
Yet I serve all with great humility;
I aid both priest and statesmen, philosopher and clown,
Grandam and infant, rich and poor, in country, and in town.

487   I'm active, I'm sluggish, I'm quick, I am slow,
I've a slumbering existence in wreaths of white snow;
In the tropics I dwell, on the land, in the stream;
Men say at earth's centre I revel supreme.

I have saved many lives, and I thousands have slain,
Without me the artizan's craft would be vain;
I creep in the veins of weak man in his rage,
Till blood oft is spilt, his mad wrath to assuage.
The paper thou holdest by me is impress'd,
By me it is spread o'er the east and the west;
O'er the north and the south, wheresoever the mind
Of man with true knowledge is blest and refined.
For the monster of iron, with power so vast,
That flies o'er the land like the hurricane blast,
Without me is useless, immovable, still,
Its power is my offspring, and lives by my will.

488   I'm always found at home, no matter when or where;
In houses large, or harbours small, you'll find me always there.
I am no kindred of the great, nor care I for the small;
I visit not the parlour, but I'm always in the hall.
In kitchens I can find a place, and there I'm quite at home;
Of beauty I can't boast a bit, yet, it's no disgrace, you'll own.
In heaven I shall find some rest. In hope I take delight;
I'm out all day, nor am I tired, but always in at-night.
With holy, reverential care, in churches I am found;
But visit not the grave-yard, nor consecrated ground.

Inside the chests of merchants bold, you'll find me 'neath the lid;
But I will shun the miser's gold; in fact, I always did.
Honest friends I dearly love; though I commit some havoc,
I'm never in the soldier's cot, but in the sailor's hammock.
On sea I never ventured yet, nor into field of battle;
But I'm the first in honour's cause, e'en when great guns do
    rattle.
All human aid is used by me, mechanic's skill I favour,
Machines and telegraphic wires, the hand with which you
    labour.
I own all these, and many more; now put your brain in motion,
And try and find a name for me out of this wild commotion.

489   I'm very oft seen on the ground –
On water and land I am found;
I'm flat, and I'm smooth, as you'll see;
And always the water finds me.

I'm used by men in various trades;
When found, I place men in their grades;
And, now, five letters tell my name;
Forward or backwards, I'm the same.

490   Sometimes I'm hard, at others soft,
In various shapes you've seen me oft;
I'm round, and square, and oval too,
Or any pattern named by you;
Both large and small, each size between,
In colours numerous I'm seen.

You tread on me when out you walk;
I'm sometimes near akin to chalk;
Men give to me a kind of grace;
In every town I have a place,
Wherever houses may be found –
But I'm not always on the ground.
I tower high above your head,
And yet I'm on the ocean's bed;
Oft am I thrown by girl or boy;
Much priz'd and valued as a toy.
A weight I am, well known in trade;
In fruit I'm often found, 'tis said;
Yet to be mineral I claim –
And ask you now to give my name.

EUBULUS (*fl.* 4th century BC)

Ancient Greek poet and dramatist. Riddle cited in Athenaeus's
Deipnosophistae.

491   It has no tongue, yet it talks, its name is the same for male or
        female, steward of its own winds, hairy, or sometimes hairless;
        saying things unintelligible to them that understand, drawing out
        one melody after another, one thing it is, yet many, and if one
        wound it, it is unwounded. Tell me, what is it? Why are you
        puzzled?

492   I know one that is heavy when he is young, and when he
        becomes old, though wingless, he lightly flies and leaves the land
        invisible.

EUSEBIUS (d.747)

Abbot of Wearmouth. Riddles published with those of Tatwine (q.v.).

493   *Natura simplex stans, non sapio undique quicquam,*
        Sed mea nunc sapiens vestigia quisque sequetur;
        Nunc tellurem habitans, prius ethera celsa vagabar;
        Candida conspicior, vestigia tetra relinquens.

        (By nature I am simple and have no wisdom in any way, but
        now every wise man will follow my tracks; now I dwell on
        earth, erewhile I roamed on high through the heavens; I am
        white in appearance, though I leave black traces.)

494   *Per me mors adquiritur et bona vita tenetur.*
        Me multi fugiunt, multique frequenter adorant;
        Sumque timenda malis, non sum tamen horrida justis.
        Damnavi virum, sic multos carcere solvi.

        (Through me death is acquired and good life is maintained.
        Many flee me, and many frequently worship me; I am to be
        feared by bad men, but I am not terrifying to the just. I have
        condemned a man and thus released many from prison.)

One of Routledge & Co's regular children's annuals, edited by Alicia A.
Leith. Contains a variety of puzzles.

495   The rain-clouds hung over land and sea,
       The way was dark and the wind blew free,
       And the sky was my *first* as it frowned o'er me.

       I was far from home in the driving sleet,
       And I thought to myself, O rest were sweet
       On my *next*, as I pressed it with weary feet.

       But the thought of the sport I'd had that day
       Chased every shadow of gloom away,
       And my *whole* in my basket was stowed away.

496   My *first*, the pride of every ancient dame,
       O'er to old England in my *second* came;
       My *whole* in every household bears a part;
       Thou art not science, but thou teachest Art.

497   A note upon the piano here you see!
       Crowned, here you have part of the verb to be.
       Crown me again, a timid thing I flee;
       And crowned once more, a portion here for thee.

498   My *first* was deadly once in war,
       In sieges it was used;
       My *second* take, I pray you friend,
       Whene'er I am abused.

       Upon my *whole* the sentinel
       Doth step with paces slow;
       To guard the silent sleeping town
       He marches to and fro.

499   He stood himself beside himself, and looked into the sea;
       Within himself he saw himself, and at himself gazed he;
       So, when himself he saw himself, and in himself go round,
       Into himself he threw himself, and in himself was drowned.
       Now if he had not been himself, but other beast beside,
       He would himself have cut himself, nor in himself have died.

500   What goddess would we welcome on a hot summer's day?

501   Happy and bright life spreadeth out,
       With Hope's fair wings unfurled,
       In early youth, ere care has dimmed
       The aspect of the world.
       O base are those who do my *first* to all this cloudless joy,
       And with a cruel and reckless hand such visions bright destroy!

       Beside my *whole*, which doth belong
       To ocean vast and drear,
       A creature stood in reckless mood,
       Unmoved by touch of fear.

My *second* held her spirit chained,
  A wretched slave was she;
For potent spells were round her cast,
  Herself she could not free.

502 I am a scene of labour. Take away a letter and I am a place
     mentioned in Shakespeare. Take away another letter, and I am
     the home of an animal. Take away one more letter and, trans-
     posed, I am a fitting conclusion.

503 The sweet ingenuous girl is *this*, in worldly ways unversed.

     The burglar laughs at *this* when in his wicked deeds immersed.

     A Shakespeare character my *whole*, whose fate by none is pitied.
     He over-reached himself and fell – by woman's brains outwitted.

504 I am a virtue. Take away a letter, and I am the present century.
     Take away two letters, and I am an emotion. Take away
     another letter and I am a possession of the poor.

EVERYBODY'S ILLUSTRATED BOOK OF PUZZLES (1890)
Over 700 puzzles, edited by 'The Sphinx'.

505 Enigma guessers, tell me what I am.
     I've been a drake, a fox, a hare, a lamb –
     You all possess me, and in every street
     In varied shape and form with me you'll meet
     With Christians I am never single known,
     Am green, or scarlet, brown, white, gray or stone.
     I dwelt in Paradise with Mother Eve,
     And went with her, when she, alas! did leave.
     To Britain with Caractacus I came,
     And made Augustus Cæsar known to fame.

506 Alone, no life can be without me;
     With C, I hold the wildest beast;
     With G, I measure land and sea;
     With P, I serve the nobleman;
     With R, I rave with passion dread;
     With S, I know the depths of wisdom;
     With W, I earn my daily bread.

507 They say my first is very bright,
       And what they say is true;
     But only in my second can
       My first be seen by you.
     My second would without my first
       Be far from being bright;
     My whole is what the working man
       Welcomes with great delight.

508 Complete can be found along the great sea,
     Near rivers and brooks it also may be;
     Curtail, then a planet comes to your sight
     That's seen from above on a clear, starry night;

Again curtail, a word you will see
Which means to impair; you'll agree with me
That another curtailment shows you a word
That's a nickname for mamma, in fond homes 'tis heard.

509   With thieves I consort,
       With the vilest, in short,
         I'm quite at my ease in depravity;
       Yet all divines use me,
       And savants can't lose me,
         For I am the centre of gravity.

510   You may find me there before you at anybody's door,
       In the palace of the rich or the cottage of the poor;
       You may find me in the earth and air, but in the mighty sea
       Would surely be a place, my friends, you need not look for me.
       I've lived out in the country, and I've lived within the town,
       And moved so oft from house to house I long to settle down.
       Both men and women shun me, the youthful and the old
       (But oh! how glad to grasp me when I am made of gold).
       How often on the doorstep, I fain would enter in, when
       Betty spied my presence and sent me off again.
       Men hate me and they scorn me, and they throw me here and
           there;
       You may see me lying helpless in the gutter – on the stair.
       You may see me where they throw me, so if you'll look again,
       Can't you see me in the eyes of some simple guileless men?
       I hate the winter's ice and snow and hate to have it rain;
       I'm very fond of travelling and always on a train.

511   My first of anything is half,
         My second is complete;
       And so remains until once more
         My first and second meet.

512   My 1, 2, 3 across the land
         My 4, 5, 6 doth carry.
       On 1 to 6 we both will stand
         The day we both shall marry.

513   I'm the offspring of shame, by modesty bred,
         I'm the symbol of virtue and vice;
       Neither written nor printed, yet constantly red;
         A critic discerning and nice.

       I'm a marplot, and terribly self-willed withal,
         I'm not to be argued or tasked;
       And although I obey not a positive call,
         I come when not wanted or asked.

514   Write one hundred and add one,
         And then with five unite;
       When one and fifty you have joined,
         You'll have what is polite.

146

515   I've hands and feet and features fine,
To you I often tell the time;
I'm sometimes seen upon the moon,
The cattle seek me oft at noon.
Around each house I creep at night,
From me the guilty hastes his flight;
I help to prove the earth is round;
I swiftly move without a sound.
I walk with you each pleasant day;
I chase the children when at play –
They cannot catch me if they try,
Yet they are as fleet of foot as I.
I am not light, I'm sure you'd say,
And yet 'tis true I nothing weigh.
Whene'er the morn is clear and bright,
My form towers to a wondrous height;
But when the dinner hour is nigh,
More broad and short and thick am I.
If before you I proceed,
And if you wish to take the lead,
Then turn and go an opposite way,
Or wait till a different time of day.

516   The roseate clouds drift through the sky,
      The sun goes down;
And soft the total's gentle cry
      Sounds through the town.

A second is he, wise and old,
      So people say;
Who carries with him, I've been told,
      First, white and gray,

To sprinkle on all wakeful eyes –
      Black, blue or brown;
As on his busy round he lies
      Straight through the town.

517   I am often worn by horsemen,
      Sometimes a snag may be,
A mountain, part of a flower,
      Or skimmer of the sea.
Wall of a fort, a fungus growth,
      Incitement, investigation;
Found at the bottom of each tree
      In each and every nation.
That which excites, impels, drives on
      To action every man,
Although I am of letters four,
      Come, guess me if you can.

518   If you would travel o'er our land,
To Vermont's hills or Georgia's strand,
      Or where Maine's breezes blow,

Get in my first and you will speed
Far faster than the swiftest steed,
　　Where'er you wish to go.

Upon my second patriots turn,
For it their hearts with ardour burn,
　　For it they live and die,
For it in toil they spend their years,
For it they give their prayers and tears,
　　For it as captives sigh.

My whole is in the garden found,
When the sweet summer months come round,
And flowers wake at their call.
Yellow sometimes and sometimes rose,
Snow white, deep red its colour glows,
　　Its perfume pleases all.

519　If to one thousand you add one,
　　　Then fifty and five hundred,
　　You'll have what's gentle, good and kind,
　　　Or else I must have blundered.

520　　　　　　*FIRST*
　　Secrets it shares with me and you
　　　Although for deafness noted;
　　And whoso to his own is true
　　　Will lead a life devoted.

　　　　　　SECOND
　　A soul too grand for earth is his,
　　　Yet base beyond relation;
　　He often *writes*, and always *is*,
　　　A curious complication.

　　　　　　WHOLE
　　The caller all rejoice to see;
　　　Desired before his betters;
　　The reigning favorite is he
　　　Among all men of letters.

521　I am borne on the gale in the stillness of night,
　　A sentinel's signal that all is not right.
　　I am not a swallow, yet skim o'er the wave;
　　I am not a doctor, yet patients I save;
　　When the sapling has grown to a flourishing tree
　　It finds a protector henceforward in me?

522   In rat, but not in kitten;
        In oar, but not in sail;
    In gloves, but not in mitten;
        In pitcher, but not in pail;
    In trumpets, but not in tune;
        The whole appears in June.

523   Places of trust I oft obtain,
        And protect the house from vermin;
    I act as shepherd on the plain,
        And at fairs I'm shown for learning;
    In northern climes a horse I'm seen,
    And a roasting jack I, too, have been;
    Strange as it seems, it's no less true,
    That I eat on four legs and beg on two.

524   No wings have I, yet I have sped
        To earth's remotest places;
    No feet have I, yet I have led
        Full many mighty races;
    No tongue have I, and yet I speak
        And e'en the deaf ones hear me;
    I rest the weary, cheer the weak,
        While knaves and bigots fear me;
    From me may draw a thousand men
        Strength, joy and inspiration;
    Yet to me thousands come again
        And find no alteration.
    Yet oft I prove a curse to be
        To mankind's sons and daughters
    More deadly than the upas tree,
        Bitter as Mara's waters.

525   My *first* each morning greets the ear
        With sweetest music, rich and clear;
    My *second* will the rider need
        To urge along his lagging steed;
    While 'mid old fashioned flowers, maybe,
        The petals of my whole you'll see.

526   My first is in sit, but not in lie.
    My second is in cake, but not in pie.
    My third is in beat, but not in slap.
    My fourth is in sleep, but not in nap.
    My fifth is in well, but not in good.
    My whole is an object made of wood.

527   A friend of mine once gave to me
        A faithful hunting dog;
    He searched for game where'er 'twas hid
        In marsh or wood or bog.

One day when I was in high rage,
    A word to him I said;
He came to me, I seized a knife,
    And then cut off his head.

As soon as this bad deed I'd done
    I realized my sin;
I turned my head away from him –
    How wicked I must have been!

And when I turned and looked again
    My poor dog wasn't there;
But what I saw was just a bird,
    Which rose into the air.

528   Ned is always doing errands, and he never gets them done,
As he usually has *total* what his mother sent him *one*.
When he comes to count his purchases, 'tis certain as can be
That for every article he *two* he wholly *one-two-three*.

529   My first is in careful, but not in save;
My second in water, and also in wave;
My third is in table, but not in chair;
My fourth is in lovely, but not in fair;
My fifth is in ringing, but not in bell;
My sixth is in pitcher, but not in well;
My seventh is in sovereign, but not in gold;
My eighth is in youthful, and also in old;
My ninth is in doleful, but not in sad;
My tenth is in happy, and also in glad;
My eleventh in reaping, but not in sow;
My whole, the grub of an insect, is ugly and slow.

530   What each one has received
    Quite early in his life;
What brave ones have achieved
    By earnest toil and strife;

What every man bestows
    On her whom he espouses;
What people sometimes chose
    To put upon their houses;

What not a cent has cost,
    Yet may not be disdained;
For if once it is lost
    It cannot be regained.

531   My *first*, a word most near to every heart;
My *next*, a very large and heavy cart;
My *last*, an implement that makes a bed;
My *whole*, a story widely loved and read.

        C
       ———
532   junction

533   I travel o'er land, I travel 'neath sea,
Hill, plain and ocean are all known to me.
I speak, and my speech is short and brief,
    Yet it reaches the wide world o'er.
To homes that are happy I bring sudden grief,
    And my slightest commands are law.
Things of importance that secret be
Are all revealed and intrusted to me.
Quick as lightning my work I fulfill,
Yet strange to say I am always still.

534   The other night I dreamed this dream:
    I stood upon a mountain,
An 'unobstructed view' I had,
    Clear as any fountain.

A vision through the space I saw –
    A father first did come;
He passed, then all again was still;
    I gazed entranced, dumb.

A charming sister next did pass,
    With bright and golden hair;
I looked at her in mute delight,
    Then she vanished in the air.

A loving mother came the last –
    Always true and kind;
Soon she passed on, then I awoke,
    This dream stamped on my mind.

535   In letter, not in sign;
In porter, not in wine;
In napkin, not in cloth;
In tiger, not in moth;
In fresh, not in old;
In heat, not in cold;
In lozenge, not in stone;
In laugh, not in moan;
In Harold, not in Kate;
In worship, not in hate.
My whole a poet great.

536   Wheresoever I may be,
Every man must follow me;
He must go where I may lead,
Though it be to change his creed.
Though I vary in my size,
I am still beneath your eyes;
And though you may go astray,
I must ever lead the way.
Every creature in the land
Has me close at his command,
For I lead to things unseen
By my properties so keen.

And I often may detect
What you never would suspect,
For my value is immense
When you're guided by my sense.
Though I'm sometimes raised in scorn,
Sometimes drooping and forlorn,
Yet each deems his own the best,
Nor would swap for all the rest.

537 In the haunted room to read I tried,
   With my dread *first* for a chum;
  If I had *second* of my *first*, I sighed,
   My *whole* I should become.

EXETER BOOK, The (10th century)
Anglo-Saxon miscellany presented to Exeter Cathedral in 1072. Riddles
once believed to have been the work of the Anglo-Saxon poet Cynewulf.

538 In former days my father and mother
  Abandoned me a dead thing lacking breath,
  Or life or being. Then one began,
  A kinswoman kind, to care for, and love me;
  Covered me with her clothing, wrapped me in her raiment,
  With the same affection she felt for her own;
  Until, by the law of my life's shaping,
  Under an alien bosom I quickened with breath.
  My foster mother fed me thereafter
  Until I grew sturdy and strengthened for flight.
  Then of her dear ones, of daughters and sons,
  She had the fewer for what she did.

539 By foot I travel, and I tear the earth,
  The grassy fields, as long as I have life.
  But when my spirit leaves me I bind fast
  The dark Welsh slaves or sometimes better men.
  Sometimes I give a noble warrior
  Drink from my breast; sometimes the haughty bride
  Treads on me. Sometimes the dark-haired Welsh maid
  Brought from afar carries and presses me,
  A foolish drunken girl at dark of night
  Wets me with water, sometimes pleasantly
  Warms me beside the fire, sticks in my bosom
  Her wanton hand, constantly turns me round,
  Strokes me all night. Tell me what I am called,
  That while I live may plunder all the land,
  And after death give service to mankind.

540 My beak is below, I burrow and nose
  Under the ground. I go as I'm guided
  By my master the farmer, old foe of the forest;
  Bent and bowed, at my back he walks,
  Forward pushing me over the field;
  Sows on my path where I've passed along.
  I came from the wood, a wagon carried me;

I was fitted with skill, I am full of wonders.
As grubbing I go, there's green on one side,
But black on the other my path is seen.
A curious prong pierces my back;
Beneath me in front, another grows down
And forward pointing is fixed to my head.
I tear and gash the ground with my teeth,
If my master steer me with skill from behind.

541 I'm a strange creature, for I satisfy women,
A service to the neighbours! No one suffers
At my hands except for my slayer.
I grow very tall, erect in a bed,
I'm hairy underneath. From time to time
A beautiful girl, the brave daughter
Of some churl dares to hold me,
Grips my russet skin, robs me of my head
And puts me in the pantry. At once that girl
With plaited hair who has confined me
Remembers our meeting. Her eye moistens.

542 I'm prized by men, in the meadows I'm found,
Gathered on hill-sides, and hunted in groves;
From dale and from down, by day I am brought.
Airy wings carry me, cunningly store me,
Hoarding me safe. Yet soon men take me;
Drained into vats, I'm dangerous grown.
I tie up my victim, and trip him, and throw him;
Often I floor a foolish old churl.
Who wrestles with me, and rashly would measure
His strength against mine, will straightway find himself
Flung to the ground, flat on his back,
Unless he leave his folly in time,
Put from his senses and power of speech,
Robbed of his might, bereft of his mind,
Of his hands and feet. Now find me my name,
Who can bind and enslave men so upon earth,
And bring fools low in broad daylight.

543 There's a troop of tiny folk travelling swift,
Brought by the breeze o'er the brink of the hill,
Buzzing black-coated bold little people –
Noisy musicians; well-known is their song.
They scour the thickets, but sometimes invade
The rooms of the town. Now tell me their names.

544 Wounded I am, and weary with fighting;
Gashed by the iron, gored by the point of it,
Sick of battle-work, battered and scarred.
Many a fearful fight have I seen, when
Hope there was none, or help in the thick of it,
Ere I was down and fordone in the fray.
Offspring of hammers, hardest of battle-blades,
Smithied in forges, fell on me savagely,

Doomed to bear the brunt and the shock of it,
Fierce encounter of clashing foes.
Leech cannot heal my hurts with his simples,
Salves for my sores have I sought in vain.
Blade-cuts dolorous, deep in the side of me,
Daily and nightly redouble my wounds.

545   A strange thing hangs by man's hip,
Hidden by a garment. It has a hole
In its head. It is stiff and strong
And its firm bearing reaps a reward.
When the retainer hitches his clothing
High above his knee, he wants the head
Of that hanging thing to find the old hole
That it, outstretched, has often filled before.

546   I'm told a certain object grows
In the corner, rises and expands, throws up
A crust. A proud wife carried off
That boneless wonder, the daughter of a king
Covered that swollen thing with a cloth.

547   A moth ate a word! To me that seemed
A strange thing to happen, when I heard that wonder –
A worm that would swallow the speech of a man,
Sayings of strength steal in the dark,
Thoughts of the mighty; yet the thieving sprite
Was none the wiser for the words he had eaten!

548   I war with the wind, with the waves I wrestle;
I must battle with both when the bottom I seek,
My strange habitation by surges o'er-roofed.
I am strong in the strife, while still I remain;
As soon as I stir, they are stronger than I.
They wrench and they wrest, till I run from my foes;
What was put in my keeping they carry away.
If my back be not broken, I baffle them still;
The rocks are my helpers, when hard I am pressed;
Grimly I grip them. Guess what I'm called.

549   My robe is silent, when I rest on earth,
Or run by the shore, or ruffle the pools;
But oft on my pinions upward I mount,
Borne to the skies on the buoyant air,
High o'er the haunts and houses of men,
Faring afar with the fleeting clouds.
Then sudden my feathers are filled with music.
They sing in the wind, as I sail aloft
O'er wave and wood, a wandering sprite.

550   I was an armèd warrior, but now
The youthful courtier covers my proud neck
With twisted filigree of gold and silver.
Sometimes I'm kissed by heroes, and again
I woo to battle with my melody

Comrades in full accord. At times the courser
Bears me across the border, and again
Over the floods the stallion of the sea
Conveys me radiant with ornaments.
Sometimes a maiden, garlanded with jewels,
Brims full my winding bosom, and again
Perforce I lie – hard, headless, solitary
Upon the board. Sometimes, set off with trappings,
In comely guise upon the wall I hang
Where heroes drink. Again, horsed warriors
On forays wear me, glorious apparel;
Then, dappled with gold, I must inspire the wind
From some one's bosom. Whilom stately men
I summon to banquetings and wine; sometimes
My voice resounds with freedom to the captive,
Flight to the foe. Now find out what I'm called.

551   I saw a creature in the homes of men
Which feeds the cattle. It has many teeth.
Its beak is useful to it. It points downwards.
It plunders gently and goes home again,
Wanders among the mounds and seeks out herbs.
It always finds out those that are not firm.
It lets the fair ones stand upon their roots,
Firm, undisturbed in their established place,
And brightly shine and blossom and grow tall.

EZRA, Abraham ibn (1089–1164)
Spanish Hebrew poet and grammarian from Cordova.

552   There was a she-mule in my house: I opened the door, and she became a heifer.

553   Take thirty from thirty and the remainder is sixty.

EZRA, Moses ibn (c. 1070–c.1138)
Spanish Hebrew philosopher, linguist and poet. Wrote occasional riddles.

554   What is the sister of the sun, though made for the night? The fire causes her tears to fall, and when she is near dying they cut off her head.

FAMILY AMUSEMENTS FOR WINTER EVENINGS (n.d.)
Puzzles, parlour magic, riddles, Book of Fate etc. Published by John Cameron, Glasgow.

555   My first a baby does when you pinch it,
My second a lady says, but does not mean it,
My third exists, and no one e'er has seen it,
My whole contains the world's best half within it.

556   My *first* is Latin for a book,
Which boys at least must know quite well;

My *second*'s two-thirds of to knot,
    And this you'll also quickly tell.
My *whole*'s the proudest boast of those
    Who dwell within this favoured land;
'Tis England's boon to every slave
    Whose foot has pressed our sea-girt strand.

557　My whole is a thing
With a terrible sting;
But cut off my head,
And still more you'll me dread.

558　My *first* a curling tail displays,
My *second* is a tail always,
My *whole*'s a tail of other days.

559　A sudden blaze, it is my *whole*,
Behead me, then I pray beware,
For I can strike, so have a care;
Behead me yet again, and see
There rises up a well known tree.

560　I am a robber on the sea, –
Behead me, I shall furious be, –
Again behead me, and a price
You fix upon me in a trice.
Now of my head once more bereft,
I'm swallowed up – there's nothing left.

561　Before a circle let appear
Twice twenty-five, and five in rear,
One-fifth of eight join, if you can,
And then you'll find what conquers man.

FANSHAWE, Catherine Maria (1765–1834)
English poet. Best remembered for the first riddle, once mistakenly
ascribed to Lord Byron. (This is the original version with the original
opening line. See also Appendix.)

562　'Twas in heaven pronounced, and 'twas muttered in hell,
And echo caught faintly the sound as it fell:
On the confines of earth 'twas permitted to rest,
And the depths of the ocean its presence confest;
'Twill be found in the sphere when 'tis riven asunder,
Be seen in the lightning, and heard in the thunder.
'Twas allotted to man with his earliest breath,
Attends at his birth, and awaits him in death,
Presides o'er his happiness, honor, and health,
Is the prop of his house, and the end of his wealth.
In the heaps of the miser 'tis hoarded with care,
But is sure to be lost on his prodigal heir.
It begins every hope, every wish it must bound,
With the husbandman toils, and with monarchs is crown'd.
Without it the soldier, the seaman may roam,
But wo to the wretch who expels it from home!

In the whispers of conscience its voice will be found,
Nor e'en in the whirlwind of passion be drown'd.
'Twill not soften the heart; but though deaf be the ear,
It will make it acutely and instantly hear.
Yet in shade let it rest like a delicate flower,
Ah breathe on it softly – it dies in an hour.

563 Inscrib'd on many a learned page,
In mystic characters and sage,
  Long time my *first* has stood;
And though its golden age be past,
In wooden walls it yet may last,
  Till cloth'd with flesh and blood.

My *second* is a glorious prize
For all who love their wondering eyes
  With curious sights to pamper;
But 'tis a sight – which should they meet
All' improviso in the street,
  Ye gods! how they would scamper!

My *tout*'s a sort of wandering throne,
To woman limited alone,
  The Salique law reversing;
But while th' imaginary queen
Prepares to act this novel scene,
  Her royal part rehearsing,
O'erturning her presumptuous plan,
Up climbs the old usurper – man,
And she jogs after as she can.

FECHNER, Gustav (1801–87)
German physicist, philosopher, and psychologist. Riddles occur in
Räthselbuchlein (1850) under the pseudonym 'Dr Mises'.

564

> Die beiden Ersten machen
> Den Weibern oft es nach,
> Jetzt sieht man sie noch lachen
> Und weinen gleich danach.
> Ein Sultan ist die Dritte,
> Geht stets gespornt einher
> Mit stolzem Herrschertritte,
> Doch niemals reitet er.
> Das Ganze ist beweglich
> Zwar, wenn es still steht, stumm,
> Doch schreit's mitunter kläglich
> Sobald sich's dreht herum.

(My two first are like women, one minute they're laughing the
next they're crying. My third is a sultan who always struts
around in spurs with a proud monarch's step, yet he never rides.
My whole is ever moving and when it's still is dumb though
sometimes when it spins around it makes a plaintive sound.)

565

Die erste Silbe ist ein klingend Instrument,
Das älteste gewiß von allen, die man kennt;
Ein Jeder trägt's und braucht's das liebe lange Jahr;
Die schönen Damen auch? frägst du. Ich dachte gar.
Die beiden andern sind ein klingend Instrument,
Das muntre Beine macht, doch müde macht die Händ';
Am meisten hat mich stets bei seinem Schall erbaut,
Daß das, was so erklingt, nicht meine eigne Haut.
Das Ganze endlich ist ein klingend Instrument,
Das von dem Ersten du nie hörest abgetrennt;
Es taugt nicht zum Concert, taugt auch nicht für den Ball;
Doch streit ich nicht mit dir, wenn dir gefällt sein Schall.

(My first is a noisy instrument, indeed the oldest known to man; everyone has one and plays it the whole year long. The fair ladies too? I hear you ask. Oh yes, indeed. My last two syllables also make a noisy instrument that wakes up the legs yet tires the hands; I am just glad that it is not my skin that makes such a noise. My whole, finally, is also a noisy instrument, one which you will never hear separated from my first. It is no good for a concert, not any use at a ball, but I certainly won't disagree with you if you enjoy its sound.)

566

Wer aus den ersten Beiden
Sehr oft die Dritte thut,
Den könnt ihr unterscheiden
An seiner Nase Glut.
Sonst geht stets aus den Höhen
Herab des Steines Lauf;
Das Ganze läßt ihn gehen
Hoch in die Luft hinauf.

(He who from my first two frequently takes my third will soon discern a reddening of his nose. More usually it can be seen moving stones. My whole indeed can lift them high in the air.)

567

Die ersten sind ein Unterthan,
Die Dritte ist ein Unterthan;
Das Ganze ist ein Unterthan,
Der von dem andern Unterthan
Wird unter den ersten Unterthan
Ganz unterthänig gethan.

(My two first are an underling, my third is an underling, my whole is an underling that becomes completely subjugated beneath my first.)

568

Es stellt als Frucht das erste Paar,
Als Pflanze sich das andre dar.
Doch wenn ihr beide wollt verbinden,
So wird alsbald ein Thier sich finden.

(The first pair make a fruit, the last pair make a plant, but when both pairs are bound together they make a beast.)

569

Sagt, wie das stimmt:
Die Erste schwimmt,
Die Zweite läuft,
Das Ganze steift.

(Tell me, how can this be: my first swims, my second runs, yet my whole is as stiff as a post.)

570

Die beiden Ersten sind mehr als gut,
Mit der Dritten wehrt sich die Gassenbrut.
Das Ganze ist die adelige Klasse
Unter einer sonst sehr gemeinen Race.

(My first two are worthiness itself, with my last the ragamuffin defends himself. My whole is a noble order of things found deep below the vulgar human race.)

571

Die erste ist ein Wort zum fragen,
Die Zweite gut um zuzuschlagen.
Das Ganze läßt den Gaumen zagen,
Oft aber heilsam für den Magen.

(My first is a word for asking, my second is useful in battle. My whole makes the palate flinch yet is remarkably healing for the stomach.)

572

Es ist ein krummes Schwert, das hauet mitten drein
In eine große Schaar, doch schneidet nicht ins Bein;
Es theilt sich bloß die Schaar, da wo das Schwert hinschlug,
Und steht ein Weilchen still, wofern sie war im Zug;
So stellt es Ordnung her im Raum und in der Zeit,
Sofern der, der es führt, nur selber ist gescheut.
Die Frauen aber, wenn auch sonst der Ordnung Hut,
Gebrauchen allzumeist das Schwert nicht allzugut.

(It is a crooked sword that slashes in the midst of a huge crowd yet never harms a limb; wherever the blade strikes it merely divides the throng, and pauses for a little while. In such a manner it creates order in space and time as long as whoever wields it keeps his nerve. Women, however, have never mastered its power.)

FIRDUSI or FIRDAUSI (c.950–1020)
Pseudonym of Abul Qasim Mansur, Persian poet. Riddles occur in the epic *Shanamah*.

573   Twelve cypresses stand in a circle and shine in resplendent green; each has thirty branches, and neither their esteem nor their number becomes less in the land of the Parsees.

574   There are two splendid horses, one black as pitch, the other of shining crystal; each runs ahead of the other but never catches it.

575   There is a green garden full of birds; a man with a large scythe goes about it, busily mowing green and dry plants; neither complaints nor submission to his will divert him from his purpose. There two cypresses rise from the waves of the sea like reeds; a bird has its nest in them. When it is sitting in them, there is a fragrance like musk. One of the trees is always green and bears fruit, the other is wilting.

FLORIO, John (c.1553–1625)
Translator of Montaigne, friend of Ben Jonson, and Reader in Italian to James I's wife. Riddles occur in *Firste Fruites* (1578), with Italian version facing English.

576   *Voi non hauete errato, ma ditemi, quale è la piu veloce cosa che sia?*

You haue not erred: but tel me, what is the swiftest thing that is?

La piu veloce cosa che sia, credo sia l'animo de l'huomo, perche in vn momento straccare tutto il mondo intorno, hora è quá, hora é lá, adesso in vn luogho, adesso in vn altro.

The swiftest thing that is, I beleeue it be the mynd of man, for in a moment he runneth al the world about, nowe he is here, and now he is there, now in one place, now in another.

577   *Quale è la piu libera cosa che sia?*

Which is the freest thing that is?

Io credo, pensiere.

I beleeue, thought.

578
Quale è la più forte coſa de que-
ſte tre, ó vino, ó una donna,
ouero la verità? ditemi di gra-
tia.

A dirui la verità, ſecondo il mio
baſſo parere, non eſſendo dot-
to, la verita mi pare, la più
forte.

Coſi credo anche io, perche le al-
tre due ſi poſſono vincer legi-
ermente.

E vero ſignor mio.

Which of theſe three thinges is
ſtrongeſt, either wine, or women, or els the truth? of cur-
teſie tel me.

To tel you the truth, after my
fooliſh opinion, and not being learned, Truth, me thin-
keth, is ſtrongeſt.

So thinke I alſo, becauſe the o-
ther two may lightly be o-
uercome.

It is true ſir.

579
Quale è la miglior coſa, che ſia
al mondo?
Io credo virtu, perche ſenza
virtu, non ſi puo far niente,
che ſia bono.

What is the beſt thing that is in
the world?
I beleeue vertue, for without
vertue, nothing can be done,
that is good.

FOX, Charles James (1749–1806)
English Whig Statesman. Credited with occasional enigmas.

580   I went to the Crimea; I stopped there, and I never went
there, and I came back again.

581   My *first* is expressive of no disrespect,
But I never call you by it when you are by;
If my *second* you still are resolved to reject,
As dead as my *whole*, I shall presently lie.

582   What is pretty and useful, in various ways,
Though it tempts some poor mortals to shorten their days;
Take one letter from it, and then will appear
What youngsters admire every day in the year;
Take two letters from it, and then, without doubt,
You are what that is, if you don't find it out.

583   Formed long ago, yet made to-day,
And most employed when others sleep;
What few would wish to give away,
And none would wish to keep.

584   You eat me, you drink me, describe me who can,
For I'm sometimes a woman, and sometimes a man.

585   What tho' some boast thro' ages dark
Their pedigree from Noah's Ark,
Painted on parchment nice;
I'm older still, for I was there,
And before Adam did appear
With Eve in Paradise.

For I was Adam, Adam I,
And I was Eve, and Eve was I,
    In spite of wind and weather;
Yet, mark me, Adam was not I,
Neither was Mrs. Adam I,
    Unless we were together.

Suppose then, Eve and Adam talking,
With all my heart; but if they're walking,
    There ends my simile;
For tho' I've tongue and often talk,
And tho' I've legs, yet when I walk
    It puts an end to me.

Not such an end but that I've breath;
Therefore to such a kind of death
    I make but small objection;
For soon I'm at my post anew,
And tho' oft Christian, yet 'tis true
    I die by Resurrection.

586   I will dedicate my *first* to the owner of my *second* provided he
       present me with my *whole* for my pains.

587   My first and second are the lot
           Of each delighted guest,
       When every sorrow is forgot
           At SPENCER'S social feast;
       But both together form a word
           Which, when those hours are pass'd
       We grieve to find, howe'er deferr'd,
           Must be pronounced at last.

FREDERICK II, King of Prussia (1712–86)

A noted patron of the arts Frederick the Great once invited Voltaire
(q.v.) to his palace using the following literary rebus. (Voltaire's reply
was equally ingenious: '*G a*' or '*J'ai grand appetit*'.)

588    $\dfrac{p}{venez}$ $à$ $\dfrac{ci}{100}$

FRENCH FOLK RIDDLES

Riddles mostly taken from Eugene Rolland's anthology *Devinettes ou
Enigmes Populaires de la France* (1877).

589   *Qui est-ce qui est noir et blanc,*
       Qui sautille a travers champs
       Et qui ressemble à monsieur le curé,
       Quand il est en train de chanter?

       (Who is it that is black and white and hops across fields and
       who sounds like the parson when he starts to sing?)

590   *Il y a un arbre derrière la maison qui porte des pommes hiver*
       comme été.

162

(There is a tree behind the house that bears apples both summer and winter.)

591 *Tantôt noir, tantôt blanc, J'ai des veines, mai point de sang!*

(Sometimes black, sometimes white, I have veins, but no blood!)

592 *Une dame rouge est enfermée dans une chambre, ou lui ouvre souvent la porte, mais elle ne peut sortir.*

(There is a red lady locked up in a room whose door is often opened yet she can never escape.)

593 *Je suis mère de mille enfants,*
Je porte une couronne en naissant,
Ceux qui veulent savoir mon sort,
Il faut m'ouvrir après ma mort.

(I am the mother of a thousand children and wear a crown at birth. Those who wish to know my destiny must open me up after my death.)

594 *Qu'est-ce qui n'a ni os ni arête,*
Qui porte du feu sur sa tête?

(Who is it who has neither bones nor spine and carries fire on his head?)

595 *Tant la fait le vif qui le mort,*
Chacun le peut aisément voir,
Personne ne le peut toucher.

(What is made by both the quick and the dead and which everyone can see clearly yet which nobody may touch?)

596 *Qui est celuy qui a un chapeau rouge et n'est point cardinal, a barbe et n'est point homme, les esperons et n'est point chevalier, sonne et se lève de grand matin et n'est point secretain?*

(Who is he who has a red hat yet is not a cardinal, has a beard yet is not a man, has spurs but is not a knight, wakes up early and calls out the time but is not a town crier?)

597 *Blanc, long, rond, velu par l'un des bouts, meurt sans enfants et naist pendu.*

(What is long, white and cylindrical, has hair at one end, dies without reproducing itself and is born hanging down?)

598 *Qui sont ceux qui tuent les gens sans être repris?*

(Who are they who kill with impunity?)

599 *Je suis capitaine de vingt-quatre soldats,*
Et sans moi Paris seroit pris.

(I am the captain of twenty-four soldiers and without me Paris would be captured.)

600   *Je sais que vous n'avez pas mon premier, mais je sais que vous êtes mon second, et je vous donnerai mon tout!*

(I know that you do not have my first but I know that you are my second, and I shall give you my whole!)

601   *Il faut être toujours mon premier, et mon second, et alors je vous donnerai mon tout!*

(You should always be my first, as well as my second, and then I shall give you my whole!)

FROLICS OF THE SPHINX, The (1812)
Collection of original riddles published by Munday & Slater, Oxford.

602   My first either male or female we find,
'Tis that which divides yet unites human kind;
My next those devoted to fashion pursue,
Both in dress and address they have it in view;
My whole on the verge, with one foot in the grave,
Oft' healthy and merry, diseases can brave.

603   Without my first man could not get his bread,
Its loss we loud lament and sorely dread,
And yet we find it painful, irksome, sore,
Oft' ask a riddance and its stay deplore.
My next has brought the bravest heroes low,
No courage, speed, nor force, could save the blow;

Yet still they live to fame and to renown,
And future triumphs may their efforts crown;
My whole at home is right above our head,
It decks the parlour, and adorns the bed.

604   My first is the half of, not end nor beginning,
My second that woman we kiss without sinning;
My whole is a known introducer of strangers,
A time-server too, and assistant in dangers.

605   My first adds a relish to savoury meat;
My second receives it before it is eat;
And yet 'tis a god who rules o'er rustic swains,
And tempts them to join in the sports of the plains;
My verse now descends from the flights of the muse,
To write that my whole is what kitchen maids use.

606   My first is a chaise, tho' of no modern fashion,
Nor like a barouche, form'd to splash and to dash on;
As my next is the thing he has daily to do,
A lawyer will make out much sooner than you;
I freely declare by my honour and soul,
As long as I *live* I shall ne'er be my whole.

607   His tail and great coat shew my first how to guess;
My next may be half, may be more, may be less;
My whole is a substance both solid and hard,
Which, saving in war, might be easily spar'd.

164

GAELIC FOLK RIDDLES

Riddles and translations taken from *Gaelic Riddles and Enigmas* (1938) by Alexander Nicholson.

608   *Tha toimhseachan agam ort,*
Chan e do cheann, chan e do chas,
Chan e d'eideadh, chan e d'fhalt,
Chan e ball a tha ad chorp,
Ach tha e ort, 's cha thomhais thu e.

(You owe me (an answer to) a riddle –
It is not your head, nor your foot,
It is not your clothing, nor your hair,
It is not a member of your body,
Yet it is on you, and you cannot guess it.)

609   *Is buige e na am brochan,*
Is cruaidhe e na an t-aran,
Bithidh e an comhnuidh an cuideachd an righ;
'Us chan 'eil iad air thalamh
Nach feum bhith 'ga ghabhail,
Is cha tig iad ro-mhath as a dhith.

(Softer than porridge,
Harder than bread,
It is always in the presence of the king;
And they are not on earth
But must partake of it,
And they cannot do well without it.)

610   *Tha suilean ann 's chan fhaic e ni,*
Tha e feumail a chum bidh'
Tha rusg 'g a chomhdachadh 's gach ball
Cha chaora 'us cha chraobh a th'ann.

(It has eyes, yet cannot see,
It is useful as food,
A skin covers its every part,
It is neither sheep nor tree.)

611   *Tha mi na's airde na beanntan an domhain,*
Agus gun bhreug tha mo leud gun thomhas,
Cumaidh an sealgair mi suas an cluais a ghunna,
Ged tha mi na's truime na mile tunna.

(I am higher than the mountains of the world,
And truly my breadth is immeasurable,
The hunter can sustain me in the nipple of his gun,
Though I am heavier than a thousand tons.)

612   *Theid mi null air mo dhrochaid ghlainne,*
Thig mi nall air mo dhrochaid ghlainne,
'Us ma bhriseas mo drochaid ghlainne,
Chan'eil an Albainn no an Eirinn
A chaireas, mo dhrochaid ghlainne.

(I shall go over my bridge of glass,
I shall return over my bridge of glass,
And if my bridge of glass breaks,
There is no one in Scotland or Ireland
Who will repair my bridge of glass.)

613   *Thainig eun gun iteag*
'Us laigh e air lag tobhtaig'.
Thainig eun gun bheul
'Us dh'ith e eun gun iteag.

(A bird without wing came
And lay on the hollow of a yard;
A bird without mouth came
And devoured the bird without wing.)

614   *Tha mile dearceag air an t-sliabh*
Nach itheadh neach a rugadh riamh;
Fasaidh iad ri oidhche bhriagh
Ach siubhlaidh iad 'nuair dhealras grian.

(A thousand berries on the moor
That none ever born would eat,
They grow during a beautiful night,
But they will vanish when the sun shines.)

615   *Chi mi, chi mi fada bhuam,*
Leth-cheud sineadh thar a' chuain.
Luchd gun fhuil, gun fheoil, gun anam,
A' leumadraich air talamh cruaidh.

(I see, I see far from me,
Fifty fathoms over the ocean,
Folk without blood, flesh, or soul,
Leaping on the hard ground.)

GALILEI, Galileo (1564–1642)
Italian scientist. Wrote occasional riddles.

616   *Mostro son io più strano, è più difforme*
    Che l'Arpia, la Sirena, o la Chimera;
    Nè in terra, in aria, in acqua è alcuna fiera,
    Ch'abbia di membra così varie forme.
Parte a parte non ho che sia conforme,
    Più che s'una sia bianca, o l'altra nera;
    Spesso di cacciator dietro ho una schiera,
    Che de' miei piè van rintracciando l'orme.
Nelle tenebre oscure è il mio soggiorno;
    Che se dall'ombre al chiaro lume passo,
    Tosto l'alma da me sen fugge, come
Sen fugge il sogno all'apparir del giorno,
    E le mie membra disunite lasso,
    E l'esser perdo con la vita, e'l nome.

(I am a monster, stranger and more alien than the Harpy, the Siren or the Chimera. Neither on land, in the air or in the sea is there a beast whose limbs can have so many shapes; no one piece of me conforms with another, anymore than if one is white, the other is black. A band of hunters often follows behind me looking for the tracks made by my feet. I inhabit the darkest places, and if I pass from the shadows into bright light my soul quickly slips away with the coming of the day and my tired limbs fall away, and I lose my being with my life and with my name.)

GARRICK, David (1717–79)

Playwright and actor/manager. Famous riddle ascribed to him, the first line of which appears in *Emma* by Jane Austen (q.v.).

617   Kitty, a fair but frozen maid,
       Kindl'd a flame I still deplore;
    The hood-wink'd boy I call'd in aid,
    Much of his next approach afraid,
       So fatal to my suit before.

At length, propitious to my pray'r,
    The little urchin came;
At once he sought the mid-way air
And soon he clear'd with dexterous care,
    The bitter relicks of my flame.

To Kitty Fanny now succeeds:
    She kindles slow but lasting fires;
With care my appetite she feeds;
Each day some willing victim bleeds,
    To satisfy my strange desires.

Say by what title or what name,
    Must I this youth address?
Cupid and he are not the same,
Tho' both can raise or quench a flame –
    I'll kiss you if you guess.

GASCOIGNE, George (c.1534–77)

English soldier-poet. Riddle composed in imitation of one on the same theme by Wyatt (q.v.) and published in *Hearbes* (1575).

618   A lady once did aske of me
       This preatie thing in privitie:
    'Good sir,' quod she, 'faine would I crave,
    One thing which you your selfe not have:
    Nor never had yet in times past,
    Nor never shall while life doth last.
    And if you seeke to find it out,
    You loose your labour out of doubt:
    Yet if you love me as you say,
    Then give it me for sure you may.'

GELLIUS, Aulus (130–*c*.180)
Roman lawyer and man of letters. Riddle occurs in *Noctes Atticae* Book XII, vi.

619   *Semel minusne an bis minus sit, nescio;*
       An utrumque eorum, ut quondam audivi dicier,
       Iovi ipsi regi noluit concedere.

       (I know not if he's minus once or twice,
       Or both of these, who would not give his place;
       As I once heard it said, to Jove himself.)

GERMAN FOLK RIDDLES
Folk riddles taken from Wossidlo *Mecklenburgische Volksüberlieferungen* (1897).

620   *Auf einem weissen See,*
       Da steht eine Rose rot,
       Und wer den weissen See will sprechen,
       Der muss die roten Rose brechen.

       (Upon a white lake there sits a red rose,
       But he who would speak with the white lake
       Must first break the red rose.)

621   *In meines Vaters Garten stehen Bäume, jeder Baum hat Zweige,*
       an den Zweigen hängen Wiegen, und in der Wiege liegen Kinder.

       (In my father's garden stand many trees. Each tree has many
       branches and on each branch hang cradles and in the cradles lie
       children.)

622   *Als ich war jung und schön,*
       Trug ich eine blaue Kron;
       Als ich war alt und steif,
       Banden sie mir einen Band um's Leib;
       Dann war ich geknüppelt und geschlagen,
       Und von Kaiser und König getragen.

       (When I was young and beautiful
       I wore a blue crown.
       When I was old and stiff
       They tied a rope around my body.
       Then I was cudgelled and beaten
       And dragged away from house and home.)

623   *Ich hab ein kleines Häuschen, wohn auch selber drein, ohne*
       Thür und ohne Fenster. Wenn ich raus will, brech ich durch die
       Wand.

       (I have a little house which I live in all alone,
       Without doors, without windows,
       And if I want to go out I have to break through the wall.)

624   *Ich bin ein armer Schmiedeknecht,*
       Hab keine Arm, zeig immer recht,

Hab keine Füss, muss immer gehen,
Und Tag und Nacht auf Schildwach stehen,
Und leg mich einmal zur Ruh,
Dann brummt noch jedermann dazu.

(I am a poor iron knight,
I have no arms but always point right.
I have no feet but I must always go
And must stand on duty both day and night through,
If ever I rest, all will complain.)

625 *Ich trage die meisten Lasten und habe keinen Rücken, durch*
mich kommen Menschen und Tiere von weitem über, und ich
allein bleib auf einer Stelle.

(I carry the heaviest loads and yet I have no back. Men and
beasts from far and wide tramp over me and I always stay in the
same place.)

626 *Wenn ich stillstehe und nicht gehe,*
Dann sind meine Bewohnten oft unzufrieden;
Wenn ich aber gehe und nicht stillstehe,
Dann kann ich sie oft in's Schweigen krigen.

(If I stand still and don't move
My occupants always complain,
But if I move and don't stand still
Then I can usually make them be silent.)

627 *Der Vater war kaum zur Welt, da sass der Sohn schon auf dem*
Dache.

(Scarcely was his father in this world when the son could be
found sitting on the roof.)

628 *Es sind vier Brüder in der Welt,*
Die haben sich zusammengestellt,
Der eine läuft und wird nicht matt,
Der zweite frisst und wird nicht satt,
Der dritte trinkt und wird nicht voll,
Der vierte singt, das klingt nicht wohl.

(There are four brothers in this world
That were all born together:
The first he runs and never wearies,
The second eats and is never full.
The third he drinks and is ever thirsty
And the fourth sings a song that is never good.)

629 *Hängt an der Wand, ohne Nagel und ohne Band.*

(There is a thing that hangs on the wall without nail or string.)

630 *Fleck auf Fleck und doch kein Nadelstich.*

(Patch upon patch and never a stitch.)

631   *Ich gehe alle Tag aus und bleibe dennoch stets zu Hause.*

(I'm out and about all day and yet I always stay at home.)

632   *Wenn man mich nicht hat, sucht man mich,*
Wenn man mich hat, bewahrt man mich nicht recht.

(He who lacks it seeks it,
He who has it mistreats it.)

633   *Ich bin gestorben und nicht geboren,*
Ich heirate meinen Vater, als ich einen Tag alt war,
Und eine Mutter hab ich nicht.

(I died without being born
And married my father when I was only a day old,
Yet I never had a mother.)

634   *Ich sass und ass, und von mir ass,*
Und unter mir ass, und oben mir ass,
Ratet überall, meine Herren, was ist das.

(I sat and I ate and from me one ate,
And below me one ate and above me one ate.
Tell me good sir what is that?)

635   *Es lag ein Mensch begraben tief,*
Sein Grab mit ihm herum lief,
Er war nicht im Himmel, er war nicht auf Erden,
Wo mag der Mensch gefunden werden?

(There is a man lies buried deep,
His grave spread all around him,
He was not in heaven, he was not on earth,
Where can that man be found?)

636   *Ungesaten, ungebraten, wird auf keinen Tisch getragen,*
doch Kaiser, König und Prinzessen müssen von der Speise
essen.

(Unseasoned, uncooked and served up at no table, yet emperors,
kings and princesses all partake of this fare.)

637   *Da sitzt was an der Wand, was gemacht ist ohne Hand,*
Es ist gemacht ohne Hand und ohne Waffen,
Wer das ratet, der soll die Nacht bei mir schlafen.

(Something hangs on the wall that was made by no hand.
Untouched it was made without hands, without tools. He who
can solve my riddle may sleep with me this night.)

638   *Die Wolke ist mein Mütterlein,*
Der Wind der soll mein Vater sein,
Mein Söhnlein ist der kühle Bach,
Die Frucht folgt mir als Tochter nach;
Der Regenbogen ist mein Bett,
Die Erde meine Ruhestätt,
Der Mensch, der ist mein Plagegeist,
Der mich bald gehn, bald kommen heisst.

(A cloud was my mother,
The wind is my father,
My son is the cool stream
And my daughter is the fruit of the land.
A rainbow is my bed,
The earth my final resting place
And I'm the torment of man.)

639   *In dem Winkel an der Mauern*
Pfleg ich auf mein Wild zu laueren,
Ohne Hund und Schiessgewehr,
Nezte spann ich um mich her,
Und mein Tisch bleibt selten leer.

(In a corner on the wall
I lie in wait for my prey
Without hounds or firearms.
I stretch my nets around me
And my table is seldom bare.)

640   *Arabien ist mein Vaterland,*
In Deutschland werd ich braun gebrannt,
In einer Mühle klein gemahlen,
Dann fühl ich heisse Wasserqualen,
Zuletzt giesst man Milch dazu,
Und trinkt mich dann in guter Ruh.

(My fatherland is Arabia,
Though in England they roast me brown.
I'm ground up inside a mill
And tortured with scalding water
And then they pour milk over me
And drink me at their leisure.)

641   *Erst war ich Pflanze, jetzt Staub,*
Dann schliesst mich Gold, Silber, Blei nach jeder Willkür ein.
Dem einen bin ich sehr beschwerlich,
Dem andern aber unentbehrlich.

(First I was a plant, then I was dust,
Then I was locked up in gold, silver or tin –
Each according to his whim.
To some I am a nuisance,
To others indispensable.)

642   *Sticht man mir die Augen aus,*
Dann reiss ich den Rachen auf.
Leinewand, Feder und Bapier,
Fress ich alles mit Pegier.

(Poke your fingers in my eyes,
And I will open wide my jaws.
Linen cloth, quills or paper,
My greedy lust devours them all.)

643   *Ein weisses Ei in einem grünen Haus,*
Brich's Haus entzwei und hol das Ei heraus.

Auf Weichem sammt, auf Weissem sammt, ist es gar schön
  gehegt,
Drum sage ich euch allesamt: kein Vogel hat's gelegt.

(There is a white egg in a green house,
And if you break open the house you can take the egg out.
But I tell you to a man, no bird ever laid it.)

644   *Die Sonne kocht's, die Hand bricht's,*
      Der Fuss tritt's, der Mund geniesst's.

(The sun cooked it, the hand broke it off,
The foot trod on it and the mouth enjoyed it.)

645   *Vier Beine hat's und läuft doch nicht,*
      Federn hat's und fliegt doch nicht,
      Immer steht es Mäuschenstill,
      Weiter nichts als Ruhe will.

(It has four legs but cannot run.
It has many feathers but cannot fly
And always stands as quiet as a mouse.)

GIFFORD, Humphrey (*fl.* 1580)

Minor English poet. Riddles contained in *Posie of Gillowflowers* (1580).

646   A mightie blacke horse, with gallant white winges,
      Within his graund paunch beares many straunge things:

Hée oft doth travayle for masters avayle,
And carges his bridle tyed fast to his tayle.
In going hée flyes twixt earth and the ayre,
And oft, where they would not, his riders doth beare:
Hée hath divers eies, and yet cannot sée,
I pray you doe tell mée what may this beast bée?

647   A certaine thing liveth in place néere at hande,
      Whose nature is straunge, if it bée well scand:
It sées without eyes, it flyes without winges,
It runnes without feete, it workes wondrous things.
To places far distant it often doth rome:
Yet never departeth, but taryes at home.
If thou doe it covet to féele or to sée,
Thy labour is lost, for it may not bée.

648   From south and west commeth a straunge warlike nation,
      Attirde and appareld in wonderfull fashion:
In garments milke white, these people are clad,
Which strike and oppresse both good men and bad
But favour they shew in dealing their blowes,
And save him from danger, ech on his way goes.
And on his backe caryes dead bodyes great store,
Which with their thicke buffets had beate them before,
Great furies are kindled at end of the fray:
Which makes this straunge nation all vanish away.

649 A certain dead creature in mine armes I take,
With her back to my bosome, great glée doth shée make,
As thus I doe hold her, she greatly doth chéere mée,
And wel are they pleased that sée me and heare mée.
Whilst erst it remayned in forest and field,
It silent remayning, no speech forth did yéeld.
But since she of life, by death was deprived,
With language shée speaketh, mens sprites are revived.

650 Two are we in name, though in substaunce but one,
First framed by arte then finisht with mone.
Before we are ready, for those that will buy,
Through greatnesse of torment, wée howle and wée cry.
Yet féele we no griefe, for all this anoy.
Great numbers by us have comfort and ioy,
Who when for their profits we have done what wée may,
They then do reiect us, and cast us away.

GIRL'S OWN BOOK, The (19th century)
Compiled by Mrs Child, author of *The Mother's Book, Frugal Housewife*, etc. Examples from thirteenth edition (1844).

651 I was, but am not; ne'er shall be again;
Myriads possess'd me, and possess'd in vain;
To some I proved a friend, to some a foe;
Some I exalted, others I laid low;
To some I gave the bliss that knows no sigh,
And some condemn'd to equal misery.
If conscious that we met, and but to sever,
Now say to whom you bade farewell for ever.

652 Of a brave set of brethren I stand at the head,
And to keep them quite warm I cram three in a bed;
Six of them in prison I cruelly put;
And three I confine in a mean little hut;
To escape my fell grasp three reside in the sky;
And, tho' strange it may seem, we have all but one eye;
Our shapes are as various as wondrous our use is,
Of Science the source, the soul of the Muses.

653 I'm a singular creature, pray tell me my name –
I partake of my countrymen's glory and fame,
I daily am old, and I daily am new,
I am praised, I am blamed, I am false, I am true –
I'm the talk of the nation, while I'm in my prime,
But forgotten when once I've outlasted my time.
In the morning no Miss is more courted than I,
In the evening you see me thrown carelessly by.
Take warning, ye Fair – I like you have my day,
But, alas! you like me must grow old and decay.

654 I'm seen in the moon, but not in the sun;
I'm put in a pistol, but not in a gun;
I'm found in a fork, but not in a knife;
I belong to the parson, but not to his wife;
I go with the rogue, but not with the thief;

I'm seen in a book, but not in a leaf;
I stay in a town, but not in the street;
I go with your toes, but not with your feet.

655 *Le nouvel enrichi porté sur mon premier.*
Qui peut à l'indigent refuser mon dernier,
Ne vaut pas l'animal qui mange mon entier.

(The newly wealthy man is carried around on my first. And he
who refuses the needy my second is worse than the animal which
eats my whole.)

656 My first is a preposition;
My second is a composition;
And my whole is an acquisition.

657 *Mon tout est grand, fameux en tout pays;*
Otez moi mon second, je suis aux ennemis!
Otez un pied de plus, ah! ce sera bien pis.

(My whole is great, and known throughout the world.
Take away my second and I am in the hands of the enemy.
Remove one more – ah that will be worse.)

658 My first is to multiply; my second we ought all to avoid; my
whole the most avaricious will give, and the poorest are seldom
willing to receive.

659 With all things I'm found, yet to nothing belong;
Though a stranger to crowds, yet I'm still in a throng;
And though foreign to music and all its soft powers,
In songs and in epigrams, ladies, I'm yours;

Though a friend to true glory, I'm ne'er in renown,
Though no kingdom's without me, I hold not a crown;
Both with kings and with beggars my birthright I claim,
But enough has been told to discover my name.

660 *Plus d'un auteur, dans mon entier,*
A dit des choses inutiles;
Plus d'un sage, dans mon premier,
Admire la nature et méprise les villes;
Plus d'un traître, sur mon dernier,
Cache par un baiser mille projets hostiles.

(More than one author has said worthless things in my whole.
More than one learned man has admired nature and scorned the
town in my first. More than one traitor has hidden a thousand
evil thoughts with a kiss on my last.)

661 The sage conductor of a hero's son;
That hero's name, who through great dangers run;
A noble fish which is by most admired;
A liquid that by authors is desired;
A virtue that by all should be acquired.
If these initials are connected right,
They'll bring a charming science to your sight.

662

663 The wicked must  ánd eeee

664 What word is that?

665  Mr. E.

666 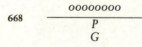 $\dfrac{liers}{sans}$

667 *L. N. E. Ne. O. P. Y.*

668 $\dfrac{ooooooo}{\dfrac{P}{G}}$

GIRL'S OWN PAPER, The (1880–1965)

Companion journal to the *Boy's Own Paper*, which as well as articles on homemaking, short stories, and history also ran a regular puzzle page. Examples taken from issues for 1882–83.

669   My first is often seen in air,
And travels through the cloudland there;
In fam'd Olympian games of yore
Conspicuous share it always bore;
But now condemned to rail or road,
It plods with varying speed and load.
My next is found beneath the crust
Of earth, in darkness, heat and dust.

Thou canst not own it, nor can he,
Because it must belong to me;
And if I were to give it thee,
Its very name would cease to be.
Combine the two – from refuse made,
A brilliant colouring is display'd.
Nothing is waste, good comes from ill,
And artists gain by patient chemists' skill.

670   My first no life nor feeling blesses;
My second everyone possesses.
And nothing more affronts my second
Than when it like my first is reckoned:
United, they a being show,
The greatest nuisance that we know.

671   Go, seek my first in heaven; my next,
In northern sea:
On earth or floating through the air,
My whole will be.

GLAUKOS RIDDLE, The (n.d.)

Oldest recorded riddle in the Greek language, found in Apollodorus. By solving the riddle, Glaukos, son of King Minos of Crete, was restored to life by the seer Polyidos.

672   In the fields grazeth a calf whose body changeth hue thrice in the space of each day. It is first white, then red, and at the last black.

GOETHE, Johann Wolfgang von (1749–1832)

Major German literary figure. Various riddles occur in his correspondence with Schiller (q.v.) and, towards the end of his life, in his letters to Marianne von Willemer (the original of 'Suleika' in the *Westöstlicher Divan* poems).

673   *Ein Bruder ist's von vielen Brüdern,*
In allem ihnen völlig gleich,
Ein nötig Glied von vielen Gliedern,
In eines großen Vaters Reich;
Jedoch erblickt man ihn nur selten,
Fast wie ein eingeschobnes Kind:
Die andern lassen ihn nur gelten
Da, wo sie unvermögend sind.

(There is a brother among many brothers, exactly like all the others; a necessary member of the family in their mighty father's kingdom. Yet he's only rarely seen, like a shy child pushed forward occasionally by the others who grant that he has a quality that they lack.)

674   *Zwei Worte sind es, kurz, bequem zu sagen,*
Die wir so oft mit holder Freude nennen,
Doch keineswegs die Dinge deutlich kennen,
Wovon sie eigentlich den Stempel tragen.

176

Es tut gar wohl in jung- und alten Tagen,
Eins an dem andern kecklich zu verbrennen;
Und kann man sie vereint zusammen nennen,
So drückt man aus ein seliges Behagen.

Nun aber such ich ihnen zu gefallen
Und bitte, mit sich selbst mich zu beglücken;
Ich hoffe still, doch hoff ich's zu erlangen:

Als Namen der Geliebten sie zu lallen,
In einem Bild sie beide zue erblicken,
In einem Wesen beide zu umfangen.

(Two words describe it, each short and easy to say and often spoken with great joy, yet we are seldom certain what they truly denote. It appears in both youth and old age, and if you can name it in both then that is bliss itself. But now, if I may, I would like to ask you to grant me this thing. I hope quietly, yet I think I will succeed and stammer out the name of my beloved. And see both its components in one picture, capture both in one being.)

GREEK ANTHOLOGY, The
Ancient Greek miscellany. Riddles occur in Book 14.

675 I am the black child of a white father; a wingless bird, flying even to the clouds of heaven. I give birth to tears of mourning in pupils that meet me, and at once on my birth I am dissolved into air.

676 One wind, two ships, ten sailors rowing, and one steersman directs both.

677 My whole is an island; my first the lowing of a cow, and my second what a creditor says.

678 I once saw a beast running straight on its back through a wood cut by the steel, and its feet touched not the earth.

679 I alone delight in intercourse with women at their husbands' own request.

680 Slain, I slew the slayer, but even so he went not to Hades; but I died.

681 I slew my brother, my brother again slew me; our death is caused by our father, and after our death we both kill our mother.

682 There are two sisters german; one gives birth to the other, and herself having brought forth is born from the other, so that being sisters and of one blood they are actually sisters and mothers in common.

683 My name, if you add a letter to it, produces a blow of the foot, but, if not, it will never allow man's feet to stumble.

684   Only to me it is allowed to have open intercourse with women at the request of their husbands, and I alone mount young men, grown men, and old men, and virgins, while their parents grieve.

685   If you look at me I look at you too. You look with eyes, but I not with eyes, for I have no eyes. And if you like, I speak without a voice, for you have a voice, but I only have lips that open in vain.

686   Wood gave birth to me and iron reformed me, and I am the mystic receptacle of the Muses. When shut I am silent, but I speak when you unfold me. Ares alone is the confidant of my conversation.

687   I was born in the mountains and a tree was my mother; the fire was my father and I am a blackened mass. If my father melts me inside a deep vessel of clay, I protect from wounds the chariot of the sea.

688   I have nothing inside me and everything is inside me, and I grant the use of my virtue to all without charge.

689   No one sees me when he sees, but he sees me when he sees not; he who speaks not speaks, and he who runs not runs, and I am untruthful though I tell all truth.

690   If you had taken me in my youth, haply you would have drunk the blood shed from me; but now that time has finished making me old, eat me, wrinkled as I am, with no moisture in me, crushing my bones together with my flesh.

GRIMM, Jacob (1785–1863) and Wilhelm (1786–1859)
German folklorists best known for the fairytale collection *Kinder- und Hausmärchen* (1812–15) first published in English in 1823. This enigmatic question requires special knowledge (cf. Ilo Riddle) and occurs in the story 'The Riddle'. (This version taken from *The Green Fairy Book c.*1892) by Andrew Lang.)

691   What is this? . . . One slew none and yet killed twelve?

GUESS BOOK, The (c.1820)
Chapbook printed by William Davison of Alnwick (1781–1858).

692   Made of two bodies join'd,
        Without foot or hand;
        And yet you will find
        I can both run and stand.

693   In almost every house I'm seen,
        (No wonder, then, I'm common),
        I'm neither man, nor maid, nor child,
        Not yer a married woman.

694   To rich and poor we useful are;
        And yet for our reward,
        By both at last we're thrown away,
        Without the least regard.

695   I am a busy active creature,
        Fashion'd for the sport of nature,
        Nimbly skip from tree to tree,
        Under a well-wrought canopy;
        Bid Chloe then to Mira tell
        What's my name and where I dwell.

696   My sides are firmly lac'd about,
          Yet nothing is within;
        You'll think my head is strange indeed,
          Being nothing else but skin.

GUESS ME (c.1872)

Compiled and arranged by Frederick D'Arros Planche and illustrated by George Cruikshank, amongst others. A useful compendium of literary and pictorial puzzles.

697   Wealth and power immense I give,
        No feeling have, and yet I live.
        Before mankind the earth had trod,
        I held possession of the sod.
        Now in the tomb of ages sought,
        Again to earth's fair surface brought
        A proof of the Eternal's plan.
        I have so much to do with man,
        Enliven all his chequer'd lot,
        I cheer the palace and the cot.
        And raise for mortals every hour
        A spirit of tremendous power.
        Though short my life, yet I supply,
        A thousand blessings e'er I die.
        And in the scriptures you may see
        A prophet once referred to me.

698   Two brothers are we, with five children a piece,
        A number which rarely is known to increase;
        We are large, hard, and black, we are soft, white, and small,
        But without us, mankind could do nothing at all.
        We laboured with Adam in tilling the ground,
        Yet in the queen's court we may always be found.
        Without us, no vessel the ocean could roam,
        Yet though we go forth, you will find us at home,
        Although for our colour and size you may flout us.
        You never would hire a maid servant without us.
        Although by the chemists we're used every day,
        Yet we aided Brinvilliers her victims to slay.
        If you can't find us out, why to cut short our story,
        When you sit down to dinner you have us before ye.

699   My *first* I may in truth declare –
        Its name and nature both is air;
        My *second* is a perfect bore,
        Yet make sweet music evermore;
        My *whole* in many a crowded street
        Lies in its bed beneath your feet.

700   A busy insect we in summer see,
       Pattern of patient industry;
       Next we have a little word,
       Applied to man, creation's lord;
       My *third*'s an insect, small and gray,
       Type of luxury and decay.
       Join these together, and you'll see
       A beast of power and majesty.

701   Without my *first*, be you black or white,
       Day would be dreary as the night;
       When in the battle danger beckoned,
       The brave were always in my *second*.
       Whene'er the weeds begin to grow,
       To use my *third* pray don't be slow.
       My *whole*, a famous British story,
       Is often called its author's glory.

702   In cultur'd plot or woodland wild,
       Where Flora, deck'd in gorgeous bloom,
       Profusely strews her choicest gems,
       And violets shed their sweet perfume.

       Where erst rests his mighty frame,
       And all his slimy spoils are stor'd;
       Where Father Thames his tribute brings,
       Anon to swell old Neptune's hoard.

       Where earth primeval forest stood,
       Now deep interr'd beneath the ground;
       Each scene with diligence explore,
       In each, in all, may I be found.

       In one the weary find a friend,
       I yield relief, assuage their pain,
       In sickness soothe, in death support,
       E'en after death, awhile, sustain.

703   I dwell in hall and castle;
           In country and in town,
       And e'en in lowly cottage
           My presence may be found.

       I'm often gay and witty,
           Sometimes cast down and sad;
       All mankind are my captives,
           From ancient sire to lad.

       I count among my victims,
           The young of noble dower;
       While e'en yon peasant maid has felt
           Ere now my subtle power.

       I'm not confined to country,
           To age, rank, time, or place;
       In high, in low, in rich or poor,
           I show my changing face.

704 I float in the air and I creep o'er the earth;
I'm at home in the skies, yet a tear gives me birth.
I dance in the sunbeams, I sleep in the shade,
Yet the mightiest engines to me look for aid,
I'm simple in aspect, yet deep as a well,
And when ruffled in temper a terrible swell.
I run without legs, and I fly without wings,
No acrobat lithe so familiar with springs.
In swiftness my pace has been seldom outdone,
And no race-horse can equal me in a long run.
Though as I haste on, I get many a fall;
Such mishaps scarce retard my great progress at all.
Like a lion I range through the woods with a roar,
Like an eagle high up in the sunshine I soar,
I am hot, I am cold, I am rough, I am smooth,
Though my anger affrights, yet my melodies soothe.
Art, Science, and Commerce to me bend the knee,
But o'er land, sea, and sky, I go fearless and free.
A traveller condemned through all nations to roam,
Yet I'm constant in charming and cleansing your home.
Great, glorious, ethereal, grand, mighty, and wild –
Still I'm merely a toy in the hands of a child.

705

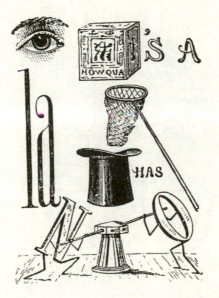

706

707

708

HALEVI, Jehudah (*c*.1086–1141)
Spanish Hebrew poet. Riddles contained in *Cuzari* (*Al-Khazari*).

709   What is it that one lays naked in the grave and yet it does not suffer death, it begets children there, it cares for them attentively, until they appear fully dressed?

710   A little staff, yet of inestimable value, green in colour as if consumed by love-sorrow, a hollow body yet with a brave heart, it casts down heroes, it brings pain to many, it hastens to fill itself properly, it does not accomplish its task with empty mouth. And five servants are ready at one time, cheerfully executing its commands. Now it likes to communicate song and elegance, now it is able to soften a prince's heart, it can make peace, it can bring about war. Tell what it is, what it means.

711   What is it, then, at which our heart laughs merrily when it weeps, but makes our heart sad and mournful when it shines brightly?

712   What is it that's blind with an eye in its head,
        But the race of mankind its use cannot spare;
    Spends all its life in clothing the dead,
        But always itself is naked and bare?

HERVARAR SAGA, The

Ancient Norse saga. Riddles occur in the story of Heidrek and
Gestumblindi.

713   I would that I had that which I had yesterday. Guess O King, what
that was: – Exhauster of men, retarder of words, yet originator of
speech.

714   What was the drink that I had yesterday? It was neither wine nor
water, mead nor ale, nor any kind of food; and yet I went away
with my thirst quenched.

715   Who is that clanging one who traverses hard paths which he has
trod before? He kisses very rapidly, has two mouths and walks on
gold alone.

716   What is that huge one that passes over the earth, swallowing lakes
and pools? He fears the wind, but he fears not man, and carries on
hostilities against the sun.

717   What is that huge one that controls many things and of which half
faces towards Hell? It saves people's lives and grapples with the
earth, if it has a trusty friend.

718   What lives in high mountains? What falls in deep valleys? What
lives without breathing? What is never silent?

719   What is the marvel which I have seen outside Delling's doorway?
It points its head towards Hell and turns its feet to the sun.

720   What is the marvel which I have seen outside Delling's doorway?
– White fliers smiting the rock, and black fliers burying themselves
in sand!

721   What is the marvel which I have seen outside Delling's doorway?
This creature has ten tongues, twenty eyes, forty feet, and walks
with difficulty.

722   What is the marvel which I have seen outside Delling's doorway?
It flies high, with a whistling sound like the whirring of an eagle.
Hard it is to clutch.

723   What is the marvel which I have seen outside Delling's doorway?
It has eight feet and four eyes, and carries its knees higher than its
body.

724   Who are the girls who fight without weapons around their lord?
The dark red ones always protect him, and the fair ones seek to
destroy him.

725   Who are the merry-maids who glide over the land for their father's
pleasure? They bear a white shield in winter and a black one in
summer.

726   Four walking, four hanging, two pointing the way, two warding
off the dogs, one, generally dirty, dangling behind!

727   Who is that solitary one who sleeps in the grey ash, and is made
from stone only? This greedy one has neither father nor mother.
There will he spend his life.

728   I saw maidens like dust. Rocks were their beds. They were black and swarthy in the sunshine, but the darker it grew, the fairer they appeared.

HOLME RIDDLES, The (1650–75)
Anthology of riddles collected by the Randle Holme family of Chester.

729   who weare those that fought before the[y] were borne

730   that wch thou lookest on o traveller is a sepulcher wthout a carcasse & a carcasse wthout a sepulcher & how can that be

731   w^{t} is that mak[e]s tears without sorow tak[e]s his journey to heaven but dys by the way is begot wth another yet that other is not begot wthout it

732   j was round and small like a p[e]arle then long & slender as brave as an earle since like a hermit j lived in a cell & now like a rogue in the wide world j dwell

733   ther is a body wthout a hart that hath a tongue & yet no head buried it was ere it was made & loud doth speek & yet is dead

734   ther is a thing no biger than a plumb that l[e]ads the king from towne to towne

735   w^{t} is that as lords keep in there pockets & begrs throw a way

736   though j be throwne from place to place & al unseemly as j am the nisest dame in the towne canot liue wthout me

737   sisly sage sits in her kage & all her children dys for age yet she is a live & lusty

738   As j was walking late at night, j through a window chanced to spy: a gallant with his hearts delight he knew not that j was so nigh: he kissed her & close did sit to little pretty wanton Gill untill he did her favour get & likewise did obtaine his wille.

739   There is a bush fit for the nonce
That beareth pricks and precious stones
The fruit in fear some ladies pull.
Tis smooth and round and plump and full . . .
They put it in, and then they move it,
Which makes it melt, and then they love it.
So what was round, plump, full and hard
Grows lank and thin and dull and marred . . .

740   there is a thing wch hath five chins 2 hath beards 2 hath none, & one it hath but half an one.

HOME AMUSEMENTS (c.1890)

Collection of over 400 riddles of various kinds plus forfeits, parlour games, etc. Compiled by 'Peter Puzzlewell Esq, of Rebus Hall'.

741 To a word of consent, add one half of a fright;
Next subjoin what you never beheld in the night;
These rightly connected, you'll quickly obtain
What numbers have seen, but will ne'er see again.

742 I from Siberia's frozen realms am brought,
Or in the wilds of Canada am sought:
But soon, by art, a domicile I form,
At once convenient, elegant and warm.
Within the compass of this pretty cell,
But two inhabitants can hope to dwell;
Here, snug and warm, in spite of wind and weather,
They both may live most lovingly together.
When spring returns, with blooming flow'rets gay,
My fickle inmates from my shelter stray;
And through the summer months inconstant roam,
Till winter's cold recalls the wanderers home.

743 My body's taper'd fine and neat,
I've but one eye, yet am complete;
You'd judge me, by my equipage,
The greatest warrior of the age;
For when you have survey'd me round,
Nothing but steel is to be found;
Yet men I ne'er was known to kill,
Though ladies' blood I often spill.

744 In wealth I abound; in water I stand;
As a fencer I'm valued all over the land;
At Venice I'm famous; by farmers I'm prized;
Respected by law, yet by huntsmen despised;
Consternation and ruin ensue when I break;
And the beasts of the forest advantage on't take.

745 Though from York and from Yarmouth I'm never away,
You'll find me always at the end of the day:
In years though I am, and have been all my life,
I'm found with a hautboy, though not with a fife:
I'm always in play – and with some little boy
Am constantly found, deep engaged with his toy.

746 My first a blessing sent to earth,
Of plants and flowers to aid the birth;
My second surely was design'd
To hurl destruction on mankind:
My whole a pledge from pardoning heaven,
Of wrath appeased and crimes forgiven.

747 He that in music takes delight,
And he that sleeps secure by night,
And he who sails too near the land,
And he that's caught by law's strong hand;

He who his time in taverns spends,
And he that courts of law attends;
He that explains heraldic signs,
And he that works in silver mines, –
Are all acquainted well with me:
My name you surely now must see.

748   My first is a substance that's light;
My second makes many things tight:
My whole is the key to delight.

749   My first's the source of various good,
To man and beast supplying food;
My next results from cold or fear,
But quickly flies when aid is near:
My whole strikes terror to the heart,
And sometimes rends my first apart.

750   I am by nature soft as silk,
By nature too as white as milk;
I am a constant friend to man,
And serve him every way I can.
When dipped in wax or plunged in oil,
I make his winter evenings smile:
By India taught, I spread his bed,
Or deck his fav'rite Celia's head;
Her gayest garbs I oft compose,
And, ah! – sometimes – I wipe her nose.

751   A word that's composed of three letters alone,
    And is backward and forward the same;
Without speaking a word makes its sentiments known,
    And to beauty lays principal claim.

752   A word if you find, that will silence proclaim,
Which spelt backward or forward will still be the same;
And next you must search for a feminine name,
That spelt backward or forward will still be the same;
And then for an act or a writing, whose name
Spelt backward or forward will still be the same;
A fruit that is rare, whose botanical name
Spelt backward or forward is ever the same;
A note used in music, that time will proclaim,
And backward or forward alike is its name;
The initials connected a title will frame,
Which is justly the due of the fair married dame,
And which backward or forward will still be the same.

753   Five hundred, a thousand, and one,
    With proper attention dispose;
And that kind of light will appear,
    Which the sun in a fog often shows.

754   Ye riddling folk, disclose my name,
    No doubt you quickly will descry it;
The self-same characters proclaim
    The fruit, and how you'd wish to buy it.

755   In camps about the centre I appear;
       In smiling meadows seen throughout the year;
       The silent angler views me in the streams,
       And all must trace me in their morning dreams;
       First in each mob conspicuous I stand,
       Proud of the lead and ever in command;
       Without my power no mercy can be shown,
       Or soft compassion to their hearts be known;
       Each sees me in himself, yet all agree
       Their hearts and persons have no charm for me;
       The chemist proves my virtue upon ore,
       For, touch'd by me, he changes it to more.

756   Though my first's a simple thing,
       Yet many hundreds from it spring,
       To men and animals a treat,
       For each will freely of it eat.
       Now I declare it is a flower
       That sweetly scents the verdant bower. –
       And when Aurora's tints are spread,
       Behold my second leave its bed;
       Undaunted by a sense of fear,
       Its courage now will soon appear;
       For, when contesting for a prize.
       It never yields, though sometimes lies. –
       My whole, I now beg leave to say,
       Is always deck'd in gay array.

HOMER'S RIDDLE
The riddle put to Homer by fishermen on Ios that is said to have caused his death.

757   What we caught we threw away; what we didn't catch we kept.

HOOD, Tom (1835–74)
Son of the satirical poet and magazine editor, Thomas Hood (1799–1845). Wrote novels, verse, and a number of children's books (which he also illustrated) as well as editing *Fun* magazine. Examples taken from the posthumously published *Excursions into Puzzledom* (1879), written with his sister, Mrs F. F. Broderip (herself the author of many children's books).

758   We sought again the pleasant cot,
           And there revealed the worst,
       That we poor travellers could not
       Get out at all, unless we got
           What I shall call my First.

       That her goodman was not thereat,
           The wife was sorely vext;
       But by the fire awhile we sat,
       And pussy, dozing on the mat,
           Indulged us with my Next.

We had not very long to wait;
  The goodman, worthy soul,
Returned, and then with pleasure great
Unlocked for us the wicket-gate:
  For which we thanked my Whole.

759   Go, seek me on the coast,
  You'll find me on the sea;
The wooden walls we boast
  Can show you lots of me.
In men-of-war I'm found,
  And yet, the truth to speak,
In tempests I'll be bound
  In me for them you'll seek.
Nay – one remark I'll make;
  Whate'er may be your mien,
When you your 'bearings' take,
  Therein shall I be seen,
Come guess me if you can,
  My mazy meaning follow;
Then seize me like a man,
  And pour me out, and swallow!

760   I'm in the earth, I'm in the sea,
The air from me is never free;
The fire alone, the only one
Of all the elements I shun.
And yet in heat I may be found,
Though I the Arctic region bound;
In Europe's little continent
I do not dwell; – I am content
With the vast globe's three larger shares,
And there I settle my affairs.
I'm leader of a chosen band,
Who do their work in every land,
Under five captains; – chief am I
By reason of priority.
Yet, though I'm vague, indefinite,
Not certain of my meaning quite,
By me in every action led,
I'm in your heart, and in your head!
I point your aims, if not your ends,
I'm with your slaves, if not your friends,
I lead your armies, not your fleets,
Live in your lands, not in your streets.
I dwell in hate, but not in love,
Mix in your rage, your anger move.
If in your youth I ne'er engage,
You're sure to find me in your age!

761   In early Spring, one silent night,
      The bold Sir Wilfred strayed
Beneath his lady's lattice bright,
      To sing a serenade.
He sat him down upon my First,
And there his loving lay rehearsed.

A silvery mist hung o'er the scene,
      Where thus he breathed his vows;
And dewdrops gemmed the herbage green,
      And decked the budding boughs.
But ah! Sir Wilfred should have reckoned
The grass was sure to be my Second.

Next morn he did his foot-page call,
      And bade at once repair
To gay Lord Guthlac's festive hall,
      And him this message bear –
'Tell hib I'be ill – upol by soul –
Al cal't to-dight atteld by Whole!'

762   When first it was created, earth
With this at once began its birth;
And so with this, whatever thence
Springs into being, must commence;
And with it, too, you may depend,
This vast terrestrial orb must end;
It dwells not in palatial halls,
But 'mid the humble cabin's walls.
Nor land nor sea can it contain,
It shuns the heart, but haunts the brain;
It breathes in slumber, but it flies
The vigil of the sleepless eyes;
In one of man's most famous works –
    The telegraphic links that bind
    The distant races of mankind –
It in the cable's centre lurks.
In labour it delights, yet still
It shuns the mart, the mine, the mill;
It closes in, with solemn gloom,
The farthest vista of the tomb,
So silently, it makes no sound
To break a stillness so profound;
Yet in life's hubbub takes its place
With treble zest and rapid pace.
Say, would you at its home arrive?
Go seek it in the busy hive!

763   I'm the dream of the maiden who wishes to wed,
And my name may be Dick, Tom, Jim, Harry, or Ned;
Yet when she's a lover too shy he may be
To say to a biped – not featherless – me;
And his ears, as an infant, my chimes may have heard,
And custom has therefore his title conferred.

No matter, young Love, by my aid 'tis confessed,
Has planted a dart in her innocent breast,
So her future she trusts, for good fortune or ill,
To that fortunate worshipper, happen what will;
For if clouds of disaster should darken Heav'n's cope
She thinks I shall shine as the beacon of hope.
So they marry at last – may their future be pleasant –
And I, all in white, at the wedding am present.

764   Above us on the cliff the samphire springs,
      Salt with the brine of many a stormy night;
Close to the chalk the hornèd poppy clings;
      The grey gull shrieks and holds its seaward flight.
And see, low-roofed, where doth to seaward front
My humble First, exposed to tempest's brunt.

Thence starts at break of day the fisher brave,
      Launches his skiff, and quickly is afloat
To spread his toils beneath the heaving wave,
      And load with finny spoil his little boat:
And aye with curious eye a watch doth keep
Upon my Second's treasures from the deep.

What is it glitters in the dripping mesh?
      A ring – perchance from Cæsar's galley lost!
Lost years ago, it visits earth afresh; –
      Say, what collector would begrudge its cost?
The wealthy antiquary, lucky soul,
Buys it at once to grace my costly Whole.

765

766

191

HOROZCO, Sebastian de (16th century)
Spanish poet. Riddles occur in *Cancionero*.

767 *Dezidme, qual es la cosa milagrosa*
que de bocas tres alcanza,
y es en sí tan tenebrosa
y espantosa
que por todas fuego lanza?
Una boca desta alhaja come paja,
nunca bebe con ninguna;
otra tiene tal ventaja;
aunque trabaja,
que con pan se desayuna.

Aunque parece ser cosa espantosa,
y que su ser no se alcança,
quedará sin ser dudosa
ni escabrosa,
y sin ninguna dudança.

(Tell me, what is the miraculous thing which has three mouths
and is so dark and dreadful that it spits fire through each of
them? One mouth eats straw and never drinks, another eats
bread for breakfast. Although it seems a terrible monster and its
identity is hidden from view, its nature can soon be discovered
and established beyond any doubt.)

768 *Doze hijos quasi iguales*
vi á un padre que tenía
y cada qual destos tales,
legítimas, naturales
sus treynta hijas habia.
La mitad de aquestas era
de clara y blanca color,
y por contraria manera
la otra mitad saliera
de turbio y triste negror.

Y vi qu'estas hijas tales
de tal suerte procedian
que todas eran mortales,
tambien eran inmortales
segun que se sucedian.
Y trataban comunmente
con los hombres como amigas,
pero despues de repente
en el tipo mas urgente
huyan como enemigas.

(I saw a father who had twelve almost identical sons, each of
which had thirty legitimate daughters. Of these, half were shining white whilst the other half were a gloomy black. And I saw
that these daughters were both mortal and immortal, and though
at first friendly towards men would later flee like enemies.)

192

ILO RIDDLE, The (n.d.)
Well-known German *Halslösungsrätsel* of folk origin.

769   *Auf Ilo geh ich,*
Auf Ilo steh ich,
Auf Ilo bin ich hübsch und fein,
Rat't, meine Herren, was soll das sein.

(On Ilo I walk, on Ilo I am handsome and smart. Tell me, good sirs, what can that be.)

INDIAN FOLK RIDDLES
Folk riddles from various sources, including *Popular Poetry of the Baloches* (1907) by M. L. Dames.

770   You are a tribe blind at night, united in oppression and violence. You are strong in attack, but you are wretched creatures in form.

771   The good God has caused a tree to grow by his will on the face of the earth. Its root is one, its branches two. One is dust, the other ashes.

772   I saw two sisters embracing, very happy at the embrace. There is not the slightest difference in their appearance; one is blind and the other can see.

773   I saw a fort with closed doors, full of bitter enemies, their heads strengthened with stings, and furious to fight. First they destroy themselves, and then set fire to their enemies.

JERROLD, Douglas (1803–57)
Playwright, journalist, and friend of Dickens.

774   Sam Bowsprit was a seaman true
   As ever loved his girl or bowl;
No landsman's tricks Sam Bowsprit knew,
   Nor ever skulk'd through lubber's hole.

Sam Bowsprit now would oft the land,
   From top-gallant and head, descry;
And with a helmsman's skilful hand
   Could steer through a mosquito's eye.

And now, close off Trafalgar bay,
   The Gallic squadrons heave in sight;
England expects; and we obey:
   No British seaman shuns the fight.

But, ah! though England gains the day,
   The loss to England we deplore;
Since victory bears my *first* away –
   The gallant Nelson is no more.

A quarter-master now behold
   As Sam stands by the hour-glass,
My *second* and *whole* he does unfold
   While the minutes cheerless pass.

Yet let not fearful terrors spread,
  The foe we yet shall dare to meet;
For though our gallant Nelson's dead,
  His spirit lives throughout the fleet.

JOHN FALKIRK'S CARICHES (n.d.)

Chapbook attributed to Dougal Graham (*c*.1724–?), Glasgow bellman, writer, and publisher. (Reprinted in *John Cheap the Chapmans Library*, 1877.)

775   Why is a drawn tooth like a thing that is forgot?

776   Why is a church bell like a story that is handed about?

777   How is swearing like a shabby coat?

778   What is that which was born without a soul, lived and had a soul, yet died without a soul.

779   Why is a churchyard like an inn?

JOYCE, James (1882–1941)

Irish novelist. Riddles occur in *Ulysses* (1922).

780   What opera is like a railway line?

781   . . .my uncle John has a long thing I heard those cornerboys saying passing the corner of Marrowbone lane my aunt Mary has a thing hairy because it was dark and they knew a girl was passing it didnt make me blush why should it either its only nature and he puts this thing long into my aunt Mary's etcetera and turns out to be you put the handle in a sweepingbrush. . .

782   Brothers and sisters had he none,
       Yet that man's father was his grandfather's son.

JUNIUS, Hadrian (1511–75)

German poet and emblematist. Riddles appear in *Emblematum et aenigmatum libellus* (1565).

783   *Porrigor in ramos quinos, et quilibet horum*
       Diditur in triplices nodos, nisi quintus egeret
       Uno, qui solus respondet robore cunctis,
       Undique colliculis surgo, in vallemque resido,
       Ast abaci, desit si forte, ega munia praesto.

       (I stretch out into five branches, and each of these is made into threefold parts, except the fifth which lacks one, and it alone answers to all in strength; and I rise in little hills and I sink down into a valley and I discharge the duties of an abacus, if by chance you have not got one.)

KÖRNER, Theodor (1791–1813)

German poet and dramatist and son of C. G. Körner the close friend of Schiller (q.v.). Also wrote riddles.

784

Was grünend den ersten Silben entquillt,
Erquickt nur die gierige Heerde:
Die menschenernährende Wurzel verhüllt
Sich bescheiden im Schooße der Erde.

Doch was sieben und zwölf ist, was dreizehn und neun,
Das muß die dritte der Silben sein.
Einst hauste das Ganze mit Zaubergewalt
In unterirdischen Reichen,
Erschien den Menschen in mancher Gestalt,
Ein Schadenfroh sonder Gleichen.
Doch hat er sich längst von der Erde getrennt,
So daß ihn die Sage der Vorzeit nur kennt.

(The greenstuff sprouting from the first two syllables refreshes only the cravings of cattle. The human-nourishing root is modestly cloaked in the womb of the earth. Yet such things as seven and twelve, thirty and nine make up the third syllable. In olden times the whole had magic power and lived in subterranean kingdoms and appeared to men in many strange forms, a malicious being without equal. But they departed from the earth many years ago and now only appear in old myths and sagas.)

785

Die Ersten lenken die rüstige Fahrt;
Die Letzte schmückt sich mit stattlichem Bart.
Und geht's in die Brandung des Lebens hinein,
So mag die Liebe das Ganze sein.

(My first directs the hearty journey; my last sports a splendid beard and if it plunges headlong into the foaming tumult of life it may well be that Love is my whole.)

786

In stiller Anmuth kommt's gezogen,
Wie Rosenhecken blüht es auf,
Und durch des Aethers blaue Wogen
Steigt es mit goldner Pracht herauf.
Kannst du des Räthsels Lösung finden?
Zwei Silben mögen dir's verkünden.
Wohl giebt es eine mächt'ge Heerde,
Von keinem Auge noch gezählt,
Sie weidet herrlich fern der Erde
Vom Glanz des ew'gen Lichts beseelt;
Willst du der Lämmer Namen kennen,
Die dritte Silbe wird ihn nennen.
Am frühen Tag erscheint das Ganze
Und steigt empor mit heitrem Sinn,
Und in des Morgens jungem Glanze
Verkündet's die Gebieterin,
Und folgt ihr nach durch alle Weiten:
Sprich, kannst du mir das Räthsel deuten?

(In still serenity it appears like a rosy hedgerow it bursts into blossom and through the blue waves of the ether it ascends in golden splendour. Can you find the solution to the riddle? Two syllables will give it to you. There is an immense flock still uncounted by any eye. They graze amazingly far from the earth shepherded by the beam of heavenly lights. If you want to learn the names of the sheep the third syllable will tell you. In the early dawn appears the whole and rises aloft with a shining soul and in the glittering of the new morn announces the arrival of its mistress and follows her through all the vastness. Speak: can you tell me the meaning of the riddle?)

787

Die erste Silb', ein Gott, beherrscht des Landes Auen,
Die zweit' und dritte ist ein Name, oft belacht.
Das schwache Ganze wird in der Gewalt der Frauen
Der Donnerkeil des Zeus, und spottet aller Macht.

(My first is a god that rules the fields, my second and third make a ludicrous name, my dainty whole once in the hands of women becomes a thunderbolt from Zeus that mocks all authority.)

LABRAT, Dunash ben (*c*.920–*c*.990)
Spanish Hebrew poet from Cordova.

788 There is a box that is not full and not empty and all the boxes are created. It has black daughters and also reddish ones and they are covered with a greenish handkerchief.

789 What speaks in all languages in his riding, and his mouth spits the poison of life or death? It is silent when it rests, and is deaf like a boy or one of the poor.

790 What weeps tears without an eye, and makes everything visible and does not see its own garment? At the time when it approaches its death that which cuts off its head revives it?

LANDSEER, Sir Edwin (1802–73)
Painter best remembered for his animal paintings such as *The Monarch of the Glen*. Picture-letter reproduced in *Strand Magazine* (q.v.) in 1891. The letter was addressed to the engraver Charles George Lewis in response to an invitation (the first house drawn is Lewis's, the second Landseer's).

LAUTERBACH, Johannes (1531–93)
Teacher in Heilbronn, Germany. Riddles published in *Aenigmata* (1601).

792 *Sum brevis in medio, capite ac in calce diei*
  Longior, ut surgit sole caditve jubar.
 Urgentes fugio, fugientes insequor, istas
  Me videt alternis quisque subire vices.
 Defessos recreo gratas dum largior auras,
  Dumque fatigatis praebeo frigus humo.
 Nil fraudes vereor, mala nil discrimina, meque
  Sede, prior moveat se nisi, nemo movet.

(I am short in the middle, and longer at the beginning and end of the day, as the brightness of the sun increases or declines. I flee those who pursue me, I follow those who run away and everyone sees me approaching those exchanges by turns. I revive the weary when I scatter welcome breezes, and I cool those who lie exhausted on the ground. I fear no deception, no evil quarrels, and no one moves me from my seat unless he first moves himself.)

LEIDEN RIDDLE, The (9th century)

Riddle composed in Old Northumbrian which appears at the end of the Leiden University MS of the enigmas of Aldhelm (q.v.). Has some similarity to Aldhelm's *De Lorica* and Riddle 35 of *Exeter Book* (q.v.) but its author remains unknown.

793   Mec se ueta uonʒ   uundrum freoriʒ
ob his innaðae   aerest cændæ.

Ni uaat ic mec biuorhtæ   uullan fliusum,
herum ðerh hehcraeft   hyʒiðoncum min.
Uundnae me ni biað ueflæ,   ni ic uarp hafæ,
ni ðerih ðreatum ʒiðraec   ðret me hlimmith.
Ne me hrutendu   hrisil scelfath,
ni mec ouana   aam sceal cnyssa.
Uyrmas mec ni auefun   uyrdi craeftum,
ða ði ʒeolu ʒodueb   ʒeatum fraetuath.
Uil mec huethrae suaeðeh   uidæ ofaer eorðu
hatan mith heliðum   hyhtlic ʒiuæde;
Ni anoeʒum ic me aeriʒfaerae   eʒsan brogum
ðeh ði numen siæ   niudlicae ob cocrum.

(Me the wet plain, wondrous cold
From its womb first brought forth.
I know I am not wrought from the fleece of wool,
From hairs with high skill (I know in my mind).
The woof is not wound about me, nor have I the warp,
Nor through the thrust of many strokes does a thread of mine
    resound.
Nor does the whirring shuttle move or shake me,
Nor in any place shall the weaver's rod smite me.
Silkworms did not weave me through the skill of Fate,
That the yellow precious cloth deck with adornments.
Nevertheless one will, far and wide over the earth,
Among the heroes call me a delightful garment.
Nor [need] I fear the showers of arrows terribly frightening
Though they be taken in times of need from the quivers.)

LEMON, Mark (1809–70)
Founder and editor of *Punch*. Also wrote plays and verse.

794   Old Charlie Brown, who a big rogue was reckon'd,
        Was brought up at my *first* for making my *second*.
        He was fined, and because he no money would pay,
        Had to work with my *whole* on the Queen's highway.

LEO XIII, Pope (1810–1903)
Original name Gioacchino Pecci. Also composed riddles in Latin. The
second given here appeared in *Vox Urbis* and was dedicated to Joseph
Lovatello.

795   *Pars prior interdum velis ornatur et auro,*
        Altera pars prisco tempore nummus erat.
        Uno juncta simul verbo pars utraque gentem
        Rapto viventem belligeramque notat.

        (My first is sometimes adorned with cloths and gold. My second
        was in former times a coin. Joined together they denote a
        warlike race living by plunder.)

796   Primum, *mi Lovatelle, cum bibissem,*
            Phthisi convalui ocius fugata.
        Cymbam, quæ liquidis natabat undis,
        Alterum maris in profunda mersit.
        Quid totum, *tibi nosse dant ocelli*
        Turgentes, faciesque luctuosa,
        Et quæ nescia comprimi aut domari
        Heu matre exanimi, intimas medullas
        Angit, excruciatque vis doloris.

        (When I drank my first, Lovatello, I swiftly recovered from
        illness. My second sank to the ocean depths the boat floating on
        the waves. What my whole is you may guess from my swollen
        eyes and sorrowful face. They cannot be suppressed or subdued
        – O my poor dead mother! – my soul suffers, I am tortured by
        grief.)

LINCOLNSHIRE HOUSEHOLD RIDDLES
A series of folk riddles submitted for publication in *Notes and Queries*
(December, 1865).

797   As I was going over London Brig,
        I spies a little red thing;
        I picks it up, I sucks its blood,
        And leaves its skin to dry.

798   As I was going over Westminster Brig,
            I met a Westminster Scholar;
        He pull'd off his hat, an' drew off his glove,
            And wished me good morrow.
        Pray tell me his name, for I've told it to you.

799   As I was goin' over Humber,
I heard a great rumble;
Three pots a boilin'
An' no fire under.

800   When I was going over a field of wheat,
I picked up something good to eat,
Neither fish, flesh, fowl nor bone,
I kep' it till it ran alone.

801   Round the house and round the house,
And leaves a white glove i' th' window.

802   Round the house and round the house,
And leaves a black glove i' th' window.

803   Grows i' the wood, an' whinnies i' the moor,
And goes up an' down our house-floor.

804   It is in the rock, but not in the stone;
It is in the marrow, but not in the bone;
It is in the bolster, but not in the bed;
It is not in the living, nor yet in the dead.

LITTLE FOLKS (1871–1932)

Magazine of stories and puzzles for small children. Artists included Kate Greenaway and Arthur Rackham.

805   A preposition my first will show,
    And another forms my second,
My third's a number which all will know,
    A suffix my fourth is reckon'd;
And if you read this with my whole, no doubt
The answer to me you will ne'er find out.

806   In my first a wine will be seen –
    From foreign parts 'tis often brought;
In many churches third has been;
    My second when guessed is but nought;
A vowel's my fourth you all will own;
A Scottish town by my whole is shown.

807   My first is in crow, but not in rook;
My second's in nurse, but not in cook;
My third is in sword, but not in sheath;
My fourth is in moor, but not in heath;
My fifth is in heat, but not in cold;
My sixth is in brave, but not in bold.
On the coast of Norfolk my whole you'll see,
So here I'll end my riddle-me-ree.

LONDON MAGAZINE AND MONTHLY CHRONICLER, The (1732–85)

Monthly literary journal set up in opposition to the *Gentleman's Magazine* (q.v.). Riddles by various hands.

809   It is my fate, like many more to be
    A slave to one that wears my livery,
    A person of vile character; in brief,
    A noted sabbath-breaker and a thief.
    In saucy manner, I have heard it said,
    He once did entertain a crowned head.
    No wonder then, you hear me oft complain;

Whilst I'm at work the rascal to maintain,
He lazy walks about, or lolls at ease,
But takes due care my labour shall not cease.
With endless tasks he keeps me still employ'd;
As if my strength cou'd never be destroy'd.
But toils extreme frequent disorders breed,
And wear my constitution out with speed.
My bowels (sure prognostick of decay!)
With wind or water rumble night and day.
   What then my ailment is, perhaps you'll query?
Tis what the doctors call a lientery,
And diabetes join'd; for as my case is,
The symptoms plain appear of both diseases.
My thirst is sometimes so intense, that I,
You'd almost swear, wou'd drink a river dry.
And what is most remarkable is this,
As often as I drink, so oft I piss.
An inward waste I have; but am not sick
At stomach, my discharges too are quick.
But then my meat does me but little good;
For why my excrements are perfect food,
And therefore 'tis become a common rule
To watch me well, whene'er I go to stool.
For if my guts a signal make, take care;
Or you may chance to go without your share,
But if within my distance you presume,
You will be powder'd with no sweet perfume.

810   So capricious am I, that if monarchs should offer
Their kingdoms, I scarce would accept of their proffer;
Since no land in the world I ever could find,
That suited exactly the turn of my mind.
Yet guiltless I often am plac'd under ground,
But return from my prison both healthy and sound.
At dinner I'm often receiv'd by the great,
When I go on command, but as quickly retreat;
For no art they can use, will oblige me to stay,
And I always contrive to slip softly away.
On the tops of high trees I sometimes reside,
When I tremble with fear, tho' I sparkle with pride.
I delight in a river, but this I must say,
I seldom adventure to sail on the sea.
The stars are my friends, but as for the sun,
With precipitation his ardour I shun.
I'm fear'd by the ancient, and lov'd by the boy,
Who rides on my back, and beholds me with joy.

811   To you, fair maidens, I address;
    Sent to adorn your life:
And she who first my name can guess,
    Shall first be made a wife.

202

From the dark womb of mother earth,
  To mortals aid I come,
But e'er I can receive my birth,
  I many shapes assume.

Passive my nature, yet I'm made
  As active as the roe;
And oftentimes, with equal speed,
  Thro' flow'ry lawns I go.

When wicked men their wealth consume,
  And leave their children poor,
To me their daughters often come,
  And I increase their store.

The women of the wiser kind
  Did never yet refuse me;
And yet I never once could find,
  That maids of honour use me.

The lily hand, the brilliant eye,
  Can charm without my aid;
Beauty may prompt the lover's sighs,
  And celebrate the maid:

But let th' inchanting nymph be told,
  Unless I grace her life,
She must have wondrous store of gold;
  Or make a wretched wife.

Altho' I never hope for rest,
  With christians I go forth,
And while they worship towards the east,
  I prostrate to the north.

If you suspect hypocrisy,
  Or think me insincere,
Produce the zealot, who like me,
  Can tremble and adhere.

812   Draw up the curtains; let the ladies see
A fight well worth their curiosity;
No monster fierce, no strange outlandish creature,
But yet a very paradox in nature.
  Forty years old I am, and more, some say;
And yet in truth I was made yesterday.
Odd is my shape; and first mine head appears
Without a mouth, or eyes, or nose, or ears.
A body, you will own, I never had,
Although with clothes I constantly am clad.
Yet feet I have, but not at my command;
With them I cannot walk, nor on them stand.
My sides cannot be mov'd; and yet with ease
A child may shift and change them, when you please.
Both sexes join in me, a wondrous sight!
You'd almost swear I was hermaphrodite;

203

Had not the many brats begot on me
Declar'd unto the world the contrary.

Guard me, ye maids; for men will play the fool,
And I'm, you know, a soft and easy tool.
I cann't say nay; and yet if I'm disgrac'd,
The crime is yours; for whilst you're pure, I'm chaste:
But if, which heav'n forbid, you prove with child;
Then I am stain'd, polluted and defil'd.
Wed then, and to your husbands constant be;
So you'll be honour'd, and you'll honour me.
But when you take *for better and for worse,*
The first great blessing, and the first great curse,
You'll find in me, and (ah! I speak too plain)
The sweetest pleasure, and the sharpest pain.

813   Let arbitrary princes boast no more
Their haughty schemes of independent pow'r;
Nor propagate (to keep mankind at distance)
The slavish principles of non-resistance;
Since I possess a more despotick sway,
And absolute command, by far, than they.
No laws, injunctions, nor restraints I know,
But such as from myself spontaneous flow.
How oft have I in mazy fetters bound
Th' intrepid sons of war, with vict'ry crown'd?
What potent heroes, valiant in the field,
Have I led captive, and oblig'd to yield?
Altho' I am no formidable name,
An universal deference I claim:
The greatest potentates my pow'r revere,
And men of all degrees my liv'ry wear:
Yet no constrain'd obedience I exact;
'Tis ev'ry man's own voluntary act.
Oft I occasion quarrels and disputes,
Intestine jars, and law-contending suits:

Reason, with all her mild persuasions, can
Avail but little, when I've laid the plan.
In publick life my influence is such,
Men hardly can be guided by't too much;
But 'tis not seldom the unhappy rise,
Of private (unforeseen) calamities.
I'll only add (t' exemplify my worth
And clear my sully'd same) I'm of celestial birth.

814   Unseen by mortal eyes, I roll
M' extensive course from pole to pole,
Do wond'rous feats, by sea and land;
Obsequious to divine command.
In prison I am oft' confin'd,
By artful projects of mankind;
Yet, maugre all their sublime skill,
I'm acted by th' eternal will.

Depriv'd of my propitious aid,
The blooming rosy cheeks soon fade;
Convulsions seize the heaving breast;
Thus far my nature I've exprest:
I'll only add (t' enhance the fame
Of my renown'd tremendous name)
No pow'r, but what vouchsaf'd me birth,
Can e'er expel me from the earth.

815 Of publick use I am, by nature free;
And yet condemn'd to lose my liberty
By law severe, and a state-prisoner made,
Until a very heavy fine be paid.
Of ill designs against the government
The child unborn is not more innocent.
And had a jury try'd me, sure enough
I had been quit: but now the want of proof
A cruel act of parliament supplies,
And subjects me to pains and penalties.
And, what yet makes my case exceeding hard,
Mine own revenues must maintain my guard.
So harmless *Huguenots* are forc'd to grieve,
Whilst rude dragoons upon free quarters live.
    But when my fine is paid a wond'rous change
I feel, permitted where I please to range.
Esteem'd where e'er I come, my usage kind,
At ev'ry house I entertainment find.
If at a feast I chance not to be there,
In haste for me is sent a messenger.
Both king and queen wou'd most uneasy be,
Shou'd they sit down without my company.
The meanest subject too, when he shou'd eat,
If I be absent will not taste his meat.
    And here perhaps you'll call me trencher-friend,
Because at meals I constantly attend.
I taste your dishes all, I must confess,
Sometimes indeed to very great excess:
But none can say, herein I take delight;
For I'm no hungry, greedy parasite.
To serve and please you is my sole intent,
And daily task, until I am quite spent.
    In short, I am an universal good,
Almost as necessary as your food,
Pure, without spot, and from corruption free;
And saints themselves have been compar'd to me.
Yet, ladies, to confess one truth I am forc'd,
My best of qualities wou'd be your worst.

LORENZO, Professor (fl. 1870s)

Author of *Amateur Amusements* (New York, 1878), from which the following riddles are taken. The book contains over 400 riddles as well as 'shadow pantomimes' card tricks, ventriloquism, etc.

816   In almost every house I'm seen,
        (No wonder then I'm common)
    I'm neither man, nor maid, nor child,
        Nor yet a married woman.

    I'm pennyless and poor as Job,
        Yet such my pride by nature,
    I always wear a kingly robe,
        Though a dependent creature.

817   I am the terror of mankind;
        My breath is flame, and by its pow'r,
    I urge my messenger to find
        A way into the strongest tow'r.

818   I lived in a house of glass,
        Where I with glorious beams was blest;
    But such my fate, it came to pass,
        At length that I was dispossess'd,
    Then being brought to open view,
        Indeed, the nak'd truth I'll tell,
    I was both flay'd and quarter'd too,
        By those that lov'd me passing well.

819   An hundred years I once did live,
    And often wholesome food did give,
    Yet all that time I ne'er did roam,
    So much as half a mile from home,
    My days were spent devoid of strife,
    Until at last I lost my life.
    And since my death – I pray give ear,
    I oft have travell'd far and near.

820   In these corrupt degenerate times,
    When men are raised for their crimes,
        Utility I boast;
    And if my path they will pursue,
    By easy steps I lead them to,
        Possess the highest post.

    There are [those], who with good address,
    Pursu'd my steps with eagerness,
        And did their hopes obtain;
    But finding what a pond'rous weight
    They had to bear, resign'd it strait,
        And soon retir'd again.

821   My first, ye fair, adorns your head,
    You wear not anything instead;
    Within the convent's gloomy walls,
    My second to devotion calls;
    In July's eve, my whole is sound,
    Decking, with azure tint, the ground.

822   When scudding with a pleasant breeze,
        Jack calls my first his friend;
        Drinks to my next and is at ease,
          Such hours he loves to spend.
        But when my first doth chance to fail,
          Or otherwise doth prove;
        Straight from my whole to furl each sail,
          With haste the tar will move.

823   When first my maker form'd me to his mind,
        He gave me eyes, but left me dark and blind;
        He form'd a nose, but left me without smell;
        A mouth, but neither voice nor tongue to tell
        The world my use; yet oft the fair thro' me
        (Although I hide the face) do plainly see.

824   My first to male or female doth relate;
        My second, ladies, is a pond'rous weight;
        When of his prey, grim death hath made him certain,
        My whole our bed prepares, and draws the curtain.

825   My first is term'd a vital juice,
        The heath my second does produce,
        The sturdiest oak that e'er was seen,
        My tender total once has been.

826   My first is a term that's distinctive of joy,
        For all plans that are form'd it has power to destroy.
        'Tis fear'd in the palace as well as the cot,
        And yet had a hand in the gunpowder plot.
        My second of life has been sometimes the bane,
        And still has a mighty effect on the brain.
        I scarce know what order my whole now must rank
        But I yet declare it is nought but a blank.

827   My first is as senseless as iron or steel,
          But my second is very acute.
        The highest sensations it often can feel,
          And yet 'tis a part of a brute.

        My whole no idea that's brilliant can know,
          And from the first hour of its birth,
        He scarcely can tell e'en a friend from a foe,
          In short, 'tis a mere lump of earth.

828   My first, an adjective of frequent use;
          My second, is of no avail on land;
        My whole, you may complain of, if you choose,
          When cruelty uplifts her iron hand.

829   My first is a prayer, or service divine,
          By my next, is a portion of land understood,
        My total, alas! you may truly define,
          A horrid effusion of innocent blood.

830   My first makes all nature appear with one face;
        My second has music, and beauty and grace;

My whole, when the winter hangs dull o'er the earth,
Is the source of much pleasure, of mischief, and mirth.

831   My first is an useful animal, my second is a root, and my whole
is a root.

832   My first is unaffected seen,
    My next a ponderous weight will show;
My whole appears with vacant mien,
    Almost an idiot you'll allow.

833   My habitation's in a wood,
    And I'm at any one's command,
I often do more harm than good,
    If once I get the upper hand.
I never fear a champion's frown,
    Stout things I oftentimes have done;
Brave soldiers I have oft laid down,
    I never fear their sword or gun.

LORICHIUS SECUNDUS, Johannes (d.1569)

Lawyer to William of Orange. Also known as 'Hadamerius'. Riddles published in *Aenigmatus libris tres* (1545).

834   *Qui manibus compinget opus, non indiget illo,*
Quique emit, hoc uti non vult, quique utitur ipso,
Ignorat, quamvis habeat, tu solve, quid hoc sit.

(He who with his hands puts it together will not be poor, and he who buys it, does not wish to use it, and he who uses it, does not know it; now you guess what it is.)

835   *Dum juvenis fui, quattuor fontes siccavi;*
Cum autem senui, montes et valles versavi;
Post mortem meam, vivos homines ligavi.

(When I was young, I drained four springs; but when I became old, I travelled over mountains and valleys; after my death, I bound living men.)

LOYD, Samuel (1841–1911)

The 'Prince of Puzzle Makers', Loyd's success as an inventor of puzzles has been rivalled only by the Englishman Henry E. Dudeney (q.v.). His most famous puzzles were 'Trick Donkeys' (1858) and the 'Get off the Earth Puzzle' (1896). Riddles taken from *Cyclopedia of Puzzles* (1914) and *Sam Loyd's Puzzles* (1912).

836   In yon vast field of cultivated space,
    I there am found with members of my race;
Decapitate me – if you've no objection –
You then will find what brings me to perfection;
Take one more cut, and then you'll plainly see,
What I am destined, day by day, to be.

837   Upon the check'rd battle field,
    I'm foremost in the ranks;
My second makes a certain gain
    'Mongst railways, stocks and banks.

My whole though sanctioned by the law
  To succor the distress'd,
Is but, at least I think it so,
  A doubtful good at best.

838   A troubadour from foreign lands,
        To a lady fair came singing;
      'O lady bright, from thine own true knight
        A message I am bringing:
      He lies in the mountains near my first,
        He dares not come to thee;
      The foe accurst would on him burst,
        He therefore sendeth me.
      And he biddeth me tell thee to seek my next,
        Where he will surely meet thee;
      O! be not vexed, nor with fear perplex'd
        For thine own true love shall greet thee.'
      Like a timid fawn, at early dawn,
        To my second the lady hied;
      And at his word, she met her lord,
        Who had my whole supplied.

839   In every hedge my second is,
        As well on every tree.
      And when the schoolboy acts amiss,
        It often is his fee.
      My first, likewise, is always wicked,
        Although it does no sin.
      My total for my first is fitted,
        Is made of brass or tin.

840   My whole is both common and useful I ween,
        Or yet may be precious and rare;
      It both in the cottage and palace is seen,
        And often adorneth the fair;
      Behead; 'tis either exquisitely sweet
        Or harsh and ungrateful it sounds.
      Curtailed; it is massive – to make it complete,
        You must furnish a good many pounds.

841   My first without wings is enabled to fly,
        It never once tires in the midst of its flight,
      Piled on it vast masses of luggage still lie,
        Which it never sinks under by day or by night.

      See fear is upon you, my next is come on;
        Yourself pray compose, it is only your nerves
      That cause this annoyance; now, now it is gone;
        Alas! what a trifle its purposes serve!

      My whole is of thousands of mortals in the d[r]ead;
        'Mid stillness engendered, it works in the dark;
      O'er its awful effects many tears have been shed,
        And wide devastation its ravages mark.

842   My primal is found where the wild waves are dashing,
        And thick falls the cold briny spray;
      My final is seen, where the fierce eyes are flashing,
        And fortunes are oft thrown away.

209

To draw your conclusions by spanning my whole,
  As to what lies beneath or concealed,
Will oft prove as false as the base flatterer's soul,
  When facts, stubborn facts are revealed.

843   My first, gentle lady, you give to the youth,
         Who now breathes the fond wish of his soul;
       Whom with ardent affection, and honor and truth,
         You perceive is indeed in my whole.

       In my snug little second, secure from the storm,
         We the helpless and innocent find;
       And my whole when a contract or bargain you form,
         You should give, the agreement to bind.

844   In fruitful field my first they grew,
       My busy next there labored, too;
       A hardy race my whole you'll find,
       To husbandry and peace inclined.

845   Perhaps you may know
       That two centuries ago
       My name in the world was unknown;
       But now 'tis allowed
       In the midst of a crowd
       I am met with in every town.
       Though varied each lot
       In life I have got,
       Yet nothing my course e'er endangers;
       And wherever I go
       So familiar I grow
       That I am nodded to even by strangers.
       I am cunning and bold.
       For young or for old
       I fear not but brawl out aloud;
       Pugnacious you'll say,
       For I knock down by scores in a crowd.

846   Though small I am, yet, when entire
       I often set a house on fire;
       Take off one letter and 'tis clear
       I then could hold a herd of deer;
       Dismiss one more, and you will know
       That once I held a strange cargo.

847   On the casement pane the wind beat high,
       Never a star was in the sky;
       All Kenneth Hold was wrapt in gloom,
       And Sir Everard slept in a haunted room.
       I sat and sang beside his bed;
       Never a single word I said,
       Yet did I scare his slumber;
       And a fitful light on his eye full glistened,
       And his cheek grew pale as he lay and listened,
       For he thought and he dreamed that the fiends and jays

210

Were reckoning o'er his fleeting days,
  And telling out their number.
Was it my second's ceaseless tone?
On whose small hand he laid his own –
The hand which trembled in his grasp,
Was crushed by his convulsive clasp.
Sir Everard did not fear my first,
He had seen it in shapes that men deem worst,
  In many a field and flood;
Yet, in the darkness of his dread,
His tongue was parched – his reason fled;
And he watched, as the lamp burned low and dim,
To see some phantom, great and grim,
Come dabbled o'er with blood.
Sir Everard kneeled, and strove to pray,
He prayed for the light of early day,
  Till terror checked his prayer;
And ever I muttered clear and well,
'Click, click,' like a tolling bell,
Till, bound in fancy's magic spell,
  Sir Everard fainted there!

848   So vast my amount fills the mind with dismay!
Behead me and thus take a thousand away;
Reverse what remains, and I'll daily dispense
To thousands the gift of a kind Providence.

849   My first is a letter, an insect, a word
That means to exist; it moves like a bird.
My next is a letter, a small part of man,
'Tis found in all climes; search when you can.
My third is a something seen in all brawls,
My next you will find in elegant halls.
My last is the first of the last part of day,
Is ever in earnest, but never in play.
My whole gives a light by some men abhorred,
The blessings from which no pen can record.

850   My first is a creature of wonderful form;
My second gives shelter in sunshine and storm;
The empire of Flora embraces my whole,
Entire you may find me where sea-billows roll.

851

MACAULAY, Thomas Babington (1800–59)

English historian, poet and civil servant. Riddles attributed to him.

852   Cut off my head, how singular I act!
Cut off my tail, and plural I appear!
Cut off my head and tail – most curious fact!
Although my middle's left, there's nothing there!
What is my head, cut off? A sounding sea!
What is my tail, cut off? A flowing river!
Amid their mingling depth, I fearless play,
Parent of softest sounds, though mute forever.

853   Here's plenty of water you'll all of you say,
And, minus the h, a thing used every day,
And here is nice beverage, put them together;
What is it, with claws, but with never a feather?

854   Come, let's look at it closely,
'Tis a very ugly word,
And one that makes one shudder
Whenever it is heard.

It may'nt be always wicked,
It must be always bad,
And speaks of sin and suffering
Enough to make one mad.

They say it is a compound word,
And that is very true,
And then they decompose it,
Which of course they're free to do.

If of the dozen letters
We take off the first three,
We leave the nine remaining
As sad as they can be;

For though it seems to make it less,
In fact it makes it more,
For it takes the brute creation in,
Which was left out before.

Let's try if we can't mend it;
It's possible we may,
If only we divide it
In some new-fashioned way.

Instead of three and nine,
Let's make it four and eight.
You'll say that makes no difference,
At least not very great.

But only see the consequence:
That's all that need be done
To change this mass of sadness
To unmitigated fun.

It clears off swords and pistols,
Revolvers, bowie knives,
And all the horrid weapons
By which men lose their lives.

It wakens holier feelings,
And how joyfully is heard
The native sound of gladness
Compressed into one word.

Yes! four and eight, my friends,
Let that be yours and mine,
Though all the host of demons
Rejoice in three and nine.

855 Cut down, yet saved with much ado and pain;
Scatter'd, dispersed, yet gather'd up again!
Wither'd though young, though dying, yet perfumed,
Laid up with care, but kept to be consumed.

MAGASIN ENIGMATIQUE (1767)

Published by 'la veuve Duchesne' of rue St Jaques, Paris and containing
a selection of the best riddles of the time ('*choisies entre toutes celles qui
ont paru depuis près d'un siecle*'). 437 riddles.

856 *Fermé, chacun me touche; ouvert, je suis à craindre;*
Qui m'exerce sur soi perd le droit de se plaindre;
Le Vieillard par mes soins prend un air moins hideux,
Et je le rajeunis, mais pour un jour ou deux.
Contre mon Conducteur l'on s'emporte, l'on jure,
S'il tâtonne en jasant, s'il n'a pas la main sûre.
Pour me connoître mieux, j'ajoûterai ces mots;
Je sers de pacotille aux Cadets de Bordeaux.

(Shut, anyone can touch me, open I am to be feared. He who
uses me on himself can't grumble. And thanks to me the old
man looks younger and less repulsive, though only for a day or
two. People lose their tempers and curse my master if he fumbles
during his chatter or if his hand is unsteady. To know me better
I will just add: there is a ready market for me amongst junior
naval officers at Bordeaux.)

857 *Je n'ai pour attelier qu'une noire prison;*
Tous les ans je reviens ainsi que l'Hirondelle,
   En certaine saison.
   Je ne porte point d'aîle,
  Et cependant au haut d'une maison
Je prodigue souvent mes chants aussi bien qu'elle.

(My workshop is a dark prison and every year, in season, I
return like a swallow. I have no wings yet often sing from the
rooftops as well as any swallow.)

858 *Je regne dans les airs & ne sçais point voler,*
   On me consulte, & je ne puis parler.
Je suis bon Sentinelle, & jamais je ne veille,

Comprenez-vous cette merveille?
Ce n'est pas tout; je suis regardé par des gens,
Comme si je faisois la pluie & le beau tems.
  Je suis encor grand Nouvelliste;
  De tout Pays je tiens la liste;
Par trente-deux Couriers à point nommé servi,
  Tantôt du Nord, & tantôt du Midi,
Du Ponant, du Levant je reçois des nouvelles.
Mon Trône n'est jamais rempli par des Femelles.
Politique, dispos, je le donne aux plus fins;
  Ce sont tous de Maîtres Gonins.
Aux marches que je fais le Diable ne voit goutte.
Tel m'a vû de Turin le soir prendre la route,
  Qui se trouve bien étonné
De me voir le matin vers Londres retourné,
De peuple chaque jour une foule assidue
  Paroît sous mes pieds tête nue,
Genoux à terre; eh quoi! me voilà donc un Dieu!
Non, non; ce n'est pas moi qu'on adore en ce lieu.

(I am lord of the air, yet I cannot fly. I am consulted by all, yet I cannot speak. I always stand sentinel, yet I have nothing to guard. Can you understand such a marvel? And that's not all: people think I can control the weather. I am also a great spreader of news: my thirty-two couriers always let me know the very latest that is in the wind, from north, south, east and west. My throne is never usurped by women. And both shrewd and of an alert disposition I only give my information to the most astute people – themselves masters of their art. The devil himself never sees me take a step yet I constantly move. Indeed the man who sees me go in the direction of Turin in the evening is often astonished to see me turning towards London the next morning. And every day a crowd of people kneel bare-headed at my feet – so am I then a god? No, no – it's not me that they worship.)

859 *Iris, je dois ma naissance*
Au Mortel industrieux
Qui des flots d'un gouffre immense,
Sauva vos premiers Ayeux.
Mon plus ordinaire asyle
Est la plaine ou le côteau,
Et l'on ne m'aime à la Ville,
Qu'à table ou dans le berceau.
Si mon teint faisoit ma gloire,
J'ai par fois l'éclat de l'or;
Mais que je sois blonde ou noire,
Je suis toujours un trésor.
Sans être utile à la guerre,
Ni propre au moindre combat,
J'ai de quoi mettre par terre
Le plus vigoureux Soldat.
Je n'accorde mes largesses

Qu'à des soins multipliés,
Et pour avoir mes richesses,
Il faut me fouler aux piés.

(I owe my birth to that remarkable man who saved all our ancestors from the great floods of history. My usual dwelling is on the plain or the hillside, and in towns I only find favour at the table or in the conservatory. If my complexion is the cause of my fame it may be because I am sometimes the colour of gold. But whether I am pale or dusky I am always prized. Useless in war and totally unsuited for the least combat I yet have the power to knock out the strongest soldier. I only dispense my favours after considerable courting and to obtain my rich delights you must first trample on me.)

860   *Je suis utile à tout le monde,*
Et mon corps représente une coupe profonde.
    Ami de l'ombre & du repos,
J'habite du sommeil le ténébreux enclos.
    Pour me parer, d'une toile on me cache;
    Pour me fixer, d'un ruban l'on m'attache.
Je suis triste, dit-on, mais je suis si discret,
    Que de chacun je couvre le secret.
J'ai place chez le Roi, mais je hais la couronne,
Et lorsque je le sers, je veux qu'il l'abandonne.

(I am useful to all and my body is like a tall-sided bowl. The friend of darkness and rest, I dwell in the shadowy cells of repose. I am trimmed with linen and tied with a ribbon. People say I am a sorry-looking thing but I am so discreet that I can be trusted to conceal everyone's little secret. I can be found in the king's household but I hate his crown and when I serve him I insist he takes it off.)

861   *De l'esprit & du corps je présente un miroir:*
Je fais ouvrir les yeux, & l'on ne peut me voir.
Pour ma production, ô merveille étonnante!
Un seul sexe suffit, sans douleur il m'enfante.
Je ne puis exister sans l'esprit & le corps;
Sans être aucun des deux, ce sont-là mes ressorts.

(I am a mirror of the mind and the body. I open people's eyes yet they cannot see me. To produce me – oh wondrous miracle! – only one sex is necessary, and I am delivered without pain. I cannot exist without the mind and the body yet am neither of these, though both control me.)

862   *Il n'est presque rien sous les Cieux,*
Malgré mon titre de foiblesse,
Plus rempli de force & d'adresse;
Je suis toujours cher à vos yeux.

Je désarme les furieux,
Quand ce seroit une Tigresse;
J'appaise & touche ma Maitresse;
Je puis fléchir même les Dieux.

Quelle chose au Monde est parfaite!
Par malheur, une horrible Bête
Me cause un odieux renom;

Comme elle me rend inhumaine,
On n'a pour moi que de la haine,
Lorsque je parois sous son nom.

(Despite my reputation for weakness, there is almost nothing beneath the heavens that has more strength and cunning than me. I am always dear to your eyes. I can disarm the enraged – even a tigress! – and can soothe and move to pity my mistress. I can even make the gods themselves grow weak. What a perfect thing! Unfortunately a horrible beast has given me a bad reputation. This monster makes me cruel, and people hate me when I appear along with its name.)

863
    Je suis de toutes les couleurs,
      Et ma famille est innombrable;
L'art me fait imiter le coloris des fleurs,
    Mais mon éclat est peu durable.
Je suis souvent ami des Jeux & des Plaisirs:
    Lorsque je suis mis à la gêne,
Je fais briller le teint de la jeune Climene,
Et je pare le sein de la charmante Iris.
J'inspire quelquefois une humeur sombre & noire;
J'accompagne en tous lieux la tristesse & la mort.
Je fais encore plus, Lecteur, peux-tu le croire?
    (Juge à ce trait de mon bizarre sort)
    Quoiqu'inventé pour embellir les Graces,
De Bellone je suis les dangereuses traces;
Et dans ces jours affreux détestés des Humains,
Intrépides Guerriers, l'on me voit dans vos mains.

(I come in all colours and my family is countless. Art makes me imitate the hues of flowers but my brilliance doesn't last. I am often a playmate in games and pastimes and when I am tied up I make young Climene's complexion glow and adorn the breast of charming Iris. But sometimes I induce darkness and gloom and I always accompany sadness and death. And I can do still more, dear Reader, if you can believe it. Although I was created to adorn the lovely Graces yet I also follow the footsteps of the warring goddess Bellona. And in those fearful times so dreaded by men then, bold warriors, you'll often find me grasped in your hand.)

864
Souvent en embuscade, à l'abri des dangers,
Malheur à l'ennemi que mes filets légers
Arrêtent tout-à-coup dans sa course rapide;
De ma cruelle soif victime trop timide,

Dans les flots de son sang je m'enivre soudain
Et s'il veut m'échapper, il se débat envain.
Mais admirez ici ma perfide industrie
A surprendre ma proie, & prolonger ma vie;
Pour ne point effrayer l'ennemi qui me fuit,
Je plonge le cadavre en un sombre réduit,
J'use de cent détours dans ma course légere,
Et je crains fort la main de quelque ménagere.

(Often waiting in ambush and hidden from danger, woe betide him who is suddenly stopped in his tracks by my light nets. For he becomes the victim of my cruel thirst and I quickly become drunk on the spurts of his blood. If he tries to escape he struggles in vain. But you must admire my double skill in both intercepting my prey whilst protecting my own life. And so as not to frighten off other victims I hide the corpses in a dark recess, taking a hundred twisting turns in my lightfooted journey. But yet I dread still the hand of the unarmed housewife.)

865   *J'ignore absolument où j'ai pris la naissance;*
Je ne sçais qui je suis, & ne le puis sçavoir;
Je n'ai point de raison, cependant je fais voir
Que je suis raisonnable en quelque circonstance.
   Selon les objets que je vois,
Je les reçois de bonne ou de mauvaise grace;
Je ne sçais ce que c'est de faire la grimace,
   Je la fais pourtant quelquefois.
   En quelque lieu que l'on me voie,
Toujours même penchant m'occupe jour & nuit;
Qui veut m'en arracher me fait faire du bruit;
Car je fais le plaisir de ce qui fait ma joie.
   Dans un attachement si doux,
   Je m'abandonne à ma tendresse;
Tel qui de mon bonheur est bien souvent jaloux,
   Vaut moins que moi dans son espece.
Pour sçavoir qui je suis, quand je vous vois rêver,
Vous me voyez peut-être & je vous vois de même;
Cherchez-moi, cher Lecteur, avec un soin extrême,
   J'affligerois bien ce que j'aime,
   Si l'on ne pouvoit me trouver.

(I haven't a clue where I was born, I don't know who I am and I've no means of finding out. I have no powers of reason yet sometimes I appear to behave rationally. Depending on what presents itself before me I receive it with either good or bad grace. Though I have never been taught to pull faces I do sometimes grimace. And whenever you see me I always seem to be up to something, day or night. And anyone who wants to drag me away will have to make a hell of a noise, because I am usually perfectly happy just doing what I want to do. He who envies my happiness is lower than me in the eyes of his own race. If you want to know who I am, you might spot me

217

when you're dozing off – and I might spot you. But look
carefully for me, dear Reader. I tend to get upset when I am
lost.)

MAGAZINE OF SHORT STORIES, The (1889–93)
Weekly magazine of short stories, anecdotes, etc., published by E. & H.
Bennett, London. From 1893 to 1904 it was known simply as *Short
Stories*. From 21 February 1891 (issue 112) it contained a weekly
competition with a cash prize for the correct and most poetic solutions
to charades composed by the editor. Examples taken from issue 112
(the prize for solving all was ten guineas).

866   Six weeks ago on New Year's Day
Young Simkiss cried in accents gay,
   'At last I am my FIRST:
Thou dreary, dusty, gloomy WHOLE;
I hate thee from my very soul
But now I slip from thy control,
   Thy galling chain I burst!'

Behold him now upon my NEXT,
Which, like a plain before him stretched,
   'My FIRST!' he cried. 'Hoo'ray!'
Then, as a bird, or as a train,
Or as a ship across the main,
Or, as some seek my WHOLE to gain,
   Headlong he made his way.

Then, all the folks who saw him, cried:
'Such foolish tricks should not be tried,
   He is the FIRST, indeed;'
But this time 'tis his feet – good lack!
It was a most tremendous crack!
And there he lay upon his back,
   Arrested in his speed.

'Oh, dear!' he groaned, 'Oh, dear! oh, dear!
My head is now my FIRST, I fear!'
   And then began to cry:–
'Me FIRST please from the SECOND take,
I made, you see, a sad mistake;
In every bone I feel an ache,
   Farewell! my NEXT, good-bye!'

So back again to Lincoln's Inn,
With damaged limbs and broken skin,
   Next morning Simkiss stole;
And then, at once my FIRST he swore,
He'd venture on my NEXT no more;
So down he sat him, bruised and sore,
   Contented in my WHOLE.

867   My FIRST is by nature and art both made,
   It is also a part of you;
And though many find it a scene of toil,

'Tis a place of pleasure, too.

My SECOND is something that all may have,
  The rich and poor alike;
And though a misfortune 'tis welcome at times,
  And is often the end of a strike.

My WHOLE is a hidden and dreadful thing,
  To be shunned where'er it be;
Though the greatest care and the strictest watch
  May fail to keep you free.

868   My FIRST is what most people do
  When called on for my WHOLE;
'Tis not Poor Rate nor Income Tax –
  A claim more than a toll.

My FIRST oft grows into my LAST
  When this demand is made;
But FIRST and LAST are both in vain,
  My WHOLE must still be paid.

869   My FIRST is said of kings,
    And of many other things, –
Such as soldiers, ships or faces, or the hand;
    It may be long or short,
    It may serve for a support,
Or answer for my WHOLE you understand.

    But my SECOND needs support,
    As it may be long or short;
To the present, past, or future may belong;
    It is golden, green and ripe,
    And is often known to pipe,
And so has formed a theme for poet's song.

    Then my WHOLE is just my FIRST,
    This may puzzle you the worst,
For you'll find that it is really thrice as long,
    And it always is the boast,
    Of the folks who 'rule the roast,'
Who oft made it their excuse for doing wrong.

870   My WHOLE had failed; disasters dire and deep,
Foul-fingered treachery, and the oppressor's strength
Had crushed it to the earth. Grim-faced despair,
With bony arm outstretched, had seized on all;
Hope shuddering fled – the fateful game was lost,
And so my FIRST – though like my SECOND – brave,
Now sought concealment from his vengeful foes.
'Alas!' he cried, 'how hard a lot is ours!
Disgraced and humbled both. Yet, if success
Had touched us with his sceptre – like the wand
Of some adept magician that transforms
All likeness to unlikeness – then my WHOLE,
No more a hateful monster in the land,

Would be with glory gilded, and myself
No longer called my FIRST, from stigma freed,
Would shine resplendent on the scroll of fame.'

MAHABHARATA, The
Hindu epic. Riddles occur in the 'Vana Parva'.

871 *Yaksha*:
What soul hath a man's which is his, yet another's?
What friend do the gods grant, the best of all others?
What joy in existence is greatest? and how
May poor men be rich and abundant? say thou.

King:
Sons are the second souls of man,
And wives the heaven-sent friends; nor can
Among all joys health be surpassed;
Contentment answereth thy last.

Yaksha:
Still, tell me what foeman is worst to subdue?
And what is the sickness lasts lifetime all through?
Of men that are upright, say which is the best?
And of those that are wicked, who passeth the rest?

King:
Anger is man's unconquered foe;
The ache of greed doth never go;
Who loveth most of saints is first;
Of bad men cruel men are worst.

MALATESTI, Antonio (1610–c.1672)
Italian dramatist and poet. Riddles published in *La Sfinge* in three parts
(1640, 1643, 1683).

872 *Di nulla è fatt'il Mondo, e nulla i' sono*
   E in questo nulla alfin torna ogni cosa;
   L'uom si spaventa del mio nome al suono,
   Ma s'in ch'ei non mi trova ei non ha posa.
Tenuta bella son, brutta, o dannosa,
   Secondo ch'un è pazzo, o tristo, o buono
   Chi m'ha, d'abbandonarmi unqua non osa,
   E chi non m'ha, può darmi ad altri in dono.
Chiamami alcun, quando il dolor l'assale;
   Ma poi vorria piuttosto altri in mia vece,
   Eppur medica son d'ogni gran male,
Fo quel ch'i' voglio, e quel ch'i' voglio lece;
   E cotanto son giusta, e liberale
   Ch'io diedi infin me stessa a chi mi fece.

(The world is made of nothing, and I am nothing, and in the
end everything returns to this nothing. Man is afraid of the
sound of my name, but until he finds me cannot rest. I am held
to be beautiful, ugly, or injurious, according to whether one is
mad, sad, or good. He who has me does not dare to

renounce me, and he who has not got me can give me to others. Anyone can call me when pain assails them, but then he would rather have something else in my place, and yet I am a cure for every great ill. I do what I want and I am so just and liberal that I give even myself to him who made me.)

873 *Chi vuol vedere quel che fuggir non può,*
　　　venga venga una volta innanzi a me,
　　　che s'avrà gli occhi e la ragion con sè,
　　　conoscerà quel ch'io gli monstrerò.
　　In virtù dell'argento il tutto fo
　　　non avend'io religïon, nè fè;
　　　ignudo mostro il corpo com'egli è,
　　　se dal fiato dell'uom panni non ò.
　　Nè m'importa, se un brutto in odio m'à,
　　　mentre un bello si val di mia virtù,
　　　perchè chiara i'vo'dir la verità.
　　Piccola o grande vaglio meno e più;
　　　ma se non fusse la fragilità,
　　　varrei più, che non val tutto il Perù.

(He who wants to see what is escaping, and cannot, let him come once first to me, for if he has got his eyes and his reason with him, he will know what I will show him. I do everything in the virtue of silver, having no religion or faith; I show the body, naked as it is, if I am not clothed by the breath of man. Nor does it matter to me, if I am held in hatred by someone ugly whilst a beautiful person values my worth, because I will speak the truth clearly. The small or the large I consider less and more; and if it were not for my fragility, I would be worth more than the whole of Peru.)

MARCH'S PENNY RIDDLE BOOK (c.1855)

Also called 'Peter Puzzle's Riddles, New Conundrums and Funny Jokes' this little booklet is no.14 in March's Penny Library published by J. March, London. (Other titles include fairy tales, histories, book of sports, etc.)

874 What is that which goes with a carriage, comes with a carriage; is of no use to the carriage, and yet the carriage cannot go without it?

875 Though for wisdom famed all the world over,
　　　Book learning I never could boast;
　　I rumple the leaves, break the cover,
　　　But if I am found, I am lost.

876 Of us thrice eight are but eleven,
　　　Two three, three five, and five are four,
　　Six are three, fifteen are seven,
　　　And a hundred are no more.

877 I'm in both corners of your eye,
  But if the weather snows or blows,
 No one then will dare deny
  I'm on the tip of each man's nose.

878 In ONE alone I'll prove there's none,
  In NINE, but one can count;
 In SEVEN but five; yet SIX alone
  Do unto nine amount;
 In FIVE, I only four can see,
  Pray tell me then, how can this be?

MASQUERADE, The (1797–1801)
Five volumes each containing various kinds of riddle and puzzle (mostly charades). Examples taken from the fourth edition (1812).

879 A piece of wood,
  Which should be good,
 Aye, tough as ash, I think;
  With which men play,
  The live long day,
 To see who'll get the chink;
  Will name a thing,
  That's on the wing,
 When Sol his head lays low;
  Yet, tho' it flies,
  And high doth rise,
 It is no bird, I trow.

880 To music's notes my first attention lends.
 To find my next the youth his leisure spends.
 My whole, the merchant, when intent on gain,
 Oft gives, in hopes his bargain to maintain.

881 My first, the trembling culprit
  For his offences fears;
 When, close behind pursuing,
  The Bow-street men he hears.

 And if in Spain the villain
  His roguery had done;
 The second he had suffer'd,
  With many an aching bone.

 My whole, the weary soldier,
  Long forced abroad to roam,
 Greets with an eye of rapture, –
  His welcome winter's home.

882 My first's the last destructive foe
 Of nature's fairest form below.
 My second is proud Albion's boast;
 And both defends and decks her coast.
 My whole, (such change from union flows)
 The bitterest boon the earth bestows.

883   Take me entire, my salutary juice
In medicine will prove of sovereign use.
Divide me, – that does such a change create,
I'm found pure water in a double state.

884   My first is half an appellation for the child of my second, and
my whole loses its name if it shews its legs.

885   My first is a body that's light;
My next a mechanical pow'r;
    My whole should be found
    Where the bottle goes round,
Which enlivens the sociable hour.

886   Form'd half beneath, and half above the earth,
We sisters owe to art our second birth;
The smith and carpenter's adopted daughters;
Made on the earth, to travel on the waters,
Swifter we move as tighter we are bound;
Yet neither touch the sea, the air, nor ground.
We serve the poor for use, the rich for whim;
Sink when it rains, and, when it freezes, swim.

887   Seldom am I the theme of poet's lays;
Seldom does singer warble forth my praise:
My worth's not great, my beauty's nothing rare,
Yet some there are who think me worth their care.
In peaceful state once undisturb'd I lay,
'Til that sad hour, that inauspicious day,
When I was torn from peace and balmy rest,
For oh! the helpless ever are opprest!
Dragg'd from my dark abode by some unpolish'd wight,
Exposed to common view and glaring light;
Yet when my form is torn by sharpen'd steel,
Tho' by the hands of those perhaps unused to feel,
They who unmoved the saddest tale can hear,
May turn their heads aside, and drop a tear.

888   My first, as ancient poets feign,
Was god among the sylvan train;
My second's provender for routs,
Assemblies, balls, and gadabouts;
My whole's a thorough English dish,
And follows after flesh and fish.

889   I have arms, but no legs, yet I run a great way,
I sleep all the night, ay, and sometimes all day.
I'm a native of Germany, some say of France,
'Tis certain that there I was first taught to dance.
When in England, am cramp'd by the fogs of November,
But brought back to life by the frosts of December;
I am there taught to speak, yet 'tis strange, and my way;
Those who set my tongue wagging don't know what I say!

890   Life's purest treasure with my first unite,
Cheer the lone walk, and gild the gloom of night;
When ah! my second, Britain's boast and pride,
From the fond bosom tears this pleasing guide;
But space nor climate can my whole destroy,
Di'monds are not so bright, and gold has more alloy.

891   My first is the centre of gravity;
My second the foundation of perplexity;
And the whole my utter aversion.

892   My first no life nor feeling blesses;
My second ev'ry sense possesses;
And nothing more affronts my second,
Than when it like my first is reckon'd;
Together they a being show,
The greatest nuisance that we know.

MEE, Arthur (1875–1943)

Journalist and editor with prodigious general knowledge. Whilst at the
Daily Mail he compiled the *Harmsworth Self-Educator* (1905) and went
on to found *The Children's Encyclopedia* (1908) and the *Children's
Newspaper* (1919–65). Examples taken from the puzzle pages of *The
Children's Encyclopedia*.

893   My first is nothing but a name;
     My second still more small;
My whole of so much smaller fame,
     It has no name at all.

894   I know a word with letters three,
Add two and fewer there will be.

895   A chain of mountains will appear
     If you the name transpose
Of those who were in ancient days
     Britain's piratic foes.

896   The sun shines clear, serene the golden sky,
Where'er you go or run as fast I fly:
With your bright day my progress, too, does end;
See here, vain man, the picture of a friend.

897   Often talked of, never seen,
Ever coming, never been,
Daily looked for, never here,
Still approaching in the rear.
Thousands for my presence wait,
But, by the decree of fate,
Though expected to appear,
They will never see me here.

898   My first is in apple and also in pear,
My second's in desperate and also in dare,
My third is in sparrow and also in lark,
My fourth is in cashier and also in clerk,

My fifth is in seven and also in ten,
My whole has now come as a gift unto men.

899 My first is in saddle and also in strap,
My second's in programme and also in map,
My third is in letter and also in send,
My fourth is in tearing and also in rend,
My fifth is in linden and also in lime,
My sixth is in clamber and also in climb,
My seventh's in clatter and also in roar,
My whole is a land great in peace and in war.

900 In the dark you will see that I falter,
Behead and I now am a halter.
Behead once again and you'll know it,
I'm open and used by the poet.

901 Inscribe an *m* above a line
    And write an *e* below,
This woodland flower is hung so fine,
    It bends when zephyrs blow.

MEGALOMITES, Basilios (11th century)
Byzantine poet contemporary with Michael Psellus.

902 There is such a male as the one who came out of a white stone;
at a distance his beard sparkles like flame; the earth trembles
under his feet; when he cries out, the devils run for shelter; a
gust of wind comes from under his wings.

MENESTRIER, Claude François (1631–1705)
French Jesuit historian and heraldic scholar. Riddles appear in *La
philosophie des images énigmatiques* (1694).

903 *Je suis de divers lieux, je nais dans les Forêts,*
Tantôt près de ruisseaux, tantôt près des marais,
Je suis de toute taille & de seche figure,
Je n'ai jambes ni bras, cependant la nature
Ne m'a pas fait un monstre, & j'en vaux beaucoup mieux,
Reparant ce deffaut par un grand nombre d'yeux;
Qu'ils soient toûjours ouverts, il n'est pas necessaire,
Qu'ils soient fermez ou non, ils sçavent toûjours plaire.
Comme un Cameleon je me nourris de l'air.
Quoi que je ne puisse parler
J'ai le don de me faire entendre
Et par une vertu qui pourra vous surprendre
Ce qu'en ouvrant la bouche on voit faire en tous lieux
A mille gens qui par là savent plaire,
Moi de qui la methode à la leur est contraire
Je le fais en fermant la plûpart de mes yeux.

(I come from various places: I was born in the forest,
sometimes near streams, sometimes near marshes. I can be of
any size and have a dry body. I have neither legs nor arms, but
nature hasn't made me a monster, and I am worth much

more than that, compensating for this defect by giving me a great many eyes. It is not necessary for them always to be open – open or shut they always know how to please. Like a chameleon I live on air. Though I cannot speak I have the gift of making people listen to me, and in a manner that would surprise you: instead of opening my mouth – by which a thousand folk know how to please – I, whose method is the opposite, do so by shutting most of my eyes.)

904   *Avec une tête assez grosse*
D'un pied je me tiens sans effort.
Bien que petit de taille, & rien moins qu'un Colosse
J'ai quelquefois terrassé le plus fort.
Quoi que je sois dans l'impuissance
De faire un seul pas pour marcher,
Je viens pourtant toûjours en grande diligence;
Mais qui me veut peut me venir chercher.
De tels dons j'étois les delices
Et qui m'avoient ouvert leur coeur
Je n'ai que trop souvent fait de grands sacrifices
Pour m'avoir pris dans ma mauvaise humeur.
Chercher, tâchez de me comprendre;
Mais quand vous m'aurez deviné
A mes freres bâtards gardez de vous meprendre,
C'est un coup seur d'en être assassiné.

(With quite a big head I stand easily on one foot. Although I am small, and anything but a Colossus, I have been known to knock down the strongest. Though I am unable to walk a single step, I still keep turning up each day with great speed; but anyone who wants me must come and find me. For those to whom I am a delicacy and who open their hearts to me I have only too often made great sacrifices for having taken me when I was in a bad mood. Now look and try to find me out; but when you have guessed my meaning make sure you do not mistake me for my bastard brothers, for this is certain death.)

905   *Inconstante & legere*
Je me fais aimer constamment,
Et le plus agréable Amant
Sans moi ne sçauroit plaire.
    Fille de Roturier,
Des plus nobles Galans je reçois les hommages,
Je cede aux fous, & je command aux sages,
Je ne fais rien & suis de tout métier,
La raison contre moi n'est jamais la plus forte,
Le Roy même a souvent reconnu mon pouvoir.
Je decide à la Cour de tout sans rien savoir,
Et malgré les Sçavans mon suffrage l'emporte.
    On ne sçauroit compter mes ans.

> *Mon extreme vieillesse*
> > *Egale celle du tems,*
> *Je plais pourtant par ma jeunesse.*

(Fickle and flighty I constantly make myself loved and even the most charming suitor could not succeed without me. Daughter of a commoner, I receive tribute from the noblest gallants; I suffer fools gladly yet I rule wise men; I do nothing and yet am a member of every profession; reason will never win against me, even the king himself has often admitted my power. I decide everything at court without knowing anything, and, in spite of the scholars, it's my word that counts. No one could tell how old I am. My great age is the age of time itself, but even so I charm with my youthfulness.)

906   *On ne voit point dans la nature*
De corps plus petit que le mien,
Et cependant je fais si bien
Que je suis plus fecond qu'aucune creature
J'aurois trop de fureur dans les grandes chaleurs,
L'hiver est destiné pour me metre en usage,
J'ai l'humeur si piquante, & l'esprit si sauvage
Que plus on me cherit, plus on verse de pleurs.
Pour se servir de moi qu'on me mette en poussiere,
Qu'on emploïe à me batre & las nuit & le jour
Je n'en serai pas moins audacieuse & fiere,
Malheur aux gens qui me font trop de cour.

(You'll never see anything in the whole of Nature with a body smaller than mine, yet I am so good at creating things that I am more fertile than any other creature. I would be too fiery in the hot season, winter is the best time to put me to use. My disposition is so sharp, and my spirit so wild that the more I am cherished, the more I cause tears. He who would employ me must first render me to dust, and beat me both night and day. But still I shall be not less audacious and proud, woe betide those who court me too much.)

MERCURE DE FRANCE, Le (1672–1965)
French fortnightly review which included enigmas, logogriphs, and charades up to 1810.

907   *Je brille avec six pieds, avec cinq je te couvre.*

(With six I shine, with five I cover.)

908   *Par quatre pieds j'entends, et par trois je réponds.*

(With four I listen, with three I reply.)

909   *Pour lier avec moi longue société,*
> *Un habitant d'un rivage écarté*
A traversé des mers l'espace formidable;
Et tandis que, brûlant d'une âme durable,
Il périt dans mon sein, de ses feux tourmenté,

De qui nous réunit il fait la volupté.
C'est du même élément le pouvoir redoutable
Qui me donne, qui m'ôte et me rend ma beauté.
   Quand une fois j'ai la tête allumée,
Je fais à mes amis une grande leçon.
Philosophe muet, je prêche à ma façon
   Que tout ici n'est que fumée.

(To bind itself in long companionship with me, a resident of a far-flung shore has crossed the vast space of the seas; and whilst burning with a lasting flame it slowly dies in my breast tormented by its own fires, it gives pleasure to the one who joins us. It is the formidable power of this same ingredient that gives, takes away and gives me back my beauty. Once my head is set alight I give my friends a great lesson. A dumb philosopher, in my own way I preach that there is nothing here but smoke.)

910   Avec six pieds, je suis un mets fort restaurant;
Avec cinq, des traités je deviens le garant;
Avec quatre, mes flots roulent avec vitesse;
Avec trois, en fuyant j'emporte la jeunesse.

(With six feet, I am a very fortifying dish; with five, I become the guarantee of the treaty; with four, my waters run swift; with three, in fleeing I steal away youth.)

911   Nous sommes quatre enfants d'une grande famille,
   Et nous avons deux espèces de sœurs.
   A notre tête est la troisième fille,
   Et notre aînée a les seconds honneurs.
Celle qui de nous quatre a la taille plus grande,
A la troisième place a soumis sa fierté,
Et par distinction la dernière demande
   Un petit ornement sur son chef ajouté.
   Nous composons un tout; mettez-vous à sa quête,
   Et si vous le trouvez, demandez-le d'abord
      Pour vous guérir du mal de tête
Que vous aura causé peut-être cet effort.

(We are four children of a big family, and we have two kinds of sister. At our head is the third daughter, and the eldest has second place. She who is the tallest of us four has condescended to take the third place, and in order to be noticed the last asks for a small ornament on her head. Together we form a single whole: go and search for the solution and if you find it, ask at once for some of it to cure the headache that this effort may have given you.)

912   De filer le produit de ma riche semence,
Le secret, par Isis, aux mortels fut donné;
Je naquis, dit l'histoire, aux bords d'un fleuve immense,
Dont le nom mémorable est mon nom retourné.

(The secret of spinning the product of my rich seed was given
to mortals by Isis. I was born, says history, on the banks of a
vast river, whose memorable name is my name back to
front.)

MINCE PIES FOR CHRISTMAS (1805)
Printed 'for Tabart & Co at the Juvenile and School Library by T.
Gillet' to 'Exercise the Ingenuity of sensible masters and misses' this
anthology of poetic riddles was compiled by 'an old friend'.

913   We are a score, nay something more,
        Within a cave reside;
    Though we but seldom disagree,
        We very oft divide.

    If we fall out, it is a doubt
        If e'er we'll meet again.
    Both beau and belle our worth can tell,
        Though oft we cause them pain.

    In white array, the ladies gay
        And sprightly often show us:
    From what is said, we are afraid,
        You will too quickly know us.

914   Four things there are, all of a height,
    One of them crook'd, the rest upright.
    Take three away, and you will find
    Exactly ten remain behind.
    But if you cut the four in twain,
    You'll find one-half doth eight retain.

915   I'm up, and down, and round about,
    No mortal e'er found my end out;
    Tho' hundreds have employ'd their leisure,
    They never could disclose my measure.
    I'm found in almost every garden;
    Nay in the compass of a farthing:
    There's neither chariot, coach, nor mill
    Can move an inch except I will.

916   My first in various senses stands,
        My second melody implies;
    My whole full oft with partial hands,
        Its favours scatters or denies;
    Yet all invoke the fickle thing,
    And wish to mount its airy wing.

917   My first is the genial source of much good,
        Though often the cause of much evil;
    My second oft raises a spurious brood,
        And my whole worships angel or devil.

918   To a semi-circle add a circle,
        The same again repeat;
    To all these add a triangle,
        And then you'll have a treat.

919   If you the heart of man erase,
And let a hen's supply its place,
Adding a leopard's tail thereto;
They'll quickly bring before your view,
What's requisite for all to do.

920   Join the name of a beast to a quarter of beef,
And a tree you will have with an ever-green leaf.

MIRTUNZIO, Fosildo (18th century)
Pseudonymous Italian riddler. Enigmas published in *Veglie autunnali*
(1796).

921   *Forrier di pace, e di tranquilla quiete,*
      Dopo tempeste strepitose, e dense,
      Tu mi vedi apparir su d'alte mete
      Pinto in vario color, che mi condense,
      Mi dileguo in brev'or per vie secrete,
      Incapibili omai, perchè già immense:
      Mi tinge un Astro, ed al sparir di quello,
      Finisco anch'io, e in questo dir mi svello.

(Portender of peace, and of quiet tranquillity, after loud, large
storms, you see me appear on high, painted in various colours
which condense me, I fade away shortly by secret paths, no
longer understandable, because already vast. A star paints me,
and when it disappears, I too finish, and in saying this I reveal
myself.)

922   *Ancella fida son di notte, e giorno,*
      Compagna indivisibil sempre a lato;
      Moto, e gesto non fai, che già d'intorno
      Gli rassomiglio oscura per usato;
      Con te già vivo, e faccio il mio soggiorno,
      Nè posso mai cambiar si nobil stato,
      Perchè mi scorta in te luce diurna
      E mi guida talor face notturna.

(I am a faithful maid by night and by day, an inseparable
companion always by your side. You make no movement or
gesture, without my being there looking like you, but obscured
as usual. I already live with you, and I make my sojourn with
you, nor can I ever change such a noble state, because daily light
makes me follow you, and sometimes even the face of night
guides me.)

MODERN SPHINX, The (1873)
General history and anthology of riddles by anonymous author
published by Griffith & Farran, London. Contains 1152 riddles of every
variety with discussion of each form.

923   Never wearied, see us stand,
A glittering and a stately band –
Of sturdy stuff, but graceful form,
In summer cold, in winter warm;

From hottest duty never swerving,
Night and day our place preserving;
Each serving to a different use,
Not to be changed without abuse.
And, pray, mark well another fact –
In unison we never act,
Except, as on occasion dread,
We watch the ashes of the dead;
When we are ranged, as you may see,
As awful sentries, one, two, three.

924 For my learning, it will a mere paradox show –
Though I understand great things, yet nothing I know.
Though thus mean in myself, even kings I support,
Have access to the fair, am familiar at court,
And at balls have the principal share in the sport.

925 I am not of flesh and blood,
         Yet have I many a bone;
     No limbs, except one leg,
         And can't stand on that alone.

My friends are many, and dwell
    In all lands of the human race;
But they poke my poor nose into the mud,
    And shamefully spatter my face.

Thrust me into each other's ribs,
    Stick me in gutter and rut;
I have never a window, and never a door,
    Yet I oft myself am shut.

926 A man of fourscore winters white
         Sat dozing in his chair;
     His frosted brow was quite my *first*.
         With glorious silver hair.

My *whole* lay playing at his feet,
    And a glance upward stole;
My *second*, I can wager you,
    Was father of my *whole*.

927 I took my *first* upon the field,
         Resolved to do or die;
     I clutch'd my *whole*; resolved to yield
         To none – to low nor high.
     My task was *second*, yet I dared
     That task to do; I stood prepared.

928 My *first*, though small, much work performs,
         All for my *second*'s sake;
     It pauses oft, but never tires,
         Nor seeks a rest to take.

My *third* is a large, well-known thing,
  Which for my *second* toils;
Unwearied, it e'er labours on,
  Nor from its task recoils.

My *whole*, my *second* doth attain,
  I am by all required;
And when of goodly quality,
  Am much to be admired.

929 As an emblem of sweetness my *first* is esteem'd;
     At the toilet my *next* of great service is deem'd;
     When united, so well put together am I,
     No builder on earth can my fabric outvie.

930 If from five you take five
       (Rightly, I mean),
     A word of dislike you'll have
       Left, I ween.

931 One thousand, two hundred,
       Nothing, and one,
     Transposed, give a word
       Expressive of fun.

932 It's found in the house, though it be but a hut,
     And without it no razor, howe'er sharp, can cut;
     It's always in sugar, but never in tea,
     It's a part of yourself, but it's no part of me.

933 I strengthen the weak, I cross the wide sea,
     I frighten the thief, and I grow on a tree.

934 'Tis easy to show me,
                 ME
     'Tis easy to show me;
     ME you always may find ME.
     These words pray rehearse,
     And turn into verse.

935 If the B m t, put:
     but if a B. putting:

936 EEE & xxxx UR XXI, XXX & eee.

937 There is ᵃⁿ vice difference virtue.
              whelming

938 Al
     |
     l.

939 To nothing add nothing, with a harbour between
     And then a famed city will quickly be seen.

940   I'm found in loss, but not in gain,
If you search there, 'twill be in vain;
I'm found in hour, but not in day;
What I am, perhaps you'll say.

MOORE, Thomas (1779–1852)
Irish poet and civil servant born in Dublin.

941   *Quest*: Why is a Pump like Viscount Castlereagh?
    Answ: Because it is a slender thing of wood
        That up and down it's awkward arm doth sway,
        And coolly spout and spout and spout away,
        In one weak, washy, everlasting flood!

MORE, Hannah (1745–1833)
Poet, novelist, tract-writer, and leading member of 'Blue Stocking Circle'
that also included Mrs Delany (q.v.).

942   I'm a strange contradiction: I'm new and I'm old,
I'm sometimes in tatters and sometimes in gold,
Though I never could read, yet letter'd I'm found
Though blind, I enlighten, though free I am bound.
I'm English, I'm German, I'm French, and I'm Dutch;
Some love me too dearly, some slight me too much.
I often die young, though I sometimes live ages,
And as Queen is attended by so many pages.

MOTHER GOOSE IN HIEROGLYPHICKS (1849)
Picture-rebus version of *Mother Goose's Tales* (q.v.), first published by
George S. Appleton of Philadelphia in 1849.

943

Old woman, old old woman, says

Whither, O whither, O whither high ?

To sweep the from the

And shall back again, by and by.

MOTHER GOOSE'S TALES (c.1729)

Translation by Samber of Perrault's children's anthology *Contes de ma mère l'Oye* (1697) containing riddle-rhymes.

944   Black I am and much admired,
Men seek me until they're tired;
When they find me, break my head,
And take me from my resting bed.

945   A house full, a hole full,
And you cannot gather a bowl full.

946   Highty tighty, paradighty,
Clothed all in green,
The king could not read it,
No more could the queen;
They sent for the wise men
From out of the East,
Who said it had horns,
But it was not a beast.

947   I'm called by the name of a man,
Yet am as little as a mouse;
When winter comes I love to be
With my red target near the house.

948   Two brothers we are,
Great burdens we bear,
On which we are bitterly pressed;
The truth is to say,
We are full all the day,
And empty when we go to rest.

949   Clothed in yellow, red, and green,
I prate before the king and queen;
Of neither house nor land possessed,
By lords and knights I am caressed.

950   Little Nancy Etticoat
In a white petticoat
And a red nose;
The longer she stands
The shorter she grows.

951   In spring I am gay,
In handsome array;
In summer more clothing I wear;
When colder it grows,
I fling off my clothes,
And in winter quite naked appear.

952   I have a little sister called Peep, Peep, Peep,
She wades in the water deep, deep, deep.
She climbs the mountain high, high, high,
My poor little sister has but one eye.

953   Old Mother Twitchett had but one eye,
And a long tail which she let fly;
And every time she went over a gap,
She left a bit of her tail in a trap.

954   Little Billy Breek
Sits by the reek
He has more horns
Than all the king's sheep.

955   Thirty white horses upon a red hill,
Now they champ, now they clamp,
And now they stand still.

956   As I was going over London Bridge,
I heard something crack;
Not a man in all England
Can mend that!

957   Flour of England, fruit of Spain,
Met together in a shower of rain;
Put in a bag, tied round with string.
If you tell me this riddle
I'll give you a ring.

NECTANEBO, King (6th century)

King of Egypt renowned for his riddling battles with Lycerus, King of
Babylon. As described by the Byzantine scholar Maximus Planudes in
his *Life of Aesop*, Lycerus usually won as Aesop served at his court.

958   There is a grand temple which rests upon a single column,
which column is encircled by twelve cities; every city has
against its walls thirty flying buttresses, and each buttress has
two women, one white and one black, that go round about

235

it in turns. Say what that temple is called.

NEW MONTHLY MAGAZINE AND HUMORIST, The (1814–84)

Literary journal founded by Henry Colburn in opposition to the Jacobin *Monthly Magazine*. Editors included Theodore Hook and Thomas Hood with charades by C. S. Calverley (q.v.) and W. M. Praed (q.v.) amongst others. Examples given taken from issues for 1840–1 by 'P' and 'AYN'.

959   Say – what is that look which excites the despair
       Of a lover while watching the eyes of his fair?
       'Tis my '*first*,' which, endued with a magical spell,
       Turns my '*second*,' while strolling in dingle or dell;
       Or running a truant, unheard and alone,
       To a petrified form, or a crystalline stone.
       United, my '*whole*' gives a name you must guess,
       That's ever in order, yet oft in a mess.

960   My *first*'s a conveyance that's oft on the stand,
       And yet none more private careers in your land.
       Nor wheels, nor e'en horses are for it e'er needed,
       And still by five couriers 'tis ever preceded.
       So quick has it moved, that, in England on Sunday,
       It's been found in the midst of Morocco on Monday.
       When through rough work and wearing 'tis no longer sound,
       By applying my *second* a cure has been found;
       My *whole* is a terror to all those who travel,
       So pray, gentle reader, this riddle unravel.

961   From wand'ring in a distant clime,
         My FIRST returns once more;
       He hath worshipped at the Holy Shrine
         That Christian hearts adore.

       He hath been where the sky is ever blue,
         And the flow'rets are ever bright;
       He hath watched the fire-fly's brilliant hue
         'Mid the glory of eastern night.

       He hath been where mighty rivers spring
         Over sands of sparkling gold;
       And radiant birds with starry wings,
         Flit thro' the forests old.

       But bowed is his stately figure now,
         And grey is his raven hair,
       And deep are the lines on his noble brow,
         For my SECOND is throned there!

       And the laughing glance of his eye is flown,
         His life's wild dream is past;
       Weary and sad to his childhood's home
         The Wanderer comes at last.

       He stands in the midst of his fathers' halls,
         Lit by the sun's last rays,

But no kindly voice rings through the walls,
  With the sounds of other days.

And they showed him to a lonely tomb,
  Where the loved of his boyhood slept;
And in bitter grief, thro' the midnight gloom,
  His vigil there he kept.

They sought him when bright morning smiled,
  But his heart's pulse beat no more;
Peaceful he lay as a sleeping child,
  For his weary WHOLE was o'er.

NEW RIDDLE BOOK, A (n.d.)

Halfpenny chapbook published by R. Burdekin of York. 16 riddles with answers given in form of woodcut pictures.

962   Legs I have got, yet seldom do I walk;
I backbite many, yet I never talk;
In secret places most I seek to hide me,
For he who feeds me never can abide me.

963   I ne'er offend thee,
    Yet thou dost me whip,
Which don't amend me,
    Though I dance and skip,
When I'm upright, me you always like best,
And barbarously whip me when I want rest.

964   Though good fellows we are
We can't hope to be sav'd;
From our very first day,
To our last we're enslaved;
Our office is hardest,
And food sure the worst,
Being cramm'd with raw flesh,
Till we're ready to burst;
Tho' low in our state,
Even Kings we support;
And at balls have
The principle share of the sport.

965   Four wings I have,
Which swiftly mount on high,
On sturdy pinions yet I never fly,
And though my body often moves around,
Upon the self same spot I'm always found;
And, like a nurse who chews the infants meat,
I chew for man before that he can eat.

966   'Tis true I have both face and hands,
And move before your eyes;
Yet when I go my body stands,
And when I stand I lie.

967   A head and a body large I have,
         Stomach and bowels too;
      One wincing gut of mighty length
         Where all my food goes thro',
      But what's more strange, my food I take,
         In at the lower end;
      And all just like a drunken rake,
         Out at my mouth I send.

NEW RIDDLE BOOK FOR THE AMUSEMENT AND INSTRUCTION OF LITTLE MISSES AND MASTERS, The
(19th century)
Chapbook by 'Master Wiseman', printed by James Kendrew of York.

968   I'm a busy active creature,
      Full of mirth and play by nature;
      Nimbly I skip from tree to tree,
      To get the food that's fit for me;
      Then let me hear if you can tell,
      What is my name, and where I dwell.

969   I'm captain of a party small,
         Whose number is but five,
      But yet do great exploits for all,
         And ev'ry man alive.
      With Adam I was seen to live,
         Ere he knew what was evil;
      But no connection have with Eve,
         The serpent, or the devil.
      I on our Saviour's law attend,
         And fly deceit and vice;
      Patriot and Protestant befriend,
         But Infidels despise.

970   Midst numbers round I spy'd a beauty fair,
      More charming than her sisters were:
      With blushing cheek she tempting of me stood,
      At last I cropt her bloom and suck'd her blood,
      Sweet meat she was, but neither flesh nor bone,
      Yet in her tender heart she had a stone.

971   Four wings I have, and sometimes more,
         By which I move and fly;
      Yet never stir until I'm drove,
         So indolent am I.

972   I daily am in France and Spain,
      At times do all the world explore,
      Since time I've held my reign,
      And shall till time will be no more.
      I never in my life beheld,
      A garden, field, or river clear;
      Yet neither garden, spring, or field,
      Can flourish if I am not there.

973   My body is thin,
And has no guts within,
I have neither head, face, nor eye;
But a tail I have got,
As long as – what not,
And without any wings I can fly.

NEW SPHINX, The (c.1832)

507 enigmas, charades, etc. published in London by T. Tegg & Son.

974   My first is a vapour that lightly descends,
Enriching the valleys and fields;
My next is a liquid, or fluid, or both,
Which often a fragrancy yields:
My whole in the sunbeams looks sparkling and gay,
Adorning with brilliants each bramble and spray;
And greatly resembles the crystalline tear,
Which falls from the eye of the penitent fair.

975   My hardy first now ploughs the main,
My second is a term to gain;
Oft at my whole a soldier aims,
And for his skill a prize he claims.

976   My first a state of equality shows;
A title in Spain my next will disclose;
The Scriptures declare my whole will be giv'n
To penitent man, to fit him for heav'n.

977   My first is valued more than gold,
Because 'tis seldom found;
Many there be the name that hold,
With whom 'tis nought but sound.
My second skims the swelling flood,
And noble is its air;
It oft has witness'd sights of blood,
And moments of despair.
My third, 'mid life's distressing cares,
A solace sweet and kind;
Happy who call the blessing theirs:
But few that solace find.

978   My first is a part of the day;
My second at feasts overflows;
In the cottage my whole is oft seen,
To measure old Time as he goes.

979   Two brothers, wisely kept apart,
Together are employ'd;
Though to one purpose they are bent,
Each takes a different side.
To them nor head nor mouth belong,
Yet plain their tongues appear;
With which they never spoke a word,
Without them useless are.

In blood and wounds they deal, yet good
  In temper they are proved;
From passion they are always free,
  Yet oft with anger mov'd.

980   Something – nothing – as you use me;
       Small, or bulky, as you choose me;
       Eternity I bring to view,
       The sun and all the planets, too;
       The morn and I may disagree,
       But all the world resembles me.

981   Like eastern monarchs, screen'd from vulgar eye,
       With triple wall secur'd, at ease I lie;
       So grand my station, title so elate,
       E'en kings submissive my precedence wait.
       Awful's my presence, form exceeding bright,
       Emitting broken rays of borrow'd light;
       Which, when collected, in a focus end,
       A speedy flight, or instant death portend;
       To me the hero bends the stubborn knee,
       And dignifies remote posterity.
       The scourge of tyrants I, the patriot's guard,
       The city's glorious prize, and just reward;
       In point of honour nice, but friend sincere;
       The badge of brav'ry, but the tool of fear.
       But why should I attempt to veil my pride,
       Or longer my perfections strive to hide,
       When, naked I command respect aloud,
       And strike a terror to the obsequious crowd;
       But gaily clad, I figure for your sport,
       And shine a harmless bauble at the court.

982   Three feet I have, but ne'er attempt to go,
       And many nails thereon, tho' ne'er a toe.
       Tempestuous winds and storms I've oft been in,
       And still go naked, tho' I deal in linen.
       I both in city and in country dwell,
       And have no head; yet I can reckon well.
       I often cheat the ladies of their due;
       You'll think it strange, but yet 'tis very true.

983   What beauties with a grace may do;
       What, when you're dress'd, looks well on you;
       What many a wretch, who has a wife,
       Submits to for a quiet life;
       What every prudent man would be,
       To please the present company;
       What miss would for a husband give,
       On what a parson's horse will live;
       What ladies use for similies,
       When fingers smart, or head-ache tease;
       All these may surely well explain
       What 'tis by all these that I mean.

NEWTON, Sir Isaac (1642–1727)
Eminent scientist and President of the Royal Society. Riddle ascribed to him cited in a letter from Horace Walpole (q.v.) to Lady Ossory.

984   Four people sat down at a table to play;
They play'd all that night, and some part of next day;
This one thing observ'd, that when all were seated,
Nobody play'd with them, and nobody betted;
Yet, when they got up, each was winner a Guinea;
Who tells me this riddle, I'm sure is no ninny.

NORTH AMERICAN FOLK RIDDLES
Folk riddles from Canada and USA including American Indian, Negro, and 'hillbilly' examples from various sources, all cited in Archer Taylor *English Riddles from Oral Tradition* (1951).

985   Riddlum, riddlum, raddy,
All head and no body.

986   Them has got eyes ain't got no head, an' what got head ain't got eyes.

987   What has a face, but no mouth?

988   What has feet and legs and nothing else?

989   Sometimes with a head,
Sometimes with no head at all,
Sometimes with a tail,
Sometimes with no tail at all.
What am I?

990   It stands on its one leg with its heart in its head.

991   What is this? Only two backbones, a thousand ribs.

992   What is it has four legs, one head and a foot?

993   Long legs, crooked toes,
Glassy eyes, snotty nose

994   There was a thing just four weeks old,
When Adam was no more;
Before that thing was five weeks old,
Old Adam was fourscore.

995   Something was here since the world was first made, and just a month old. What's that?

996   Cut me up in pieces and bury me alive,
The young ones will live and the old ones die.

997   What has a bed but never sleeps;
And has a mouth, yet never eats?

998   What is it that has a tongue but never talks,
Has no legs but always walks?

999   What has got eyes but never sees?
What has got a tongue but never talks?
What has a soul that can't be saved?

1000   What has four eyes and cannot see?

1001   What has a thousand legs and can't walk?

1002   What is it which flies high and flies low, has no feet and yet wears shoes?

1003   A white dove flew down by the castle. Along came a king and picked it up handless, ate it up toothless, and carried it away wingless.

1004   Goes over the fields all day, sits in the cupboard at night.

1005   What goes all down the street and comes back home, and sits in the corner and waits for a bone with its tongue hanging out?

1006   Runs over fields and woods all day.
       Under the bed at night sits not alone,
       With long tongue hanging out
       A-waiting for a bone.

1007   Little Polly Pickett
       Run through the thicket,
       Out and in and back again
       With one leg tied to the door jamb.

1008   Long neck and no hands,
       Hundred legs and can't stand,
       Runs through the house of a morning,
       Stands behind the door when company comes.

1009   Long-legged lifeless came to the door staffless,
       More afraid of a rooster and hen
       Than he was of a dog and ten men.

1010   Why is a baby like a wheatfield?

1011   They took me from my mother's side
       Where I was bravely bred
       And when to age I did become
       They did cut off my head.
       They gave to me some diet drink
       That often made me mad
       But it made peace between two kings
       And made two lovers glad.

1012   I sailed here from the old land,
       And am bound with iron bonds;
       Murder have I not done;
       Stolen not; cheated not;
       Yet a peg is beaten into my head.

1013   Use me well and I am everybody;
       Scratch my back and I am nobody.

1014   As I was on my way to London Town
       To buy my wife a soda cracker,
       I saw a host: some black, some brown,
       The rest the colour of tobacker.

242

1015   There was a green house.
Inside the green house there was a white house.
Inside the white house there was a red house.
Inside the red house there were a lot of little black babies.

1016   I washed my hands with water,
Which was neither rain nor run,
I dried them on a towel,
Which was neither woven nor spun.

1017   As I went across the bridge, I met a man with a load of wood
which was neither straight nor crooked. What kind of wood was
it?

1018   What belongs to you, but others use it more than you do?

1019   What is it that you can keep after giving it to someone else?

1020   What goes to sleep with its shoes on?

1021   What goes up the chimney down, but can't go down the
chimney up?

1022   Light as a feather,
Nothing in it.
A stout man can't hold it
More than a minute.

1023   What is it that you will break even if you name it?

1024   What fastens two people yet touches only one?

1025   What is it the more you take away the larger it becomes?

1026   What grows larger the more you contract it?

NOTES AND QUERIES (1849–date)

Periodical founded by the antiquary W. J. Thoms (1803–85). Riddles by
readers and queries on old enigmas, etc. *passim*.

1027   I see my *first*, I see my *next*,
    And both I sigh and see
Join'd to my *third*, which much perplex'd
    And sorely puzzled me.
'Twas fifty and 'twas something more,
    Revers'd 'twas scarce an ell;
With *first* and *next* it form'd my *whole*,
    Clearer than crystal well.
What is my *whole*? 'A splen-
    Did tear,' upheld in cruel thrall.
Blow soft, ye gales; bright suns, appear,
    And bid it gently fall!

1028   We rule the world, we letters 5,
And thus we sing and thus we strive.

    The crowned king and belted knight,
    The churl of low degree,
    The priest, the statesman, and the squire,
    Are ruled by letters 3.

The Chartist league, the Premier grave,
And devils black and blue,
And little beaux and grave debates
Are checked by letters 2.

Where lightly flies the gondola
Over the moonlit sea,
There master-spirits of the earth
Are ruled by letters 3.

They whirl about, they turn about,
And vex the world they do,
The letters 3, and most they love
To vex the letters 2.

Ha, ha! the 2 they ponder deep,
Plus therefore Q.E.D.,
They class themselves and dance about
With us, the letters 3.

From Heaven's blue vault we letters 3
On showers of roses came,
And caught upon our downward flight
The colours of the same.

Olympian Jove in high divan
He split his skull half through,
And the bright Goddess sprang to light
Who loves the letters 2.

Now fair befall the letters 5,
The letters 3 and 2;
Forsooth it were a happy world
If ye had each your due!

Fill high the bowl! ye letters 5,
Your Albion drinks to you:
Long may her daughters own the 3,
Her braver sons the 2!

1029   To five and five and forty-five
        The first of letters add,
    'Twill give a thing
    That killed a king,
        And drove a wise man mad.

OPIE, Mrs Amelia (1769–1853)
Novelist and poet satirized in *Headlong Hall* by Peacock (q.v.).

1030   Fair ladies, doubtless in my *whole* you'll find
    A pleasing entertainment for the mind;
    But if before my *first* my *second*'s placed,
    'Twill poison mind and body; – shun the taste.

PANARCES (n.d.)
Ancient Greek poet, cited by Athenaeus in *Deipnosophistae*. A version
of the riddle is also mentioned by Plato in *Republic*, Book V.

1031   A man that was not a man hit a bird that was not a bird,
        perched on wood that was not wood, with a stone that was not
        stone.

PARLOUR PASTIMES FOR THE YOUNG (1857)
Published by James Blackwood, London, and edited by 'Uncle George'.
Various puzzles, games, magic, etc. plus a number of riddles, mostly
conundrums.

1032   In number we are fifty-two,
            A motley, quaint, and jovial crew;
        We go wherever fortune sends,
            By some deemed foes, by others friends.
        In festive scenes we oft are found,
        In dissipation's halls abound;
        Four monarchies, with rogues in court,
        Each in apparel of a sort;
        One makes his kingdom in the heart,
        Another takes the delving part,
        A third is armed quite savagely,
        A fourth lights up the other three.
        We have a pope, we have a deuce –
        I pray th' expression you'll excuse;
        Our commons have their apple seed;
        But, 'stead of fruit, a noxious weed
        Springs up to choke the mind's best soil,
        And a false pleasure proves fierce toil;
        A pack of wolves – we fleece the sheep,
        And leave them wasted hours to reap.

1033   My whole is in cottage, and palace, and hall,
        And is constantly used by the great and the small,
        Beheaded, it still is attached to a head,
        And of various colours, black, brown, white, or red.
        Behead it again, and all heads would lie low,
        If deprived of its aid, as you probably know.

1034   Five hundred begins, five hundred ends it,
            Five in the middle is seen;
        The first of all figures, the first of all letters,
            Take up their stations between.
        Join all together, and then you will bring
        Before you the name of an eminent king.

1035   Tho' but small my size and figure,
            Yet I am in general use;
        To ev'ry blessing I contribute,
            To all happiness conduce.

No delight exists without me;
  I attend each beau and belle;
Also grace the shepherd's cottage,
  And the hermit's lonely cell.

From the king I'm ever banish'd,
  In his court I'm never seen;
But I with redoubled duty
  Daily wait upon the queen.

1036 Her body's sound, her brave attire complete,
And her attendants are both small and great;
Two friends she hath, by whom she seeks her chance,
The one supports, the other does advance
Her in her progress; but they both at last
Her enemies turn, and she's in danger cast.

Her hope was firm, her strength did not decay,
Though these two friends assailed her night and day;
She was directed by a little guide
In that, her great distress, to turn aside
Unto a place to which she was addressed,
Where she with her attendants take their rest.

1037 Proudly I'm borne o'er the billowy sea,
And far-distant nations have trembled at me;
Yet my office, at times, is so mean and so low,
I am subject to many an insult and blow.

By the side of the millstream I fearlessly rest,
And gracefully bend o'er the lake's glassy breast;
Yet the glory of England I bear far and wide,
And under me thousands have fought and have died.

Though 'tis true that, whene'er I appear in the street,
I am trampled in scorn by the crowd's busy feet,
I am often exalted in station and place,
And to strike me has ever been held a disgrace!

How often I claim your attention and care,
And repay you with smiles in your blooming parterre;
Then what can I be, who am known near and far,
And so gentle in peace, and so fearful in war?

PASSOVER RIDDLE, The (n.d.)
Ancient riddle recited at Jewish Passover Eve celebrations.

1038 Who knoweth one? I (saith Israel) know One:
  One is God, who is over heaven and earth.
Who knoweth two? I (saith Israel) know two:
  Two tables of the covenant; but One is our God
Who is over the heavens and the earth.

[And so on to the last verse, which is:
  Who knoweth thirteen? I (saith Israel) know thirteen:
Thirteen divine attributes, twelve tribes, eleven stars, ten

commandments, nine months preceding childbirth, eight days preceding circumcision, seven days of the week, six books of the Mishnah, five books of the Law, four matrons, three patriarchs, two tables of the covenant; but One is our God who is over the heavens and the earth.]

PEACOCK, Thomas Love (1785–1866)
British satirist, essayist, and poet. Charade reprinted in *Compleat Works*. (See also *Aelia Lelia Crispis* for Peacock's translation and solution.)

1039   Take three-quarters of fortune connected with chance
And one-half of a sprightly agreeable dance,
To these add two-thirds of what serves to restrain,
And a General who brings twenty-five in his train;
In all three united at once may be seen
The glory of Rome and of Shacklewell Green.

PEARSON, A. Cyril (fl. 1900s)
Former puzzle editor of the *Evening Standard* and author of numerous puzzle books. Examples taken from *The Twentieth Century Standard Puzzle Book* (1907) and *Pictured Puzzles and Word Play* (1908).

1040   A word of five though I may be,
    My charms are quite a lot;
Combine my fifth and second, and
    'See!' That's what you have got.
My first and fourth and third compose
    'A brilliant line of light.'
My fifth and fourth and third make up
    'To put or place aright.'

    My second, fourth, and first you take
    To push a boat along;
My first and second, fourth and first
    Cry out too loud and long.
When you my whole in hand possess
    You hold a precious thing,
The best of friends, whose title means,
    'Pertaining to the King.'

1041   I sit in a corner,
    And never was heard
To make a petition
    Nor utter a word.
Yet I travel by night,
    And I travel by day,
And carry your message
    Whatever you say.
I am blue, I am green,
    I am pink, I am red –
The smallest of prices
    Is set on my head.

When I start on my journey,
    Though I stick to my place,
I am sure to receive
    A hard blow in the face.
I am generally square
    But my character's such
That you'd best not compel me
    To work overmuch.
For I'll run you one errand,
    And, that errand run,
My life work is ended,
    My usefulness done.

1042   Complete, though not of human race,
            A soul in me may dwell;
        Behead, I held a higher place,
            Until, like man, I fell.
        Again behead, and in the song
            Of Burns I'm all your own;
        Behead once more, it would be wrong
            To find me out when known.

1043   When winter comes with frost and cold,
        My first is welcome, as of old;
        And though its grip may make you thinner,
        It helps to cook your Christmas dinner.

        Let me but hear my next rejoice
        At early dawn with cheerful voice,
        I haste to find, with eager pleasure,
        Some specimen of hidden treasure.

        A traveller my whole may find
        Far from his English kith and kind;
        Though some at home, to England's shame,
        Are this in fact, if not in name.

1044   Complete, I grow within a field
        And pleasant pasture often yield;
        Behead me once, a suitor then
        Is quickly brought before your ken;
        Behead again, I am a word
        That on the cricket-ground is heard.
        Restore my heads, cut off my tail,
        To name a spice you'll not then fail;
        Behead me now, and you will find
        The master passion left behind.
        Put on my head, my tail restore,
        Complete me as I was before,
        My second letter take away,
        An envelope I am, you'll say;
        But now curtail me just once more,
        I am an inlet on the shore.

248

1045   When my whole takes a flight in the air you will find
       That my next is not left a great distance behind;
       But join them together, and plain to your view
       It all is as firm and as tight as a screw.

1046   Veiling the leas, my first may steep
           Late autumn's listless air;
       And with my tainting second creep
           On idle spade and share.

       When happy days link soul to soul,
           And sunny faces shine,
       May both combined, a subtle whole,
           Be far from me and mine!

1047   When a monk in old times, unexpectedly heated,
           Endangered the peace of his soul,
       To atone for my second my first he repeated
           Quite ten times a day on my whole.

1048   My first a simple verb, or half a verb, may be;
       Almost the same my next, or half the same, we see.
       My whole may weigh a ton or more, and yet be light,
       Dull, and bereft of motion; swift, exceeding bright.

1049   My first reversed will plainly show
           An apple in its embryo.
       Reverse my second, and we see
           That which in sight can never be.
       Replace them both, and write me down
           Six letters that will spell a town.

1050   My first is worn by night and day,
           And very useful reckoned;
       London, or Bath, or Bristol may
           With truth be styled my second.
       Now if you cannot find me out
           You lack my whole without a doubt.

1051   My first now marks the soldier's face,
           Who was my next's defender;
       But when my whole attacked the place
           It drove him to surrender.

1052   My first is an insect,
           My second a border;
       My whole puts the face
           Into tuneful disorder.

PETER PRIMROSE'S BOOKS FOR BOYS AND GIRLS:
RIDDLES (c.1850)
Chapbook printed by William Walker of Oxley, Yorkshire.

1053   Many a lady in the land
       Has grasp'd me in her lily hand;
       I'm sometimes made a little bright,
       And often us'd to make more light.

1054   To cross the water I'm the way,
       For water I'm above:
    I touch it not, and, truth to say,
    I neither swim nor move.

1055   Horns tho' I wear, in yonder sky
    Astronomers have plac'd me high;
    The seeds of cruelty I nourish,
    And 'mongst Hibernia's children flourish.

1056   My tongue is long,
    My voice is strong,
       And yet I breed no strife;
    You will me hear,
    Both far and near,
       And yet I have no life.

1057   My first does innocence express;
    My second, 'tis a part of dress:
    United, they a period show
    That's free from vices, guilt and woe.

1058   I live in a study, but know not a letter;
    I feast on the muses but am ne'er the better:
    Can run over English, o'er Latin, o'er Greek,
    But none of the languages ever could speak.

1059   I am the beginning of sorrow, and the end of sickness. You
    cannot express happiness without me; yet I am in the midst of
    crosses. I am always in risk, yet never in danger. You may find
    me in the sun, but I am never out of darkness.

1060   I at fires attend,
    Am a kitchen friend;
    When my nose I blow,
    How the embers glow!
    When the wind compels,
    How my belly swells!

PETRONIUS, Gaius (fl. 1st century AD)
Roman satirist. The following triple enigma occurs in *Satyricon*.

1061   'What part of us am I? I come far, I come wide. Now find me.'
    I can tell you what part of us runs and does not move from its
    place; what grows out of us and grows smaller.

PITT, William, 1st Earl of Chatham (1708–78)
Whig statesman. Riddles ascribed to him.

1062   To discover the name that my verse would express
    A letter you'll first from the alphabet guess;
    Which letter, by this may be easily known,
    Its shape is the very reverse of your own.
    My next, if a fair one too rashly exposes
    A beauteous complexion of lilies and roses,
    What the beams of the sun will infallibly do

To deaden their lustre and sully their hue.
Add to these, what induces the amorous swain
To persist in his vows, though received with disdain.
These, joined all together, will make up the name
Of a family known in the annals of fame.

1063   My *first* is French, my *second* English, and my *whole* is Latin.

POE, Edgar Allan (1809–49)

American poet and story-writer. Riddles and acrostics appeared in
various literary magazines. (To translate the first two, read the first
letter of the first line in connection with the second letter of the second
line, the third letter of the third line, the fourth of the fourth, and so
on to the end. The names will thus appear. To solve the third riddle,
take the first letter of the name of each writer described in the text –
together they also form a word.)

1064   For her this rhyme is penned, whose luminous eyes,
     Brightly expressive as the twins of Læda,
  Shall find her own sweet name, that, nestling lies
     Upon the page, enwrapped from every reader.
  Search narrowly the lines! – they hold a treasure
     Divine – a talisman – an amulet.
  That must be worn *at heart*. Search well the measure –
     The words – the syllables! Do not forget
  The trivialest point, or you may lose your labour!
     And yet there is in this no Gordian knot
  Which one might not undo without a sabre,
     If one could merely comprehend the plot.
  Enwritten upon the leaf where now are peering
     Eyes scintillating soul, there lie *perdus*
  Three eloquent words oft uttered in the hearing
     Of poets, by poets – as the name is a poet's, too.
  Its letters, although naturally lying
     Like the knight Pinto – Mendez Ferdinando –
  Still form a synonym for Truth. – Cease trying!
     You will not read the riddle, though you do the best you
      can do.

1065   'Seldom we find,' says Solomon Don Dunce,
     'Half an idea in the profoundest sonnet.
  Through all the flimsy things we see at once
     As easily as through a Naples bonnet –
     Trash of all trash! – how *can* a lady don it?
  Yet heavier far than your Petrarchan stuff –
  Owl-downy nonsense that the faintest puff
     Twirls into trunk-paper the while you con it.'
  And, veritably, Sol is right enough.
  The general tuckermanities are arrant
  Bubbles – ephemeral and *so* transparent –
     But *this* is, now, – you may depend upon it –
  Stable, opaque, immortal – all by dint
  Of the dear names that lie concealed within 't.

The noblest name in Allegory's page,
The hand that traced inexorable rage;
A pleasing moralist whose page refined,
Displays the deepest knowledge of the mind;
A tender poet of a foreign tongue,
(Indited in the language that he sung).
A bard of brilliant but unlicensed page
At once the shame and glory of our age,
The prince of harmony and stirling sense,
The ancient dramatist of eminence,
The bard that paints imagination's powers,
And him whose song revives departed hours,
Once more an ancient tragic bard recall,
In boldness of design surpassing all.
These names when rightly read, a name [make] known
Which gathers all their glories in its own.

POLITE JESTER, or The Theatre for Wit (1796)

Printed by and for J. Drew of Fetter Lane, London. Contains 'Diverting Jests, Smart Repartees, Brilliant Bon Mots, Sensible Puns, Keen Epigrams, Pleasing Tales, Comical Bulls, Choice Riddles, Good Conundrums, Witty Epitaphs etc., interspersed with a great variety of Comic Poetry. The whole intended for chearful Amusement and is free from indelicacy.'

1067   My size is large, my shape's uncouth,
    I have neither limb nor feature;
Men's hands have form'd my skin so smooth:
    My guts were made by nature.

Nor male nor female is my sex,
    You'll scarce believe my troth:
For when I've told you all my tricks
    You'll swear 't must needs be both.

For oft my master lies with me,
    His wife I oft enjoy;
Yet she's no whore, no cuckold he,
    And true to both am I.

My cloaths, nor women fit, nor men,
    They're neither coat nor gown;
Yet oft both men and maidens, when
    They're naked, have them on.

When I'm upon my legs, I lie,
    Yet legs in truth I have none;
And never am I seen so high
    To rise as when I'm down.

What's oft my belly is oft my back,
    And what my feet, my head;
And though I'm up, I have a knack
    Of being still a-bed.

1068   Why is Richmond like the letter R?

1069   My face resembles all mankind;
I'm ever blind when with the blind;
When I'm approach'd by ladies fair,
I'm just as handsome I declare;
And when an ugly girl I view,
By Jove, I'm just as ugly too:
If a beggar to me draw near,
Then quick a beggar I appear;
And when a king I chance to see,
I am as great a king as he.

1070   I'm parent of mirth, and the child of art;
A stranger to myself in ev'ry part;
I'm either weak or strong, sour or sweet,
To suit the taste of those I chance to meet;
And various countries have combin'd
To make me pleasant unto all mankind:
My faithful friends upon my ruin thrive,
And see me dying as they grow alive.

1071   He who begot me did conceive me too:
Within one month to a man's height I grew;
And should I to an hundred years remain,
I to my stature not one inch should gain.
Numbers of brethren I have here on earth;
And all, like me, of this surprizing birth.
Some, curious garments do their limbs adorn,
And some as naked are as they were born,
Yet both alike are cold, alike are warm.
Some want an eye, and others have no feet,
Some have no arms, others no legs, and yet
Most men esteem them equally with me,
Though I in all my limbs unblemish'd be.
To sum up all as briefly as I can,
I am man's offspring, tho' I'm not a man.

POTTER, Beatrix (1866–1943)
Author and illustrator of popular children's books. Traditional folk riddles, sometimes in slightly unusual form (as in the 'Humpty Dumpty' variant given here) occur in *The Tale of Squirrel Nutkin* (1903), her third book and first real success. (See also *Mother Goose's Tales*.)

1072   Riddle me, riddle me, rot-tot-tote!
A little wee man, in a red red coat!
A staff in his hand, and a stone in his throat;
If you'll tell me this riddle, I'll give you a groat.

1073   Humpty Dumpty lies in the beck,
With a white counterpane round his neck,
Forty doctors and forty wrights,
Cannot put Humpty Dumpty to rights!

PRAED, Winthrop Mackworth (1802–39)
Humorous poet and MP who was Secretary to the Board of Control
from 1834. Renowned for his elegant charades which first began to
appear in *Knights Quarterly Magazine* in 1823 under the pseudonym
'Vyvyan Joyeuse'. Also published in *The New Monthly Magazine* and
Athenaeum.

1074   Sir Hilary charged at Agincourt, –
            Sooth 'twas an awful day!
        And though in that old age of sport
        The rufflers of the camp and court
            Had little time to-pray,
        'Tis said Sir Hilary muttered there
        Two syllables by way of prayer.

        My *First* to all the brave and proud
            Who see to-morrow's sun;
        My *Next* with her cold and quiet cloud
        To those who find their dewy shroud
            Before to-day's be done;
        And both together to all blue eyes
        That weep when a warrior nobly dies.

1075   Row on, row on! – The First may light
        My shallop o'er the wave to-night;
        But she will hide in a little while,
        The lustre of her silent smile;
        For fickle she is, and changeful still,
        As a madman's wish, or a woman's will.

        Row on, row on! – The Second is high
        In my own bright lady's balcony;
        And she beside it, pale and mute,
        Untold her beads, untouched her lute,
        Is wondering why her lover's skiff
        So slowly glides to the lonely cliff.

        Row on, row on! – When the Whole is fled,
        The song will be hushed, and the rapture dead;
        And I must go in my grief again
        To the toils of day, and the haunts of men,
        To a future of fear, and a present of care,
        And memory's dream of the things that were.

1076   Come from my First, aye, come!
            The battle dawn is nigh;
        And the screaming trump and the thundering drum
            Are calling thee to die!
        Fight as thy father fought,
            Fall as thy father fell;
        Thy task is taught, thy shroud is wrought:
            So – forward! and farewell!

Toll ye my Second, toll!
  Fling high the flambeau's light;
And sing the hymn for a parted soul
  Beneath the silent night!
The wreath upon his head,
  The cross upon his breast, –
Let the prayer be said, and the tear be shed:
  So – take him to his rest!

Call ye my Whole, aye, call!
  The lord of lute and lay;
And let him greet the sable pall
  With a noble song to-day.
Go, call him by his name;
  No fitter hand may crave
To light the flame of a soldier's fame
  On the turf of a soldier's grave!

1077   Morning is beaming o'er brake and bower,
Hark! to the chimes from yonder tower,
Call ye my First from her chamber now,
With her snowy veil and her jeweled brow.

Lo! where my Second, in gorgeous array,
Leads from his stable her beautiful bay,
Looking for her, as he curvets by,
With an arching neck, and a glancing eye.

Spread is the banquet, and studied the song;
Ranged in meet order the menial throng,
Jerome is ready with book and stole,
And the maidens fling flowers, but where is my Whole.

Look to the hill, is he climbing its side?
Look to the stream – is he crossing its tide?
Out on the false one! he comes not yet –
Lady, forget him, yea, scorn and forget.

1078   Alas! for that forgotten day
  When Chivalry was nourished,
When none but friars learned to pray
  And beef and beauty flourished!
And fraud in kings was held accurst,
  And falsehood sin was reckoned!
And mighty chargers bore my First,
  And fat monks wore my Second!

Oh, then I carried sword and shield,
  And casque with flaunting feather,
And earned my spurs on battle field,
  In winter and rough weather;
And polished many a sonnet up
  To ladies' eyes and tresses,
And learned to drain my father's cup,
  And loose my falcon's jesses:

But dim is now my grandeur's gleam;
  The mongrel mob grows prouder;
And everything is done by steam,
  And men are killed by powder.
And now I feel my swift decay,
  And give unheeded orders,
And rot in paltry state away,
  With sheriffs and recorders.

PRIZE, The (1863–1931)

Founded as the *Children's Prize* by Rev. J. Erskine Clarke, who later launched the highly successful *Chatterbox*. Contained fact, fiction, humour, and verse with religious tone. (Examples taken from 1907 issues.)

1079   Who wrung out dew where all was dry?
        Who dryness found where earth was wet?
        Who chose his army carefully,
        And found they were too many yet?
        Who dreamed of bread and of a tent,
        And told the dream when night was spent?
        Who made his men stand round the camp
        Each with his pitcher, trumpet, lamp,
        And with a great and mighty shout
        Put all the enemy to rout?

1080   A good old prophet's worthless elder son;
        A Hebrew by the greed of gold undone;
        A very great and glorious Persian king;
        A place whence ships did gold in plenty bring:
        A seer who blessed when he was told to curse,
        Will bring us to the ending of our verse.

        Take the first letters, you will surely see
        A plain man, living in simplicity;
        Though crafty, too, and cunning he could be.

PSELLUS, Michael (*fl.*1075–1100)

Greek encyclopedist and diplomat.

1081   I am justice. I am the height of justice. I have six ribs, but only
        two legs.

PUCCINI, Giacomo (1858–1924)

Italian opera composer. Riddles contained in Act 2 of *Turandot* (1926), based on plays by Gozzi and Schiller (libretto by G. Adami and R. Simoni).

1082   In the dark night flies a many-hued phantom. It soars and
        spreads its wings above the gloomy human crowd. The whole
        world calls to it, the whole world implores it. At dawn the
        phantom vanishes to be reborn in every heart. And every night
        't is born anew and every day it dies!

1083   It kindles like a flame but it is not flame. At times it is a frenzy. It is fever, force, passion! Inertia makes it flag. If you lose heart or die it grows cold, but dream of conquest and it flares up. Its voice you heed in trepidation, it glows like the setting sun!

1084   Ice which gives you fire and which your fire freezes still more! Lily-white and dark, if it allows you your freedom it makes you a slave; if it accepts you as a slave it makes you a King!

PUNCH, or The London Charivari (1841–date)
English illustrated weekly comic periodical. Conundrums taken from an issue of 1843.

1085   Why are washerwomen the greatest navigators of the globe?

1086   Why is 'Yes' the most ignorant word in the language?

1087   Why is a railroad like a bug?

1088   Why is a man who has too many servants like an oyster?

1089   Why is a rook's throat like a road?

1090   Why is a cornfield gayer than any other?

1091   Why is a cow's tail like a swan's bosom?

1092   Why is a pig in a parlour like a house on fire?

1093   Why is the sun like a good loaf?

1094   Why is a bird a greedy creature?

1095   When is a fowl's neck like a bell?

1096   Why isn't a boy like a pretty bonnet?

1097   When is a lady like a trout?

PUTTENHAM, Richard (1520–1601)
English author and critic. Riddles occur in *The Arte of English Poesie* (1589).

1098   It is my mother well I wot
       And yet the daughter that I begot.

1099   I haue a thing and rough it is
       And in the midst a hole I wis:
       There came a yong man with his ginne,
       And he put it a handfull in.

PUZZLE BOOK The (c.1820)
Chapbook printed by William Davison of Alnwick (1781–1858).

1100   I timely go to rest at night,
          And with the sun I rise;
       All day I try to reach in flight,
          That place where no one dies.

1101   Old Mother old stands in the cold,
        Her children die with age:
        Yet she still lives, and brings forth young,
        And every one without a tongue.

1102   I daily view the world around,
        And in one place I'm seldom found;
        I never eat, yet by my power,
        Procure what millions do devour.

1103   My virtue is such, that I
        Can do the things with ease,
        Which strength and force will never do,
        Employ them as you please.

1104   Tho' I both foul and dirty am,
          As black as black as can be,
        There's many a Lady that will come,
          And by the hand take me.

1105   We dwell in cottages of straw,
        And labour much for little gains;
        Sweet meat from us our masters draw,
        And then with death reward our pains.

1106   Tho' I have neither legs nor feet,
          My use is for to go;
        Altho' I cannot speak, I tell
          What others want to know.

PUZZLECAP'S AMUSING RIDDLE BOOK (c.1870)
Chapbook published by S. & J. Keys of Devonport, England.

1107   Two twins we are, and let it not surprise,
        Alike in every feature, shape, and size;
        We're square or round, of brass or iron made,
        Sometimes of wood, and useful found in trade:
        But to conclude, for all our daily pains,
        We by the neck are often hung in chains.

1108   A tall and slender shape I bear:
        No lady's skin more white or fair.
        My life is short and doth decay
        So soon, it seldom lasts a day;

        If in the evening brought to light,
        I make my exit in the night;
        Yet to mankind I'm useful ever,
        And many hidden things discover.

1109   There's a little short gentleman,
          That wears the yellow trews,
        A dirk below his doublet
          For sticking of his foes.
        Yet in a singing posture,
          Where'er you do him see,

And if you offer violence,
   He'll stab his dirk in thee.

1110   I know my owner, serve my feeder,
       But am ignorant of my breeder,
       Who sought the means to change my nature;
       And from a fierce, unruly creature,
       Made me as useful to the nation
       As some who move in higher station;
       As I mankind do render stronger,
       And die that they may live the longer.

PUZZLING CAP, The (*c*.1780)
British chapbook.

1111   Tho' it be cold, I wear no cloaths,
          The frost and snow I never fear;
       I value neither shoes nor hose,
          And yet I wander far and near:
       My diet is for ever free,
          I drink no cyder, port or sack:
       What Providence doth send to me,
          I neither buy, nor sell, nor lack.

1112   Without a bridle or a saddle
       Across a ridge I ride and straddle;
       And ev'ry one, by help of me,
       Tho' almost blind are made to see.
       Then tell me, ev'ry pretty dame,
       And witty Master, what's my name.

1113   Preferment lately was bestow'd,
          Upon a man tho' mean and small;
       A thousand then about him flow'd,
          Yet he return'd no thanks at all;
       But yet their hands are ready still,
          To help him with their kind good will.

QUEEN OF SHEBA'S RIDDLES, The (n.d.)
Riddles later ascribed to the Queen of Sheba (apocryphal).

1114   Seven there are that issue and nine that enter; two yield the
       draught and one drinks.

1115   There is an enclosure with ten doors; when one is open, nine are
       shut; when nine are open, one is shut.

1116   A woman said to her son, 'Thy father is my father, and
       thy grandfather my husband; thou art my son, and I am thy
       sister.'

1117   What land is that that has but once seen the sun?

1118   There is something which when living moves not, yet when its
       head is cut off it moves?

1119   What is that which is produced from the ground, yet man produces it, while its food is of the fruit of the ground.

RABELAIS, François (1494–1553)
French humanist, satirist and physician. Riddles occur in *Pantagruel* (1532), *Gargantua* (1534) and the 'Fifth Book' (1562–4) from which this example is taken.

1120   *Une bien jeune et toute blondelette*
Conceut un fils Æthiopien, sans pere,
Puis l'enfanta sans douleur la tendrette,
Quoiqu'il sortist comme faict la vipere,
L'ayant rongé, en mout grand vitupere,
Tout l'un des flancs, pour son impatience.
Depuis passa monts et vaux sans fiance,
Par l'air volant, en terre cheminant:
Tant qu'estonna l'amy de Sapience,
Qui l'estima estre humain animant.

(A pretty creature, young and fair and slender
Conceived, without a sire, a swarthy son
And bore him painlessly, the little tender
Suckling, although his birth was a strange one.
For, like a viper, through her side he bored
Impatiently, a truly hideous thing,
And then o'er hill and valley boldly soared,
Riding the air, or o'er land journeying;
Which drove the Friend of Wisdom out of his mind,
For he had thought him of the human kind.)

RECEUIL DES ÉNIGMES DE CES TEMPS (1659)
French riddle collection edited by Abbé C. Cotin.

1121   *De mille ouvriers i'occupe le loisir,*
Ie porte un masque au visage semblable,
Qui me cachant, irrite le desir,
Car au grand iour ie suis moins agreable.

Souvent i'eschappe à qui me croit saisir,
Et les beaux traits qui me rendent aymable
Font de la peine, & causent du plaisir,
Mais trop de fard me rend reconnoissable.

En plein midy mon sçavoir nompareil,
Peut mettre un voile au devant du Soleil.
Vous qui percez l'obscuritè plus forte.

Ie vous invite à démesler ce poinct,
Qui me connoist m'appelle en mesme sorte,
Que l'ignorant qui ne me connoist point.

(I occupy the leisure of a thousand workers. I wear a mask like a face which, hiding me, inflames desire, for I am less attractive in broad daylight. I often escape those who think they can catch me, and the good features that make me lovable are both sources of pain, and yet also cause pleasure. But too much make-up makes me recognizable. At high noon my unparalleled knowledge can even put a veil in front of the sun. You, who can pierce a stronger darkness, I ask you to untangle this puzzle. He who knows me calls me by the same name as the ignoramus who doesn't know me at all.)

1122   *Mon pere n'est qu'esprit, & gouverne la terre,*
Son estre est immortel, il est fait pour les Cieux,
Il me produit obscure, & reserve à ses yeux
L'honneur de penetrer le voille qui m'enserre,
Dans une sombre nuict ie cache mes tresors,
Ie fais ce que ie puis, de peur d'estre apperceuë,
Mais dedans ce dessein souvent ie suis deceuë,
Un seul mot me confond, & descouvre mon corps.

(My father is just a spirit, and he governs the earth. His being is immortal, he is made for the heavens. He makes me obscure and keeps for his own eyes the honour of piercing the veil which encloses me. In a dark night I conceal my treasures. I do whatever I can, for fear of discovery, but I am often disappointed in my purpose. A single word confounds me and exposes me.)

REUSNER, Nicolaus (1545–1602)

Rector of Jena University, Germany. Riddles published in *Aenigmata* (1602). Also edited an anthology, *Aenigmatographia.*

1123   *Foemina, piscis, avis sum, nautas fallere docta, sum scopulus, non sum foemina, piscis, avis.*

(I am a woman, a fish and a bird, well taught to deceive sailors. I am a rock, I am not a woman, or a fish or a bird.)

1124   *Sunt gemina germana, harum alteram et altera gignit, perque vices sic fit, filia nata, parens.*

(They are twin sisters; each of them gives birth to the other, and thus it happens that, by turns, a daughter is born, then a parent.)

1125   *Lacryma multa mihi, sed nulla est causa doloris, coeli affecto vitam, sed gravis aer obest.*

(Many are the tears I give but there is no cause for grief. I strive for life in the sky, but the weighty air engulfs me.)

RIDDLE BALLADS, English (18th century)

Some slightly abridged texts of famous English riddle ballads.

1126   'A Noble Riddle Wisely Expounded'

There was a lady of the North Country,
  Lay the bent to the bonny broom
And she had lovely daughters three.
  Fa la la la, fa la la la ra re

There was a knight of noble worth
Which also lived in the North.

The knight, of courage stout and brave,
A wife he did desire to have.

He knocked at the ladie's gate
One evening when it was late.

The eldest sister let him in,
And pin'd the door with a silver pin.

The second sister she made his bed,
And laid soft pillows under his head.

The youngest daughter that same night,
She went to bed to this young knight.

And in the morning, when it was day,
These words unto him she did say:

'Now you have had your will,' quoth she,
'I pray, sir knight, will you marry me?'

The young brave knight to her replyed,
'Thy suit, fair maid, shall not be deny'd.

'If thou canst answer me questions three,
This very day will I marry thee.

'Kind sir, in love, O then,' quoth she,
'Tell me what your [three] questions be.'

'O what is longer than the way,
Or what is deeper than the sea?

'Or what is louder than the horn,
Or what is sharper than a thorn?

'Or what is greener than the grass,
Or what is worse than a woman was?'

'O love is longer than the way,
And hell is deeper than the sea.

'And thunder is louder than the horn,
And hunger is sharper than a thorn.

'And poyson is greener than the grass,
And the Devil is worse than woman was.

When she these questions answered had,
The knight became exceeding glad.

And having [truly] try'd her wit,
He much commended her for it.

And after, as it is verifi'd,
He made of her his lovely bride.

So now, fair maidens all, adieu,
This song I dedicate to you.

I wish that you may constant prove
Unto the man that you do love.

'Captain Wedderburn's Courtship'

The Lord of Rosslyn's daughter gaed through the wud her
    lane,
And there she met Captain Wedderburn, a servant to the
    king.
He said unto his livery-man, 'Were 't na agen the law,
I wad tak her to my ain bed, and lay her at the wa.'

Then he lap aff his milk-white steed, and set the lady
    on,
And a' the way he walkd on foot, he held her by the hand;
He held her by the middle jimp, for fear that she should
    fa;
Saying, 'I'll tak ye to my ain bed, and lay thee at the
    wa.'

'O haud awa frae me, kind sir, I pray ye lat me be,
For I'll na lie in your bed till I get dishes three;
Dishes three maun be dressd for me, gif I should eat them a',
Before I lie in your bed, at either stock or wa.

''T is I maun hae to my supper a chicken without a bane;
And I maun hae to my supper a cherry without a stane;
And I maun hae to my supper a bird without a gaw,
Before I lie in your bed, at either stock or wa.'

'Whan the chicken's in the shell, I am sure it has na bane;
And when the cherry's in the bloom, I wat it has na stane;
The dove she is a genty bird, she flees without a gaw;
Sae we'll baith lie in ae bed, and ye'll be at the wa.'

'O haud awa frae me, kind sir, I pray don't me perplex,
For I'll na lie in your bed till ye answer questions six:
Questions six ye maun answer me, and that is four and twa,
Before I lie in your bed, at either stock or wa.

'O what is greener than the gress, what's higher than thae
    trees?
O what is worse than women's wish, what's deeper than the
    seas?
What bird craws first, what tree buds first, what first does on
    them fa?
Before I lie in your bed, at either stock or wa.'

'Death is greener than the gress, heaven higher than thae
    trees;
The devil's waur than women's wish, hell's deeper than the
    seas;
The cock craws first, the cedar buds first, dew first on them
    does fa;
Sae we'll baith lie in ae bed, and ye 'se lie at the wa.'

Little did this lady think, that morning whan she raise,
That this was for to be the last o a' her maiden days.
But there's na into the king's realm to be found a blither twa,
And now she's Mrs Wedderburn, and she lies at the wa.

'Proud Lady Margaret'

1128 'T was on a night, an evening bright,
    When the dew began to fa,
Lady Margaret was walking up and down,
    Looking oer her castle wa.

She looked east and she looked west,
    To see what she could spy,
When a gallant knight came in her sight,
    And to the gate drew nigh.

'You seem to be no gentleman,
    You wear your boots so wide;
But you seem to be some cunning hunter,
    You wear the horn so syde.'

'I am no cunning hunter,' he said,
    'Nor neer intend to be;
But I am come to this castle
    To seek the love of thee.
And if you do not grant me love,
    This night for thee I'll die.'

'If you should die for me, sir knight,
    There's few for you will meane;
For mony a better has died for me,
    Whose graves are growing green.

'But ye maun read my riddle,' she said,
    'And answer my questions three;
And but ye read them right,' she said,
    'Gae stretch ye out and die.

'Now what is the flower, the ae first flower,
    Springs either on moor or dale?
And what is the bird, the bonnie bonnie bird,
    Sings on the evening gale?'

'The primrose is the ae first flower
    Springs either on moor or dale,
And the thristlecock is the bonniest bird
    Sings on the evening gale.'

'I think you maun be my match,' she said,
    'My match and something mair;
You are the first eer got the grant
    Of love frae my father's heir.'

RIDDLE BALLADS, Faroese (n.d.)

Abridged text of Ancient Faroese ballad, *Gátu Ríma*.

1129   Guest goes wandering from the hall,
        Silent and blind is he;
    Meets he with an eldern man
        All with hair so grey.

    Meets he with an eldern man,
        All with hair so grey;
    'Why art thou so silent, Guest the Blind,
        And wherefore dost thou stray?'

    'It is not so wonderful
        Though I of speech am slow;
    For riddles have brought me to an evil pass,
        And I lose my head tomorrow.'

    'How much of the red, red gold
        Wilt thou give to me,
    If I go in before King Heithrek
        And ask thy riddles for thee?'

    'Twelve marks of the red, red gold
        Will I give to thee,
    If thou wilt go in before King Heithrek,
        And ransom my head for me.'

    'Go thou into thy courtyard
        And look to thy dwelling, thou,
    While I go in before King Heithrek,
        And ask him riddles now.'

    'O hearken now, Heithrek my King,
        And what can this be now? –
    Soft as down and hard as horn,
        And white as glistening snow!'

    'Hear thou this now, Guest the Blind;
        This riddle I understand. –
    The sea it is both soft and hard,
        And flings white spray upon the land.'

    'O hearken now, Heithrek my King,
        Where does the sapling grow, –
    Its root is turned towards high Heaven,
        And its head turned down below?'

    'The icicle on the high crags,
        No sapling it is I trow,
    Yet its root is turned towards high heaven,
        And its head turned down below.'

    'O hearken now, Heithrek my King,
        Where does that forest grow, –
    It is cut on every holy day,
        And yet there is wood enow?'

'The beard which grows on each man's chin,
    No forest is that I trow,
Though shaved on every holy day,
    And yet there is wood enow.'

'O hearken now, Heithrek my King,
    Where dost thou know the brothers, –
Both of them live in the same hall,
    And have neither fathers nor mothers?'

'Turf clods and brimstones,
    Neither of the twain are brothers.
Both of them live in the same hall,
    And have neither fathers nor mothers.'

Othin has turned into a wild fowl,
    And has flown far out to sea;
He has burnt King Heithrek in his hall,
    And all his company.

RIDDLE BALLADS, Russian

Russian song based on *zagádki* (riddles) quoted in W. R. S. Ralston's
The Songs of the Russian People (1872).

1130   A maiden fair was strolling in a garden,
Gathering rosy flow'rets was the maiden.
By that way a merchant's son came driving.
'Now may God be with thee, beauteous maiden,
God be with thee, rosy flow'rets gathering!'
'Many thanks! O merchant's son! Thanks many!'
'Shall I ask thee riddles, beauteous maiden?
Six wise riddles shall I ask thee?'
'Ask them, ask them, merchant's son,
Prithee ask the six wise riddles.'
'Well, then, maiden, what is higher than the forest?
Also, what is brighter than the light?
Also, maiden, what is thicker than the forest?
Also, maiden, what is there that's rootless?
Also, maiden, what is never silent?
Also, what is there past finding out?'
'I will answer, merchant's son, will answer,
All the six wise riddles will I answer.
Higher than the forest – is the moon,
Brighter than the light – the ruddy sun.
Thicker than the forest – are the stars.
Rootless is, O merchant's son, a stone.
Never silent, merchant's son, the sea,
And God's will is past all finding out.'
'Thou hast guessed, O maiden fair, guessed rightly,
All the six wise riddles hast thou answered.
Therefore now to me shalt thou be wedded,
Therefore, maiden, shalt thou be the merchant's wife.'

RIDDLE BOOK; or Fireside Amusements, The (18th century)
Chapbook published by Thomas Richardson.

1131   Why is ink like scandal?

1132   My face is smooth and wondrous bright,
        Which mostly I keep out of sight
        Within my house; how that is made
        Shall with much brevity be said:
        Compos'd with timber and with skin,
        Cover'd with blankets warm within:
        Here I lie snug, unless in anger,
        I look out sharp suspecting danger;
        For I'm a blade of mighty wrath,
        Whene'er provok'd I sally forth;
        Yet quarrels frequently decide,
        But n'er am known to change my side,
        Tho e'er so much our party vary,
        In all disputes my point I carry.
        Thousands by me are daily fed,
        As many laid among the dead.
        I travel into foreign parts;
        But not in coach convey'd, or carts.
        Ladies, for you I often war,
        Then in return my name declare.

1133   Why is a large wig like a fierce engagement?

1134   In places where mirth and good-humour abound,
        Who so welcome as I, or so commonly found?
        If I get among gamblers, I never am winner;
        Eat nothing, yet who can afford better dinner.
        At church of my privilege n'er bate an ace;
        Not e'en to churchwarden or parson give place.
        In verse or in prose, there are few who indite,
        But to me they apply e'er they venture to write.
        In council I'm present, nor absent at sea,
        Nymphs who're courted by all, come and pay court to me.
        Then seek out my title, each spirit lover,
        Who dares such a favourite rival discover:
        If I move not on four, as I usually do,
        You may find me on one leg, but never on two.

RIDDLE OF THE SPHINX, The (n.d.)
Traditional Greek riddle. Mentioned in Athenaeus's *Deipnosophistae* but
also occurs in *Greek Anthology* and elsewhere.

1135   What is it that goes on four legs in the morning, two legs at
        noon and three legs in the evening?

RIDDLE SONGS
The first of these two examples is taken from *The National Song Book*
edited by Charles Villiers Stanford (1906). The second is a traditional
folk song.

RAISE US A RIDDLE.
(THE FLOATING TRIBUTE.)

Poem by A. P. GRAVES.

Fairly quick.

mf CHORUS OR 2ND VOICE.

1. Raise us a rid - dle as spin - ning we sit.
2. Sure - ly hid trea - sure is in..... your head.

mf * SOLO OR 1ST VOICE.

1. P'r'aps I have one that your fan - cy will fit.
2. Wrong - ly my rid - dle this time you have read.

f CHORUS.   SOLO.

1. Come, then, advance it with all of your wit.   Some have got the
2. Come, give us hold of a strong - er thread.   How is this my

1. bar - ley show - in', Some a pur - ty patch of oats,
2. herds can ut - ter Of them-selves the milk all day,

1. O - thers just the pra - ties grow - in', With a moun - tain
2. Churn and turn it in - to but - ter, Faix and fir - kin it

1. side for goats.   Come with me thro' mea - dows flow'r - y,
2. safe a - way.   Ker - ry cows up - on their brows

1. Up where furze and heath - er blow,   If my se - cret
2. Bear a pair of branch - ing horns;   But my kind they

1. gold - en dow - ry, Lass - es, you would like to know.
2. wear be - hind,..... One, on - ly one, like U - ni - corns

D.C.

f CHORUS.   SOLO.

Ah! then your herds are the bees on the height. 'Deed and this time you've

f CHORUS.

guessed a - right.   Plea - sant the rid - dle you put us to-night.

THE RIDDLE SONG

1137   I gave my love a cher-ry that
has no stones, I gave my love a chick-en that
has no bones, I gave my lov a ring _____ that
has no end, I gave my love a ba-by that's no cry-en.

How can there be a cherry that has no stones?
How can there be a chicken that has no bones?
How can there be a ring that has no end?
How can there be a baby that's no cry-en?

A cherry when it's blooming it has no stones.
A chicken when it's pipping it has no bones.
A ring when it's rolling it has no end.
A baby when it's sleeping there's no cry-en.

RIDDLES AND THEIR SOLUTION (c.1905)
Booklet no.1 of 'Dick's Penny Series' which also included American
Humour and Puzzles. Published by John Dicks, London. Over 1000
riddles.

1138   Since time began my age I date,
Yet still retain my youthful state;
And if I live till all things moulder,
I never shall be one day older;
I'm that which none can ever see,
Or what now is shall ever be;
I always rise with every morn,
And yet must die before I'm born;
For me the ardent lover sighs;
The needy hope from me supplies;
Parties I ask to dine with me,
But with them I can never be;
As long as time remains the same,
So long shall I retain my name;
And though my life is but a span,
Yet time must die before I can;
Assured I cannot live for ever,
'Tis clear that time and I must sever:
To find me out this clue I'll give –
If time were dead I could not live.

1139   I'm cold as death, yet can't be heated;
My name is old, and oft repeated;
I'm pure as dew in April morning;
I rest on hills, their tops adorning;
Should you only once discover
To handle me, I'm gone for ever.

1140   I am a word of letters five,
And am consumed by all alive;
Take six away, and then you'll see,
That little word of letters three.

269

1141   I am seen in all quarters with ladies of quality,
       And always was fond of a tranquil retreat;
    I never could join in gay scenes of frivolity,
       Though in the quadrille I my friends often meet,
    I am in each metropolitan theatre *heard*,
       Though I am only seen in the *Queen's*, 'pon my word.
    I'm frequently heard of in all billiard-rooms,
       And I'm placed in bouquets of the richest perfumes.

1142   My *first* you use in many a way,
    In fact you use me night and day,
    As right and left I am well known,
    And when you play at whist I'm shown;
    My *next*'s a pronoun as you'll find,
    One of a very personal kind;
    My *last* upon the head is seen,
    Worn by a beggar or a queen;
    My *whole* will name a well-known race,
    If you the sporting papers trace.

1143   My *first* transposed, with hateful skill
       Its web perfidious weaves in vain;
    Firm as a rock, secure from ill,
    O truth, thou art my *second* still,
       And ever wilt remain.
    If business press, or duty call,
    Try not, ye fair, to find my *whole*;
    But when you've no more work to do,
    All duties well performed, may you
    Both find it and enjoy it too!

1144   There is a thing in truth unknown,
    Which yet is by experience shown;
    It is not found in earth or air;
    'Tis in no weather, foul or fair;
    It is a wayward, curious creature;
    Opposed, athwart, and cross in nature.
    Nothing without it is perplexed;
    Extreme, excited, anxious, vexed;
    In county it hath never been;
    In busy town it ne'er was seen.

    By lecture you would try in vain
    Its wondrous essence to explain;
    No chemist by his art can find it,
    Sage, magic, cannot seize and bind it;
    To war and pestilence a stranger;
    Nor was it ever seen in danger.
    It is not found in the great ocean;
    Nor in repose, nor yet in motion;
    Though not in form, state, or condition,
    'Tis seen in every exhibition.

1145   I always end the combat dire,
Although for fight I've no desire;
I join every fierce debate,
Yet never with the Church or State;
You're sure to find me in your bath;
At night I often cross your path;
I'm first in every battle fought;
I'm much afraid of being caught;
The battle-axe, without my aid,
Could ne'er ward off the warrior's blade;
In fact, no battery could stand,
Unless I lent a helping hand;
Without me girls would lose a play
They're fond of on a summer's day;
At battledore they'd never more
Be heard to count a twentieth score;
I am a quiet harmless thing;
I never bark, or loudly sing:
Two distinct species, you will find,
Are in my person nicely joined.

1146   I have no head, and a tail I lack,
But oft have arms, and legs, and back;
I dwell in the palace, the tavern, the cot –
'Tis a beggarly residence where I am not.
If a monarch were present (I tell you no fable),
I still should be placed at the head of the table.

1147   So high is my post, so exalted my station,
That I'm sure to be found with the head of the nation:
I'm sometimes as lovely as lovely can be,
And there's never a sigh but is uttered through me;
But I'm sometimes so ugly, and void of all charm,
Though I do try my best, not a heart can I warm.
By men I am treated quite harsh, I declare,
But the women protect me with infinite care.
With watches and clocks, too, I'm sure to be found,
Or useless 'twould be for the hands to go round.
At the death-bed of one who's to memory dear
Your feelings will make you shed o'er me a tear.

1148   Three letters, in England's wintry air,
May save thy life by their warmth and care;
But meet them 'neath Africa's burning sun,
Ah! speed thee away or thy race is run.

1149   Beware of my *first*! On the desolate mountain
      It sits like a demon to lead you astray;
    Or, lodged in yon vale by a murmuring fountain,
      It shows its dark visage, alas! to betray.
    My *next* is a freebooter, nursed by destroying
      The brightest of talents it tends to obscure;
    By day and by night it is always employing
      Those wasteful devices which ruin ensure.
    My *whole*, when you think me a frontless deluder,
      I seem in your looks, like a wizard, to trace;
    Ah, why should you harbour so base an intruder,
      Which every believer esteems a disgrace?

1150   I've heard that Lord Verulam's learning was great,
    That he scarce had a rival in Church or in State;
    And yet I've been known to be higher than he,
    Although at no college I took my degree.
    The young and the old of my favour can boast;
    And when ladies appear I descend from my post:
    Then adding a letter, you quickly will prove
    That I'm quite the reverse of esteem or of love.

1151   I'm fond of a row, sir, I freely confess;
    And I'm often in error; but, nevertheless,
    Though I fly from the weak and abide with the strong,
    I'm as oft in the right as I am in the wrong.
    And though in a riot I'm *first* to appear,
    I'm the *last* on the scene, sir, when danger is near.
    You may call me capricious; perhaps it is true;
    But I'll wager my life I stay longer than *you*
    In a perilous house; for I'm there to the last,
    And *you* quit very soon when the *first* half is past.
    I leave you to find out my name if you will,
    If you will not, I'll revel in mystery still.

1152   A feeling all persons detest,
    Although 'tis by everyone felt,
    By two letters fully expressed,
    By twice two invariably spelt.

1153   A riddle of riddles, it dances and skips;
    It is read in the eyes, though it cheats in the lips:
    If it meets with its match, it is easily caught;
    But if money will buy it, it's not worth a groat.

RIDDLES, CHARADES, AND CONUNDRUMS (1822)

1154   What is that which a coach always goes with, cannot go
    without, and yet is of no use to the coach?

1155   What is put on a table, cut, but never eaten?

1156   What has three feet and cannot walk?

RIDDLES OF HERACLITUS AND DEMOCRITUS (1598)

Anonymous riddle collection printed in London.

1157   Many a man doth speake of mee,
But no man ever shall me see,
For all in one doe full agree
That no where must my dwelling bee.

1158   I wrinkled am and passing olde,
    But gallant is my motion,
Abhorring aie to be controulde
    By any ones devotion.
Come all that list on me to mount,
    Sure I will not forsake them,
But let them make their just account,
    That finely I shall shake them.
Ne doe I aske men ought for hose,
    For shooes, for drinke, or meating,
Come all that list with me to close
    Sans paying or intreating.
And they may chaunce finde in my wombe
To make them wish they were at home.

1159   A female, produced first in a rude lumpe, as they say a yong
beare is, not by licking, but by pressing became beautifull. For
she hath as many friendes as the Queene of England, as many
subjectes as the King of Spaine, as many rulers as Athens ever
had, or Venice hath. And though shee can neither write nor
reade, yet is she lettered, a phisition, a rhetorician, and a
chronicler.

1160   We are in number not five times five,
    No one of us two handfull long,
Nor any of us takes care to thrive,
    Yet all together we doe so throng,
That if a man would lift to strive
    T'extinguish or to doe us wrong
Were he the greatest prince alive,
    We should be found for him too strong,
And could make him infamous in time to come,
Though most of us beene deafe and dombe.

1161   This is the age that I would have,
    These times for me are woondrous fit;
Each ladie that is fine and brave
    With me delights to goe and sit.
My living lieth not in my lands,
    Yet I am daintie, fine and sweete.
The ladies take me in their hands,
    Their lips and mine full often meete.

Their paps, their cheekes I well may touch,
  In smiling sort with me they play,
Their husbands thereat thinke not much,
  No, though I downe with them doe lay:
In sooth, it is a foolish sin,
When foolish husbands iealous bin.

1162   Two forward went, and one did seeme to stay them;
       Foure after ran, and five did overlay them,
       Of which one dead foure quicke was comprehending:
       And all these twelve unto one marke were tending.

1163   First I was small, and round like a pearle;
       Then long and slender, as brave as an earle;
       Since, like an hermit, I livde in a cell,
       And now, like a rogue, in the wide world I dwell.

1164   There is a bodie without a hart, that hath a toong, and yet no
           head;
       Buried it was, ere it was made, and lowde it speakes, and yet
           is dead.

1165   A lowe bred squire,
       Borne in the mire,
       That never knew who was his sire,

       Being armed light,
       After midnight
       (No remedie) would needes go fight.

       In corslet bad
       The youth was clad,
       And sarcenet sleeves for sooth he had.

       But at a word:
       He had no sword,
       Nor other weapon woorth a *etc* [*sic*].

       Ne was he strong,
       Nor large nor long,
       But foorth he came with a hideous song.

       And Tartar leeke
       He me did seeke,
       Lighting at first full on my cheeke.

       This thing of naught
       At face still raught,
       As Cesar once his souldiours taught,

       When they should fight
       Against that knight,
       Pompey defending countries right:

       So in like case
       This varlet base
       Was ever poring at my face.

I could not rest
Within my nest,
The rascall did me so molest.

I had the Jacke
Soone brought to wracke,
Had he not ever retired backe.

But he comes, he goes,
He fell, he rose,
He bit me by the very nose.

It made me sweare,
And God to teare,
I could not for my life forbeare.

That such a knave
Should be so brave,
Would make (I trowe) a saint to rave.

But clod or stone,
Or sticke or bone,
Or gunne or crosbowe had I none.

That, truth to showe,
I did not knowe,
Which way I might him overthrowe.

So that at last
I waxt agast,
And, longing t'have the combate past,

I hid my head
Within a bed
And slept like one that had been dead.

1166   Mounsier Monoculus, with that one eie,
It's not for his personage or his sweete face,
That wherefoere I goe, I doe him espie,
   With maidens and wives in speciall grace.
He is a surgeon, he can let blood,
His pricke is a thing that doth them good.

1167   That which a sheepe did inward hide,
I use to weare on my outside;
And that which a tree did outward weare,
   Within me alwaies I doe beare.
By drowning first I tooke effence,
   And hanged was since for none offence:
Still ready, by a blast of breath,
To finde a life causing my death.

1168   Al day leeke one that's in disgrace
   He resteth in some secret place,
And seldome putteth foorth the head,
   Untill daylight be fully fled;

Then in the maides or goodwives hand
  The gallant ginnes first up to stand:
Whom to a hole they doe apply,
Wherein he will both live and die.

RIG-VEDA, The (*c*.1000 BC)
Hindu religious text.

1169   The one who made him does not know him. He escapes from the one who has seen him. Enveloped in his mother's womb, he is subject to annihilation, while he has many descendants.

1170   Breathing, it lies there and is nevertheless quick in its gait, moving and yet fixed in the rivers. The soul of the dead man goes about as it likes. The immortal one has the same origin as the mortal one.

1171   I saw a restless shepherd travelling back and forth on his paths. He garbs himself in that which goes in the same and in an opposite direction. He goes hither and thither among creatures.

1172   The wheel of nature with twelve spokes turns around the heavens without ever going to ruin. On it stand, O Agni, sons in pairs to the number of seven hundred and twenty.

ROSSETTI, Christina (1830–94)
Poet and prose writer (sister of D. G. and W. M. Rossetti). Riddles first appeared in *Marshall's Ladies' Daily Remembrancer* (1850) and *Sing-Song, A Nursery Rhyme Book* (1872).

1173   Name any gentleman you spy,
    And there's a chance that he is I.
    Go out to angle, and you may
    Catch me on a propitious day.
    Booted and spurred, their journey ended,
    The weary are by me befriended.
    If roasted meat should be your wish,
    I am more needful than a dish.
    I am acknowledgedly poor;
    Yet my resources are no fewer
    Than all the trades – there is not one
    But I profess, beneath the sun.
    I bear a part in many a game;
    My worth may change, I am the same:
    Sometimes, by you expelled, I roam
    Forth from the sanctuary of home.

1174   Me you often meet
        In London's crowded street,
    And merry children's voices my resting-place proclaim.
        Pictures and prose and verse
        Compose me – I rehearse
    Evil and good and folly, and call each by its name.

I make men glad, and I
　Can bid their senses fly,
And festive echoes know me of Isis and of Cam.
　But give me to a friend,
　And amity will end,
Though he may have the temper and meekness of a lamb.

1175　My first is no proof of my second,
　Though my second's a proof of my first.
If I were my whole, I should tell you
　Quite freely my best and my worst.

One clue more:– If you fail to discover
　My meaning, you're blind as a mole;
But if you will frankly confess it,
　You show yourself clearly my whole.

1176　How many authors are my first!
　And I shall be so too
Unless I finish speedily
　That which I have to do.

My second is a lofty tree
　And a delicious fruit;
This in the hot-house flourishes –
　That amid rocks takes root.

My whole is an immortal queen
　Renowned in classic lore:
Her a god won without her will,
　And her a goddess bore.

1177　There is one that has a head without an eye,
　And there's one that has an eye without a head.
You may find the answer if you try;
　And when all is said,
　Half the answer hangs upon a thread.

ROUSSEAU, Jean Jacques (1712–78)
French political philosopher and educationalist. Riddle published in
1776. (Verse translation by Dr Johnson's friend, Mrs Thrale
(1741–1821).)

1178　*Enfant de l'Art, Enfant de la Nature,*
　Sans prolonger les jours j'empêche de mourir:
　Plus je suis vrai, plus je fais d'imposture,
　Et je deviens trop jeune à force de vieillir.

(Art's offspring, whom Nature delights here to foster,
　Can Death's dart defy, though not lengthen life's stage;
Most correct at the moment when most an impostor,
　Still freshening in youth as advancing in age.)

ROWLEY, Hugh (1833–1908)

Compiler and illustrator of *Puniana, or Thoughts Wise and Other-wise* (1867) and a sequel, *More Puniana* (1875). The books, which contain mostly conundrums and charades, are divided into eighty-five and fifty 'canters', respectively. (See also Appendix for parody of Fanshawe riddle.)

1179   I am white, and I'm brown; I am large, and I'm small;
       Male and female I am, and yet that's not all –
       I've a head without brains, and a mouth without wit;
       I can stand without legs, but I never can sit.
       Although I've no mind, I am false and I'm true,
       Can be faithful and constant to time and to you;
       I am praised and I'm blamed for faults not my own,
       But I feel both as little as if I were stone.

1180   O'Donoghue came to the hermit's cell;
       He climbed the ladder, he pulled the bell;
       'I have ridden,' said he, 'with the saint to dine
       On his richest meal and his reddest wine.'

       The hermit hasted my *first* to fill
       With water from the limpid rill;
       And 'Drink,' quoth he, 'of the juice, brave knight,
       Which breeds no fever, and prompts no fight.'

       The hermit hasted my *second* to spread
       With stalks of lettuce and crusts of bread;
       And 'Taste,' quoth he, 'of the cates, fair guest,
       Which bring no surfeit, and break no rest.'

       Hasty and hungry the chief explored
       My *whole* with the point of his ready sword,
       And found, as yielded the latch and lock,
       A pasty of game and a flagon of hock.

1181   In many a curious wreath, around
       A well-turned pillar I am bound;
       With which no Grecian orders vie
       For beauty and just symmetry.
       Though I'm allowed to rival all,
       My rise is owing to a fall;
       And now advanced, in Courts I live,
       From whence no honour I receive;
       Yet honours to the great I give.
       Me the coy virgin strives to hide,
       But soon discloses when a bride.
       Me the discarded love finds
       A certain cure for love-sick minds.

1182   The night was dark, the night was damp;
       St. Bruno read by his lonely lamp:
       The Fiend dropped in to make a call,
       As he posted away to a fancy ball;
       And 'Can't I find,' said the Father of Lies,
       'Some present a saint may not despise?'

Wine he brought him, such as yet
Was ne'er on Pontiff's table set:
Weary and faint was the holy man,
But he crossed with a cross the tempter's can,
And saw, ere my First to his parched lip came,
That it was red with liquid flame.

Jewels he showed him – many a gem
Fit for a Sultan's diadem:
Dazzled, I trow, was the anchorite;
But he told his beads with all his might;
And, instead of my Second, so rich and rare,
A pinch of worthless dust lay there.

A lady at last he handed in,
With a bright black eye and a fair white skin;
The stern ascetic flung, 'tis said,
A ponderous missal at her head;
She vanished away; and what a smell
Of my Whole she left in the hermit's cell!

1183   Through thy short and shadowy span,
I am with thee, child of man,
With thee still, from first to last,
In pain and pleasure, feast and fast,
At thy cradle and thy death,
Thine earliest wail and dying breath,
Seek thou not to shun or save,
On the earth or in the grave;
The worm and I, the worm and I
In the grave together lie.

ROYAL RIDDLE BOOK, The (1820)
Scottish chapbook published in Glasgow by J. Lumsden & Son.

1184   In the bed it stands, in the bed it lies,
Its lofty neb looks to the skies:
The bigger it is the good wife loves 't better,
She pluckt it and suckt it, till her eyes did water.
She took it into her hand, and said it was good,
Put it in her belly and it stirred up her blood.

1185   Much higher than the trees I am,
        My bulk exceeds a house;
And yet I seem unto most men,
        No larger than a mouse.

1186   In a green coat a thing is clad,
Wing'd for flight not seldom made;
Small, yet capers well, and sings,
Pray tell me what may be this thing.

1187   There is a little thing
        That's found in divers lands,
    Altho' it teacheth multitudes,
        Yet nothing understands:
    'Tis found in every kingdom,
        Yet not in earth or sea,
    'Tis in all sorts of timber,
        But not in any tree,
    And in all sorts of metal,
        But yet as I am told,
    'Tis not in iron, brass,
        Tin, silver, or in gold.
    Wild Africa this wonder wants,
        And so doth Asia,
    But yet, as travellers do affirm,
        'Tis in America;
    Germany enjoys it,
        Yet does not France or Spain,
    In Hungary and Poland
        To seek for it is vain;
    In Amsterdam 'tis common
        Yet Holland wants it still;
    'Tis in every mountain,
        Yet not in any hill;
    It never was in Italy,
        In Rome it still appears,
    It comes in every minute,
        Yet not in twenty years,
    All Scotland cannot shew it,
        Nor England, but men say,
    In Westminster and Cambridge,
        You see it every day,
    And tho' you do not think on it
        'Tis never out of mind,
    And always in its proper place,
        Indeed you may it find.

1188   Belly to belly, and hands at the back,
    Pull out a raw morsel, and stop a red gap.

1189   There were four sisters ran a race,
    And each did strive to mend their pace,
    Not one the other could o'ertake,
    Although they strove great haste to make.

1190   No teeth I have, and yet I bite,
        And when the bite is seen,
    According to my tender might,
        There is a mark of spleen.

1191   Twelve and twelve white cows,
        Stand equal in a stall,
    Forth came a red bull,
        And overlick'd them all.

ROYAL RIDDLER, The (1855)

Written by the anonymous author of *Parlour Pantomime or Charades in Action* and published by Dean & Son, London.

1192   In things of note I'm plainly seen,
        But yet in Nothing am I found;
    In water, fire, earth, or air,
        I'm not, – yet still I'm in the ground;
    At night I always stay at home,
    But from the day I'm known to roam.
    The ring that ties the marriage knot,
        My presence doth proclaim:
    No matter what my foes may say,
        I'm seen in every name.

    In the heavens, the moon, and sun, –
    The planets, who their courses run, –
    The gallant seaman, who crosses the ocean, –
    The engine that keeps the train in motion,
    The train that bears the people away,
    The men who go in the carriage to-day;
    In all these, – if you look, – I ween,
    My name may easily be seen.

1193   A child sees me with infant joy,
    And views me only as a toy;
    But youth and man own me with pride,
    And take me as a faithful guide.

1194   In every house I find a home,
        Because I'm useful found,
    The morning sees me clothed in white,
        The family seated round.

    Thus several times throughout each day,
        A porter's load I bear;
    And every time I'm loaded thus,
        The family all appear.

1195   Ladies are very found of my first,
        Which to us from China's brought;
    For my next, a spinning top transpose
        Which by boys is often bought.
    My whole all persons surely take
    Whene'er they wish my first to make.

1196   Though simple I am, I much power possess,
    And my name, I expect, you won't easily guess.
        The lawyer, who can plead so well,
        My powers to aid his cause, can tell;
        The student, when he his task indites,
        Admits I aid whate'er he writes;
        Divest me of my mystic dress,
        You soon may then my title guess.

1197   Skilful riddlers, say the name
       Which I, with some right, do claim;
       I swallow nails, – nay, do not start!
       They form of me a goodly part;
       From morn till night I bear a load
       Through mud and mire – o'er dusty road,
       Unlike a porter, (what I say is true,)
       I bear the porter, and his burden too!
       Life I contain, – good flesh and blood,
       From stalwart men to infant bud;
       Sometimes I'm cut and hacked about
       When handled by a foolish lout.
       When people die, I still must slave,
       And help to bear them to their grave.

1198   My first means to throw,
       As soon you will know,
       If rightly the answer you guess;
         An article next
         Will add to the text,
       To unravel this mystical dress.

       Then close to them place
       With right comely grace
       What fishermen use when at sea;
         My whole has oft been
         Used when dancing, I ween,
       And must be well known unto thee.

1199   'Tis gladsome to hear me,
         At gay Christmas time,
       When gay lads and lasses
         Are then in their prime;
       Add but one letter, – 'tis all you need do,
       Sad scenes of sorrow are then brought to view.

1200   A warlike weapon in me you behold,
       Which is of an ancient date, we are told;
       Behead me, – a fruit will be brought into sight,
       Behead me again, – you may then hear aright.

1201   Come, ye, who in riddles can take a delight,
       You'll surely detect me – and at first sight:
       In your service I've been for many a day,
       You use me e'en when you make things for your play.

       If your pretty doll you should wish to well dress
       My aid you require. – What I am, can you guess?
       In every house, – aye, and in cottage, I ween,
       And in palace as well – I am sure to be seen.

RUSSIAN FOLK RIDDLES

A selection of folk riddles from various sources, largely from an anonymous article in *Chambers Journal* (July 1893).

1202   *Edva primetnyi cherv', no dlia mekhov opasnyi*
        Est' pervoe moe. Znak v azbuke bezglasnyi –
        Vtoroe. A poet i komik-charodei
        Est' tseloe sharady sei.

        (A worm that's barely noticeable but dangerous to furs
        Is my first part. A mute symbol in the alphabet
        Is the second. And a poet and comic wizard
        Is the whole of this charade.)

1203   In the ocean-sea,
        On the island Buyán,
        Sits the bird Yustritsa.
        She boasts and brags
        That she has seen all,
        Has eaten much of all.
        She has seen the Tsar in Moscow,
        The king in Lithuania,
        The elder in his cell,
        The babe in his cradle.
        And she has not eaten that
        Which is wanting in the sea.

1204   *Stoit pop nizok,*
        Na nem sto rizok.

        (The priest is short, the vestments many.)

1205   I went down the street, I came to two forked roads, and I walked along them both at the same time.

1206   I am blind, but show others the way; deaf and dumb, but know how to count.

1207   It has neither eyes nor ears, yet it leads the blind.

1208   It flies silently and alights in silence; but when dead and rotten, it roars aloud.

1209   People pray for me, and long for my coming; but directly I appear, they hide themselves.

1210   There is a little dog which turns round and then lies still. It neither barks nor bites, but it keeps you out of the house.

1211   It lives without body, speaks without tongue; none ever saw, but all have heard me.

1212   If I eat grass my teeth grow blunt; chewing stone, they grow sharp again.

1213   Black, but no crow; horned, but not a bull; with six legs, but no hoofs – what am I?

1214   I am not bird or beast, but sharp-nosed, thin, and shrill-voiced; killing me you shed your own blood.

1215 Who are the two brothers that live on opposite sides of the road yet never see each other?

ST NICHOLAS (1873 to date)
Children's monthly magazine published by Scribner's of New York. Contained regular puzzle page, 'The Riddle Box'. Examples taken from issues for 1873 and 1874.

1216 Two heads I have, and when my voice
    Is heard afar, like thunder,
The lads and maids arrested stand,
    And watch and wait with wonder.

Quite promptly I'm obeyed, and yet
    'Tis only fair to say,
My master bangs me, right and left,
    And him I must obey.

1217 My *second* went to the side of my *first*,
And stayed through the *whole*, for the air;
    There were croquet and swinging,
    And bathing and singing
And chatting with maidens fair.

1218 My first comes from the Emerald Isle,
    Or else is given in play;
My second is a useful grain,
    Or else a crooked way.

My last is silver, paper, shell.
    Sometimes 'tis ruddy gold;
Or else it is a Scottish word –
    At least, so we are told.

My whole, though hoarded by the sire,
    Is wasted by the son.
With all the hints that I now give,
    My meaning must be won.

1219 My first you will certainly find on the farm,
    If the crops have been good this year;
My second you sometimes will find in the brooks,
    When the season is cold and drear;
My whole by the builder is carried aloft,
    By the architect skilfully planned,
For the mansion, the court-house or palace, perhaps,
    An ornament graceful or grand.

1220 My first, the dark Señora
    Wields with uncommon grace,
And, blushing, hides behind me
    The beauty of her face.

My second is a school-boy,
    The first in every game;
And yet – you'll scarce believe me –
    'Tis nothing but a name.

My whole is but a fancy,
A vision or a dream,
And very seldom – if at all –
Has my whole form been seen.

1221   My first is in battle, but not in fight;
My second is in eve, but not in night;
My third is in hearing, but not in sight;
My fourth is in darkness, but not in light;
My fifth is in wrong, and also in right;
My sixth is in red, but not in white;
My seventh is in flee, but not in flight;
My eighth is in read, and also in write;
My ninth is in danger, but not in fright.
My whole is a beautiful tree.

1222   A gorgeous bird, whose plumage bright,
Makes tropic forests gay;
A bright-winged thing, whose hanging nest
The passing breezes sway;
A warbler sweet of sunny isles,
Too oft a prisoner here;
A bird, whose wing scarce seems to move
While sailing through the air;
A pretty little warbling finch,
Familiar, gay and bright;
A songster rare, whose mellow notes
Are sweetly sung at night;
A bird with breast of golden dye,
And wings of darker hue;
A favourite nestling of our woods,
All clothed in feathers blue;
An idol, once to Egypt dear,
And named in ancient lore;
An English pet, that comes in spring,
And chirps about the door;
A gentle, tender, meek-eyed bird,
Oft seen upon the wing,
Whose note is plaintive soft and pure,
Whose praises poets sing.

These songsters sweet, from every land,
Who form a fluttering, bright-hued band,
Have here in kindness flown;
For each one now an offering brings,
To form the name of one who sings,
And makes their songs his own:
The bird, to Southern woods most dear,
With voice sweet, mellow, rich and clear.

SCALIGER, Julius Caesar (1484–1558)
Italian poet. Latin riddles published in *Poetices* (1561) and *Poemata* (1591).

1223   *Ore gero gladium, matrisque in pectore condo*
        Ut mox, qua nunc sunt mortua, viva colas.
        Dux meus a tergo caudamque trahens retrahensque
        Hasta non me ut eam verberat ast alios.

(I carry a sword in my mouth, and I bury it in my mother's breast so that soon you may cultivate, alive, what is now dead. My leader from behind me sticks a tail on me and drags it back and forth, and lashes not me but others, in order to beat her.)

1224   *Quale animal, dic, esse putes, quod nobile totum.*
        Est oculus, neque pars praetera ulla manet?
        Quotidie gignit natum sine matre creatum
        Qui tamen una ipsa hac interit ille die.
        Cuius item soror absente est genitore creata,
        Partita imperium fratris, et interitum.

(Tell me, what creature is this that is excellent in all degrees: is it an eye, with no other part remaining? Every day he is re-born without a mother to give him birth, and every day he dies. And his sister is also reared without a parent, and shares the empire of her brother, and shares his death.)

SCHILLER, Johann Christoph Friedrich von (1759–1805)
German dramatist/poet and leading figure of European Romantic movement. Riddles contained in *Turandot* (1802) and *Parabeln und Rätsel* (1803).

1225   *Es führt dich meilenweit von dannen*
            Und bleibt doch stets an seinem Ort,
        Es hat nicht Flügel auszuspannen,
            Und trägt dich durch die Lüfte fort.
        Es ist die allerschnellste Fähre,
            Die jemals einen Wandrer trug,
        Und durch das größte aller Meere
            Trägt es dich mit Gedankenflug,
        Ihn ist ein Augenblick genug!

(It bears thee many a mile away,
    And yet its place it changes ne'er;
It has no pinions to display,
    And yet conducts thee through the air.

It is the bark of swiftest motion
    That every weary wanderer bore;
With speed of thought the greatest ocean
    It carries thee in safety o'er;
    One moment wafts thee to the shore.)

1226   *Es steht ein groß geräumig Haus*
            Auf unsichtbaren Säulen,
        Es mißt's und geht's kein Wandrer aus,
            Und keiner darf drin weilen.

286

Nach einem unbegriffnen Plan
  Ist es mit Kunst gezimmert,
Es steckt sich selbst die Lampe an,
  Die es mit Pracht durchschimmert.
Es hat ein Dach, kristallenrein,
Von einem einz'gen Edelstein,
Doch noch kein Auge schaute
Den Meister, der es baute.

(There stands a dwelling, vast and tall,
  On unseen columns fair;
No wanderer treads or leaves its hall,
  And none can linger there.

Its wondrous structure first was plann'd
  With art no mortal knows;
It lights the lamps with its own hand
  'Mongst which it brightly glows.

It has a roof, as crystal bright,
Form'd of one gem of dazzling light;
  Yet mortal eye has ne'er
  Seen Him who placed it there.)

1227   Zwei Eimer sieht man ab und auf
  In einem Brunnen steigen,
Und schwebt der eine voll herauf,
  Muß sich der andre neigen.
Sie wandern rastlos hin und her,
Abwechselnd woll und wieder leer,
Und bringst du diesen an den Mund
Hängt jener in dem tiefsten Grund,
  Nie können sie mit ihren Gaben
  In gleichem Augenblick dich laben.

(Within a well two buckets lie,
  One mounts, and one descends;
When one is full, and rises high,
  The other downward wends.

They wander ever to and fro –
Now empty are, now overflow.
If to the mouth thou liftest *this*,
That hangs within the dark abyss.
In the same moment they can ne'er
Refresh thee with their treasures fair.)

1228   Kennst du das Bild auf zartem Grunde,
  Es gibt sich selber Licht und Glanz.
Ein andres ist's zu jeder Stunde,
  Und immer ist es frisch und ganz.
Im engsten Raum ist's ausgeführet,
  Der kleinste Rahmen faßt es ein,
Doch alle Größe, die dich rühret,
  Kennst du durch dieses Bild allein.

Und kannst du den Kristall mir nennen,
  Ihm gleicht an Wert kein Edelstein,
Er leuchtet ohne je zu brennen,
  Das ganze Weltall saugt er ein,
Der Himmel selbst ist abgemalet
  In seinem wundervollen Ring,
Und doch ist, was er von sich strahlet,
  Noch schöner als was er empfing.

(Know'st thou the form on tender ground?
  It gives itself its glow, its light;
And though each moment changing found,
  Is ever whole and ever bright.
In narrow compass 'tis confin'd,
  Within the smallest frame it lies;
Yet all things great that move thy mind,
  That form alone to thee supplies.

And canst thou, too, the crystal name?
  No gem can equal it in worth;
It gleams, yet kindles ne'er to flame,
  It sucks in even all the earth.
Within its bright and wondrous ring
  Is pictur'd forth the glow of heaven,
And yet it mirrors back each thing
  Far fairer than to it 'twas given.)

1229 *Ein Gebäude steht da von uralten Zeiten,*
Es ist kein Tempel, es ist kein Haus,
Ein Reiter kann hundert Tage reiten,
Er umwandert es nicht, er reitet's nicht aus.

Jahrhunderte sind vorübergeflogen,
Es trotzte der Zeit und der Stürme Heer,
Frei steht es unter dem himmlischen Bogen,
Es reicht in die Wolken, es netzt sich im Meer.

Nicht eitle Prahlsucht hat es getürmet,
Es dienet zum Heil es rettet und schirmet,
Seinesgleichen ist nicht auf Erden bekannt,
Und doch ist's ein Werk von Menschenhand.

(For ages an edifice here has been found,
  It is not a dwelling, it is not a fane;
A horseman for hundreds of days may ride round,
  Yet the end of his journey he ne'er can attain.

Full many a century o'er it has pass'd,
  The might of the storm and of time it defies;
'Neath the rainbow of Heaven stands free to the last, –
  In the ocean it dips, and soars up to the skies.

It was not vain glory that bade its erection,
It serves as a refuge, a shield, a protection;
Its like on the earth never yet has been known
And yet by man's hand it is fashion'd alone.)

Unter allen Schlangen ist eine,
   Auf Erden nicht gezeugt,
Mit der an Schnelle keine,
   An Wut sich keine vergleicht.

Sie stürzt mit furchtbarer Stimme
   Auf ihren Raub sich los,
Vertilgt in einem Grimme
   Den Reiter und sein Roß.

Sie liebt die höchsten Spitzen,
   Nicht Schloß, nicht Riegel kann
Vor ihrem Anfall schützen,
   Der Harnisch – lockt sie an.

Sie bricht wie dünne Halmen
   Den stärksten Baum entzwei,
Sie kann das Erz zermalmen,
   Wie dicht und fest es sei,

Und dieses Ungeheuer
   Hat zweimal nur gedroht –
Es stirbt im eig'nen Feuer,
   Wie's tötet, ist es tot!

(Amongst all serpents there is one,
   Born of no earthly breed;
In fury wild it stands alone,
   And in its matchless speed.

With fearful voice and headlong force
   It rushes on its prey,
And sweeps the rider and his horse
   In one fell swoop away.

The highest point it loves to gain;
   And neither bar nor lock
Its fiery onslaught can restrain;
   And arms – invite its shock.

It tears in twain like tender grass,
   The strongest forest-tree;
It grinds to dust the harden'd brass,
   Though stout and firm it be.

And yet this beast, that none can tame,
   Its threat ne'er twice fulfils;
It dies in its self-kindled flame,
   And dies e'en when it kills.)

Der Baum, auf dem die Kinder
Der Sterblichen verblühn,
Steinalt, nichtsdestominder
Stets wieder jung und grün.
Er kehrt auf einer Seite
Die Blätter zu dem Licht,
Doch kohlschwarz ist die zweite,

Und sieht die Sonne nicht.
  Er setzet neue Ringe
Sooft er blühet, an,
Das Alter aller Dinge
Zeigt er den Menschen an.
In seine grüne Rinden
Drückt sich ein Name leicht,
Der nicht mehr ist zu finden,
Wenn sie verdorrt und bleicht.

(The tree whereon decay
  All those from mortals sprung, –
Full old, and yet whose spray
  Is ever green and young;
To catch the light, it rolls
  Each leaf upon one side;
The other, black as coals,
  The sun has ne'er descried.
It places on new rings
  As often as it blows;
The age, too, of all things
  To mortal gaze it shows.
Upon its bark so green
  A name oft meets the eye.
Yet 'tis no longer seen,
  When it grows old and dry.
This tree – what can it mean?
  I wait for thy reply.)

1232   *Wie heißt das Ding, das wenige schätzen,*
Doch ziert's des größten Kaisers Hand,
Es ist gemacht, um zu verletzen,
Am nächsten ist's dem Schwert verwandt.

  Kein Blut vergießt's und macht doch tausend Wunden,
Niemand beraubt's und macht doch reich,
Es hat den Erdkreis überwunden,
Es macht das Leben sanft und gleich.

  Die größten Reiche hat's gegründet,
Die ältsten Städte hat's erbaut,
Doch niemals hat es Krieg entzündet,
Und Heil dem Volk, das ihm vertraut!

(What is the thing esteem'd by few?
  The monarch's hand it decks with pride,
Yet it is made to injure too,
  And to the sword is most allied.

No blood it sheds, yet many a wound
  Inflicts, – gives wealth, yet takes from none;
Has vanquish'd e'en the earth's wide round,
  And makes life's current smoothly run.

The greatest kingdoms it has fram'd,
　The oldest cities rear'd from dust,
Yet war's fierce torch has ne'er inflam'd;
　Happy are they who in it trust!)

1233　*Ich wohne in einem steinernen Haus,*
Da lieg ich verborgen und schlafe,
Doch ich trete hervor, ich eile heraus,
Gefodert mit eiserner Waffe.
Erst bin ich unscheinbar und schwach und klein,
Mich kann dein Atem bezwingen,
Ein Regentropfen schon saugt mich ein,
Doch mir wachsen im Siege die Schwingen,
Wenn die mächtige Schwester sich zu mir gesellt,
Erwachs ich zum furchtbarn Gebieter der Welt.

(I live within a dwelling of stone,
　There buried in slumber I dally;
Yet, arm'd with a weapon of iron alone,
　The foe to encounter I sally.
At first I'm invisible, feeble, and mean,
　And o'er me thy breath has dominion;
I'm easily drown'd in a rain-drop e'en,
　Yet in victory waxes my pinion.
When my sister, all-powerful, gives me her hand,
To the terrible lord of the world I expand.)

1234　*Ich drehe mich auf einer Scheibe,*
　Ich wandle ohne Rast und Ruh,
Klein ist das Feld, das ich umschreibe,
　Du deckst es mit zwei Händen zu –
Doch brauch ich viele tausend Meilen,
　Bis ich das kleine Feld durchzogen,
Flieg ich gleich fort mit Sturmeseilen,
　Und schneller als der Pfeil vom Bogen.

(Upon a disk my course I trace,
　There restlessly for ever flit;
Small is the circuit I embrace,
　Two hands suffice to cover it.
Yet ere that field I traverse, I
　Full many a thousand mile must go,
E'en though with tempest-speed I fly,
　Swifter than arrow from a bow.)

1235　*Ein Vogel ist es und an Schnelle*
　Buhlt es mit eines Adlers Flug,
Ein Fisch ist's und zerteilt die Welle,
　Die noch kein größres Untier trug,
Ein Elefant ist's, welcher Türme
　Auf seinem schweren Rücken trägt,
Der Spinnen kriechendem Gewürme
　Gleicht es, wenn es die Füße regt,
Und hat es fest sich eingebissen
　Mit seinem spitz'gen Eisenzahn,

So steht's gleichwie auf festen Füßen
Und trotzt dem wütenden Orkan.

(A bird it is, whose rapid motion
  With eagle's flight divides the air;
A fish it is, and parts the ocean,
  That bore a greater monster ne'er;
An elephant it is, whose rider
  On his broad back a tower has put:
'Tis like the reptile base, the spider,
  Whenever it extends its foot;
And when, with iron tooth projecting,
  It seeks its own life-blood to drain,
On footing firm, itself erecting,
  It braves the raging hurricane.)

1236   *Von Perlen baut sich eine Brücke*
        Hoch über einen grauen See,
      Sie baut sich auf im Augenblicke,
        Und schwindelnd steigt sie in die Höh.

      Der höchsten Schiffe höchste Masten
        Ziehn unter ihrem Bogen hin,
      Sie selber trug noch keine Lasten,
        Und scheint, wie du ihr nahst, zu fliehn.

      Sie wird erst mit dem Strom, und schwindet
        Sowie des Wassers Flut versiegt.
      So sprich, wo sich die Brücke findet,
        Und wer sie künstlich hat gefügt?

      (A bridge of pearls its form uprears
        High o'er a grey and misty sea;
      E'en in a moment it appears,
        And rises upwards giddily.

      Beneath its arch can find a road
        The loftiest vessel's mast most high,
      Itself hath never borne a load,
        And seems, when thou draw'st near, to fly.

      It comes first with the stream, and goes
        Soon as the wat'ry flood is dried.
      Where may be found this bridge, disclose,
        And who its beauteous form supplied!)

SIBYLLINE RIDDLE, The

Famous ancient riddle contained in Book I of the so-called *Sibylline Oracles* first assembled in the sixth century but dating back at least to the first century. The riddle, for which many solutions have been offered in the past, is dealt with at length and satisfactorily resolved by W. H. Scott in *The Atlantis* (1859). (See Appendix.)

1237   Be wise, discern me; He that is am I;
        The earth my footstool, and my robe the sky;
        With air encircled, girdled with the main;
        And all around me runs the starry train.

Discern me well; four syllables are mine;
In each two letters, out of letters nine;
Save that three letters to the last belong;
And five are consonants the nine among.
But of my perfect number there will be
Hundreds twice eight, and decads three times three;
Add seven to these, and if thou read'st me right,
True heavenly wisdom will have purged thy sight.

SMITH, Horace (1779–1849)
Novelist, playwright, and poet best known for *Rejected Addresses* (1812) written with his brother James.

1238   In arts and sciences behold my *first* the watchword still,
All prejudice must bow the knee before its iron will;
Yet 'Onward' is the Briton's cry – a cry that doth express
A holy work but half begun, and speaks of hopefulness;
In palace or in lonely cot its name alike is heard,
And in the Senate's lordly halls sit my *second* and my *third*;
Strange paradox, though for my *first* my total is design'd,
Sad marks of vice and ignorance we in that *whole* may find.

SOPHOCLES (*c.*496–406 BC)
Athenian tragic dramatist. Riddle occurs in his satyr-play *Ichneutae* (The Trackers), of which only fragments survive.

1239   *Cyllene.* Be no longer faithless, for with faithful words a goddess speaketh graciously unto thee.
Chorus. But how shall I believe that the voice of that which is dead can roar thus loudly?
Cy. Believe: for in death the beast hath gotten a voice, but in life was speechless.
Ch. What was the manner of his outward appearance? Was it a long beast, or a bent, or a short?
Cy. Short, after the fashion of a pitcher, and covered with a spotted hide.
Ch. Is his shape peradventure as a cat's, or as the shape of a leopard?
Cy. The difference is great exceedingly: for the thing is round and the legs thereof are short.
Ch. Nor yet is it shapen like a weasel or like a spider of the sea?
Cy. Neither again is it such an one. Nay, search out some other similitude.
Ch. Lo, is his form, I pray thee, as the form of a beetle that hath horns, even the beetle of Mount Etna?
Cy. Now art thou come nigh unto knowledge of that whereto the creature is most like.
Ch. Declare thou again and tell me what part thereof it is that soundeth, whether the part that is within or the part that is without.
Cy. It is, as it were, his coat, yea, a thing that is as sister in the mountains to the speechless mother of pearls.

Ch. Wilt thou not declare the name? Do thou set it forth, if so
be thou have further knowledge.

Cy. The child calleth the beast a tortoise, and the part again
that soundeth a lute.

SPHINX, or Allegorical Lozenges, The (1812)

Author described as 'a Descendant of Cleobulina, an ancient composer
of enigmas etc'. Published on 1 August 1812 by Wm Darton Jnr in
Holborn, London.

1240   Without a pair of hands I pinch,
       Unseen I nip the nose;
The school-boy oft at me doth winch,
       When I attack his toes.
Nay, there are times, when I lay hold
       Of fingers fair and small;
And am so impudent and bold,
       I seize the strait and tall.
I care not for the size of man,
       Nor yet of ladies fair;
They all must feel, do what they can,
       My power when I'm near.

1241   My *first*, with soft refreshing pow'r,
Revives each drooping plant and flow'r;
My *second* speeds, with fatal art,
A deathful weapon to the heart;
My *whole*, in colours deck'd more gay
Than belle or coxcomb at a play,
Attracts the sight to gaze on high,
Ere yet its transient beauties die.

1242   I'm not in the gouty, though in the rheumatic,
Nor yet in the kitchen, though I'm in the attic;
I'm not in the light, tho' I blaze in the candle,
I'm not in the knife, tho' found in the handle;
You'll not find me at dinner, though always at table,
Displeas'd with the idle, tho' friend to the able;
I'm not with the clock, tho' found with the case,
And not in your nose, though I'm close in your face.

1243   My *first*, without an edge, can wound,
       And most severely cut;
My *second*'s edge should sharp be found,
       And safest when close shut;
Without my *whole*, my first can ne'er
       Its properties fulfill,
Or soil the white transparent glare,
       With its most blackening skill.

1244   By European cruelty I'm from my country torn,
And forc'd across the spacious sea in ships by canvas borne;
All the long voyage I am kept from light and from the air,
Confin'd within a prison safe, and guarded well with care:

When safely brought on Albion's land, each nation takes a share,
Pouring o'er me the boiling wave, to finish my career.

1245　　There's many a rogue deserves my *first*
　　　　　Should with a rope unite;
　　　　My *second*'s made by female hands,
　　　　　And either black or white.
　　　　Sometimes my *third* is orient pearl,
　　　　　Sometimes the brilliants glare,
　　　　Sometimes I'm brightly burnished gold,
　　　　　As best may suit the fair.

1246　　My form delighteth every eye,
　　　　And no one can my worth deny;
　　　　Whate'er my colour I'm of use,
　　　　Though subject oft to much abuse;
　　　　The cause of anguish and of joy,
　　　　For most will smile when I am by.
　　　　When I am absent, small the power
　　　　To cheer the melancholy hour;
　　　　Possessing me to some doth prove
　　　　Their life, their soul, the all they love.
　　　　Others with me can ne'er agree,
　　　　But quickly give me liberty;
　　　　Few think of me enough they've got,
　　　　But all can tell when they have not.

1247　　With my colour a negro may easily vie,
　　　　And so may the beetle, and common house-fly;
　　　　A river my substance can readily show,
　　　　For like it I frequently murmuring flow;
　　　　The learned are all well inform'd of my use,
　　　　And claim my assistance, thro' help of a goose.

1248　　I'm north, I'm south, I'm east or west,
　　　　Whichever pleases me the best;
　　　　Seldom in any quarter stay,
　　　　So fond of changing is my way;
　　　　With every Zephyr's breath I rove,
　　　　And every gale can make me move.

1249　　When Petrarch for his Laura wept,
　　　　　He used my tenderest strain;
　　　　Catullus too my numbers kept,
　　　　　When Lesbia mourn'd in vain.
　　　　One told my softest notes of woe,
　　　　　Heart-struck by Cupid's arrow;
　　　　The other's elegiac flow
　　　　　Was for a dying sparrow.
　　　　My friendly power, in Vaucluse shade,
　　　　　To Petrarch gave relief;
　　　　And Lesbia, by my soothing aid,
　　　　　Recover'd from her grief.

1250 Those, who my *first* attempt to touch,
  Will find themselves defil'd;
 It is a fact that's certain known,
  To almost every child.
 My *second*'s sometimes ivory,
  Of polish'd steel also;
 Sometimes I'm silver shining bright,
  As those who use me know.
 My *whole* is often in the field,
  The stable, and the yard;
 The barn and dung-heap often yield
  Their produce to my guard.

1251 In the black art, it plain appears,
  My *first* must surely deal;
 For, though your thoughts it never hears,
  It always can reveal.

 My *second*, while it holds its breath,
  Will never cease its noise;
 It serves us as a guide to death,
  And herald to our joys.

 My *tout ensemble* is possest
  By every Grub-street poet,
 And there my pen shall take its rest,
  For surely now you know it.

1252 What bears me rises from the earth,
 And gives my vegetable birth;
 From whence I'm chang'd to liquid state,
 In which I'm us'd by poor and great;
 And, was there but enough of me,
 I soon should calm the troubled sea.

1253 My *first*, unless the vintage smiles,
  And plenteous crops appear,
 Can ne'er be had to fill my next,
  With bright and sparkling cheer.

 My *second* is a compound made
  By man's ingenious art,
 Which can reflect the human form,
  Or liquid good impart.

 My *whole* enables many a one
  Convivial joys to know;
 With wishes kind salutes the friend,
  Confusion to the foe.

1254 Dear friends, take two *no*'s,
   And pray them transpose,
 Then divide by five hundred (so witty),
  And then, as 'tis said,
   If fifty you add,
 It will show a large populous city.

STIGLIANI, Tommaso (1573–1651)
Italian poet and enigmatographer. Riddles contained in *Rime* (1601),
deemed worthy of placing on the Vatican's *Index librorum prohibitorum*
in 1605. A cleaned-up version, *Canzoniero*, appeared in 1623.

1255   *Se ben nessun mi batte, io grido forte,*
     Ed hò barba di carne, e bocca d'osso.
     Sto fra Christiani, e per tenermi posso,
     Com'il gran Turco, più d'una Consorte.
   Son crestoso in un luogo, e di tal sorte,
     Che giù mi pendon, quad'il peso è grosso,
     E sempre, ò che mi fermi, ò che sia mosso,
     Avien, che l'horologio in gola porte.
   Son Capitan d'essercito pedone,
     E per usare una mia foggia sgherra
     L'elmo hò in testa, ed in groppa un pennacchione.
   Son senza braccia, e con altrui fò guerra;
     Son senza denti, e mozzico in tenzone;
   Porto gli sproni, e vò co i piè per terra.
     Canto spesso sotterra,
     Per trovar mia ventura, e mio destino:
     E pur stimo un Rubin men d'un Lupino.

(Even if no one beats me, I cry loudly, and I have a beard of
flesh and a mouth of bone. I live amongst Christians but, like
the grand Turk, I can keep more than one consort. I have a crest
in such a place, and of such a kind, that it hangs down from
me when its weight is heavy and always, whether I am still or
moving, I carry a clock in my throat. I am the captain of an
army of foot-soldiers and, to look like a real desperado, I have
a helmet on my head and on my back a great plume. I am
without arms, yet I make war on others; I am without teeth, yet
I tear others to pieces in combat; I wear spurs, yet I go with my
feet on the ground. I often sing underground, to find my fortune
and my destiny; and yet I value a ruby less than a lupin.)

1256   *Hò cent'occhi e non vedo,*
     Son senza groppa, e siedo,
     Mangio d'un cibo, e mai non hò appetito.
     Con le palpebre il trito,
     E con gli occhi il trangugio poco appresso:
     Vomitandol per dietro a un tempo stesso.

(I have a hundred eyes and yet I cannot see; I have no back and
yet I sit down; I eat food and yet I have no appetite. I chew with
my eyelids and swallow with my eyes whilst vomiting behind at
the same time.)

STRAPAROLA, Giovanni Francesco (d. c.1557)
Italian novelist. Riddles contained in *Tredeci Piacevoli Notti* (1557).

1257   *Nel mezzo della notte un leva su,*
     Tutto barbuto, e mai barba non fe'.
     Il tempo accenna, né strologo fu;
     Porta corona, né si può dir re.

Né prete, e l'ore canta; ed ancor più:
Calza li sproni, e cavalier non è.
Pasce figliuoli, e moglie in ver non ha;
Molto è sottil ch'indovinar lo sa.

(In the middle of the night,
Rises one with beard bedight.
Though no astrologer he be,
He marks the hours which pass and flee;
He wears a crown, although no king;
No priest, yet he the hour doth sing;
Though spurred at heel, he is no knight;
No wife he calls his own by right,
Yet children many round him dwell.
Sharp wits you need this thing to tell.)

1258 *Il candido mio nervo duro e forte,*
Parte peloso e parte perforato,
Entròvi bianco e asciutto, o dura sorte!
E fuori doppo usci nero e bagnato.
Onde servir altrui mai non si stanca,
Se 'l duce che lo guida non li manca.

(A useful thing, firm, hard, and white,
Outside in shaggy robe bedight;
Hollowed within right cleverly,
It goes to work both white and dry.
When after labour it comes back,
You'll find it moist and very black;
For service it is ready ever,
And fails the hand that guides it never.)

1259 *L'amante mio, che troppo m'ama e prezza,*
Con diletto or mi stringe ed or mi tocca;
Ora mi bascia ed ora m'accarezza
Ed or la lingua sua mi mette in bocca.
Dal menar nasce poscia una dolcezza
Cosi soave, che l'alma trabocca.
E forza è trarlo, per sciugarlo, fuore.
Dite, donne, se ciò è quel fin d'amore.

(Of lovers mine is sure the best;
He holds me close upon his breast;
He fondles me; our lips then meet
With kisses and caressing sweet;
His tongue my mouth in fondness seeks,
And with such tender accent speaks,
That hearts with love are all afire.
But brief the space of our desire;
For soon his lips from mine must stray,
To wipe the dews of toil away;
And from me gently he doth move.
Now say, is this the end of love?)

1260 *Per me sto ferma, e se tal'un m'assale*
Vo su per tetti e spesso urto nel muro.
Le percosse mi fan volar senz'ale
E saltar senza piedi al chiaro al scuro.
Non cesso mai, se 'l mio contrario tale
Non resta che 'l desir suo sia sicuro:
In me principio o fin pur non si vede
E cosa viva fui, né alcun me 'l crede.

(Left in peace I never move;
But should a foe desire to prove
His mettle on me, straight I fly
Right over wall and roof-tree high.
If driven by a stroke of might,
I take, though wingless, upward flight;
No feet have I, yet 'tis my way
To jump and dance both night and day;
No rest I feel what time my foe
May will that I a-flying go.
No end and no beginning mine,
So strange my nature and design,
And they who see me on the wing
May deem me well a living thing.)

1261 *In un ampio, fiorito e verde prato*
Si pasce un vago e gentil arenino.
Copresi di un bel manto, e molto ornato,
Di color giallo, verde e celestino.
Porta corona ed ha 'l capo elevato;
Da veder molto è vago e pellegrino.
La coda leva e mira e 'l suo amor sfida,
Ma i piè si guarda e da vergogna grida.

(In a flowering meadow green,
A lovely gentle thing is seen;
Gorgeous be its robes to view,
Bright with yellow, green, and blue.
It wears upon its head a crown,
And proudly paces up and down;
Its splendid train it raises high,
And seeks its love with jealous cry;
But gazing at its feet below,
It shrieks aloud for shame and woe.)

1262 *Due siamo in nome e sol una in presenza,*
Fatte con arte e fornite con guai.
Fra donne conversiam senza avertenza
Ma siam maggior fra genti rozze assai.
Ed infiniti non posson far senza
Nostro valor, né si dogliamo mai.
E consumate per l'altrui lavoro
Guardate non siam più d'alcun di loro.

(Twofold be we in our name,
But single-natured all the same;
Made with skill and art amain,
And perfected with bitter pain.
Fair dames our service meanly prize,
And poor folk like us large in size.
To countless men we lend our aid,
And never our hard fate upbraid;
But when our useful task is done,
No thanks we get from anyone.)

1263   *Vivo co 'l capo in sabbia sotterrato*
E sto giocondo e senza alcun pensiero.
Giovane son, né appena fui ben nato
Che tutto bianco, anzi canuto io ero.
La coda verde, e poco apprecciato
Son dal popolo grande, ricco, altero;
Caro sol m'ha la gente vile e bassa
Ché mia bontà fra gran signor non passa.

(In the ground my head is buried,
Yet with care I'm never harried.
In my early youth and fresh,
White and tender is my flesh,
Green my tail; of lowly plight,
The rich man's scorn, the boor's delight.
The peasant on me sets good store,
The noble casts me from his door.)

1264   *D'ogniun prendo se non la forma mia;*
Guardate ben qual è lo stato mio.
Se mi si fa dinanzi alcun che stia
Lieto o doglioso, io sto com'ha il disio.
E perché mostro il ver de la bugia
Molti mi chiaman frodolente e rio.
Questo par impossibil, gli è pur vero,
Ch'io non so dimostrar bianco per nero.

(From everyone I something take,
But on myself no claim I make.
Mark well my nature. If you gaze
Into my face I mock your ways:
For if you sorrow, I am sad;
But if you smile, you make me glad.
Because I tell truth from a lie,
Men call me wicked, false, and sly;
Strange saying this, but true I ween.
So I, to let it clear be seen
That truth nor honesty I lack,
Will never tell you white is black.)

1265　*Vassi a seder la donna con gran fretta;*
　　　Ed io levole e panni a mano a mano,
　　　E perché certo son ch'ella m'aspetta
　　　Indi m'acconcio con la cosa in mano.
　　　La gamba i' levo, ed ella; – Troppo stretta,
　　　Ahimé, mi va tal cosa: fa più piano. –
　　　E perch'ella ne senta più diletto
　　　Sovente la ritraggio e la rimetto.

　　　(My lady seats her in a chair,
　　　And raises then her skirt with care;
　　　And as I know she waits for me,
　　　I bring her what she fain would see,
　　　Then soft I lift her dainty leg,
　　　Whereon she cries, 'Hold, hold, I beg!
　　　It is too strait, and eke too small;
　　　Be gentle, or you'll ruin all.'
　　　And so to give her smallest pain,
　　　I try once more, and eke again.)

1266　*Cortesi donne mie, vommi a trovare*
　　　L'amico che mi dà tanto diletto.
　　　Ed ivi giunta tosto me 'l fo dare
　　　E tra una coscia e l'altra me lo metto.
　　　Quella novella poi, che rallegrare
　　　Tutte vi face, piglio; e inanzi e indietro
　　　Menandola, ne manda un dolce fuore
　　　Che languire vi fa spesso d'amore.

　　　(Gentle dames, I go to find
　　　What aye to me is blithe and kind,
　　　And having found it, next I ween
　　　I set it straight my knees between;
　　　And then I rouse the life that dwells
　　　Within, and soon its virtue tells.
　　　As to and fro my hand I sway,
　　　Beneath my touch sweet ardours play –
　　　Delights which might a savage move,
　　　And make you faint through too much love.)

STRASSBURGER RÄTHSELBUCH, Der (1505)
336 question-and-answer riddles grouped under various headings, e.g.
Birds, Fish, Water, God. Examples taken from section entitled '*Von den
Menschen*'.

1267　*Wer ein mutter gehabt hab vnd kein vatter.*

　　　(Who had a mother but no father?)

1268　*Wer nach seim todt gessen hab.*

　　　(Who ate after he was dead?)

1269　*Wer da leb vnd nit geborn sey.*

　　　(Who are they that live without being born?)

1270   *Welcher Mensch hat ein gantz vierteill der welt getödt oder vmbracht.*

(Who killed a quarter of the world's population?)

SWIFT, Jonathan (1667–1745)
Irish satirist. Riddles published in various literary magazines.

1271   In Youth exalted high in Air,
Or bathing in the Waters fair;
Nature to form me took Delight,
And clad my Body all in White:
My Person tall, and slender Waste,
On either Side with Fringes grac'd;
Till me that Tyrant Man espy'd,
And drag'd me from my Mother's Side:
No Wonder now I look so thin;
The Tyrant strip't me to the Skin:
My Skin he flay'd, my Hair he cropt:
At Head and Foot my Body lopt:
And then, with Heart more hard than Stone,
He pick't my Marrow from the Bone.
To vex me more, he took a Freak,
To slit my Tongue, and made me speak:
But, that which wonderful appears,
I speak to Eyes and not to Ears.
He oft employs me in Disguise,
And makes me tell a Thousand Lyes:
To me he chiefly gives in Trust
To please his Malice, or his Lust.
From me no Secret he can hide;
I see his Vanity and Pride:
And my Delight is to expose
His Follies to his greatest Foes.

All Languages I can command,
Yet not a Word I understand.
Without my Aid, the best Divine
In Learning would not know a Line:
The Lawyer must forget his Pleading,
The Scholar could not shew his Reading.
Nay; Man, my Master, is my Slave:
I give Command to kill or save.
Can grant ten Thousand Pounds a Year,
And make a Beggar's Brat a Peer.

But, while I thus my Life relate,
I only hasten on my Fate.
My Tongue is black, my Mouth is furr'd,
I hardly now can force a Word.
I dye unpity'd and forgot;
And on some Dunghill left to rot.

1272   All-ruling Tyrant of the Earth,
To vilest Slaves I owe my Birth.
How is the greatest Monarch blest,
When in my gaudy Liv'ry drest!
No haughty Nymph has Pow'r to run
From me; or my Embraces shun.
Stabb'd to the Heart, condemned to Flame,
My Constancy is still the same.
The fav'rite Messenger of *Jove*,
And *Lemnian* God consulting strove,
To make me glorious to the Sight
Of Mortals, and the Gods Delight.
Soon would their Altars Flame expire,
If I refus'd to lend them Fire.

1273   By Fate *exalted high* in Place;
Lo, here I stand with *double Face*;
Superior none on Earth I find;
But see *below me* all Mankind.
Yet, as it oft attends the Great,
I almost *sink* with my own *Weight*;
At every *Motion* undertook,
The Vulgar all consult my *Look*.
I sometimes give Advice in *Writing*,
But never of my own *inditing*.

     I am a Courtier in my Way;
For those who *rais'd* me, I *betray*;
And some give out, that I entice
To Lust and Luxury, and Dice:
Who Punishments on me inflict,
Because they find their Pockets pick't.

     By riding *Post* I lose my Health;
And only to get others Wealth.

1274   Though I, alas! a Pris'ner be,
My Trade is, Pris'ners to set free.
No Slave his Lord's Commands obeys,
With such *insinuating* Ways.
My Genius *piercing, sharp* and *bright*,
Wherein the Men of Wit delight.
The Clergy keep me for their Ease,
And *turn* and *wind* me as they please.
A new and wond'rous Art I show
Of raising Spirits from below;
In *Scarlet* some, and some in *White*;
They rise, walk round, yet never fright.
In at each *Mouth* the *Spirits* pass,
Distinctly seen as through a Glass:
O'er *Head* and *Body* make a Rout,
And drive at last all *Secrets* out:
And still, the more I show my Art,
The more they *open every Heart*.

A greater Chymist none, than I,
Who from *Materials hard and dry*,
Have taught Men to *extract* with Skill,
More precious Juice than from a Still.

Although I'm often *out of Case*,
I'm not asham'd to show my *Face*,
Though at the Tables of the Great,
I near the Side-board take my Seat;
Yet, the plain Squire, when Dinner's done,
I never pleas'd till I make one;
He kindly bids me near him stand;
And often takes me by the *Hand*.

I twice a Day a *hunting* go;
Nor ever fail to *seize my Foe*;
And, when I have him by the *Pole*,
I drag him upwards from his *Hole*.
Though some are of so stubborn Kind,
I'm forc'd to leave a *Limb* behind.

I hourly wait some fatal End;
For, I can *break*, but scorn to *bend*.

1275 Begotten, and Born, and dying with Noise,
The Terror of Women, and Pleasure of Boys,
Like the Fiction of Poets concerning the Wind,
I'm chiefly unruly, when strongest confin'd.
For Silver and Gold I don't trouble my Head,
But all I delight in is Pieces of Lead;
Except when I trade with a Ship or a Town,
Why then I make pieces of Iron go down.
One Property more I would have you remark,
No Lady was ever more fond of a Spark;
The Moment I get one my Soul's all a-fire,
And I roar out my Joy, and in Transport expire.

1276 There is a Gate, we know full well,
That stands 'twixt Heav'n, and Earth, and Hell,
Where many for a Passage venture,
But very few are found to enter;
Altho' 'tis open Night and Day,
They for that Reason shun this Way:
Both Dukes and Lords abhor its Wood,
They can't come near it for their Blood.
What other Way they take to go,
Another Time I'll let you know.
Yet Commoners with greatest Ease,
Can find an Entrance when they please.
The poorest hither march in State,
(Or they can never pass the Gate)
Like *Roman* Generals triumphant,
And then they take a Turn and jump on't.

If gravest Parsons here advance,
They cannot pass before they dance;
There's not a Soul, that does resort here,
But strips himself to pay the Porter.

1277   I am jet-Black, as you may see,
The Son of Pitch, and gloomy Night;
Yet all that know me will agree,
 I'm dead except I live in Light.

Sometimes in Panegyrick high,
 Like lofty *Pindar* I can soar,
And raise a Virgin to the Sky,
 Or sink her to a pocky Whore.

My Blood this Day is very sweet,
 To-morrow of a bitter Juice,
Like Milk 'tis cry'd about the Street,
 And so apply'd to diff'rent Use.

Most wond'rous is my Magick Power;
 For with one Colour I can paint;
I'll make the Dev'l a Saint this Hour,
 Next make a Devil of a Saint.

Thro' distant Regions I can fly,
 Provide me but with Paper Wings,
And fairly shew a Reason, why
 There shou'd be Quarrels among Kings.

And after all you'll think it odd,
 When learned Doctors will dispute,
That I shou'd point the Word of GOD,
 And shew where they can best confute.

Let Lawyers bawl and strain their Throats,
 'Tis I that must the Lands convey,
And strip their Clients to their Coats;
 Nay give their very Souls away.

1278   We are little airy Creatures,
All of diff'rent Voice and Features,
One of us in Glass is set,
One of us you'll find in Jet,
T'other you may see in Tin,
And the fourth a Box within,
If the fifth you shou'd pursue
It can never fly from you.

1279   Never speaking, still awake,
Pleasing most when most I speak,
The Delight of old and young,
Tho' I speak without a Tongue.
Nought but one Thing can confound me,
Many Voices joining round me;
Then I fret, and rave and gabble,
Like the Labourers of *Babel*.

Now I am a Dog, or Cow,
I can bark, or I can low,
I can bleat, or I can sing,
Like the Warblers of the Spring.
Let the Love-sick Bard complain,
And I mourn the cruel Pain;
Let the happy Swain rejoice,
And I join my helping Voice;
Both are welcome, Grief or Joy,
I with either sport and toy.
Tho' a Lady, I am stout,
Drums and Trumpets bring me out;
Then I clash and roar, and rattle,
Join in all the Din of Battle.
Jove, with all his loudest Thunder,
When I'm vext, can't keep me under;
Yet so tender is my Ear,
That the lowest Voice I fear;
Much I dread the Courtier's Fate,
When his Merit's out of Date,
For I hate a silent Breath,
And a Whisper is my Death.

1280　We are little Brethren twain,
Arbiters of Loss and Gain,
Many to our Counters run,
Some are made, and some undone.
But, Men find it to their Cost,
Few are made, but Numbers lost.
Tho' we play them Tricks for ever,
Yet, they always hope, our Favour.

1281　By something form'd, I nothing am,
Yet ev'ry Thing that you can name;
In no Place have I ever been,
Yet ev'ry where I may be seen;
In all Things false, yet always true,
I'm still the same – but ever new.
Lifeless, Life's perfect Form I wear,
Can shew a Nose, Eye, Tongue, or Ear;
Yet neither Smell, See, Taste, or Hear.
All Shapes and Features I can boast,
No Flesh, no Bones, no Blood – no Ghost:
All Colours, without Paint, put on,
And change like the *Cameleon*.
Swiftly I come, and enter there,
Where not a Chink lets in the Air;
Like Thought I'm in a Moment gone,
Nor can I ever be alone;
All Things on Earth I imitate,
Faster than Nature can create;
Sometimes imperial Robes I wear,

Anon in Beggar's Rags appear;
A Giant now, and strait an Elf,
I'm ev'ry one, but ne'er my self;
Ne'er sad I mourn, ne'er glad rejoice,
I move my Lips, but want a Voice;
I ne'er was born, nor e'er can die,
Then prythee tell me what am I.

SYLVAIN, Alexandre (1535–c.1585)

French pseudonym of Belgian poet Alexander van den Bussche. French riddles published in *Cinquante aenigmes françoises* (1582).

1282   *I'ai engendré seul deuze beaux enfans,*
Les uns chagrins, les autres triomphans,
Desquels chacun en suivant sa nature,
Sans estre aydé d'aucune creature,
Faict d'engendrer tellement son devoir
Que trente fils beaux & clairs nous faict voir:
Oultre ce fils engendrent trente filles

Brunes: mais tant à concevoir habilles,
Que chacune a son frère pour espoux.
Et nous produict ce marriage doux
Filles encor iusques à deux douzaines,
Desquelles puis naissant aultres certaines
Filles, qui sont soixante & quatre à point:
Devinez qui ie suis, ou ne suis point?

(I have given birth to twelve beautiful children all by myself, some of them gloomy, others triumphant. Each of them in following his nature, again without the help of any other creature, performs his duty in breeding to such an extent that thirty handsome and bright sons are born. In addition to these sons thirty dark daughters are conceived so skilfully that each one has her brother for a husband. And this sweet wedding produces still more daughters for us until there are two dozen, from whom are conceived certain other daughters, who number exactly sixty-four [*sic*]. Now see whether or not you can guess who I am.)

1283   *Peintre ne suis, toutesfois je figure*
Facilement le pourtrait de plusieurs,
Representant bien au vray les couleurs,
En tous les poincts requis en pourtraiture.

Parfois un temps ce mien ouvrage dure,
Parfois bien peu, non pas les rigueurs
Du temps, qui fait perir herbes, & fleurs:
Car tant ne suis subject à pourriture.

Mais ceux, qui sont cause de mon labeur,
Sont cause après (voyez mon grand malheur)
Que plus il n'est, ou bien qu'il ne se monstre.

Aux femmes suis un tresor precieux,
  Qui bien souvent fait despit à leurs yeux,
  Puis veulent bien, qu'après ie les rencontre.

(I am not a painter, but I can easily create the portrait of several, representing the true colours and all the things required in portraiture. Sometimes my work lasts some time, sometimes very little, but not because of the demands of time which kills the grass and flowers, for I am not touched by decay. But those who are the subject of my labours are, afterwards, the cause (see my great misfortune) of the fact that it no longer exists, or that it does not show itself. To womankind I am a precious treasure, which none the less often affronts their eyes. Then they wish that I should meet them afterwards.)

1284   *Ie n'ay ny pieds, ny mains, ny teste, mais un corps,*
  Qui est tousiours armé d'une armure bien forte
  Qui me sert de rampart, de fenestre, & de porte,
  Et par fois est ouverte à ceux qui par dehors
  Guettent: pour me manger, car plus que moy sont forts.
  Mais pour mieux leur monstrer combien celà m'importe
  Ie les retiens captifs, & prins de telle sorte
  Que malgré leur effort souvent demeurent morts.
  Ie ne les mange point, car ce qu'est ma viande
  Est si tres delicat qu'à peine se peut voir,
  En fin ie suis mangé tant ma misere est grande,
  Qui me sçaura nommer fera bien son devoir.

(I have neither feet, nor hands, nor head, but only a body, which is always protected by very strong armour that serves as rampart, window and door, and is sometimes opened to those who are outside lying in wait: to eat me, for they are stronger than me. But in order to show them how much I resent this, I keep them captive and prisoner so that in spite of all their efforts they often die. But I do not eat them, because the kind of food I eat is so dainty that you can hardly see it. In the end, though, I am eaten and my misery is great. He who can name me will have performed his task well.)

SYLVANO, Alexandro (1535-c.1585)

Spanish pseudonym of Belgian poet Alexander van den Bussche. Spanish riddles published in *Quarenta aenigmes en lengua espannola* (1581).

1285   *Pregunto quien es aquel cavallero,*
  Rey es forçado qui siempre vencio,
  Es entre damas soldato guerrero,
  Segundo en su casa jamas consintio
  De musica, y celos, de amor se mantiene
  De cuerpo es gentil tambien generoso
  Vence à la onça, al tigre, y al osso
  Tambien el lion gran miedo lo tiene.

(I ask you who is that noble gentleman who is compelled to be king but is always vanquished? Amongst ladies he is a warlike soldier and his authority is second to none in his own home. He lives on music, jealousy and love and his body is both graceful and noble in form. He conquers the lynx, the tiger and the bear and even the lion is afraid of him.)

SYMPHOSIUS (5th century)
Latin poet and father of Anglo-Latin riddling. Once believed to be the minor Roman poet Lactantius or Firmianus Symphosius Caelius. Riddles contained in *Symphosii Aenigmata*.

1286   *Cæca mihi facies atris obscura tenebris.*
        Nox est ipsa dies, nec sol mihi cernitur ullus.
        Malo tegi terra: sic me quoque nemo videbit.

(Blind is my face in dark shadows hid; the very day is night nor is any sun by me perceived; I prefer to be covered by clods; thus no one will see me either.)

1287   *Findere me nulli possunt, præcidere multi.*
        Sed sum versicolor, albus quandoque futurus.
        Malo manere niger: minus ultima fata verebor.

(None can split me, though many cut me; but I am of changeable hue, at some time hence I shall be white. I prefer to stay black, the less I shall fear my fate.)

1288   *Virtutes magnas de viribus affero parvis.*
        Pando domos clausas: iterum sed claudo patentes;
        Servo domum domino: sed rursus servor ab ipso.

(I bring great power from little strength. I open houses when closed up; but again I shut them up when open. I keep the house safe for its owner; yet again I am kept safe by him.)

1289   *Littora semper amo, ripis vicina profundis,*
        Suave canens Musis; nigro perfusa colore,
        Nuntia sum linguæ, digitis signata magistri.

(I, the god's dear mistress, that dwell near the deep banks, sweetly singing to the Muses, overspread with black hue, I am the herald of my master's tongue when pressed light between his fingers.)

1290   *Major eram longe quondam, dum vita manebat:*
        Sed nunc exanimis, lacerata, ligata, revulsa,
        Dedita sum terræ; tumulo sed condita non sum.

(I was far larger once while life remained; but now I am lifeless after being rent, tied up and plucked away; I am devoted to the soil, yet I am not buried in a tomb.)

1291   *Mucro mihi geminus ferro conjungitur unco.*
        Cum vento luctor, cum gurgite pugno profundo;
        Scrutor aquas medias, ipsas quoque mordeo terras.

(My twin points are joined together by crooked iron; with the wind I wrestle, with the depths of the sea I fight; I search out the midmost water, and I bite the very ground itself.)

1292   *Non ego continuo morior, dum spiritus exit;*
Nam redit assidue, quamvis et sæpe recedat.
Et mihi nunc magna est animæ, nunc nulla facultas.

(I do not die forthwith when my breath leaves me; for it constantly returns, though as often it departs; and one moment I have a great store of air, the next I have no power at all.)

1293   *Littera me pavit, nec quid sit littera novi.*
In libris vixi, nec sum studiosior inde.
Exedi Musas, nec adhuc tamen ipsa profeci.

(A letter was my food, yet I know not what a letter is. In books I have lived, yet I am no more studious on that account. I devoured the Muses, yet so far I have made no progress.)

1294   *Mordeo mordentes, ultro non mordeo quemquam;*
Sed sunt mordentem multi mordere parati:
Nemo timet morsum, dentes quia non habeo ullos.

(I bite those that bite me; of my own accord I bite no one; but though I bite, many are ready to bite me. No one fears my bite, because I have no teeth.)

1295   *Est domus in terris, clara quæ voce resultat:*
Ipsa domus resonat, tacitus sed non sonat hospes;
Ambo tamen currunt, hospes simul et domus una.

(Its home is the earth, and it re-echoes with loud voice: the home itself resounds, but the host is mute and makes no sound; both however run, the host and the home run together.)

TALMUD, The
Jewish religious text.

1296   Bake him with his brother, place him in his father, eat him in his son, and then drink his father.

1297   What animal has one voice living and seven voices dead?

1298   High from heav'n her eye looks down,
Constant strife excites her frown;
Winged beings shun her sight,
She puts the youth to instant flight.
The aged, too, her looks do scout;
Oh! oh! the fugitive cries out.
And by her snares whoe'er is lured
Can never of his sin be cured.

TATWINE, (d.734)
Archbishop of Canterbury. Riddles contained in *Aenigmata* with those of Eusebius (q.v.).

1299   *Efferus exuviis populator me spoliavit,*
Vitalis pariter flatus spiramina dempsit,
In planum me iterum campum sed verterat auctor.
Frugiferos cultor sulcos mox irrigat undis,
Omnigenam nardi messem mea prata rependunt,

Qua sanis victim et lœsis prœstabo medelam.

(A ruthless pillager stripped me from a skin and likewise took away the holes through which passed the breath of life; the preparer next pounds me into a level surface; soon the dresser waters the fruitful furrows, my level fields pay back a manifold and fragrant harvest. Whereby I shall give livelihood to the healthy and healing to the sick.)

1300   *Angelicas populis epulas dispono frequenter,*
       Grandisonis aures verbis cava guttura complent,
       Succedit vox sed mihi nulla aut lingua loquendi,
       Et bino alarum fulci gestamine cernor,
       Queis sed abest penitus virtus jam tota volandi,
       Dum solus subter constat mihi pes sine passu.

(Angelic food to folk I oft dispense,
While sounds majestic fill attentive ears,
Yet neither voice have I nor tongue for speech.
In brave equipment of two wings I shine,
But wings withouten any skill to fly:
One foot I have to stand, but not a foot to go.)

1301   *Celsicolae nascor fœcunda matris in alvo,*
       Quœ superas penitus sedes habitare solescit.
       Sum petulans agilisque fera, insons corporis astu,
       Ardua ceu pennis convecta cacumina scando,
       Veloci vitans passu discrimina Martis.

(I was born in the fecund womb of my lofty-dwelling mother who is accustomed to dwelling in the highest haunts. I am a pert and agile creature, harmless and adroit of body. I climb high tree-tops as if carried on wings, avoiding with a swift step the hazards of war.)

1302   *Egregius vere nullus sine me est, neque felix;*
       Amplector cunctos quorum me corda requirunt.
       Qui absque meo graditur comitatu morte peribit;
       Et qui me gestat sospes sine fine manebit.
       Inferior terris et altior sed cœlis exsto.

(Truly no one is outstanding without me, nor fortunate; I embrace all those whose hearts ask for me. He who goes without me goes about in the company of death; and he who bears me will remain lucky for ever. But I stand lower than earth and higher than heaven.)

THEODECTES of Phaselis (c.375–334 BC)
Ancient Greek orator and poet. Riddles cited in Athenaeus's *Deipnosophistae*.

1303   What thing is that which is not among all the things that Earth, the nurse, brings forth, nor the sea, nor has any growth in its limbs like that of things mortal, yet in the time of its earliest begotten generation is largest, but at its midmost height is small, and at old age itself is again largest in shape and size?

311

1304   There be two sisters, of whom one gives birth to the other,
        while she herself, after giving birth, is brought forth by the
        other.

THEOGNIS (6th century BC)
Greek elegiac poet from Megara. Riddles occur in *Elegies*.

1305   I'm called home by a cadaver from the sea.
        Although it's dead, it speaks with living lips.

1306   My friends betray me, give me nothing when
        Men are around. So, of my own accord
        I'll come out in the evening, and go back
        At dawn, when all the roosters start to crow.

1307   I do not serve the wine to that sweet girl;
        Another (no match for me) does that, while I
        Serve fresh cold water to her parents. Still,
        She often takes me to the well and then
        Supports me groaning; while I kiss her neck
        With arms around her, and she sweetly moans.

1308   I am a champion mare and beautiful.
        I carry a bad man. This brings me pain
        And often I have almost burst the reins
        And thrown my evil rider, and escaped.

THESAURUS ÆNIGMATICUS (1725–6)
140 riddles printed in four parts for John Wilford in Little Britain,
London. The complete title runs: *Thesaurus ÆEnigmaticus or, a Collection of the most Ingenious and Diverting ÆEnigma's* [sic] *or Riddles: The whole being designed for Universal Entertainment; And in particular for the Exercise of the Fancies of the Curious.*

1309   Unseen, extended o'er the sight,
        Thro' fancies bounds I take my flight;
        Delude the Sense by ranging wide;
        In me Men shew their State and Pride;
        Open and Free with soft Access,
        I climb the greatest Precipice.
        Sound gulfy Seas of vast extent,
        Yet am within each Body pent;
        Am void of Colour, Shape, or Frame,
        Yet imp each Figure, sound, and name.
        Surmounting all, my self alone,
        Yet to my self I am unknown;
        Untoucht I ev'ry Motion give,
        Thro' my Conveyance tis you live,
        Wer't not for me each Noise wou'd cease,
        And Harmony return to Peace.

1310   Tho in silence I reign, I the Scepter nere sway'd,
        Yet easily command and am easily obey'd:
        By Nature I'm strong, yet my Body is small,
        I'm hurtful to some, yet I am useful to all;

312

War and Peace I proclaim, yet I am so nice,
That the least touch offends me and troubles my Bliss;
I sometimes am Mournful and sometimes am Gay,
My general Clothing's the Black and the Grey,
I'm fixt in a hole, yet each Moment I rove,
And travel with freedom below and above,
In the Morning I'm Brisk, in the Evening I'm dull,
And always am greedy, yet always am full,
In all my Appearance I'm dazzling and bright,
I rise with the Day and I set with the Night.

1311   What's that each Hour grows Old and Young,
Which dies each Minute, lives again,
Makes strong Men weak, and weak Men strong,
Which flies in Joy, and creeps in Pain:
Unequal Steps, too short, or long:
A fruitful train it ever bears,
Then eats it all and nothing spares.

1312   I by a gentle Breathing first begun,
And by the same my Shape is carried on.
More frail than Looking-glass, but not so true,
All present Things I represent to View.
In Colours various, still in Shape the same,
Bloated awhile I ape the Heav'nly Frame.
But when to full Perfection I am brought,
Away I fly, and vanish swift as a Thought.
Proud Mortals! whom the fawning Crowds adore,
I'm next to nothing, and you are no more.

1313   The strongest thing on Earth I be,
Not *Sampson*'s Strength can vie with me:
No mortal Man can bear my Smart,
I always prey upon the vital Part.
By none belov'd, I hated am by all,
But seldom come within the great one's Call:
All living Things yield to my Sovereign Sway.
I thousands by my Power slay,
And numbers by me fall each Day.

1314   In all rich Minerals I'm found,
Old Mother Earth with me abounds;
But yet to make the Matter plain,
Not in her Bowels nor in any Vein.
I'm often known in Air to rise,
And yet a Stranger to the Skies.
Sometimes in hottest Fires I'm seen,
But from their Flames my self I Screen.
The purling Streams are my Delight,
I live in Water Day and Night;
Yet fly the noisy foaming Main,
And from all Ponds and Lakes abstain.

1000 CONUNDRUMS (n.d.)

One of Foulsham's 'New Popular Handbooks'. Other titles in the series included *Tricks with Cards*, *Teacup Fortune Telling* and *Palmistry*. Compiled by Tom King.

1315   Why is St Paul's Cathedral like a bird's nest?

1316   Why is Denmark like the first U in cucumber?

1317   What key is best for unlocking the tongue?

1318   What is it that nobody wants but nobody wants to lose?

1319   What is it that is purchased by the yard and worn by the foot?

1320   What is it that never asks questions but has to be continually answered?

1321   Who first introduced walking-sticks?

1322   Why is the letter G like the sun?

1323   Why is an umbrella like a pancake?

1324   What trees are not changed by being burnt?

1325   Why is the letter E like London?

1326   What odd number becomes even when beheaded?

1327   What people are the slowest writers?

1328   What is that which divides by uniting?

1329   Why is I the luckiest of vowels?

1330   Why is a peacock like the figure 9?

1331   What spirit can be spelt both in English and French in three letters?

1332   What only flies when its wings are broken?

1333   What is that which is black itself and yet is used to enlighten the world?

1334   What letter would be of great use to a deaf woman?

1335   What cannot you hold for any length of time, yet is one of the lightest things in existence?

1336   What is it that you often hold but rarely touch?

1337
    done
    mutt
    and   a glutt
     i   T c d
you make me

1338   FAULTS HUSBAND DIFFERENCES WIFE FAULTS

1339   We   westand   fall

2B
A A A A A A A A A A
T C R I I O F U L S E S
STANDING
IS THE MARK OF A MEAN

1001 RIDDLES, with a few thrown in (1890)
Anonymous collection of conundrums published by George Routledge & Sons, London.

1341   Why are riddles which cannot be answered, like a man disappointed by his visitors?

1342   What is the difference between a surgeon and a conjuror?

1343   When is the moon like a load of hay?

1344   Why is a psychological romance like the train of a celebrated actress's dress?

1345   Who killed the greatest number of chickens?

1346   What three notes in Hullah's musical notation would brighten up a drawing-room?

1347   Which of the feathered tribe would be supposed to lift the heaviest weight?

1348   Why is a field of grass like a person older than yourself?

1349   Which is one of the longest words in the English language?

TOLKIEN, J. R. R. (1892–1973)
Professor of English Literature and writer. Riddles occur in *The Hobbit* (1937).

1350   What has roots as nobody sees,
       Is taller than the trees,
         Up, up it goes,
       And yet it never grows?

1351   Voiceless it cries,
       Wingless flutters,
       Toothless bites
       Mouthless mutters.

1352   An eye in a blue face
       Saw an eye in a green face.
       'That eye is like to this eye'
       Said the first eye,
       'But in low place,
       Not in high place.'

1353   It cannot be seen, cannot be felt,
       Cannot be heard, cannot be smelt.
       It lies behind stars and under hills,
         And empty holes it fills.
       It comes first and follows after.
         Ends life, kills laughter.

1354   A box without hinges, key, or lid.
        Yet golden treasure inside is hid.

1355   Alive without breath,
        As cold as death;
        Never thirsty, ever drinking,
        All in mail never clinking.

1356   This thing all things devours:
        Birds, beasts, trees, flowers;
        Gnaws iron, bites steel;
        Grinds hard stones to meal;
        Slays king, ruins town,
        And beats high mountain down.

TREE RIDDLE, The

Many versions of this extraordinary multiple riddle exist, but the most complete version was reprinted in *Notes and Queries* on 1 September 1888.

1357   What's the sociable tree,[1] and the dancing tree,[2]
        And the tree[3] that is nearest the sea;
    The most yielding tree,[4] the busiest tree,[5]
        And the tree[6] where ships may be?

    The languishing tree,[7] the least selfish tree,[8]
        And the tree[9] that bears a curse;
    The chronologist's tree,[10] the fisherman's tree,[11]
        And the tree[12] like an Irish nurse?

    The tell-tale tree,[13] and the traitor tree,[14]
        And the tree[15] that's the warmest clad;
    The layman's restraint,[16] and the housewife's tree,[17]
        And the tree[18] that makes one sad?

    The tree[19] that with death befrights you,
        The tree[20] that your wants would supply,
    The tree[21] that to travel invites you,
        And the tree[22] that forbids you to die?

    What tree[23] do the thunders resound to the skies,
        What brightens your house, does your mansion sustain;[24]
    What urged the Germans in vengeance to rise,[25]
        And strike for the victor by tyranny slain?[26]

    The tree[27] that will fight, and the tree[28] that obeys you,
        And the tree[29] that never stands still;
    The tree[30] that got up, and the tree[31] that is lazy,
        And the tree[32] neither up nor down hill?

    The tree[33] to be kissed, and the dandiest tree,[34]
        And that guides the ships to go forth;[35]
    The tree[36] of the people, the unhealthiest tree,[37]
        And the tree[38] whose wood faces the north?

The tree[39] in a battle, the tree[40] in a fog,
  And the tree[41] that bids the joints pain;
The terrible tree[42] when schoolmasters flog,
  And what of mother and child bears the name?[43]

The emulous tree,[44] the industrious tree,[45]
  And the tree[46] that warms mutton when cold;
The reddest brown tree[47] and the reddest blue tree,[48]
  And what each must become ere he's old?[49]

The treacherous tree,[50] the contemptible tree,[51]
  And that to which wines are inclined;[52]
The tree[53] that causes each townsman to flee,
  And what round fair ankles are twined?[54]

The tree[55] that's entire, and the tree[56] that is split,
  The tree[57] half given by doctors when ill;
The tree[58] that we offer to friends when we meet,
  And the tree[59] we may use as a quill?

The tree[60] that's immortal, and the trees[61] that are not,
  And the tree[62] that must pass through the fire;
The tree[63] that in Latin can ne'er be forgot,
  And in English we all most admire?[64]

The Egyptian plague tree,[65] the tree[66] that is dear,
  And what round itself doth entwine;[67]
The tree[68] that in billiards must ever be near,
  And the tree[69] that by Cockneys is turned into wine?

TRUE TRIAL OF UNDERSTANDING OR WIT NEWLY REVIV'D,
The (18th century)
English chapbook.

1358   While I did live, I food did give,
        Which many one did daily eat.
        Now being dead, you see they tread
        Me under feet about the street.

1359   Tho' it be cold I wear no cloaths,
        The frost and snow I never fear,
        I value neither shoes nor hose,
        And yet I wander far and near;
        Both meat and drink are always free,
        I drink no cyder, mum, nor beer,
        What Providence doth send to me
        I neither buy, nor sell, nor lack.

1360   Promotion lately was bestow'd
        Upon a person mean and small;
        Then many persons to him flow'd,
        Yet he return'd no thanks at all;
        But yet their hands were ready still
        To help him with their kind good will.

317

1361   My weapon is exceeding keen,
Of which I think I well may boast,
And I'll encounter Colonel Green
Together with his mighty host.
With me they could not then compare,
I conquer them both great and small,
Tho' thousands stood before me there
I stood and got no harm at all.

1362   I saw five birds all in a cage,
Each bird had but one single wing,
They were an hundred years of age,
And yet did fly and sweetly sing.
The wonder did my mind possess,
When I beheld their age and strength;
Besides, as near as I can guess, –
Their tails were thirty feet in length.

1363   Stouthearted men with naked knives
Beset my house with all their crew;
If I had ne'er so many lives,
I must be slain and eaten, too.

1364   Divided from my brother now,
I am companion for mankind;
I that lately stood for show,
Do now express my master's mind.

UNIVERSAL MAGAZINE OF KNOWLEDGE AND PLEASURE, The (1747–1815)

English pot-pourri journal appearing monthly. Its pages contained some of the best examples of English enigmatography in the eighteenth century. Riddles ceased to be published with the new series, commencing in 1814.

1365   Of fancy born, by folly bred,
From foreign countries hither led:
My form and shape I often change,
Am really nothing; yet, 'tis strange,
By all caress'd, by all admir'd,
In wealth and poverty desir'd;
Of such variety I'm made,
That I'm the great support of trade;
And tho' brought up by wisdom's foe,
I much of wisdom in me show:
For, by my fleeting changing state,
I make all money circulate;
Reward the sailor for his pains,
And much augment the merchant's gains.
I am no sooner known to be,
Than all the great take leave of me,
And I'm a mere non-entity.
To have me, all, their cares employ,
But when possess'd I quickly cloy:

I serve the ladies when alone,
To shew their handy skill upon,
And when assembled, give them pleasure,
Since I'm their chiefest talking treasure.

1366   Before I was by man a prisoner made,
I in green meads and verdant pastures stray'd;
But soon as e'er he me bereft of life,
As soon I caus'd content, as often strife.
Now dead I have no tongue, yet I can speak
All languages, *French, Hebrew, Latin, Greek*:
To most remotest parts my words are sent,
No hands I have, but what to me are lent;
I'm short of stature, my body it is slender;
And oft companion to the fair and tender:
Ladies delight to use me at their leisure,
To tell my name, you'll give the writer pleasure.

1367   Behold the *Lilliputian* throng,
Nor male, nor female, old or young;
Four inches tall, of slender size,
With neither mouth, nor nose, nor eyes,
Who never from each other stray,
But stand in order night and day,
Like soldiers marshall'd in array.
A bloody ensign each does bear,
Yet ne'er trained up to feats of war;
Their actions gentler passions move,
And aid and fan the flames of love,
Soften the unrelenting fair,
And sooth the pensive stateman's care;
Nimble as thought they skip and dance,
Yet ne'er retreat, nor ne'er advance,
Nor order change – like the world's frame,
Always unalterably the same.
Tho' nimble and to action free,
Yet move they never willingly,
But in their secret caverns sleep,
Time without end, nor stir, nor peep.
Until some heav'n-born genius comes,
To raise them from their sleepy tombs,
By pow'r unseen, then up they spring
Without the help of leg or wing,
And mount; and as they mount they sing.

1368   At two days old good *Latin* I speak,
   Tho' for it I never went to school:
Arms I have four, which come out of my *back*,
   And in *yellow* am dress'd like a fool.
All men me seek, tho' few can me get,
   When caught I'm confin'd like a fish in a net.

1369   Here is a thing that *nothing* is
'Tis foolish, wanton, sober, wise;
It hath no wings, no eyes, no ears,
And yet it flies, it sees, it hears:
It lives by loss, it feeds in smart,
It dwells in woe, it liveth not.
Yet ever more this hungry elf,
Doth feed on nothing but itself.

1370   When virtue smil'd and spread her purple wings,
O'er senates, laws, and held the crowns of Kings:
How happy I! who, by a just applause,
Converted all to one essential cause,
Bid merit rise, and held imperial sway,
Till *Athens* fell: O black and awful day!
Then lofty *Rome* to every virtue prone,
To arts and arms, with heighten'd lustre shone,
Smil'd in the records of immortal fame,
And rais'd a temple sacred to my name;
Approv'd my worth, ador'd my tender care,
And made me guardian to the charming fair.

1371   Without edge it cuts; without tongue it sings;
Foams without anger; and flies without wings.

1372   Nor wings, nor feet, unto my share have fell,
Yet I in swiftness do the best excel.
Arms I have none, nor weapons do I wear,
And yet I daily wound the brave and fair.
My name is odious, both to friends and foes,
Yet I'm admired by all the Belles and Beaus.
And when my name's concealed, I've many friends,
The best man fears me, and his fault amends.
All wise men hate me, as their common foe,
Take C from me, I keep you from the snow.
Old maids caress me, for this world I hate
As it hates them, so we receive our fate.
From these short hints, to tell my name's your task,
That well performed, I've nothing more to ask.

VANHOMRIGH, Esther (1692–1723)

The 'Vanessa' referred to in the writings of Jonathan Swift (q.v.).

1373   Cut the name of the man who his mistress denied,
And let the first of it be only applied
To join with the prophet who David did chide;
Then say what a horse is that runs very fast,
And that which deserves to be first put the last;
Spell all then, and put them together, to find
The name and the virtues of him I designed.
Like the patriarch in Egypt, he's versed in the state;
Like the prophet in Jewry, he's free with the great;
Like a racer he flies, to succour with speed,
When his friends want his aid or desert is in need.

VIRGIL (70–19 BC)

Accepted sobriquet of Publius Vergilius Maro, Roman poet. Riddles occur in the third eclogue of *Pastoral Poems* ('Are these Meliboeus' sheep?').

1374 *Damoetas*: Read me this riddle – and I shall take you for Apollo's self. Where in the world is the sky no more than three yards wide?

1375 *Menalcas*: Answer me this and Phyllis shall be yours alone. Where in the world do flowers grow with kings' names written on them?

VOLTAIRE (1694–1778)

Anagrammatic pseudonym of François-Marie Arouet ('Arouet le Jeune' gives letters AROU(V)ET L. J.), French satirist and eminent man of letters. Riddles ascribed to him.

1376 What, of all things in the world, is the longest and the shortest, the swiftest and the slowest, the most divisible and the most extended, the most neglected and the most regretted; without which nothing can be done; which devours all that is little and ennobles all that is great?

1377 *Mon premier est un tyran, mon second un horreur,*
Mon tout est le diable lui-même.
Mais si mon premier est bon, mon second ne fait rien,
Et mon tout est le bonheur suprême.

(My first is a tyrant. My second is a terror. My whole is the devil himself. But if my first is good, my second will not worry me at all, and my whole will be happiness itself.)

WALLACE, Edgar (1875–1932)

Prolific British thriller writer. This pictorial riddle occurs in the story 'The Rebus' in *Again the Three* (1928) and is discovered to be the last will and testament of an illiterate man. (The rhomboids represent the shapes of his estates, the house is his bank, the circles his money and the last three symbols mean 'all (awl) for (four strokes) Margaret (another name for daisy)'.)

1378

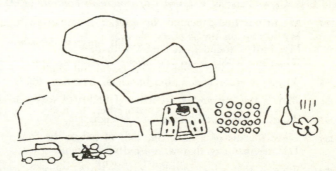

WALPOLE, Horace, 4th Earl of Orford (1717–97)
Novelist, MP, son of Whig Prime Minister Robert Walpole (1676–1745). Best remembered for his witty letters. The following occur in his correspondence with Countess Ossory, H. S. Conway (his cousin), and Rev. William Mason.

1379   *Ma première partie fait aller; ma seconde fait reculer; mon tout fait rire et pleurer.*

(My first makes things go. My second makes you recoil. My whole brings laughter and tears.)

1380   In concert, song, or serenade,
My first requires my second's aid.
To those residing near the pole
I would not recommend my whole.

1381   Charades of all things are the worst,
But yet my best have been my first.
Who with my second are concerned
Will to despise my whole have learned.

1382   *Eloigné de l'objet que j'aime,*
Lui seul calme mon ennui;
Il est plus beau que l'amour même
Mais elle est plus belle que lui.

(From the dear object of my dreams
Removed, I still that object see;
As fair as love itself it seems:
Yet she is fairer still than he.)

1383   I counterfeit all bodies, yet have none.
Bodies give shadows, shadows give me one
Loved for another's sake; that person yet
Is my chief enemy whene'er we meet;
Thinks me too old, though blest with endless youth,
And like a monarch hates my speaking truth.

WEST INDIAN FOLK RIDDLES
A selection of folk riddles from various sources including Archer Taylor *English Riddles from Oral Tradition* and articles by John H. Johnson and Elsie Clews Parsons in *Journal of American Folklore* (1921, 1925).

1384   My first is found behind the door,
My second on the winding shore,
My third is found in the park with deer,
While my whole is an isle of the western sphere.

1385   Why is a tailor and a ripe bunch of bananas alike?

1386   Why is the sun and a French loaf of bread so much alike?

1387   What is that that is never out of sight?

1388   Three fourths of a lion, one half of an ass,
Tell me that city that is covered with brass?

1389   What is that which dwells once in earth, twice in heaven and lives in the middle of men?

1390   There is a thing is the first to pity and the last to help.

1391   Hold me, an' I'm shining light; transpose me, and I'll become animals.

1392   Take 500 from the opposite of light, and tell me where your forefathers dwelt in the time of the Deluge.

1393   If I were in the sun
And you were out of the sun,
What would the sun be?

1394   There is a word if you take out the *i*, it leave the nose.

1395   There was a man comin' from Boston, an' he lost his son on der way. When he come to the Grand Central Station, he met a man who told him to take 3/7 of a chicken, 2/3 of a cat, and 1/2 of a goat, and he would find his son.

1396   There's a t'ing, it's no use to you, you cannot see it, but you cannot do without it, but you always have it with you. What's dat?

1397   What has a neck but no head?

1398   A riddle, a riddle, as I suppose;
A hundred eyes and never a nose.

1399   What has a tongue but no mouth?

1400   East and west and north and south,
One hundred teeth and never a mouth.

1401   What turns without moving?

1402   A steel horse going over a bony bridge with a silver whip to drive him.

1403   When first I appear I seem mysterious,
But when I am explained I am nothing serious.

WHATELY, Richard (1787–1863)
Archbishop of Dublin and formerly Professor of Political Economy at Oxford University. Wrote occasional riddles.

1404   My *first* is equality, my *second* inferiority; my *whole* superiority.

1405   Man cannot live without my first,
    By day and night it's used;
My second is by all accursed,
    By day and night abused;
My whole is never seen by day,
    And never used by night;
Is dear to friends when far away,
    But hated when in sight.

1406   When from the Ark's capacious round
    Mankind came forth in pairs,
Who was it that first heard the sound
    Of boots upon the stairs?

WHETSTONE FOR DULL WITS, A (18th century)
English chapbook.

1407   Without a Bridle,
Or a Saddle,
Across a thing,
I Ride a-straddle.
And those I Ride,
By help of me,
Tho' almost Blind,
Are made to see.

1408   No mouth, no eyes,
Nor yet a nose,
Two arms, two feet,
And as it goes,
The feet don't touch the ground,
But all the way,
The head runs round.

1409   A little informer,
Clothed in bright armour,
Beloved by men of degree;
It goes fine and neat,
Without leg or feet,
Now tell me what this riddle must be.

1410   Into this world I came hanging,
    And when from the same I was ganging,
I was cruelly batter'd and Squeez'd,
    And men with my blood, they were pleas'd.

1411   Tho' of great age
I'm kept in a Cage
Having a long tail and one ear,
My mouth it is round
And when Joys do abound
O' then I sing wonderful clear.

1412   The greatest travellers that e'er were known
    By Sea and land were mighty archers twain;
No armor proof, or fenced walls of stone,
    Could turn their arrows; bulwarks were in vain.
Thro' princes courts, and kingdoms far and near,
    As well in foreign parts as Christendom,
These travellers their weary steps then steer,
    But to the deserts seldom come.

1413   A thing with a thundering breech
It weighing a thousand welly,
    I have heard it roar
    Louder than Guys wild boar,
They say it hath death in its belly.

324

1414   It flies without wings,
      Between silken strings
      And leaves as you'll find
      Its guts still behind.

1415   Close in a cage a bird I'll keep,
      That sings both day and night,
      When other birds are fast asleep
      Its notes yield sweet delight.

1416   A Visage fair
      And voice is rare,
      Affording pleasant charms;
      Which is with us
      Most ominous
      Presaging future harms.

1417   To ease men of their care
      I do both rend and tear
      Their mother's bowels still;
      Yet tho' I do,
      There are but few
      That seem to take it ill.

1418   By sparks in fine lawn
      I am lustily drawn,
      But not in a chariot or Coach;
      I fly, in a word,
      More swift than a bird,
      That does the green forest approach.

1419   My back is broad, my belly is thin,
      And I am sent to pleasure youth;
      Where mortal man has never been
      Tho' strange it is a naked truth.

WHEWELL, William (1794–1866)
English philosopher. Wrote occasional riddles. (The first of those given
also appears in a Spanish version in George Borrow's *The Bible in Spain*
(1834), Chapter 32.)

1420   A handless man had a letter to write,
      And he who read it had lost his sight;
      The dumb repeated it word for word,
      And deaf was the man who listened and heard.

1421   U O A O O I O U
            O N O O O O M E T O O
            U O A O I D O S O
            I O N O O I O U T O O

WILBERFORCE, Samuel (1805–73)

Bishop of Winchester and son of William Wilberforce. The solution to the first riddle was finally published by Lewis Carroll in 1866.

1422   I have a large Box, with two lids, two caps, three established Measures, and a great number of articles a Carpenter cannot do without. – Then I have always by me a couple of good Fish, and a number of a smaller tribe, – besides two lofty Trees, fine Flowers, and the fruit of an indigenous Plant; a handsome Stag; two playful animals; and a number of a smaller and less tame Herd: – Also two Halls, or Places of Worship; some Weapons of warfare; and many Weathercocks: – The Steps of an Hotel; The House of Commons on the eve of a Dissolution; Two Students or Scholars, and some Spanish Grandees, to wait upon me.

      All pronounce me a wonderful piece of Mechanism, but few have numbered up the strange medley of things which compose my whole.

1423   I'm the sweetest of voices in orchestra heard,
      But yet in an orchestra never have been.
I'm a bird of fine plumage, but less like a bird
      Nothing in nature ever was seen.
Touching earth, I expire; in water I die;
Though I do not progress, I can run, swim, and fly.
Darkness destroys me, and light is my death;
And I can't keep alive without stopping my breath.
If my name can't be guessed by a boy or a man,
By a girl or a woman it certainly can.

WIT'S ACADEMY, or Six Peny'worth for a Penny (1656)

Anthology of riddles supposedly written by Ben Jonson: 'Ben Jonson's Last Arrow, to all Citizens' Wives and London Dames; shot from his famous Poetical Quiver, to the General view of the Courteous Reader.' Jonson had died nineteen years earlier. 77 questions and answers in six pages.

1424   Who was the first thiefe that ever was?

1425   Who was he that danced before he was born?

1426   What kind of water is the most deceitful?

1427   Why do lawyers wear round caps, and not square?

1428   Why are thieves said to die like swans?

1429   Which of the valientest Greeks had the fowlest name?

1430   Whether has a horse, or no horse, more legs?

WORCESTER MISERICORD Riddle (c.1379)

The riddle, carved in oak, appears on a misericord seat in Worcester Cathedral.

1431   Young maiden must come neither walking nor riding, nor driving, neither dressed nor naked and bearing a gift that is no gift.

WYATT, Sir Thomas (1503–42)

English poet and diplomat. Wrote occasional riddles, published in *Tottel's Miscellany* (1557). (See also *Gascoigne*.)

1432   Vulcan begat me; Minerva me taught:
Nature, my mother; Craft nourisht me year by year:
Three bodies are my foode: my strength is nought.
Anger, wrath, waste, and noise are my children dear.
Guess, my friend, what I am: and how I am wraught:
Monster of sea, or of land, or of elsewhere.
Know me, and use me: and I may thee defend:
And if I be thine enemy, I may thy life end.

1433   One is my sire: my soons, twise six they bee:
Of daughters each of them begets, you see,
Twise ten: whereof one sort be fayr of face,
The oother doth unseemly black disgrace.
Nor this hall rout is thrall unto deathdaye,
Nor worn with wastfull time, but live alwaye:
And the same alwaies (straunge case) do dye.
The fire, the daughters, and the soons distry.
In case you can so hard a knot unkniti
You shall I count an Edipus in wit.

1434   A ladye gave me a gyfte she had not
And I receyvid her guifte I toke not.
She gave it me willinglye, and yet she wold not,
And I receyvid it, albeit I coulde not.
If she geve it me, I force not;
And, yf she take it agayne, she cares not.
Conster what this is and tell not,
Ffor I am fast sworne, I maye not.

1435   What wourde is that that chaungeth not,
Though it be tourned and made in twain?
It is myn aunswer, god it wot,
And eke the causer of my payn.
A love rewardeth with disdain,
Yet is it loved. What would ye more?
It is my helth eke and my sore.

YORKSHIRE HOUSEHOLD RIDDLES
A series of folk riddles submitted by readers and published in *Notes and Queries* (October 1865).

1436   Goes up white and comes down yellow.

1437   As I were going over London Brig,
            I met a load of hay,
        I shot wi' my pistol,
            And all flew away.

1438   Black and breet [bright],
        Runs without feet.

1439   All round t' house,
        All round t' house
        And it [in the] cupboard.

1440   As I were going over London Brig,
            I pipp't into a winder,
        And I saw four-and-twenty ladies,
            Dancing on a cinder.

YOUNG ENGLAND (1880–1937)
Children's magazine containing regular 'Puzzledom' column with picture and word puzzles by various hands. Examples selected from issues published in 1880–1.

1441   Like the saint who dwelt in penance
            (Long the wonder of his land),
        On a pillar grey and mossy,
            Here beneath the sky I stand.

        Drenched with rain and chilled by dewdrops,
            Buffetted by wind and storm,
        Sport of hoar-frosts that around me
            Cabalistic patterns form.

        I endure all, dreading only
            Lot too prosperous and fair,
        For on smiling days my visage
            Will a gloomy impress bear.

        Should you question me, as Pagan
            Coming to Apollo's fane,
        See the god is first propitious,
            Or no answer you will gain.

        And that answer, while it varies –
            Varies, yet is ever right,
        Will in darkness e'er be rendered,
            Though you seek it in the light.

1442   I never was, yet am to be;
        Princes never saw me; you may never see.
        And yet I am the confidence of all
        Who live and breathe on this terrestrial ball.

The Prince of Wales, his honours not yet blown,
Still looks to me for his expected crown.
The miser hopes I shall increase his wealth;
The sick man prays me to restore his health;
The lover trusts me for his destin'd bride,
And all who hopes or wishes have beside.
Young England readers name me, but confide not, for believe,
That you and every one I still deceive.

1443   My first's an animal, you'll find,
Which, though of a most peaceful kind,
   Can make its foes to quail.
With horns which bend above a head
So hard, e'en hungry wolves will dread
   A primal to assail.

My next, though quite a little word,
Doubts every statement ever heard,
   And questions everything.
But third, though he is smaller still,
Can make all words obey his will,
   And all their tribute bring.

My next in parlour warm and snug
You oft may see upon the rug;
   'Tis seldom of much worth.
You'll find fifth in the vacant voids
Of space, or in the asteroids,
   But never in the earth.

If any doubt, we're sixth this world,
They should at once from it be hurled;
   And now watch closely, pray.
Sly total, which, though holding these,
Grows small and smaller by degrees,
   And turns and twists away.

1444   We're often lowest when we're highest;
Often drollest when we're driest;
At times in burning torrents flow;
At times fall chill as flakes of snow.
We're picked to pieces, yes, and broken,
And yet of good faith we're the token.
We're treasured up, we're thrown away,
We're made to sing, we're made to pray;
Remembered we may be for ages,
Or blotted quite from memory's pages;
We float in air, you can't see where;
We fall to ground, you may not care;
Yet some of our number have the art
To turn your foot, to stir your heart;
Once forth we go, we can't return,
Whether we freeze or whether we burn;
Such folks as are wise and wary
Use us in a way most chary.

By others we are often wasted,
For when once the joy they've tasted,
Of using us at their sweet will,
They go on using us until –
Until they cannot use us more.
Such folks, of course, we vote a bore,
Although this might them greatly vex,
They being for most of gentler sex.
We go, but none can tell how far;
Now will you tell us what we are?

1445 On every lofty mountain
   That keeps the valleys warm;
 I glisten in the lightning flash,
   I murmur in the storm.

No spring its sunshine gave me,
  In summer days unknown,
But through autumnal tints I shine,
  In frosty nights I roam.

In the still and silent moonlight,
  'Mid glittering stars I rise;
When the nightingale's sweet melody
  Is wafted to the skies.

In hell I never wander,
  Nor yet have soared to heaven;
But in a changeful earth to me
  A little space is given.

I linger not in sad farewell,
  Though from each tender heart
Called forth in tears that sadly flow,
  Though I'm the last to part.

When by the cares and ills of life
  Our hearts are sore opprest,
Without me many a weary one
  Would never find a rest.

I know no ruffling changes,
  Since time began with me,
And yet I hope to live again
  Throughout eternity.

1446 One day I trod a London street,
Though thick the *first* lay at my feet,
  In temper far from good,
'What horrid weather this,' I thought,
As 'gainst the wet and wind I fought,
  All drenched my cape and hood.
While grumbling thus, a song I heard,
The piping of some little bird.
  A *second* loudly singing.

330

A soft rebuke: it seemed to say,
'Why grumble at the rainy day?'
    Shame and reproach thus bringing.
This lesson firmly to impress,
A *whole* I saw in tattered dress,
    Deep paddling by the river;
I gave some coppers to the lad,
And hurried home, ashamed and sad.
    Now guess my whole, folks clever.

1447   My first you'll find both soft and warm;
When passive, will not do you harm;
But when in action you behold,
The very sight will turn you cold.
My second you can quickly choose –
An article the English use.
My third in barber's shops one sees;
'Tis worn by birds and made by bees.
My whole, pray tell me if you can;
It forms a resting-place for man.

1448   I am found in a valley, but ne'er in a hill,
In a stream I abide, you won't find me in rill,
I begin in an enemy, end in a foe,
But I'm always in welcome, wherever I go.
I lie in the heavens, the earth, and the sea,
I'm not tied to a house, for I always am free.
You never will see me in day or in night,
For, although I'm not shy, I don't live in the light.

SOLUTIONS TO THE RIDDLES

1 man on a horse
2 'It is the high wind issuing from the hole on which one sits.'
3 walnut
4 shadow
5 when the trees are in blossom
6 Cain when he killed Abel, leaving only Adam and Eve, who were created, not born
7 paper, ink and writer
8 lice, fingers, eyes
9 (see Appendix)
10 winged white ant (a delicacy that comes from the ground)
11 milk calabashes don't rattle when full
12 broom
13 central pole of hut and roof poles
14 axes chopping same tree
15 the eleusine plant resembles an arrow when grown, not in seed
16 eye and eyebrow
17 nose
18 river (or road)
19 raindrops
20 drum
21 salt
22 cooking-pot
23 water
24 the child in her womb
25 puff-adder
26 church bell

27 violin
28 salt
29 Minotaur
30 stork
31 cuirass
32 ostrich
33 leech
34 fire
35 heliotrope
36 candle
37 pen
38 dove
39 fish
40 glass cup
41 pregnant sow
42 man blind from birth
43 serpent
44 woman in labour with twins
45 spark
46 alphabet
47 sleep
48 bread and flint
49 *punkah* (a canvas ventilating fan)
50 rope of palm fibre
51 reed pen
52 water-wheel
53 fingernail
54 wine
55 *uqâb* ('a black eagle' and also 'a standard')
56 *saur* ('a bullock' and also 'a piece of cheese')
57 kohl pencil
58 sigh
59 rosebud
60 (solution lacking)

61 Jack and Jill
62 moon
63 heroine
64 thorn in hand
65 wo(e)man
66 VIXEN
67 barrel of beer
68 squirrel
69 tomorrow
70 pencil
71 river
72 road
73 breath
74 smoke
75 voice
76 sun
77 woman crossing a bridge with a pail on her head
78 man with sods on his head
79 egg in duck's belly
80 wind
81 nail in horseshoe
82 an axe on a man's shoulder
83 path
84 rain
85 bird in a cage
86 sawmill
87 fire
88 turnstile
89 match
90 ear of corn
91 river
92 saw
93 chair
94 man sitting on a three-legged stool milking cow is kicked by cow, so man hits cow with stool
95 stars
96 parchment, quill pen, wax
97 snail
98 duck in a puddle
99 fire in the grate
100 water
101 book
102 towel
103 key
104 fire: spark, smoke, ashes
105 bees making honey
106 flax
107 carriage wheels
108 man in coffin is dry, bearers are wet
109 ship at anchor (the leaves are its sails)
110 sieve
111 cabbage
112 newspaper
113 school
114 the letter M
115 footsteps
116 peace
117 grasshopper
118 riddle
119 Red Sea, Moses' rod, the destruction of Pharaoh's host
120 plough
121 embroidery table
122 air
123 snake
124 windmill
125 flea
126 fire
127 spoon
128 egg
129 sight
130 pipe
131 snake
132 tree stump with snow on it
133 hair
134 letter G
135 death
136 apple
137 sponge
138 red-hot poker
139 lobster
140 carpet
141 sheep
142 fiddle
143 bell
144 river
145 egg
146 coffin
147 my son
148 a mountain (it has mountaineers!)
149 charcoal
150 kitten
151 cat
152 counterfeit money
153 map
154 chestnut
155 housefly

156	because it draws and colours beautifully	204	money (messenger = death)
157	echo	205	flea
158	because all the rest are inaudible (in 'audible')	206	wine
		207	pair of spectacles
159	chestnut	208	lute
160	sponge	209	Arabic figures 1–9
161	swallow	210	river
162	soul	211	army
163	goad	212	nose (dust = snuff)
164	snail	213	al(l)bum
165	sandal	214	wisdom
166	dove, olive leaf, Noah's ark	215	wind
167	candle-snuffers	216	ice
168	horseshoe	217	horse drawn by pen
169	cherry	218	nothing
170	bark of a tree	219	heirloom
171	pump	220	Dartmouth
172	dead ashes falling on fire	221	Fleetwood
173	hare	222	chaplain (lane)
174	lobster	223	criterion
175	conundrum	224	discrete (discreet)
176	hope, hop	225	clamour
177	a letter (the 'babes' are the words)	226	necromancer
		227	lobster
178	river and fish	228	(solution in text)
179	papyrus	229	warlock
180	ships	230	cutpurse
181	anchor	231	Coldstream (guards)
182	sponge	232	wheat
183	mirror	233	ship
184	ball	234	olive
185	reed-pen	235	pitch
186	fire	236	(solutions in text)
187	leaves of a door	237	the Church (see Appendix)
188	needle	238	flea
189	serpent (land, sea, constellation)	239	thorn in a man's foot
		240	turning a spit
190	glow-worm	241	eglantine berry
191	bed	242	playing cards
192	winter	243	three flies trapped in a glass covered with a slice of bread
193	gooseberry		
194	your word	244	the ass that bore Mary out of Egypt
195	Dickens		
196	farewell	245	bee
197	holiday	246	hole in shoe
198	mattress	247	walnut
199	newspaper	248	rope-maker
200	ox	249	pillow-case
201	tissue	250	candles (unlit and lit)
202	courtship	251	bucket in a well
203	pepper	252	a rope
		253	worm

254 two millstones
255 church, steeple, bell, clapper
256 flame of a candle
257 Eve and her children
258 Noah's ark
259 snail
260 dice
261 walnut
262 sails of a windmill
263 game of bowls
264 feather
265 swan
266 man with spectacles
267 comb and louse killed on
    its back
268 a hand with rings (except
    on middle finger)
269 at the bottom of a well
270 icicle
271 spider's web
272 workmen carrying ladders
273 moon
274 hail
275 the speaker
276 bee
277 a woman's girdle
278 peacock's tail
279 parrot in a cage
280 liberty
281 Greenland
282 Armstrong
283 flea
284 horse
285 pin
286 letter A
287 eye
288 cane
289 letter O
290 Pondicherry
291 drum
292 candlesticks
293 hourglass
294 purport
295 milkmaid
296 death
297 gadfly
298 heart
299 pair of skates
300 pen
301 pearl-diver
302 cuckoo-flower
303 harebell

304 robin redbreast
305 Jonah in the whale's belly
306 hair rope
307 Eve
308 Abindon (or Abingdon),
    Berkshire
309 Eve
310 pen
311 wind
312 bed
313 magpie
314 tongs
315 nettle
316 hedgehog
317 watch
318 glove
319 gun
320 sun
321 bellows
322 clothes horse
323 bellows
324 cock
325 fart
326 gun
327 horseshoe-maker
328 orange
329 fish caught in a net
330 cock
331 fire and kettle
332 the twelve months of the
    year
333 icicle
334 paper and ink
335 egg
336 wedding ring
337 an iron pot
338 hair
339 an equal
340 reflection in a mirror
341 nail in the bottom of a ship
342 pump
343 bee
344 wasp, asp, was, as
345 snail
346 letter I
347 drugget
348 Waterloo
349 cares, caress
350 oyster
351 Galatea (gala-tea)
352 season (sea-son)
353 tablet

354 imagination	404 Eve
355 church bells	405 snow
356 a secret	406 apple
357 VIVID	407 nut
358 David	408 arrow
359 highwayman	409 knife going into a sheath
360 muffin	410 seed
361 MILE	411 eye
362 Sandringham	412 John baptizing Jesus
363 MLONE = Melon	413 days, months, Christian
364 wine	feasts, year
365 jealousy	414 the horse when it farted in
366 riddle	Noah's ark
367 man with fetters on his legs	415 darkness
368 candle-snuffer	416 stone
369 glass	417 egg
370 Member of Parliament	418 peppercorn
371 eyes	419 bees in a hive, honey
372 smile	420 rose
373 plague, ague	421 tongue
374 assassin	422 crop in a field
375 hope	423 cat and bacon
376 now, won, own	424 year, months, days and
377 thought	nights
378 equal	425 cupping-bowl
379 silence	426 violin
380 coltsfoot	427 kettle
381 courtship	428 the crown
382 Hotspur	429 bell
383 deathwatch	430 kiss
384 wedlock	431 nothing
385 snowdrop	432 flute
386 earnest	433 drum
387 backgammon	434 the earth
388 maypole	435 asparagus (sparrow-grass)
389 fish	436 because it's an oyster
390 nightingale	(hoister)
391 Antoinette is under size but	437 coffin
is not under age	438 content
392 clockwork	439 sprightly (sprite, lie)
393 pleasure	440 dew
394 catastrophe (cat, ass,	441 Because when they see the
trophy)	altars covered they think
395 penitent (pen, eye, tent)	their masters go thither to
396 dandelion (dandy, lion)	dinner
397 outrage	442 Because he knoweth not his
398 sweetheart	bed's head from the feet
399 harebell	443 sack
400 waterfall	444 hot water
401 *la noblesse* (the nobility)	445 a bridge
402 nothing	446 Because their mother is no
403 (solution lacking)	more maiden

447 When the gander is on her back
448 Cain when he slew his brother Abel
449 bowl
450 *j'ay assez obey à elle*
451 *cinqs coqs chastrez sont cinq chapons*
452 *trop subtils sont souvent bien surpris*
453 *le souhait en suspens le coeur soustient*
454 *j'ay grand appetit de soupper pour substenter mes appetits*
455 *deux coeurs en un coeur et s'entre-aymer iusques à la fin comme au commencement*
456 *il faut dix né comme souspé*
457 *amendez-vous, qu'attendez-vous la mort*
458 *bonne entreprise fait bon entreprendre*
459 Adam
460 A man's sins and his Lord's anger
461 judgement
462 earth, fire, hell, avaricious man
463 coffee
464 walnut
465 bonnet
466 pack of cards
467 fieldfare
468 nascent, ascent, scent, cent
469 drink, rink, ink
470 pinchbeck
471 sleep
472 lace (ace = one)
473 the gopher would (wood)
474 AD, am, Adam, a dam, a damson, a dam
475 Lot's wife
476 postman
477 metaphysician
478 David
479 Give attention and be convinced (G(IV)E, a T ten T(10)N, and B, C on V in CED)
480 wasp, asp, aspen
481 Think twice before you speak (Th in K twice, before Us, pea K)
482 Be independent, but not too independent (B in D, pendent, butt, knot 2 in D, pendent)
483 figure 8
484 nothing
485 thought
486 a shoe
487 heat
488 letter H
489 level
490 stone
491 the rump
492 thistle-down
493 quill pen
494 cross
495 grayling
496 tea chest
497 re, are, hare, share
498 rampart
499 eddy, Neddy
500 Isis (ices)
501 margin
502 garden, Arden, a den, end
503 Shylock
504 courage, our age, rage, rag
505 a name
506 age
507 Sunday
508 marsh, Mars, mar, ma
509 letter V
510 dust
511 semicircle
512 carpet
513 a blush
514 CIVIL
515 shadow
516 sandman
517 spur
518 carnation
519 MILD
520 postman
521 bark
522 roses
523 dog
524 book
525 larkspur
526 table
527 beagle, eagle
528 forgotten

529 caterpillar	(apple) + *Schimmel*
530 a name	(mushroom)
531 Ivanhoe	569 whalebone (used in corsets)
532 conjunction (C on junction)	= *Fisch* (fish) + *Bein* (leg)
533 telegraph	570 Jewel = *Edel* (noble) +
534 panorama (pa, Nora, ma)	*Stein* (stone)
535 Longfellow	571 wormwood = *Wer* (who)
536 nose	+ *Mut* (courage)
537 fearless	572 *Komma* (comma)
538 cuckoo	573 year
539 leather	574 day and night
540 plough	575 the world (cypresses = two
541 onion	halves of heaven; bird =
542 mead	the sun; nest = zodiacal
543 gnats	sign of the ram; death)
544 shield	576 (solution in text)
545 key	577 (solution in text)
546 dough	578 (solution in text)
547 bookmoth	579 (solution in text)
548 anchor	580 watch
549 swan	581 herring
550 horn	582 glass, lass, ass
551 rake	583 a bed
552 Hebrew פרדה (= she-	584 toast
mule) remove ד (pro-	585 bedfellow
nounced דלת = door),	586 pension (Sion House)
and there remains פרה	587 farewell
(= heifer)	588 *venez souper à Sanssounci*
553 Hebrew שלשים (= 30) take	589 *la pie* (magpie)
the ל (= 30), and the	590 *le sapin* (fir tree)
remainder is שׁים (=	591 marble
60)	592 *la langue* (tongue)
554 taper/candle	593 *une grenade* (pomegranate)
555 crinoline	594 *la chandelle* (candle)
556 liberty	595 *l'ombre* (shadow)
557 wasp, asp	596 *le coq* (cockerel)
558 pigtail	597 *la chandelle* (candle)
559 flash, lash, ash	598 *les medecins et executeurs*
560 pirate, irate, rate, ate	*de haute justice* (doctors
561 love	and executioners)
562 letter H	599 letter A (*pris* = captured)
563 (solution not known)	600 orange = *or* (gold) + *ange*
564 weathercock = *Wetter*	(angel)
(weather) + *Hahn* (cock)	601 bonnet = *bon* (good) +
565 Jew's harp = *Maul* (mouth)	*net* (honest)
+ *Trommel* (drum)	602 sexton
566 block and tackle pulley =	603 cornice
Flaschen (flask) + *Zug*	604 midwife
(swig or hoist)	605 saucepan
567 boot-jack = *Stiefel* (boot)	606 carcass
+ *Knecht* (servant)	607 rampart
568 dapple-grey horse = *Apfel*	608 your name

609 water
610 potato
611 the atmosphere
612 ice
613 snow and rain
614 dew
615 hailstones
616 riddle
617 chimney-sweep
618 kiss
619 Terminus
620 letter with a seal
621 runner beans
622 flax
623 egg
624 clock
625 bridge
626 cradle
627 fire, smoke
628 water, fire, earth, wind
629 cobweb
630 bird
631 snail
632 health
633 Eve
634 woman on a horse beneath
a cherry tree with a child at
her breast – she eats, the
child eats, a bird in the tree
eats and the horse grazes
635 Jonah in the whale
636 mother's milk
637 swallow's nest
638 rain
639 spider
640 coffee
641 tobacco
642 shears
643 bean
644 grape
645 bed
646 ship
647 a man's mind
648 Men travelling in the snow
are beaten with it, and
carry the dead bodies on
their garments until they
come to a fire, which
makes them vanish
away
649 lute
650 pair of shears

651 yesterday
652 letter A
653 a newspaper
654 letter O
655 thistle = *char* (carriage) +
don (gift / donation)
656 fortune
657 Paris, *pris* (captured), *pis*
(worse)
658 advice
659 letter G
660 preface = *pré* (field) +
face (face)
661 music (Mentor, Ulysses,
salmon, ink, charity)
662 *J'ai dansé assez* (G *dans* C,
a c)
663 expect many crosses and
little ease (X pecked, little
Es)
664 effeminacy (FM in a C)
665 inexplicable mystery
666 *J'ai traversé Paris sans
souliers* (G *traversé par I
sans sous liers*)
667 *Helène est née au pays Grec*
668 *J'ai soupé sous les orangers*
(G *sous* P *sous les Os
rangés*)
669 carmine
670 blockhead
671 starling
672 mulberry
673 *Schalttag* (intercalary day)
674 sweetheart = *Herz* (heart)
+ *Lieb* (love)
675 smoke ('pupils' = pupils in
eyes)
676 double flute (sailors =
fingers)
677 Rhodes (*dos* = 'give')
678 louse
679 clyster
680 Nessus the centaur, with
whose blood the robe that
slew Heracles was poisoned
681 Eteocles and Polynices, the
sons of Oedipus
682 day and night
683 sandal / scandal
684 clyster
685 mirror

686 writing tablet ('Ares' = stylus)
687 pitch
688 mirror
689 sleep ('untruthful' because, though unreal, dreams portend realities)
690 raisin
691 twelve robbers ate a raven that had fed on the carcass of a poisoned horse
692 hourglass
693 cat
694 pair of shoes
695 squirrel
696 drum
697 coal
698 hands
699 gaspipe
700 Behemoth (bee, he, moth)
701 Ivanhoe (eye, van, hoe)
702 bed
703 love
704 water
705 It's a long lane that has no turning
706 Dishonesty ruins both fame and fortune
707 The proof of the pudding is in the eating
708 Be merry and wise
709 grain of wheat
710 pen
711 sky
712 needle
713 ale
714 dew
715 goldsmith's hammer
716 fog
717 anchor
718 A raven always lives in high mountains, and dew falls in deep valleys, a fish lives without breathing, and the booming waterfall is never silent
719 leek
720 hail and rain
721 sow with nine piglets
722 arrow
723 spider
724 a game of chess
725 ptarmigan
726 cow
727 spark
728 embers in the hearth
729 Jacob and Esau in their mother's womb
730 the pillar of salt Lot's wife became
731 smoke
732 egg, silkworm, cocoon, butterfly
733 bell (which is cast in the earth)
734 eye
735 'snot of ther noses'
736 dishcloth
737 leaves of a tree
738 a yong man in a tavern drinking a Gill of sack to chear up his spirits & so obtained his will
739 gooseberry
740 a rose bud whose outward green leaves are some jaged others plaine
741 yesterday
742 muff
743 needle
744 bank
745 letter Y
746 rainbow
747 bar
748 corkscrew
749 earthquake
750 cotton
751 eye
752 Madam (mum, Anna, deed, anana (pineapple), minim)
753 DIM
754 peach, cheap
755 letter M
756 peacock
757 lice
758 keeper (key, purr)
759 port
760 letter A
761 banquet (bank, wet)
762 B, bee
763 beau, bo, bow
764 cabinet
765 Don't reckon your chickens before they are hatched (D

on T, wreck on ewer,
chickens, B 4 they (tea(T)
+ hay), R hatched)

766 Winds begin to howl at
night,
Leaves are falling down,
Early evening steals the
light,
Woods and dales grow
brown.
(NB Earl I)
767 stove
768 year
769 Ilo is the speaker's dog out
of whose skin he has made
shoes
770 mosquitoes
771 tree is mankind, branches
are Muslims (who are
buried at death) and
Hindus (who are burnt)
772 reflection in a mirror
773 box of matches
774 newspaper
775 because it is out of one's
head
776 because it is often toll'd
777 because it is a bad habit
778 the whale that swallowed
Jonah
779 because it receives weary
travellers
780 *The Rose of Castille* (rows
of cast steel)
781 (solution in text)
782 Bloom looking in mirror
783 hand
784 troll = *Rübe* (turnip) +
Zahl (numeral)
785 helmsmann = *Steuer*
(rudder) + *Mann* (man)
786 morningstar = *Morgan*
(morning) + *Stern* (star)
787 slipper = *Pan* (god of
fields) + *Offel* (?) (NB
Unter dem Pantoffel Stehan
means to be henpecked.)
788 watermelon
789 pen
790 candle
791 Dear Charles, I shall be
delighted to come to your
house, also Maria, William
and Henry. – Yours, Neddy
Landseer
792 shadow
793 mail coat
794 barrow
795 Arabs = *ara* (altar) + *bes*
(coin)
796 tears = *lac* (milk) + *rima*
(crack)
797 orange
798 Andrew
799 water under the boat
800 egg
801 snow
802 rain
803 sweeping brush (made of
horsehair)
804 the letter R
805 inattention
806 Portobello
807 Cromer
808 The capital of Russia lies
on both banks of the Neva
at its influx into the Gulf of
Finland; it stands partly on
the mainland and partly on
islands formed by the
divergence of the river,
which is crossed by ten
bridges, and over its
branches and canals there
are upwards of seventy
more. Its public buildings,
surmounted by gold-plated
domes, are massive and
elegant, but the Italian style
of architecture, which is
commonly adopted, is
hardly suited to the climate.
The chief street is four
miles long and one hundred
and thirty feet wide; along
it has been laid a street
railway. The winter palace
is one of the largest in the
world.
809 a mill
810 ice
811 needle
812 a bed
813 love

814 the wind
815 salt
816 cat
817 cannon
818 melon
819 oak tree
820 ladder
821 harebell
822 windlass
823 mask
824 sexton
825 sapling
826 margin
827 blockhead
828 hardship
829 massacre
830 snowball
831 horseradish
832 simpleton
833 beer in a barrel
834 coffin
835 leather
836 wheat
837 pawnbroker
838 passport
839 candlestick
840 stone
841 earthquake
842 surface
843 earnest
844 peasants
845 auctioneer
846 spark
847 deathwatch
848 myriad
849 Bible
850 shaddock
851 crab (cowl − owl + rabbit − bit)
852 cod
853 cat (sea, hay, tea)
854 manslaughter, slaughter, man's laughter
855 hay
856 razor
857 chimney sweep
858 weathercock
859 bunch of grapes
860 nightcap
861 word
862 tears
863 *ruban* (ribbon and sword blade)
864 spider
865 dog
866 office
867 pitfall
868 demurrage
869 lineage
870 rebellion
871 (solutions in text)
872 death
873 mirror
874 noise
875 fox
876 letters
877 letter E
878 roman figures
879 bat
880 earnest
881 barrack
882 wormwood
883 liquorice
884 kitcat
885 corkscrew
886 pair of skates
887 onion
888 pancake
889 telegraph
890 friendship
891 viper
892 blockhead
893 nameless
894 few, fewer
895 Danes, Andes
896 a shadow
897 tomorrow
898 peace
899 America
900 grope, rope, ope
901 anemone (an M on E)
902 cock
903 flute
904 mushroom
905 fashion
906 grain of mustard
907 *étoile* (star), *toile* (tablecloth)
908 *ouie* (ear), *oui* (yes)
909 pipe
910 *potage* (soup), *otage* (hostage), *Tage* (river Tagus), *âge* (age)
911 *café* (coffee)

912 *lin* (flax), *Nil* (river
Nile)
913 teeth
914 XIII (divided horizontally
gives VIII)
915 circle
916 fortune
917 heathen
918 COCOA
919 mend
920 box
921 rainbow
922 shadow
923 fire-irons (shovel, poker,
tongs)
924 shoe
925 umbrella
926 grandson
927 standard (stand, hard)
928 penmanship
929 honeycomb
930 fie (five − V = fie)
931 MCCOI = comic
932 letter U
933 bark
934 Above and below me,
'Tis easy to show me,
Before and behind me
You always may find me.
(solution = shadow)
935 If the grate be empty, put
coal on but if the grate be
full, stop putting coal on
936 Great ease and little crosses
before you are 21; great
crosses and little ease after
937 There is an overwhelming
difference between vice and
virtue
938 All hath an ending here
below
939 Oporto
940 letter O
941 (solution in text)
942 book
943 There was an old woman
tossed up in a blanket,
Seventy times as high as the
moon.
What she did there, I
cannot tell,
But in her hand she carried

a broom.
Old woman, old woman,
old woman, says I,
Whither, O whither, O
whither so high?
To sweep the cobwebs from
the sky
And I shall be back again,
by and by.
944 coal
945 fog/mist
946 holly
947 robin
948 pair of shoes
949 parrot
950 candle
951 tree
952 star
953 needle and thread
954 hedgehog
955 teeth and gums
956 ice
957 plum pudding
958 temple = world, column =
year; cities = months,
buttresses = days, two
women = light and
darkness
959 (solution not known)
960 (solution not known)
961 (solution not known)
962 flea
963 top
964 pair of shoes
965 windmill
966 clock
967 pump
968 squirrel
969 the letter A
970 cherry
971 shuttlecock
972 the sun
973 boy's kite
974 dewdrop
975 target
976 pardon
977 friendship
978 hourglass
979 pair of spurs
980 letter O
981 sword
982 yard

983 anything
984 musicians
985 tadpole
986 needle and pin
987 clock
988 stockings
989 wig
990 cabbage
991 track
992 bed
993 frog
994 moon
995 moon
996 potatoes
997 river
998 shoe
999 shoe
1000 Mississippi
1001 500 pairs of trousers
1002 dust
1003 snow melted by the sun
1004 milk
1005 shoe
1006 shoe
1007 shuttle
1008 broom
1009 grasshopper
1010 first it is *cradled*, then it is *threshed* and then it becomes the *flour* of the family
1011 quill pen
1012 cask
1013 mirror
1014 bees
1015 watermelon
1016 washed in dew, dried in sunshine
1017 sawdust
1018 your name
1019 your word
1020 milkman's horse
1021 umbrella
1022 breath
1023 silence
1024 wedding ring
1025 a hole
1026 a debt
1027 icicle
1028 letters BUT (beauty) and YZ (wise head)
1029 LAVA (5 + 5 + 45 = 55 = LV; Pyrrhus was killed by lava tile; Empedocles jumped into Etna)
1030 drama, a dram
1031 eunuch, bat, fennel, pumice
1032 pack of cards
1033 chair, hair, air
1034 David
1035 letter E
1036 ship
1037 flag
1038 (solutions in text)
1039 (solution not known)
1040 royal
1041 postage stamp
1042 train, rain, ain, in
1043 heathen
1044 clover, lover, over, clove, love, cover, cove
1045 dovetail
1046 mistrust
1047 average
1048 beam, be, am
1049 Dublin (bud, nil)
1050 capacity
1051 scarcity
1052 anthem
1053 fire poker
1054 bridge
1055 bull
1056 bell
1057 childhood
1058 mouse
1059 letter S
1060 bellows
1061 (solution lacking, perhaps 'foot', 'eye' or 'hair')
1062 Stanhope (S, tan, hope)
1063 Latin
1064 Frances Sargent Osgood
1065 Sarah Anna Lewis (Poe's patroness)
1066 (line 1) *Spenser*; (2) *Homer*; (3–4) *Aristotle*; (5–6) *Kallimachos*; (7–8) *Shelley*; (9) *Pope*; (10) *Euripides*; (11) Mark *Akenside*; (12) Samuel *Roger*; (13–14) *Euripides*; – which together spell 'Shakspeare' [*sic*]
1067 a bed
1068 because it is next to Kew (Q)

1069 looking-glass
1070 bowl of punch
1071 picture
1072 cherry
1073 egg
1074 goodnight
1075 moonlight
1076 Campbell
1077 bridegroom
1078 knighthood
1079 Gideon
1080 Jacob (Joel, Achan, Cyrus, Ophir, Balaam)
1081 scales
1082 hope
1083 blood
1084 Turandot
1085 because they are constantly *crossing the line* and running from *pole* to *pole*
1086 because it doesn't 'No' anything
1087 because it runs on sleepers
1088 because he's eaten out of house and home
1089 because it's a *caw's way*
1090 because it has a lot of larks
1091 because it grows down
1092 because the sooner it's *put out* the better
1093 because it's light when it rises
1094 because it never eats less than a peck
1095 when it is rung for dinner
1096 because one becomes a woman, the other doesn't
1097 when she takes a *fly* that brings her to the Bank
1098 ice and water
1099 fur glove
1100 lark
1101 tree
1102 sun
1103 key
1104 tea-kettle
1105 bees
1106 watch
1107 pair of scales
1108 candle
1109 bee
1110 ox
1111 fish
1112 pair of spectacles
1113 man in a pillory
1114 Seven are the days of a woman's defilement; Nine are the months of pregnancy; Two are the breasts that yield the draught; And one the child that drinks.
1115 That enclosure is the womb; the ten doors are the ten orifices of man – his eyes, ears, nostrils, mouth, the apertures for the discharge of the excreta and the urine, and the navel; when the child is in the embryonic state, the navel is open and the other orifices are closed, but when it issues from the womb, the navel is closed and the others are opened.
1116 Lot's daughter speaking to her son
1117 The land upon which (after the creation) the waters were gathered, and (the bed of the sea on) the day when the sea was divided.
1118 It is the ship in the sea (the living tree has no motion, the trunk from which the crowning branches have been severed supplies the material for the moving vessel).
1119 a wick
1120 black weevil in a white bean
1121 riddle
1122 riddle
1123 siren
1124 day and night
1125 smoke
1126 (solution in text)
1127 (solution in text)
1128 (solution in text)
1129 (solution in text)
1130 (solution in text)

1131 because it blackens the fairest things
1132 sword
1133 because it consumes much powder
1134 a table
1135 man
1136 (solution in text)
1137 (solution in text)
1138 tomorrow
1139 snowflake
1140 viand (VI, and)
1141 letter Q
1142 handicap
1143 leisure
1144 letter X
1145 bat
1146 chair
1147 the face
1148 boa
1149 mistrust
1150 hat, hate
1151 letter R
1152 envy (NV)
1153 heart
1154 noise
1155 pack of cards
1156 yard rule
1157 wind/vacuum
1158 sea
1159 coin
1160 letters of the alphabet
1161 feather fan
1162 two horses, coachman, four wheels, coach, four passengers
1163 butterfly
1164 bell
1165 gnat
1166 needle
1167 candle
1168 candle
1169 lightning/wind
1170 body and soul/Agni
1171 sun
1172 year, months, days and nights
1173 Jack
1174 *Punch* (punch)
1175 candid
1176 Proserpine
1177 pins and needles

1178 portrait
1179 a bust
1180 cupboard
1181 garter
1182 brimstone
1183 letter A
1184 onion
1185 star
1186 grasshopper
1187 letter M
1188 child sucking a woman
1189 sails of a windmill
1190 a bush of Nettles
1191 tongue and teeth
1192 letter N
1193 watch
1194 table
1195 teapot
1196 pen
1197 shoe
1198 castanet
1199 laughter, slaughter
1200 spear, pear, ear
1201 scissors
1202 Molière (*Mol'* (moth) + *er* (a silent letter in Old Russian) = *Mol'er* (Molière))
1203 death
1204 cabbage
1205 trousers
1206 milestone
1207 walking stick
1208 snow
1209 rain
1210 lock
1211 echo
1212 sickle
1213 beetle
1214 gnat
1215 eyes
1216 drum
1217 season
1218 patrimony
1219 cornice
1220 phantom
1221 evergreen
1222 mocking-bird (macaw, oriole, canary, kite, indigo, nightingale, goldfinch, bluebird, ibis, robin, dove
1223 plough

1224 day and night
1225 telescope
1226 cosmos/universe
1227 day and night
1228 eye
1229 Great Wall of China
1230 lightning
1231 the year
1232 plough
1233 spark
1234 shadows on a sundial
1235 ship
1236 rainbow
1237 (see Appendix)
1238 reformatory
1239 (solution in text)
1240 frost
1241 rainbow
1242 letter A
1243 penknife
1244 tea
1245 necklace
1246 money
1247 ink
1248 weathercock
1249 poetry
1250 pitchfork
1251 inkhorn
1252 olive oil
1253 wineglass
1254 London
1255 cock
1256 grater
1257 cock
1258 pen
1259 trumpet
1260 tennis ball
1261 peacock
1262 scissors
1263 leek
1264 mirror
1265 tight shoe
1266 viol da gamba
1267 Christ
1268 Christ
1269 the angels
1270 Cain when he slew Abel
1271 pen
1272 gold
1273 gold
1274 corkscrew
1275 cannons

1276 gallow
1277 ink
1278 the vowels
1279 echo
1280 pair of dice
1281 reflection in a mirror
1282 year
1283 mirror
1284 oyster
1285 cock
1286 mole
1287 hair
1288 key
1289 reed (from which a flute can be made)
1290 soldier's boot
1291 anchor
1292 bellows
1293 bookworm
1294 onion
1295 river and fish
1296 i.e., bake the fish in salt, his brother (for salt water comes with the fish from the sea), place him in his father (in water), eat him in his son (i.e. the juice or gravy), and then take a draught of water
1297 ibis
1298 (solution lacking)
1299 parchment
1300 eagle-lectern
1301 squirrel
1302 humility
1303 shadow
1304 night and day
1305 conch shell
1306 prostitute's cat (or moon)
1307 water jug
1308 town and its tyrant ruler
1309 air
1310 eye
1311 time
1312 bubble
1313 hunger
1314 letter R
1315 because it was built by a Wren
1316 because it is between two seas (Cs)
1317 whisky

1318 a lawsuit
1319 carpet
1320 the doorbell
1321 Eve when she gave Adam a little Cain
1322 because it is the centre of light
1323 because is is never seen after Lent
1324 ashes, which are still ashes when burnt
1325 because they are both the capital of England
1326 S-even
1327 convicts, because many of them have spent 20 years on one sentence
1328 blades of a pair of scissors
1329 because it is in the centre of bliss, while E is in hell and all the others are in purgatory
1330 because without a tail it is nothing
1331 BR and Y, ODV (*eau de vie*)
1332 an army
1333 ink
1334 the letter A, because it would make her hear
1335 your breath
1336 your tongue
1337 underdone mutton and onion make, between you and me, a glutton a little seedy after a capital tea
1338 differences between husband and wife: faults on either side
1339 united we stand, divided we fall
1340 to be tenacious in the midst of trifles is the mark of a mean understanding (NB.CIOUS in the midst of TRIFLES)
1341 because there is a host put out and not one guest (guessed)
1342 one is a cupper, the other a sorcerer
1343 when it's on the wane

(wain)
1344 because it's a tale (tail) of mystery (Miss Terry)
1345 Hamlet's uncle did 'murder most foul'
1346 so, la, re (solar ray)
1347 the crane
1348 because it is pasturage (past your age)
1349 smiles; because there is a mile between the first and last letters
1350 mountain
1351 wind
1352 sun and daisy
1353 dark
1354 egg
1355 fish
1356 time
1357 As follows (some missing): [1]Tea tree. [2]Caper. [3]Beech. [4]– [5]Medlar. [6]Bay. [7]Pine. [8]– [9]Apple. [10]Date. [11]Crab. [12]Honeysuckle. [13]– [14]Judas. [15]Fir. [16]– [17]Broom. [18]– [19]Nightshade. [20]Bread tree. [21]O-range. [22]O-live. [23]– [24]– [25]– [26]– [27]Box. [28]– [29]Aspen. [30]Rose. [31]Sloe. [32]Plane. [33]Mistletoe. [34]– [35]Elm (helm). [36]Poplar. [37]Plague. [38]Southernwood. [39]– [40]Hazel. [41]Rue. [42]Birch. [43]– [44]Ivy. [45]Cotton. [46]Ash. [47]Chestnut. [48]– [49]Sage. [50]Cane (Cain). [51]– [52]– [53]– [54]Sandal. [55]– [56]Clove. [57]Bark. [58]Palm. [59]Cedar. [60]Amaranth. [61]– [62]Ash. [63]– [64]– [65]– [66]– [67]Hop. [68]Mace. [69]–
1358 cow
1359 herring in the sea
1360 man in pillory
1361 man scything grass
1362 bells in a steeple
1363 oyster
1364 ox horn
1365 fashion
1366 quill pen
1367 harpsichord
1368 guinea

1369 the mind
1370 wisdom
1371 'bottle-ale'
1372 scandal
1373 Jonathan Swift
1374 at the bottom of a well or on a celestial globe
1375 hyacinthus (the plant which grew from the spot where the youth Hyacinthus accidentally died; the event recurred at the death of Ajax – the letters in question are AI AI which form part of the plant's colouring and are Greek for an expression of grief)
1376 time
1377 marriage = *mari* (husband) + *age* (old age)
1378 (solution in text)
1379 vapour = *va* (to go) + *peur* (fear)
1380 lutestring
1381 hardships
1382 portrait
1383 portrait
1384 Barbados
1385 because one fit to cut and one cut to fit
1386 because one rise in the east, and one rise with yeast
1387 letter I
1388 London
1389 letter E
1390 letter P
1391 star, rats
1392 dark – D = Ark
1393 sin
1394 noise
1395 Chicago (Chi + ca + go)
1396 your footsteps
1397 bottle
1398 potato
1399 shoe
1400 saw
1401 milk
1402 thimble, finger, needle
1403 riddle
1404 peerless
1405 *ignis fatuus* (or income-tax)
1406 To him who cons the matter o'er
A little thought reveals,
He heard it first who went before
Two pairs of soles and eels!
1407 spectacles
1408 wheelbarrow
1409 pocket watch
1410 cider apple
1411 bell (tail = rope, ear = wheel)
1412 Death and Cupid
1413 cannon
1414 weaver's shuttle
1415 clock
1416 mermaid
1417 plough
1418 arrow
1419 kite
1420 letter O nothing
1421 You sigh for a cipher, O I sigh for you,
Sigh for no cipher, O sigh for me too.
You sigh for a cipher I decipher so,
I sigh for no cipher, I sigh for you too!
1422 'The WHOLE, – is MAN. The PARTS are as follows:
A large box – The Chest.
Two lids – The Eye Lids.
Two Caps – The Knee Caps.
Three established Measures – The nails, hands, and feet.
A great number of articles a Carpenter cannot do without – Nails.
A couple of good Fish – The Soles of the Feet.
A number of a smaller tribe – The Muscles (Mussels).
Two lofty Trees – The Palms (of the hands).
Fine Flowers – Two Lips (Tulips), and Irises.
The fruit of an indigenous Plant – Hips.
A handsome Stag – The Heart (Hart).

Two playful Animals – The Calves.

A number of a smaller and less tame Herd – The Hairs (Hares).

Two Halls, or Places of Worship – The Temples.

Some Weapons of Warfare – The Arms, and Shoulder blades.

Many Weathercocks – The Veins (Vanes).

The Steps of an Hotel – The Insteps (Inn-Steps).

The House of Commons on the eve of a Dissolution – Eyes and Nose (Ayes and Noes).

Two Students or Scholars – The Pupils of the Eye.

Some Spanish Grandees – The Tendons (Ten Dons)

1423 angel (heavenly being, old English coin, fish)

1424 Adam, for he robbed God's orchard

1425 John the Baptist who leapt in the womb

1426 women's tears

1427 because square dealing would undo them

1428 because they sing a little before

1429 Ajax (a jakes/jax)

1430 no horse: for a horse has four legs, and no horse has more!

1431 (solution in text) She is covered in a net, rides a goat with one foot on the ground and bears a rabbit which runs away

1432 gun

1433 year

1434 kiss

1435 Anna

1436 egg

1437 bird

1438 an iron

1439 mouse

1440 sparks

1441 sundial

1442 tomorrow

1443 ramification

1444 words

1445 letter T

1446 mudlark

1447 catacomb

1448 letter E (composed by A. Mary T. Bryant, 1894)

APPENDIX

1. Aelia Laelia Crispis (no. 9)

T. L. Peacock's solution of the riddle:

I believe this aenigma to consist entirely in the contrast, between the general and particular consideration of the human body, and its accidents of death and burial. Abstracting from it all but what is common to all human bodies, it has neither age nor sex; it has no morals, good or bad: it dies from no specific cause: lies in no specific place: is the subject of neither joy nor grief to the survivor, who superintends its funeral: has no specific monument erected over it; is, in short, the abstraction contemplated in the one formula: 'Man that is born of a woman;' which the priest pronounces equally over the new-born babe, the mature man or woman, and the oldest of the old.

But considered in particular, that is, distinctively and individually, we see, in succession, man and woman, young and old, good and bad; we see some buried in earth, some in sea, some in polar ice, some in mountain snow. We see a funeral superintended, here by one who rejoices, there by one who mourns; we see tombs of every variety of form. The abstract superintendent of a funeral, abstractedly interring an abstract body, does not know to whom he raises the abstract monument, nor what is its form; but the particular superintendent of a particular funeral knows what the particular monument is, and to whose memory it is raised.

2. The Bishop's riddle (no. 237)

Also known as 'Hallam's Riddle'. Printed below are two of the best-known solutions, by 'Rebecca' (*Notes and Queries*, 29 June 1850) and J. P. Owen (*Notes and Queries*, 28 April 1900). I also reproduce (c) the discussion by H. E. Dudeney in his book *The World's Best Word Puzzles* (1925).

(a) Firm on the Rock of Christ, though lowly sprung,
    The Church invokes the Spirit's fiery Tongue;
    Those gracious breathings rouse but to controul
    The Storm and Struggle in the Sinner's Soul.
    Happy! ere long his carnal conflicts cease,
    And the Storm sinks in faith and gentle peace –
    Kings own its potent sway, and humbly bows
    The gilded diadem upon their brows –

Its saving voice with Mercy speeds to all,
But ah! how few who quicken at the call –
Gentiles the favour'd 'little Flock' detest,
And Abraham's children spit upon their rest.
Once only since Creation's work, has night
Curtain'd with dark'ning Clouds its saving light,
What time the Ark majestically rode,
Unscath'd upon the desolating flood –
The Silver weigh'd for it, in all its strength
For scarce three pounds were counted, while its length
Traced in the Prophet's view with measur'd reed,
Squared just a mile, as Rabbins are agreed –
And now I feel entitled well to smile,
Since Christ's Church bears the Palm in all our Isle.

(b)   *Is it 'R'?*
Yes, you sit on your rock in a blustering breeze;
Begone with your partner, disturb not mine ease;
In the world of the north men still cling to you,
Tho' elsewhere you're hated by Gentile and Jew;
When you're seen in the Conqueror's hand as a whip
How pale grows each cheek and how quivers each lip!
But, mistress, believe me, you were seen in the dark
When you played on old No' that unmaidenly lark,
And his angry spouse dropped you clean out of the Ark
('Like to like,' as she did so, I heard her remark).
Though the roe's weight I doubt, yet hark to the flow
Of Hallam's Greek puns as he rides in the Row,
Declaring the season from start unto close
Shows nothing to equal a sweet English rose.

(c) This is generally believed to be by Hallam the historian, who it is
said gave it to a lady to solve within a year, but himself died before
the year was up, leaving it unanswered. But in an old magazine
published in 1849 it is attributed to the then Bishop of Salisbury
and the statement made that 'the late Archbishop had given the
solution, as also the Bishop's own daughter.' This statement as to
the authorship is not however convincing, for the proposed answer
CHRIST-CHURCH is most unsatisfactory. Some years ago a writer
in the *Morning Post* proposed HAM, a fortress on a rock on the
Somme, where Louis Napoleon sat imprisoned for some six years,
planning to escape and trying to raise the wind. When he became
Emperor kings paid court to him. Ham was know to but few, but
ships often passed it. The land of Ham was hated by the Gentile;
the Jew hates Ham as pig. Ham slept with Noah in the Ark. The
Isle is perhaps a mile long. The letters HM stand for Her Majesty
Queen Victoria. But this will not do. It would be Ham sits on a
rock, when Ham is raising the wind, not Napoleon. To give the
approximate weight of a pig's ham as three pounds is absurd. And
the 'one night' is not explained. The answer CHURCH appeared in
The Times about 80 years ago. For 'my weight is three pounds' we
are referred to Zechariah xi. 12, and for 'my length is a mile' to
Ezekiel xlii. 20. You are asked to believe that 'my first and my last

are the pride of this isle' refers to Christchurch, Oxford. Hallam was a Christchurch man.

We think ourselves that the best proposed answer is RAVEN. The raven croaks before a storm, it was once an object of worship, and is seldom seen. It was forbidden the Jew as food (see Lev. xi. 15). It was alone with Noah in the Ark when its mate was sent forth. It weighs about three pounds and it is the name of a small South Carolina island – presumably a mile long. 'My first and my last' R.N. (the Royal Navy) are certainly 'the pride of this isle.' Readers may now take their choice.

3. Catherine Maria Fanshawe (562)

This parody of Fanshawe's riddle on the letter H appeared in *Puniana* (1867) by Hugh Rowley:

I dwells in the Hearth, and I breathes in the Hair;
If you searches the Hocean you'll find that I'm there.
The first of all Hangels in Holympus am Hi,
Yet I'm banished from 'Eaven, expelled from on 'igh.
But, though on this Horb I'm destined to grovel,
I'm ne'er seen in an 'Ouse, in an 'Ut, or an 'Ovel.
Not an 'Orse nor an 'Unter e'er bears me, alas!
But often I'm found on the top of a Hass.
I resides in a Hattic, and loves not to roam,
And yet I'm invariably absent from 'Ome.
Though 'Ushed in the 'Urricane, of the Hatmosphere part,
I enters no 'Ed, I creeps into no 'Art.
Only look, and you'll see in the Heye Hi appear.
Only 'Ark and you'll 'Ear me just breathe in the Hear.
Though in sex not an 'E, I am (strange paradox)
Not a bit of an 'Effer, but partly a Hox.
Of Heternity I'm the beginning! and mark
Though I goes not with Noar, I'm first in the Hark.
I'm never in 'Ealth, have with Fysic no power,
I dies in a month, but comes back in a Hour.

4. The Sibylline riddle (1237)

The solution to this ancient riddle as explained by W. H. Scott in *The Atlantis* (1859).

First, it is necessary to observe carefully the points of the riddle; for it is skilfully contrived, and contains several ambiguities. The statements with which it begins are simple. The name which it has in view is one of four syllables and nine letters, five of these being consonants and the rest vowels; and the syllables are severally composed of two letters, except the last syllable, which has three. Then follows the mention of a number – 'twice eight hundred, three times three decads, and seven'. This it is natural to compute as 1697; yet the 'seven' is ambiguous, and may mean, if we choose, 'seven decads', which, if so, must be added to the preceding nine decads; and the number resulting will then not be 1697, but 1760, which in fact is the one intended. Moreover, natural as it may be to conclude, as the commentators have done, that this number is the sum of the numeral value of the nine letters composing the name, this is not necessary, nor is it asserted by the riddle. And lastly, there is an ambiguity, not unintentional, in the circumstance that the riddle does not say simply that 'the whole number is 1760', but 'of the whole number there is 1760', thus obscurely implying that the whole number intended is something larger than the sum mentioned.

Turning now to the Scriptural account of the events preceding the deluge, and comparing it with the Sibylline, we see that whilst in the command of the Almighty to Noe to prepare the ark, there is no mention of the Almighty revealing His name, or of anything directly throwing light on the introduction of this riddle; there is, on the other hand, an omission in the Sibylline narrative, of the announcement accompanying the command to enter the ark: 'Yet awhile, . . . and I will rain upon the earth forty days and forty nights', although the Sibyllist was aware of it, for he afterwards speaks of Noe coming out of the ark on the forty-first day. Comparing, then, as it is natural to do, the omission with the insertion, the idea suggests itself that the Sibylline riddle may be the substitute for the Scriptural fact; or, in other words, the expression of that fact in a symbolical form.

The solution of the puzzle is now easy. The key to it is the passage in the Apocalypse, 'I am Alpha and Omega, the beginning and the end, saith the Lord God, who is, and who was, and who is to come, the Almighty'; Εγώ ειμι τὸ Α καὶ τὸ Ω, ἀρχὴ καὶ τέλος, λεγει ὁ Κύριος, ὁ ὢν, καὶ ὁ ἦν, καὶ ὁ ἐρχόμενος. Alpha and Omega (A and Ω), as being the beginning (ἀρχὴ) and the end (τέλος) of the letters, numerally taken, of the Greek alphabet, are the symbols of Him who is the first and the last, and comprehends time and creation in His own eternity. The Name, then, intended by the Sibyllist is ἀρχὴ τέλος, and the number equivalent to the name is ΑΩ. The Name precisely fulfils the conditions of the riddle, as containing nine letters, four syllables, five consonants, two letters in each of the three first syllables, and three in the fourth. And the number, rightly understood, fulfils them also; for A represents one, or one thousand, as we choose to take it, and Ω is eight hundred; A and Ω, therefore, are equivalent together to 1800, which is in excess of the number in the riddle, which I have shown to be 1760, by just forty; the explanation of which is this: A and Ω being symbols of 'the beginning and the end', are employed by the Sibyllist as the measure of the period which he describes, from the Creation to the deluge; the deluge being the 'destruction of the earth' and the 'end of all flesh', as the Creation was the beginning of it. But as the deluge itself, that is, the rain of forty days, was pending, and not actually come, when the command was given by the Almighty for the preparation of the ark, this is expressed in the riddle by the diminution of the full 1800 to the amount of 40; exactly in accordance, it will be observed, with the words of the riddle, which does not say, 'My whole number is 1760', but 'of my whole number there is 1760', as before pointed out. The purport, then, of the enigmatical name, as introduced into the riddle, is simply this: 'I am the beginning and the end (1800), and my number is even now within forty days of the end; of the whole number (τοῦ παντὸς ὁ ἀριθμού) there is at present 1760, and there remains 40'. The number 40 is thus separated off from the whole number, for the additional reason, that in Scripture it is the symbol of a time of waiting before judgment begins, and the language of the riddle is virtually analogous to the announcement of the impending catastrophe by the prophet Jonas, 'Yet forty days, and Ninive shall be destroyed'. For a similar mode of mystical interpretation, involving the *addition* and *subtraction* of a number, we may consult a passage of St Augustine on the fifth chapter of St John's Gospel. He thus comments on the 38 years during which the sick man, whom our Lord cured, had laboured under his infirmity. The number 40 '*in quadam perfectione commendatur*'; and, as being the length of the fasts of Moses, Elias, our Lord, and of Lent, it especially denotes the good Christian's life, which is a *perfect* mortification. Now what is the reward of these forty days of life-long Lent? We find from the parable of the vineyard, that it is *denarius*, i.e. a *ten*; *add* 10 to the 40 days of Lent, and we have the 50 days of Paschal time. So much for a holy life; it is represented by 40 years; but how is a life deficient in religious mortification expressed by 38? Because the great commands of the law are two, love of God and our neighbour; *subtract* them from 40, and we have the mystical number of imperfection.

That the interpretation here given of this famous riddle is the true one, may be reasonably concluded from the fact that it both fulfils the requirements of the riddle in the minutest particulars, and that it explains the introduction of the riddle, on the face of it so anomalous, in the context in which we find it. But the following considerations come in to complete the argument: – the use of ὁ ἐὼν in the first line ('I am He that is'), which is manifestly a repetition of the ὁ ὢν in the passage of the Apocalypse above quoted; the use of νόησον and νόει ('understand me'), which is imitated from the passage in the Apocalypse about the number of Antichrist: 'He that hath understanding (νουν) let him count the number'; and the similar reference in the αμυητος of the last line, to the great doctrine intimated throughout the Apocalypse in various figures, that the knowledge of divine truth is a mystery (μυστηριον) revealed by the Almighty only to His own initiate; e.g., 'the new name which no man knoweth but he that receiveth it'; and the 'canticle' which 'none could say' but 'those hundred and forty-four thousand who were purchased from the earth'; and the 'name Babylon', which is 'mystery', it being only the Church which has the gift of discerning Antichrist. Finally, it is not to be overlooked that the distinct mention in the Apocalypse of the rainbow and of the ark, taken in connection, as it must be, with the great judicial visitation which closes that prophecy, recalls the deluge, and may have prompted the adaptation of the Apocalyptic name of the Almighty to the account of it in the poem.

FURTHER READING

A comprehensive bibliography would be out of place in a book of this nature, even if space would permit it. However, listed below are a few of the more accessible reference works on the history of riddles and riddling, which are given here both to acknowledge a debt in the preparation of the present volume and perhaps also to stimulate the interested reader to further study.

De Filippis, M. (1948) *The Literary Riddle in Sixteenth-century Italy*, University of California Publications in Modern Philology
De Filippis, M. (1953) *The Literary Riddle in Seventeenth-century Italy*, University of California Publications in Modern Philology
De Filippis, M. (1967) *The Literary Riddle in Eighteenth-century Italy*, University of California Publications in Modern Philology
Opie, I. and Opie, P. (1959) *The Lore and Language of Schoolchildren*, Oxford University Press
Taylor, A. (1939) *Bibliography of Riddles*, Helsinki (this is very comprehensive and covers both books and journals from all over the world from the earliest times to 1939)
Taylor, A. (1948) *The Literary Riddle before 1600*, University of California Press
Taylor, A. (1951) *English Riddles from Oral Tradition*, University of California Press
Tupper, F. (1910) *The Riddles of the Exeter Book*, Ginn & Co. (this contains a thorough study of riddling up to 1910 together with the text and detailed analysis of the *Exeter Book* enigmas)

ACKNOWLEDGEMENTS

Grateful acknowledgement is made for the use of copyright material as follows: to George Allen & Unwin (Publishers) and Houghton Mifflin for *The Hobbit* by J. R. R. Tolkien; The Bodley Head and the Estate of Karen Blixen for *Seven Gothic Tales*; Cambridge University Press for *Stories and Ballads of the Far Past*, translated by N. Kershaw; Faber & Faber and Random House for *A Choice of Anglo-Saxon Verse*, edited and translated by R. Hamer, and *The Elder Edda*, translated by P. B. Taylor and W. H. Auden; The Folio Society for *The Exeter Book*, translated by K. Crossley-Holland; The Loeb Classical Library (Harvard University Press) for Plutarch's *Dinner of the Seven Wise Men*, Aulus Gellius's *Noctes Atticae*, Petronius's *Satyricon*, Athenaeus's *Deipnosophistae*, Aristophanes's *Wasps, The Greek Anthology*; Penguin Books for Rabelais's *Gargantua and Pantagruel*, translated by J. M. Cohen, Plato's *The Republic*, translated by D. P. Lee, Virgil's *The Pastoral Poems*, translated by E. V. Rieu, *Hesiod and Theognis*, translated by D. Wender; University of California Press for *The Literary Riddle before 1600* and *English Riddles from Oral Tradition*, by A. Taylor, *Clareti Enigmata*, edited by F. Peachy; University of Minnesota Press for *The Book of Apollonius*, translated by R. L. Grismer and E. Atkins. Every effort has been made to trace copyright holders. Advice of any omissions would be appreciated and any errors will be corrected in future editions.

INDEX

Adevineaux amoureux, Les
39–40, 67–8
*Adventures of Huckleberry Finn,
The* 7
Aelia Lelia Crispis 68–9, 247,
352
Aenigmata 31, 197, 261, 310
Aenigmatus libris tres 208
Aesop 13, 14
African riddles (original language)
69–70
Again the Three 321
Aldhelm of Malmesbury, St 3,
21, 22, 71–6, 198
Alexander the Great 14
Alexis 14, 76
Al-Hariri, Abu Muhammad Al-
Qasim 12, 27–8, 30, 76–8
Al-Khazari (see *Cuzari*)
Ali the Enigmatic 26
Alice's Adventures in Wonderland
55
All the Year Round 78–9
Amateur Amusements 206
Amusing Riddle Book, The 79
'A Noble Riddle Wisely
Expounded' 10, 50, 261
Antiphanes 14, 86
Apollodorus 176
Apollonius of Tyre 28–30, 32, 86
Apuleius 15
*Arabian Nights Entertainment,
The* 28, 87
Aristophanes 14, 87
Aristotle 3, 12, 13, 14, 132
Arouet, François-Marie (see
Voltaire)
Arte of English Poesie, The 257

Ashmore, A.C. Stevenson 87–9
Athenaeus 13, 14, 15, 76, 86,
143, 245, 267, 311
Atlantis, The 292, 354
Austen, Jane 3, 52, 89, 167
Aventures de Télémache, Les 42
Avicebron (see Gabirol, Solomon
ibn)

Bagwell, William 34, 89–90
Barbauld, Mrs A.L. 46, 91
Barham, Rev. R.H. 92
Bede, the Venerable 11, 22, 23,
92
Beeton, Mrs 54, 92, 108
Beeton, S.O. 54, 92, 108
Beeton's Boy's Annual 92–3, 108
Bellamy, William 52, 94
Bembo, Cardinal Pietro 35
Bentley, Richard 95
Bentley's Miscellany 60, 92, 95–6
Berne Riddles, The 21, 97
Bible, The 3, 17–19, 98
Bible in Spain, The 325
*Bigarrures du Seigneur des
Accords, Les* 40–1, 136
Bishop's Riddle, The 98–9, 352
'Blue Stocking Circle' 46, 135,
233
Boccaccio, Giovanni 35, 37
Boileau (Despréaux), Nicolas
41–2, 99
Boniface, St 22–3
Bononian Enigma, The (see Aelia
Lelia Crispis)
Book of Meery Riddles, The
99–100
Book of Riddles, The 102–3

Booke of Merrie Riddles, A
  100–2
Borrow, George 325
Bottini, Giovanna Statira 50–1,
  103
Bourne, Vincent 104
Boy's Newspaper, The 105–6
Boy's Own Book, The 53, 106–8
Boy's Own Paper, The 175
Boy's Own Volume, The 92,
  108–10
Brentano, Franz 12, 52
Broderip, Mrs F.F. 188
Brough, Robert B. 114
Browning, Robert 24
Buchler, Johannes 31
Bunyan, John vi, 51
Buonarroti, Michelangelo the
  Younger 38, 114
Burton, Sir Richard 87
Bussche, Alexander van den 41,
  307, 308
Byron, George Gordon 6th Baron
  46, 98, 115, 156

Caelius, Firmianius Symphosius
  (see Symphosius)
calembour 6
Calverley, Charles Stuart 52,
  115–6, 236
Camerarius, Joachim 31
Campion, Thomas 32
Cancionero 42, 192
Canning, George 45, 115
'Captain Wedderburn's Courtship'
  10, 50, 263
Carroll, Lewis 3, 54–8, 62,
  116–8, 326
*Cassells Complete Book of Sports
  and Pastimes* 118–9
'catch' riddles 7
catechic questions 11
Cenni 37
Cento nodi 50, 103
Century of Charades, A 94
Cervantes Saavedra, Miguel de 3,
  30, 42–3, 120–3
Chambers, Robert 53, 80, 110
Chambers Journal 283
charade 6
Charades, Enigmas, and Riddles
  123–7

Charades of Every Variety 127–9
Chesterfield, Philip Dormer
  Stanhope 4th Earl of 45, 130
Chesterton, G.K. 20
Chiariti 51
Child, Mrs 173
Children's Encyclopedia, The 224
*Choice Collection of Riddles,
  Charades, Rebusses, A* 46, 130
Christophorus of Mytilene 23,
  130
Cicero 13, 15
Cinquante aenigmes françoises 41,
  307
Claretus, Dr 11, 23, 130–2
Clarke, Rev. J. Erskine 256
Clearchus of Soli 13
Cleobulina 13, 132
Cleobulus 13, 132
Collection of Birds and Riddles, A
  132–3
Compleat Works 247
Contes de ma mère l'Oye 53, 234
conundrum 6
Cotin, Abbé C. 42, 260
Cowper, William 45, 104, 133
Creation Riddle, The 133–4
Croce, Giulio Cesare 36–7, 134–5
Cunliffe, John 59
Curtis, Sir William 135
Cuzari 25, 183
Cyclopedia of Puzzles 208
Cynewulf 26, 152

Dames, M.L. 193
Dante Alighieri 25, 35
Davies, Sir John 135
De Chirico, Giorgio vi, 8
Deipnosophistae 13, 14, 76, 86,
  143, 245, 267, 311
Delany, Mrs Mary 46, 135–6,
  233
*Demandes joyeuses en manière de
  quodlibets* 33, 40, 136
Demaundes Joyous, The 11, 12,
  33, 40, 136
Denison, Dr, Bishop of Salisbury
  98
*Devinettes ou énigmes populaires
  de la France* 162
Des Accords, Estienne Tabourot
  40–1, 136–7

Dialogue of Salamon and
  Saturnus, The 12, 137
Dickens, Charles 78, 95, 193
Dinesen, Isak vi
Diphilus 14
Dodgson, Rev. C.L. (see Carroll,
  Lewis)
Donne, John 32
Drawing Room Scrap Sheet, The
  137-8
Duchamp, Marcel and Picabia,
  Francis 7
Duchesne 47, 213
Dudeney, Henry E. 60, 138-41,
  208, 352

Elder Edda, The 10
Elegies 14, 312
Elgar, Edward 8
Emblematum et aenigmatum
  libellus 194
Emma 52, 89, 167
English Riddles from Oral
  Tradition 80, 241, 322
enigma 5, 6
Enigma, The 60
Enigma Variations 8
Enigmas of Every Variety 141-3
Enimmi di Moderno Autore 51
Ennimistica Moderno 60
Epistola ad Acircium 22, 71
Escobar, Luis 42
Eubulus 143
Eusebius 22, 143, 310
Every Girl's Annual 144-5
Everybody's Illustrated Book of
  Puzzles 145-52
Excursions into Puzzledom 54,
  188
Exeter Book, The 24, 26-7, 30,
  152-5, 198
Ezra, Abraham ibn 24, 155
Ezra, Moses ibn 25, 155

Facetious Nights (see Tredeci
  Piacevoli Notti)
Family Amusements for Winter
  Evenings 155-6
Fani 26
Fanshawe, Catherine Maria 46,
  156-7, 278, 354
Fechner, Gustav 52, 157-60

Fénelon, François de Salignac de
  la Mothe 42
Fiera 114
Firdusi (Firdausi) 28, 160
First Fruites 34, 160
Flores 11, 23, 92
Florio, John 34, 160-1
Folk riddles passim; African
  69-70; British 110-14; French
  162-4; Gaelic 165-6; German
  168-72; Indian 193; North
  American 241-3; Russian
  283-4; West Indian 322-3
Fontaine, Charles 41
Fox, Charles James 6, 45, 98,
  161-2
Frazer, Sir James 11, 61, 62
Frederick II, King of Prussia 162
French riddles (original language)
  6-7, 40-2, 44, 47, 67-8, 99,
  130, 136-7, 162-4, 174, 175,
  213-8, 225-9, 260-1, 277,
  307-8, 321, 322
Freud, Sigmund 3, 52
Friedreich, J.B. 51
Frolics of the Sphinx, The 54,
  164

Gabirol, Solomon ibn 24
Gaelic riddles (original language)
  165-6
Gaelic Riddles and Enigmas 165
Galatea, La 42-3, 120
Galilei, Galileo 3, 35-6, 166-7
Gargantua 40, 260
Garrick, David 45, 167
Gascoigne, George 34, 167
Gátu Ríma 17, 265
Gellius, Aulus 15, 168
Genoa University Manuscript,
  The 38
Gentleman's Magazine, The 46,
  133, 201
German riddles (original language)
  157-60, 168-72, 176-7, 193,
  195-6, 286-92, 301-2
Gifford, Humphrey 34, 172-3
Gilbert, W.S. and Sullivan,
  Arthur 8
Giraldi, Lilio Gregorio 36
Girl's Own Book, The 54, 173-5
Girl's Own Paper, The 175-6

Glaukos Riddle, The 3–4, 14, 176
Goethe, Johann Wolfgang von 3, 44, 176–7
Golden Bough, The 11, 61
Gower, John 32, 86
Gozzi, Carlo 9, 45, 256
Graham, Dougal 194
Greek Anthology, The 14, 132, 177–8, 267
Green Fairy Book, The 178
Grimm, Jacob and Grimm, Wilhelm 178
Guess Again or Easy Enigmas for Little Folk 51, 54
Guess Book, The 54, 178–9
Guess Me 179–83

Hadamerius (see Secundus, Johannes Lorichius)
Halevi, Jehudah 24–5, 183
Hallam, Henry 98, 352, 353, 354
Halliwell-Phillips, J.O. 110
Hamlet 32
Hearbes 167
Heine, Heinrich 24, 28
Helmbold, Ludovicus 30
Henry VIII, King of England 33
Heraclitus 13, 33
Hervarar Saga, The 16-17, 184–5
Hesiod 14
Hobbit, The 53, 55, 59, 315
Hollis, A.C. 69
Holme Riddles, The 35, 185
Home Amusements 186–8
Homer 3, 14, 21, 188
Hood, Thomas 188, 236
Hood, Tom 54, 188–91
Hook, Theodore 236
Horozco, Sebastian de 42, 192
Hundred Merry Riddles, A 34

Ichneutae 14, 293
Ilo Riddle, The 9, 193
Immanuel of Rome 25–6, 35
Indovinelli 114
Ingoldsby Legends, The 92
Italian riddles (original language) 35–6, 37, 39, 103, 114, 134–5, 160–1, 166–7, 220–1, 230, 297–301

Jerrold, Douglas 193–4
Jocoseria 92
John Falkirk's Cariches 46, 194
Johnson, Dr 277
Jonson, Ben 34, 160, 326
Josephus 19
Joyce, James 194
Judah the Patriarch 14–15
Junius, Hadrian 31, 194

Kinder- und Hausmärchen 178
'King John and the Abbot of Canterbury' 49–50
Knights Quarterly Magazine 254
Koran, The 3
Körner, Theodor 195–6

Labrat, Dunash ben 24, 196
Lactantius (see Symphosius)
Laertius, Diogenes 13, 132
Lamotte (Lamothe) 47
Landseer, Sir Edwin 196–7
Lang, Andrew 178
Latin riddles (original language) 22, 31, 36, 68–9, 71–6, 92, 97, 104, 130–2, 143, 168, 194, 197–8, 199, 208, 261, 286, 309–11
Lauterbach, Johannes 31, 197–8
Leiden Riddle, The 198
Lemon, Mark 199
Leo XIII, Pope 52, 199
Libro di Apolonio, El 32, 86
'Lincolnshire Household Riddles' 60, 199–200
Lippi, Lorenzo 38
Little Folks 60, 200–1
Lives of Eminent Philosophers 13, 132
logograph 6
London Magazine and Monthly Chronicler, The 47, 201–5
Lorenzo, Professor 206–8
Lorsch Riddles, The 23
Loyd, Samuel 55, 60, 138, 208–11
Lucchese, Catone l'Uticense 44, 50
Lycerus, King of Babylon 14, 235

Macaulay, Thomas Babington 52, 212–3

Madonna Daphne 37
Magasin énigmatique 47, 213–8
Magazine of Short Stories, The
218–20
Mahabharata, The 16, 220
Mahberot Immanuel 25–6, 35
Malatesti, Antonio 30, 38–9, 51,
220–1
Mansur, Abul Qasim (see Firdusi)
Maqamat 27–8, 76
March's Penny Riddle Book
221–2
Marcus Aurelius 14–15
*Marshall's Ladies Daily
Remembrancer* 276
Masquerade, The 46, 222–4
Martial 21
*Mecklenburgische
Volksüberlieferungen* 168
Medici, Lorenzo de' 11
Mee, Arthur 224–5
Megalomites, Basilios 225
Menestrier, Claude François 41,
225–7
Mercure de France, Le 6–7, 47,
48, 227–9
Merry Wives of Windsor, The
34–5
Midsummer Night's Dream, A
31
Mince Pies for Christmas 54,
229–30
Minos, King of Crete 3–4, 176
Minstrelsy 50
Mirtunzio, Fosildo 51, 230
Mises, Dr (see Fechner, Gustav)
Modern Sphinx, The 230–3
Moneti, Francesco 38
Montaigne, Michel de 39, 160
Monthly Magazine, The 236
Moore, Thomas 45, 233
More, Hannah 46, 91, 135, 233
More Puniana 278
Mother Goose in Hieroglyphicks
223–4
Mother Goose's Tales 53, 233,
234–5, 253
*Muses Mercury: or the Monthly
Miscellany, The* 47

National Song Book, The 267
'neck' riddle 9

Nectanebo, King of Egypt 14,
235–6
Neue Räthsel 12, 52
*New Monthly Magazine and
Humorist, The* 60, 92, 236–7,
254
New Riddle Book, A 237–8
*New Riddle Book for the
Amusement and Instruction of
Little Misses and Masters*
238–9
New Sphinx, The 239–40
Newton, Sir Isaac 34, 241
Nicholson, Alexander 165
Noctes Atticae 15, 168
Notes and Queries 59–60, 133,
199, 243–4, 316, 328, 352
Notte sollazzevole di cento enigmi
36, 134
Nursery Rhymes of England 110

Old Northumbrian riddle (original
language) 198
Opie, Mrs Amelia 244

Panarces 13, 245
Pantagruel 40, 260
Parabeln und Rätsel 44–5, 286
Parlour Pastimes for the Young
245–6
Parsons, Elsie Clews 322
Passover Riddle, The 11, 24,
246–7
Pastoral Poems 15, 321
Peacock, Thomas Love 52, 68–9,
244, 247, 352
Pearson, A. Cyril 247–9
Pecci, Gioacchini (see Leo XIII,
Pope)
Pericles 32
Perrault, Charles 53, 234
*Peter Primrose's Books for Boys
and Girls: Riddles* 54,
249–50
Petrarch 35
Petronius, Gaius 15, 250
*Philosophie des images
énigmatiques, La* 41, 225
pictorial riddles 8
Pictured Puzzles and Word Play
247
Pindar 13, 14

Pitt, William 1st Earl of Chatham 45, 250–1
Planche, Frederick D'Arros 179
Plato 13, 245
Plutarch 13, 15
Poe, Edgar Allan 3, 4, 52, 252–3
Poemata 36, 286
Poemata, Latine partim reddita, partim scripta 104
Polite Jester, The 46, 251–2
Pompeius 15
Popular Poetry of the Baloches 193
Popular Rhymes and Nursery Tales 110
Popular Rhymes of Scotland 53, 80, 110
Posie of Gillowflowers, A 34, 172
Potter, Beatrix 253
Praed, Winthrop Mackworth 52, 236, 254–6
Prettie Riddles 100
Pretty Riddle Book 51, 54
Prize, The 60, 256
'Proud Lady Margaret' 50, 264
Psellus, Michael 23, 225, 256
Puccini, Giacomo 3, 8, 256–7
Punch, or the London Charivari 60, 199, 257
Puniana, or Thoughts Wise and Other-wise 278, 354
Puttenham, Richard 257
Puzzle Book, The 257–8
Puzzlecap's Amusing Riddle Book 258–9
Puzzling Cap, The 259
Pythagoras 13

Quarenta aenigmas en lengua espannola 42, 308
Quarles, Francis x
Queen of Sheba's Riddles, The 19, 259–60

Rabelais, François 40, 260
Ralston, W.R.S. 266
Räthselbuchlein 157
rebus, literary 7
rébus de Picardie 11
Recueil des énigmes de ces temps 260–1
Rees, Ennis 59

Republic, The 13, 245
Reusner, Nicolaus 31, 261
Riddle ballads 10, 43, 49–50; English 261–4; Faroese 17, 265–6; Russian 266
Riddle Book; or Fireside Amusements, The 267
Riddle Magazine, The 60
Riddle of the Sphinx, The 9–10, 267
Riddle songs 267–9
Riddles Ancient & Modern ix
Riddles and their Solution 269–72
Riddles, Charades, and Conundrums 272–3
Riddles of Heraclitus and Democritus 33–4, 273–6
Rig-Veda, The 13, 15–16, 276
Rime 38, 297
Rolland, Eugene 51, 162
Romeo and Juliet 31
Rooyen, G.A. and Pellisier, S.H. 61
Rossetti, Christina 54, 276–7
Rousseau, Jean Jacques 44, 277
Routledge, George 54, 144, 315
Rowley, Hugh 278–9, 354
Royal Riddle Book, The 52, 279–80
Royal Riddler, The 281–2
Russian riddles (original language) 283

St Nicholas 284–5
Sam Loyd's Puzzles 208
Santucci, Leone (see Lucchese, Catone l'Uticense)
Satyricon 15, 250
Scaliger, Julius Caesar 36, 286
Schiller, Johann Christoph Friedrich von 3, 5, 9, 31, 44–5, 176, 195, 256, 286–92
Scott, Sir Walter 43, 50
Scott, W.H. 292, 354
Secundus, Johannes Lorichius 31, 208
Sfinge, La 38, 220
Shakespeare, William 3, 30, 31–2, 34–5
Shanamah 28, 160
Sheridan, R.B. 98
Sibylline Oracles 292

Sibylline Riddle, The 292–3, 354
Silbenrätsel 6
Sing-Song, A Nursery Rhyme Book 276
Smith, Horace 293
Sommers, Will 33
Songs of the Russian People, The 266
Sophocles 14, 293–4
Spanish riddles (original language) 120–3, 192, 308–9
Sphinx, or Allegorical Lozenges, The 294–6
Stanford, Charles Villiers 267
Stigliani, Tommaso 11, 33, 37, 38, 297
Strand Magazine, The 60, 138, 196
Straparola, Giovanni Francesco 10–11, 30, 33, 37–8, 41, 50, 297–301
Strassburger Räthselbuch, Der 30, 301–2
Swift, Jonathan 3, 44, 46–7, 135, 302–7, 320
Sylvain, Alexandre 37, 41, 307–8
Sylvano, Alexandro 42, 308–9
Symphosii Aenigmata 21, 309
Symphosius 21, 22, 309–10

Tale of Squirrel Nutkin, The 253
Talmud, The 19–20, 310
Taroni, Giovanni Battista (see Bottini, Giovanna Statira)
Tarquin the Great 15
Tatwine 12, 22, 143, 310–11
Taylor, Archer 51, 80, 241
Tchaikovsky, Peter Ilyich 8
Thackeray, William Makepeace 6, 95
Theocritus 14
Theodectes of Phaselis 311–12
Theognis 14, 312
Therander, Huldrich 31
Thesaurus Ænigmaticus 46, 312–3
Thoms, W.J. 243
1001 Conundrums 314–5
1001 Riddles, with a few thrown in 315
Thrale, Mrs 277

Through the Looking Glass 54, 116
Tolkien, J.R.R. 3, 53, 55, 59, 62, 315–6
Tottel's Miscellany 34, 327
Tractatus Logico-Philosophicus 4
Tredeci Piacevoli Notti 10–11, 37–8, 297
Tree Riddle, The 316–7
True Trial of Understanding or Wit Newly Reviv'd, The 49, 317–8
Tullius 21, 97
Turandot 8, 45, 256, 286
Twain, Mark 7
Twentieth Century Standard Puzzle Book, The 247

Ulysses 194
Universal Magazine of Knowledge and Pleasure, The 47–8, 318–20

Vanhomrigh, Esther 46, 320
Vanity Fair 6
Veglie autunnali 51, 230
Verses and Translations 115
Vinci, Leonardo da 35
Virgil 15, 321
Voltaire, François 44, 162, 321
Vox Urbis 199

Wallace, Edgar 321
Walpole, Horace 4th Earl of Orford 45, 241, 322
Wartburgkrieg 30
Wasps 14, 87
Whately, Richard 323
Whetstone for Dull Wits, A 49, 324–5
Whewell, William 52, 325
Wilberforce, Samuel 326
Williams, Kit 59
Wit's Academy, or Six Peny'worth for a Penny 34, 326
Wit's Extraction 34, 89
Wittgenstein, Ludwig 4
Worcester Misericord Riddle, The 326
Word Games and Word Puzzles 87
Worde, Wynkyn de 33, 40, 136

World's Best Word Puzzles, The 138, 352
Worträtsel 6
Wossidlo, Richard 51, 168
Wyatt, Sir Thomas 34, 167, 327

Yeoman of the Guard, The 8
'Yorkshire Household Riddles' 60, 328
Young England 328–31